LEARNING AND TEACHING THEOLOGY

SOME WAYS AHEAD

**Edited by
Les Ball & James R. Harrison**

Learning and Teaching Theology
Some Ways Ahead
Edited by Les Ball & James R. Harrison
Second edition 2024

SCD Press
PO Box 6110,
Norwest NSW 2153
scdpress@scd.edu.au

Compilation copyright © Les Ball and James R. Harrison
Copyright of individual chapters remains with the authors of those chapters

ISBN-13: 978-1-925730-51-7 (Paperback)
ISBN-13: 978-1-925730-52-4 (E-book)

Cataloguing–in-Publications entry is available from the National Library of Australia http:/catalogue.nla.gov.au/.

All rights reserved. Other than for the purposes and subject to the conditions prescribed under the Copyright Act, no part of this publication may be reproduced, stored in a retrieval system, or transmitted in any form or by any means, electronic, mechanical, photocopying, recording or otherwise, without the prior written permission of the publisher.

First published 2014

Cover and internal design and layout: Lankshear Design Pty Ltd.

LEARNING AND TEACHING THEOLOGY

SOME WAYS AHEAD

**Edited by
Les Ball & James R. Harrison**

SCD Press
2024

Publications associated with SCD Learning & Teaching Theology Conferences

1. Les Ball, *Transforming Theology. Student Experience and Transformative Learning in Undergraduate Theological Education* (Preston, Vic.: Mosaic, 2012). Second edition: Macquarie Park, SCD Press, 2022.
2. Les Ball & James R. Harrison (eds.), *Learning & Teaching Theology. Some Ways Ahead* (Northcote, Vic: Morning Star, 2014). Second edition: Norwest, NSW, SCD Press, 2024.
3. Yvette Debergue & James R. Harrison (eds.), *Teaching Theology in a Technological Age* (Cambridge: Cambridge Scholars Publishing, 2015).
4. Les Ball & Peter G. Bolt (eds.), *Wondering About God Together. Research-Led Learning & Teaching in Theological Education* (Macquarie Park, NSW: SCD Press, 2018).
5. Peter G. Bolt & Peter Laughlin (eds.), *God's Exemplary Graduates: Character-Oriented Graduate Attributes in Theological Education* (Macquarie Park, NSW: SCD Press, 2021).
6. Les Ball, *Learning to be Learners: A Mathegenical Approach to Theological Education* (Macquarie Park, NSW: SCD Press, 2022).
7. Peter G. Bolt & Peter Laughlin (eds.), *Testing Us Testing God. Assessment and Theological Competency* (Macquarie Park, NSW: SCD Press, 2022).
8. Peter G. Bolt & Peter Laughlin (eds.), *Thinking for Ourselves for God's Sake. Theological Education in an Age of Social Engineering* (Norwest, NSW: SCD Press, forthcoming).

CONTENTS

Revisiting Learning and Teaching Theology Bill Salier — vii

SECTION ONE: **SETTING OUT**

    Introduction Les Ball — xvii

    Where Are We Going? Les Ball — xxi

SECTION TWO: **A BIBLICAL ROAD MAP: PAUL AS A THEOLOGICAL TEACHER**

    1 *Higher Education in the Pauline Churches.* E.A. Judge — 1

    2 *Paul and the Ancient Gymnasiums.* James R. Harrison — 15

    3 *Paul as Theological Educator.* Robert Banks — 39

SECTION THREE: **SOME PHILOSOPHICAL BEARINGS**

    4 *An Analysis of "Soul" as the Central Construct in Dirkx's and Ruether's Transformative Learning Theory.* Neil Holm — 53

    5 *Leaving Home.* Dan Fleming and Peter Mudge — 71

    6 *Assessing Integrative Learning and Readiness for Ministry.* Nancy Ault — 87

    7 *The Contribution of Theories of Multiple Intelligences to the Promotion of Deep Learning through the Assessment of Learning.* Charles de Jongh — 103

Section Four: SOME DIFFERENT DIRECTIONS

9 *Addressing the Need for Better Integration in Theological Education.* Richard Hibbert and Evelyn Hibbert   125

9 *Responding to Complexity.* Stephen Smith and Leon O'Flynn   143

Section Five: DRIVING THE TECHNOLOGY

10 *Making the Implicit Explicit.* Diane Hockridge   159

11 *Theology for the iGeneration.* Kara Martin   181

12 *Video Game Design and the Theological Classroom.* Isaac Soon   197

13 *Embodiment and Transformation in the Context of e-Learning.* Steve Taylor   213

Section Six: GOING AHEAD: IDEAS FROM THE FIELD

14 *A Practical Approach for Teaching Foundational Theology.* Denise Goodwin   233

15 *Transformative Learning in Church History.* Tim Cooper   251

16 *Cross-cultural Mission as a Transformative Learning Experience.* Murray House   267

17 *From Place to Place.* Darren Cronshaw and Andrew Menzies   275

Section Seven: ENLARGED HORIZONS

18 *Chinese Theological Education in Australia.* Felix Chung   295

19 *Nungalinya College – Empowering Indigenous Christians.* Jude Long   315

REVISITING *LEARNING AND TEACHING THEOLOGY*

BILL SALIER

What was I expecting to think after re-visiting this collection of essays ten years on from its initial publication? Was it going to be a case of 'that was then; this is now'; a sense that this was a snapshot from a distant time of issues that once were relevant but are no longer so? Or was it going to be a case of the more things change, the more they remain the same? That we were still trawling over the same set of vital concerns in Australian theological education?

As you might guess the answer is a little bit of both, but the over-riding reaction was one of gratitude. This volume was, and remains, an impressive achievement. The essays and the conference they represent remain a real breakthrough in Australian theological education. Together, they mark a concerted attempt to promote a conversation about the process of teaching and learning in theological education in Australia.

Both elements of this statement are important.

First, it is a conversation about *learning and teaching* that is occurring. When it comes to tertiary education It is regularly observed that interest in research eclipses interest in teaching and learning. When the matter of teaching and learning does come up, the focus is often on content of teaching and not the process. This is arguably more so the case in the theological education sector where the core content of the Christian Scriptures is highly valued. And, of course, one of the key qualifications of competent tertiary teacher is competency in the field of study. The higher degree is a necessary qualification. That said, there is more to teaching and learning than content mastery and delivery. The material has to be communicated; it has to be taught and learned.

Often lecturers in theological institutions are recruited from amongst the ranks of graduates after they have spent some time working in a Christian ministry and it is easy to assume that a good Bible teacher in a ministry context makes a good classroom teacher. Certainly, there may well be an overlap in communication competency but as many students who have suffered under this paradigm will tell you, 'it ain't necessarily so'. There is more to teaching a class than simply giving a good, if not longer, sermon.

In tertiary education generally, there have been moves to emphasise the importance of good teaching and learning practices. The rise of centres of teaching and learning in the universities and the proliferation of Graduate Certificates bears testimony to this. But perhaps the theological sector has been a little slow in catching up. Standard professional development more normally consists of attendance at an academic conference in the relevant theological field, again the focus on content. Publications are highly prized. This is necessary as recency and the capacity to develop knowledge in the discipline is an essential feature of what it means to be a sound academic practitioner. But the reality for most faculty, in the relatively small theological sector, is extensive classroom engagement and this requires some facility with classroom teaching practice, some familiarity with learning theory, and space for reflection on what it means to be an effective practitioner. These are all areas worthy of reflection and development.

There exist many forums for the discussion of the content of theological education but, prior to the SCD offerings, opportunities to consider the practice of theological education were few and far between. And there was also a dearth of written material reflecting on learning and teaching in the Australian theological context. The volume reissued here, its companion volumes, and the conferences they represent are therefore a major service to the theological education sphere in the Australasian context.

And it is that context which is the second notable feature. This volume speaks with an Australian voice, an Australian accent. It speaks from, and into, the Australian context. By sheer size and volume of market the USA, and to a lesser extent the UK, tend to exert a considerable influence in thinking about teaching and learning in the theological education sphere. There have of course been significant Australian contributions in the tertiary sector generally, but when it comes to thinking about teaching and learning in the theological education space from an Australian perspective there is plenty of room for further contribution.

I don't want to overstate this as an issue as we ought to be grateful for the resources and learning that come from 'over there'. But it is good to hear flattened vowels, and local concerns. The SCD is to be congratulated for this initiative.

As the SCD conferences and publications keep coming, they are providing a substantial, and growing, body of research and reflection on the process of theological education.

Is this important? I think our students would say yes. They are the beneficiaries. The skills of engaging a class with the subject matter, communicating concepts with clarity, and achieving goals that are truly educative, and formative, are worthy of reflection, research and practice. Students know the difference when they are skilfully delivered content that is thoughtful and pedagogically informed. They appreciate the value of teaching which is focussed on their learning and understanding and not merely on the transmission of information. In fact, the simple difference of the lecturer acknowledging that they are a teacher (even better a fellow learner, albeit more experienced) and they are working with a class rather than delivering a lecture will make a world of difference. But I hear the sound of a panting hobby horse.

Let's get back to the volume we are reflecting upon. This is a real contribution to the general tertiary learning and teaching conversation. It is in the particularity of the discussion of local concerns in the discipline of theological education that they make a substantial contribution to the broader discussion.

The special focus of the volume on transformation is important and will always be relevant. At the time, the conference was building on the important investigation conducted into transformative learning by Les Ball.[1] If anything, the discussion about transformation in theological education is more urgent as a series of spectacular high-profile failures by various people in Christian ministry in the intervening ten years have shone a spotlight on moral and personal failure. The question is sharply raised by these failures concerning the importance of character and transformation as an appropriate concern for those institutions preparing candidates for ministry. While we can't expect miracles from the theological programme; it is after all only three to four years, we also do not expect nothing because it is a peculiarly focused and concentrated three to four years. The debate as to what constitutes a transformative educational experience remains a live one

---

1   Les Ball, *Transforming Theology: Student Experience and Transformative Learning in Undergraduate Theological Education* (Second edition; Norwest, NSW: SCD Press, 2023 [Original: 2012]). see also Les Ball's later volume: *Learning to be Learners: a mathegenical approach to theological education* (Norwest, NSW: SCD Press, 2022).

and one where the theological sector has an important contribution to make to the wider tertiary sector, which also grapples with similar issues.

The general movement of the volume from theory through to discussion of practices is important. It is essential that we keep exploring the 'why' questions as well as the 'how' questions, especially in a world where the attitude is often, 'we can, so why not?'

The breadth of issues addressed stood out. I appreciated again Harrison's overview and reflections on the relationship between the theological and the secular higher education sectors. The essays on integration at the macro level and at the level of curriculum planning are worth reading over and reflecting upon at length.

The essays by Taylor, Hockridge and Martin seem especially prescient as they deal with the use of technologies in education. Taylor's essay remains provocative in its attempt to give a very positive theological justification for the necessity of online learning. All of this when online learning was in its relative infancy.

The intervening years have been scarred by the Covid pandemic and marked by the next stage in the information and technological revolution that is progressing around us.

The pandemic placed a spotlight on the question of the importance, or otherwise, of face-to-face contact in the theological education mix. Many colleges, who had dabbled lightly in, or perhaps had studiously avoided, online modes of education found themselves forced to innovate quickly and provide online experiences for their students. They are now facing the question of winding back or keeping going.

Post-covid, many students have flocked back to an 'in-person' experience. Other colleges have found that students (and some lecturers) prefer the flexibility and convenience of remaining online. In arguably the worst of all possible worlds, hybrid arrangements are the norm. Classes that are simultaneously composed of students in the classroom and online require considerable thought and technological dexterity to ensure that both cohorts of students are suitably engaged. Many teachers now have the unnerving experience of talking to a series of avatars/screenshots or a list of names with the hope that there is a flesh and blood presence behind them.

All of this requires the development of new skills and the adaptation of old ones. Questions concerning what constitutes an effective online learning experience were important ten years ago and even more important now as Colleges invest more resources into online education.

The issue that drove this volume, transformative learning, is still worthy of discussion and innovation especially in the online environment, asking whether this environment is an appropriate one to facilitate personal transformation.

The more general issue of the use and integration of technology into theological education is only more complex and more acute. At the International Council for Evangelical Theological Education (ICETE) conference held in Turkey (2023), two of the main morning strands were dedicated to questions of online learning and the use of technology, with a good percentage of the conference participants electing to attend these strands for the 4 days of the conference. The upcoming conference in Albania in 2025 will again feature substantial streams on technology and its effects. In both the wider society and all levels of education the question of phones and their use is passionately discussed from all angles: pedagogical, moral, social, and scientific.

The implications of the amount of information now available to students and lecturers through technologies continues to be grappled with. As Michael Bird points out in a recent reflection, content is not the issue in theological education.[2] There is a proliferation of online materials and courses in all the classical areas of theological education. This is forcing questions to be asked. Bird suggests that the role of teacher is shifting from being a provider/creator of content to being a curator of content who helps guide students through the maze of materials available. What does this look like in course design and classroom pedagogy?

At the same time Bird stresses the importance of the College enabling a cohort to develop, with an eye to the kind of personal formation that comes through relationships in the classroom while learning. This sounds like a plea for some form of community-based process, whether full or part time residential, or perhaps intensive based or something else again. These are insights worth plumbing and pondering further as to their accuracy and implications.

The new 'kid on the block' is the rise of Artificial Intelligence and there is a vigorous discussion ensuing over the way it is to be used. At the time of writing this seems to have swamped all education systems in the blink of an eye. Have we really grasped the nettle on any of this? A recent conversation with a colleague was marked by bewilderment at how quickly the AI tsunami has hit and how disruptive and even regressive it has proven in areas like assessment. Not all disruption is bad of course and perhaps many future volumes in this series will reflect on the beneficial uses of AI to help struggling students to

---

[2] See https://michaelfbird.substack.com/p/the-future-of-seminaries-is-not-what

express themselves better and who know what other developments?[3]

All of this makes an ongoing discussion about the value and process of online education and the use of technology essential.

The final section of the volume featured welcome essays on Chinese and Indigenous theological education. These hinted at the wide vista of possible ethnic horizons in Australian theological education and posed questions about the capacity to contextualise theological education for the diversity that we meet around us. This is a diversity that is not only ethnic but also socio-economic, gendered, and more besides. In what ways should teaching and learning and all that entails be shaped to meet this diversity? The exploration of oral learning and assessments is only one continuing area of investigation to meet some of this diversity.

We live and teach in ever developing and changing contexts. Two recent statements attempt to point to the realities and challenges theological educators face. The upcoming 2025 ICETE Conference lists the following:

- the integration of next generation leaders;
- the place of women in theological education;
- orality, technology;
- contextual curriculum;
- sociopolitical unrest;
- ministry leadership;
- ethical practice;
- micro-credentialling
- the place of the arts in ministry;
- personal formation.[4]

Preparations are underway for the International Lausanne Conference on World Evangelisation in late 2024. The material published to prepare delegates to participate discusses what they see as the major global challenges facing the task of world evangelisation. This is also an instructive list with respect to the context for theological education. They list the following global trends and questions:

- The Digital Age.
- Rising middle class and urbanisation,

---

3   Coincidentally, at the time of writing the April 2025 SCD Learning and Teaching Conference is being advertised with the title: 'Digital Divinity: Working with Intelligence: Artificial, Human, and Divine?'
4   See https://icete.info/event/icete-c-25-tirana/

- Global aging,
- Global trust (lack of),
- What does is mean to be human with Artificial Intelligence and the debate over issues of human sexuality.[5]

Not everyone will not agree with the relevance of every item on these lists. But they do provide food for thought and maybe even some agendas for future discussion at future conferences. These contexts and others besides force us to think through issues of curriculum, assessment, teaching and learning; the 'why'; the 'what'; the 'how'; the 'where'; and 'when' of theological education.

In his important essay that opens the following volume Les Ball asks 'Where are we going?' This a question we should never stop asking. He makes the point that 'the academy must adapt', while at the same time retaining 'a due sense of its traditional heritage, its underlying theological base, its ecclesiological mandate, and its educational philosophy'. Rightly he speaks of a coherent tension. Or is the question even more 'meta' than that: asking how can theological institutions prepare their students for a context where the constant is change? A firm place to stand with convictions grounded in the revelation of God in his word would seem to be essential. Perhaps also the skills developed by more recent problem-based learning approaches to teaching and assessment that enable the communication and application of that traditional base to the everchanging needs of the world which the College is preparing its students for. But that sounds like another discussion to be had.

This book made a breakthrough contribution and ten years on it still makes an important contribution as does the conference and the series which it is a part of. One gets the sense that discussions on learning and teaching in the theological education space remain still far too few and far too piecemeal but that is not the fault of this volume. All of which is to say that we ought to be profoundly grateful for the conversations these essays further amongst theological education practitioners, encouraging us all to deeper levels of faith-informed reflection and practice.

Rev. Dr Bill Salier
Consultant
GAFCON Theological Education Network

---

5 These are mentioned in the Lausanne State of the Great Commission Presentation, which can be found here: https://www.youtube.com/watch?v=w3I-kxB9Z9E

SECTION ONE
SETTING OUT

INTRODUCTION

LES BALL

This volume arises out of a Learning and Teaching conference conducted at Sydney College of Divinity which addressed emerging issues and practices in the field of theological education. That conference was largely inspired by the findings of the *Transforming Theology* project led by Les Ball in 2010-2012. Hence the title of this book is suggestive of the fact that, while there is not necessarily any one "right" or "best" way of delivering theological education (in Australia as elsewhere), there is none the less much evidence that contemporary theological educators are developing new and exciting ideas and practices within the field. This volume is offered as a compendium of essays from scholars and practitioners at the leading edge of theological education in Australia and New Zealand. It aims to generate further impetus in charting effective ways to make progress along the important journey of delivering relevant contemporary educational experiences for the learners of theology.

The introductory essay in Section 1 of the collection sets the scene for the rest of the book, as Les Ball addresses several key areas that arose from his original research in *Transforming Theology*. These issues include underlying philosophies and objectives, implications for curriculum design and aspects of teaching and learning practices, with an overarching focus on those things which generate transformative learning and experiences.

In line with Ball's recommendations, the early sections of the book focus on some significant biblical and philosophical issues that undergird all theological education. In section 2, there are several scholarly essays that provide paradigmatic analyses of the background, principles and practices of the Apostle Paul as a deliverer of theological learning. Edwin Judge presents a detailed overview of the inherited higher educational worldview that so influenced Paul as he delivered his theological education in the churches of his day. Thus Judge sets up a virtual template for others to consider. James Harrison's essay continues in this vein as it provides an examination of Paul and his relation to the ancient Gymnasium. Harrison's interest lies in the extrapolation of salient principles that will inform the ethical conduct of research (and indeed teaching in general) in theological education. The section concludes with Robert Banks' essay on "Paul as Theological Educator." This essay draws Paul into the classroom by means of providing practical applications of lessons from Paul that can influence teaching practices for today and tomorrow.

Following the biblical excurses, Section 3 proceeds with some further philosophical and theoretical considerations. Neil Holm's essay on "An Analysis of Soul" examines an oft neglected topic within transformative learning, as a complement to the common focus on the work of Mezirow. In this piece, Holm eloquently seeks to restore the soul as an essential element of theological transformation, as an adjunct to (or even a corrective of) the dominant emphasis on content and techniques. In "Leaving Home" by Dan Fleming and Peter Mudge, there is a transformatively discomforting challenge to theological teachers to grasp the nettle of discomforting learners as they travel far from the secure comforts of their theological "home" to encounter enlarged horizons of theological possibilities and perspectives. Nancy Ault's discussion of the ever-present and ever-pressing issue of assessment in theological formation also challenges conventional thinking in the area. The essay advocates a less empirical but more effectual approach to linking assessment with evidences of personal resilience as a key aspect of readiness for ministry, an important outcome desired in much theological education. In a different but clearly compatible way, Charles de Jongh explores the possibilities of the psychological theories of multiple intelligences as a way of constructing assessment to facilitate, not just measure, the depth of learning that is so desirable in theological learning.

The book then moves into a more practical direction as involved practitioners suggest and report on various ways in which conventional systems of thinking and doing may be implemented. Section 4 offers some different approaches to curriculum construction and delivery, with two essays which draw on insights from other areas of higher education that may be applied in principle to theological education. Richard and Evelyn Hibbert draw lessons from medical education, and propose an approach to theological learning whereby transformative ideals may be promoted by means of the pedagogical advocacy of problem-based learning, the integration of ministry, the development of a learning community and effectual faculty mentoring. Stephen Smith and Leon O'Flynn develop their prior research in the fields of hermeneutics, knowledge management and health science to advocate a pedagogical paradigm shift from a focus on competence (what individuals know or do in terms of skills and knowledge) to a focus on capability (the capacity of individuals to adapt to change and to generate new, useful knowledge for improved practice).

Section 5 engages the essential area of how we may use emerging and powerful technologies for the enhanced educational experience of theological learners. Diane Hockridge lays out principles and processes for effective learning management through technological systems. Her focus is on ways of intentionally designing online programs and activities to achieve the desired formative ends. Kara Martin's essay on Theology for the iGeneration provides an insightful treatment of the "now and coming" generation and important ramifications for theological education, delivered in the context of a case study of a particular program designed specifically for such a clientele. Isaac Soon ventures into the realm of computer gaming in his essay on "Gamification," which does not advocate games *per se*, but rather cogently analyses the pedagogic principles that underlie gaming, which can be creatively applied within theological learning. To complete this section, Steve Taylor's essay engages in a three-way conversation among Gospel, *Transforming Theology* and e-learning literature, to arrive at the conclusion that e-learning is not merely a viable option for theological education; rather, e-learning is actually a theological necessity.

In Section 6 there is offered a selection of some of the innovative practices that have recently been developed and implemented by practitioners in the field. These are presented in order to encourage further creativity in teaching and learning methods. In a treatment of how she has come to teach foundational theology, Denise Goodwin outlines her development of a Matrix of Ideas, especially as it has operated in a specific case, involving problem-based learning and collaborative learning. Tim Cooper outlines his approach to teaching a course in church history, wherein he generates a transformative experience of perspective extension and change, by transcending (even over-turning) the traditional approaches of West-centric triumphalist history. The examples he provides of actual lesson activities are as entertaining as they are informative. In a brief report, Murray House presents an all too rare empirical analysis of a cross-cultural experience undergone by his students and the actual transformative impact the experience had on them. To complete this section, Darren Cronshaw and Andrew Menzies also present an analytical report on a program of workplace formation delivered within their colleges. This program has been intentionally designed to stretch learners beyond their normal comfort zones, and the report thus identifies significant implications for integrated practical placements and learning-in-context pedagogy.

The volume concludes with two essays featuring the recent expansion of theological teaching and learning horizons in Australia. The multi-cultural face of modern Australia now embraces theological learning in many non-Western communities. Felix Chung provides a review of Australian Chinese history, churches and multicultural ethos and, in so doing, offers suggestions for theological development. This is a useful snapshot of a particular cultural group within Australian theological education. Finally, in what has been described as possibly the most important essay in the volume, Jude Long poignantly portrays the story of Nungalinya (Aboriginal) College, and offers insightful comment on the triumphs, the challenges, and the needs of this community. Any road map of the ways ahead for Australian theological education must include earnest consideration of such cultural diversity in the national landscape.

In presenting this book to the theological educational community, the editors gratefully acknowledge the facilitative support of the Sydney College of Divinity. On behalf of the College, we trust that this work will be received as a worthwhile sentence introduced into the ongoing conversation that seeks the betterment of theological education. For the days ahead, we sincerely hope that this book will throw some spark of light on the ways ahead.

WHERE ARE WE GOING?

QUESTIONING THE FUTURE OF LEARNING AND TEACHING THEOLOGY

LES BALL

Abstract

The essay flows out of the findings of the *Transforming Theology* project which researched theological higher education in Australia. Several key questions emerged as warranting more intensive examination if theological graduates are to be produced who will competently and convincingly engage the contemporary world in the mission of the church. Serious questions of pedagogical philosophy, theological content, and methods of learning and teaching all pointed to the need for a re-evaluation of how theological curriculum should be constructed to achieve the goal of integrated contemporary and future graduates. In addressing these questions, this paper confronts some entrenched traditional thinking in ways that seek to preserve the inherent values of current theological learning and at the same time to enhance that learning to make it more personally grounded in a graduate and thereby more effectual in vocational and societal expressions.

• • •

Before We Start

Theology is not God. Right at the outset, I want to issue a warning against the seductive trap of "logolatry": the enslavement to systems of thinking which can serve insidiously to obscure or even negate the purported object of that thinking.

Theological discourse is replete with "ologies": soteriology, Christology, pneumatology, ecclesiology. Similarly, pedagogical discourse is replete with its "ologies": epistemology, methodology, and so on. Such constructs should be kept in a proper perspective, as extremely useful systems of organizing our thinking and enhancing our understanding of complex realities, including sacred and immutable realities, but they should not be held as sacred immutabilities in their own right. It is useful, I think, to view such technical terms in their composite parts. The common suffix in all these words is the "ology" component, which describes the process involved, namely, a reasoned systematic approach to thinking, understanding, studying. But the primary part of the terms is the semantic root, in our case, "theos," which denotes the focus of that thinking, namely, God. Too often, the process suffix "ology" obscures the driving subject of the focal root "theos." Whereas we rightly view God and his revelation as sacred, immutable and the true focus of theological learning and teaching, we would do well to ensure that we do not ascribe the same sanctity to our traditions of thinking and learning, which have at times come too close to a veneration born of a received tradition rather than a divine revelation. We do well also to acknowledge humbly the Pauline observation that we indeed know—and always have known—but "in part" (1 Cor 13:9). God is God. Theology is not God. It is on that basis that I am challenged to re-think many of my traditional, even entrenched ways of thinking about the pedagogy of theological learning.

Where Shall We Start? Pedagogical Philosophy

I have become increasingly convinced of late that the proper starting point of all learning and teaching is the philosophical base which undergirds that undertaking, rather than the traditional practices which have tended to shape our present situation. In theological education, there are at least four distinct, sometimes competing, yet equally legitimate philosophical bases. There is first the *historical or traditional rationale*, which essentially justifies what we do on the basis that this is what we have always done or what everyone else does. Often, this is the primary practical consideration in curriculum design (aided by accrediting bodies' obsession with benchmarking). Second and far more important is the *theological rationale* for what we are doing: the quest to know God, to understand his person, work and will for all creation, and to facilitate the growth of persons within that knowledge. You may of course add further nuances to such a theological platform. Then there is the associated yet distinct overlay of the *ecclesiological rationale* for what we do: the commitment to serving the mission of the church, in both its global and its local expressions, including its denominational requirements and its ecumenical aspirations—itself not an easy tension to sustain. Finally, there is the *pedagogical rationale* which shapes neither the theological content nor the ecclesiological purpose, but it does determine the very shape in which the learning and teaching of theology will be conducted.

In considering all these philosophical grounds, it is important to maintain a sense of balance so as not to jettison the good and necessary along with the outdated and irrelevant. We need to retain a respect for history—without which we have no continuity. We need to guard our fidelity to theology—without which we have no identity. We need to maintain a loyalty to our institutions—without which we have no structure. We need to ensure effectiveness in pedagogy—without which we have no relevance. It is this element of theological pedagogy which is my focus in this essay.

So, let me mark my pedagogical territory right from the outset. As I draw towards the end of a long educational career, I am more committed than ever before to a philosophy of student-centred learning and teaching. For decades, I practised a thorough-going delivery of content-centred curricula, where I offered to my students a compendium of knowledge and wisdom gleaned from many years of my learning and research. I decided what knowledge is the "sacred deposit" of my disciplines, I organised that material in a coherent way, and I delivered it to classes with variable levels of engagement. While I am confident that much good ensued, I came a few years ago to believe there is a better way, a way which retains the high value on the knowledge that I cherish so much, but which allows me to value just as highly the persons of the learners as parts of God's ongoing work. I am not talking about a process whereby I have been removed to a sideline position as a detached coach, but about a process of what Mascolo has called "guided participation," involving a novice (learner) and a more expert guide (teacher).[1] Here, the teacher as a leader of learning assumes responsibility for creating the structures and initiating the activities that allow the learning group to succeed.[2] Thus my teaching has

---

1   Michael Mascolo, "Beyond student-centered and teacher-centered pedagogy: Teaching and learning as guided participation," *Pedagogy and the Human Sciences 1*, No. 1 (2009), 11-12.
2   Alex Haslam, "The I and We of Leadership," *Contact* (Winter 2013), 28.

become a work in which I have been allowed to participate as a privileged co-learner in the process of facilitating a person's development, not just as an imparter of important knowledge or even as a trainer of skilled performers.

I add another observation here. As well as what might be seen as a theological base of a learner-centred pedagogy, there is a secondary sociological consideration. It is virtually axiomatic that the nature and the context of contemporary (and by extension future) theological learners are vastly different from the situation of even a couple of decades ago (which is probably the time when many of today's theological teachers received their own education). The teacher is no longer the sole or necessarily the major source—or perhaps even the main determiner—of important knowledge transmission. The learners are no longer content to accept authoritative dicta without question, especially if such dicta seem disconnected from or contradictory of their own experience. As well as the theological issue of respect for the personal worth of the learner and the learner's situation, the sociological considerations of the greater emphasis on personal and immediate relevance, the overt challenging of received authority, and the virtually infinite access to knowledge now readily available add further weight to the advocacy of a learner-centred pedagogy.

What Shall We Teach? The Content of Theological Learning and Teaching

There is of course no such thing as a contentless curriculum. A recent survey of theological education providers and their communities in Australia made it very clear that a major motivation and purpose of such education is growth in biblical and theological knowledge.[3] It is the main reason cited by students for enrolling; it is the main priority listed by faculty; it is the non-negotiable attribute demanded by church leaders. However, while the demand for theological knowledge is virtually universal, there is no equivalent identification of exactly what such a body of knowledge should be. Most courses incorporate at least a first year of survey units in traditional disciplines of Bible, systematic theology and church history or philosophy, with all students required to digest the same large corpus of knowledge, which may have some or no connection with the

---

3   The *Transforming Theology* research project (2010-2012) surveyed and interviewed faculty, students, graduates, and church leaders across all Australian States and involved 59 teaching campuses of public universities and private colleges.

students' prior or ongoing life experience.[4] This is commonly followed by a series of often disconnected units in the same main disciplines, with various inclusions of practical ministry skills or supervised field education units.

Given that such an approach manages to cover the main doctrinal and ecclesiastical requirements, it is not surprising that such a structure has been generally adopted. In general, I have no argument with the overall content and skills so included in a theological program, as the traditional, theological and ecclesiological rationales for learning are thus more or less satisfactorily developed. However, there are some areas that are often neglected in this traditionally determined content, which are emerging as increasingly significant in the global context of today's (and tomorrow's) curriculum. Neil Holm has recently reminded us of the need to take seriously the issues of inter-faith engagement and the emergence of theological discourse emanating from the Majority World, whose foci are vastly different from the usual Euro-American perspectives of traditional theological scholarship.[5] Rarely do these elements find their way into formal theological curricula, which retain their largely inherited focus, yet the 21st century will require theological graduates to be not only aware of these wider horizons but also competent to play a role in such discourse.

However, my main argument lies in the pedagogical domain which addresses just how the desired knowledge and skills base is packaged and processed. The generally passive reception of pre-determined and pre-packaged knowledge and the conventional programmatic approach to skills development are not consistent with the principles of learner-centred education and are contributory to the generally observed lack of integration that marks much theological learning.[6] The essential theological knowledge of the received Christian tradition (however determined and selected) and the effectual skills of ministry (however understood and practised) may well be the "sacred deposit" of institutional learning; however, the transmission and development of these elements need to be learner-centred if they are to be personalised in the graduate people produced by the educative process. If there needs to be conservatism in content (which

---

4 The *Transforming Theology* project found a high degree of commonality in theological undergraduate degree structures in Australian institutions.
5 Neil Holm, "Reflections on the SCD," in *Transforming Teaching*, Vol. 1 Issue 2 (May 2013), 3.
6 Stephen Haar voiced the concern of numerous theological educators when he bemoaned the non-integrated compartmentalised learning experience that typifies much theological education. Stephen Haar, "Enhancing the Capability of Theological Schools in Becoming Agents of Change and Transformation in Civil Society" (Consultation on Establishing a Regional Network of Lutheran Theological Educators: Bangkok; 18 March 2010).

itself is arguable, even though it does seem to typify theology in general), there also needs to be a progressiveness in delivery, if our learning and teaching are to be relevant and vital for contemporary learners within a contemporary context.[7]

How Shall We Teach? Methods of Learning and Teaching

To my somewhat simplistic mind, there are two basic types of approach to methods of learning and teaching: pontification and engagement. By pontification, I mean that approach which implies, "This is all ye know on earth and all ye need to know" (with apologies to John Keats). In this approach, the focus is on teaching rather than on learning. The master-teacher is the key agent in the process, with the common term "lecturer" saying much more than it probably wants to do in this regard. The teacher selects, organises and presents the content as a necessary corpus for all learners to receive in the same way. Individual learners will inevitably process this teacher input variously, despite the generally uniform parameters for such processing devised by the teacher. The main object of this approach is the comprehensive coverage of all required syllabus content. Thus it is particularly well suited to those forms of learning which require detailed knowledge of regulations, legalities or technical processes. Yet clearly the emphasis on the transmission of extensive and detailed content does little to encourage either processing skills or personal development.

So it is that I turn to engagement as a generally preferred approach to learning method, a turn which I strongly urge as a future emphasis in theological education, which is arguably more inherently concerned with the formation of persons than most other fields of education. Engagement does not devalue content; it sees content as a means to the end of personal learning rather than the end of that learning. In espousing engagement as the desirable dominant methodological approach to theological learning and teaching in the future, I will use three kinds of such engagement as examples. There are of course many more, but these will hopefully serve to make the point.

Problem-Based Learning (PBL) is a well-established educational approach, particularly suited to organisational or structural studies, such as ministry topics. Case studies of ministry incidents or issues, real or hypothetical, are useful ways of engaging learners, and they allow learners to bring their individual experiences

---

[7] See also the essay by Neil Holm, "An Analysis of 'Soul' as the Central Construct in Dirkx's and Ruether's Transformative Learning Theory."

and insights to bear on the identification and resolution of a problem. There is much to be said for the establishment of a suitable portfolio of problematic scenarios for group or individual analysis and resolution in many disciplines.[8] While the application of such an approach is obvious in field education studies, it is also applicable to classroom based units, with reference to solving textual problems, conceptual conundrums or ethical dilemmas.[9] When a learner is personally engaged in the identification, analysis and, importantly, the resolution of a critical problem, the learning will most likely become personalised and permanent. While such an approach has been commonplace in higher level research, it has much to offer at all other levels of learning as well.

A second kind of engagement is Inquiry-Based Learning (IBL). Whereas PBL assumes a problem to be solved by an external analyst (and is thereby inherently capable of offending those within the problematic situation), IBL is a more positive heuristic approach. Here, learners are motivated by a desire to discover an answer, to fill in gaps in their existing knowledge, to build on their prior experience as they continue a process of discovery. While this is generally an open-ended inquiry, it is not an unstructured process, with the structures being crafted to allow learners to connect the discovery with the realities of their own life. A particularly productive form of IBL is Appreciative Inquiry, where the learner is encouraged to identify and analyse past personal successes, then to articulate ways in which those past successes may be developed to generate ongoing successes.[10] The application of such an approach is virtually limitless. It has a most formative outcome, as it takes genuine cognisance of where a learner has come from and where the learner is potentially going.

Work-Integrated Learning (WIL) is my final example of engagement. It is worth noting that this approach is fast gaining traction in many universities as well as in theological colleges. It is particularly emerging as a key strategy for equipping graduates in human service type professions, such as teaching, nursing,

---

8   For an introduction to the approach of scenarios in problem-solving, see James Dalziel, "Developing Scenario Learning and its implementation in LAMS," in L. Cameron and J. Dalziel, eds., *Proceedings of the 7th International LAMS Conference: Surveying the Learning Design Landscape* (2012), 32-39.
9   A working example of a Problem-Based Learning teaching strategy for exploring the question of non-violence in Christian thought is provided at http://jamesdalziel.blogspot.com.au/2012/01/problem-based-learning-example.html.
10 See G.R. Bushe and A.F. Kassam, "When is Appreciative Inquiry Transformational? A Meta-Case Analysis," *The Journal of Applied Behavioural Science* 41:2 (2005), 161-181.

counselling and social work.[11] It is noteworthy that Bible Colleges have given a strong historical lead here, as they have traditionally placed students in churches or other Christian organisations as a mandatory part of their overall programs. However, such placements have also traditionally been seen as an extra-curricular additive to college life rather than as a part of the formal curriculum, and consequently have typically lacked the programmatic cohesion or pedagogical rigour applied to the more formal fields of study.[12] Yet the fact that these colleges have successfully established networks of supportive community work bases for the placement of students bodes well for further development of this rich source of personal and professional development of students.

It is not my purpose to examine the details of WIL here, as much research is currently under way into the philosophy and practices involved.[13] Rather, I will limit my remarks to a few aspects which may prompt a broadening of the scope of WIL within our theological sector. For integrated and formative learning to take place, WIL needs to connect in a structured and strategic way with the living context of the learner. That is, effectual cognisance needs to be had of both the actual past experience of the learner and the potential future experience which the learner is aspiring to have. This will of course require getting to know the learner as an individual, which is admittedly time-consuming yet vital for effectual placement and development. All learning takes place by way of being related to past understanding and experiences, and WIL is no different. It serves little purpose simply to place learners in a situation and hope they will automatically learn by experience, if that "learning experience" is disconnected from the real world of those learners. WIL should intentionally and strategically take a learner from a known experiential starting point and lead to an articulated

---

11   A review of recent curriculum structures in these fields across the major Australian universities shows a strong trend towards including work placements in real life situations as a major component of the courses, with an emphasis on clinical or other internships being a feature of the final stages of many programs.

12   In recent years, many Australian undergraduate Theology awards have included a small number of field-based elective units, but as well as forming but a small part of the award for a limited number of students, they still suffer from the common stigma of lack of integration, formal development and pedagogical rigour.

13   For an up-to-date statement on this topic, see the essay by Darren Cronshaw and Andrew Menzies, "From Place to Place: A Comparative Study of 5 Models of Workplace Formation at 2 Colleges on 1 Campus."

   WIL is a popular topic for current research projects currently funded by the Australian Government Office for Learning and Teaching, with studies currently being conducted, *inter alia*, by Charles Sturt University, Murdoch University and Queensland University of Technology. See http://www.olt.gov.au/grants-and-projects.

end tailored to the needs and aspirations of the learner.

The only other plea I make for future WIL consideration concerns the ambit of placements. It is traditional, and almost universal, to place theological students in a local church or para-church situation under the supervision of a local minister, with the aim of developing the learner's pastoral ministry skills. Yet such skills are not specifically required by the majority of contemporary theological students.[14] As noted above regarding the content of theological programs, traditional horizons need review. Preparing learners for life in a manse will not prepare the majority of students for their roles in a broader and increasingly post-Christendom world. Hopefully, even those heading for vocational ministry will be equipped to relate to this wider context. As a Christian layman, my plea is for theological WIL to expand the range of placements beyond the church, beyond Christian organisations, even beyond a Christian community, and to create opportunities for learners to attain not just Work Integrated Learning but Life Integrated Learning. While the skills of preaching and Bible teaching are well fostered in a local church, the skills of critical thinking and apologetic argument and the expanding of worldview can occur very well in a totally different scene. Since most of the world to be encountered beyond graduation is beyond the church, it seems logical that work placements could also benefit from going beyond the church into our local majority world.

How Shall We Build? Implications for Curriculum

It is in this area that I make perhaps my most controversial suggestion and where I expect to meet most resistance, since it goes against much entrenched structuralist tradition (including my own, in which I have comfortably located myself for four decades of teaching). The *Transforming Theology* project had, as its stated end, curriculum design and planning of undergraduate theological degrees. In the concluding pages of that book, I made some recommendations for fundamental curriculum reform.[15] At the risk of some repetition, I re-visit some of the thoughts expressed there.[16]

---

14 Recent Graduate Destination Surveys from Australian theological institutions show that the range of graduates entering vocational ministry is 30-50% depending on the ethos of the institution. While this remains the most significant destination, it is not the future of the majority of students.
15 Les Ball, *Transforming Theology. Student Experience and Transformative Learning in Undergraduate Theological Education* (Preston Vic: Mosaic Press, 2012), 141-144.
16 See also the essay by Evelyn and Richard Hibbert, "Addressing the Need for Better Integration in Theological Education: Proposals, Progress, and Possibilities from the Medical Education Model."

A good curriculum design is one that will facilitate the desired end of the learning process. It should therefore start from an articulated and owned philosophical base that determines that desired end, rather than simply being an inherited way of doing things. In considering the future direction of curriculum design, I am acutely aware of such inherited ways of doing things, and as a natural conservative (and an historian), I have great respect for such heritage. I am also aware of the legitimate ecclesiastical demands that impinge on curriculum design in many theological institutions. However, as an educationist, I am constantly seeking ways to enhance the educative process, without sacrificing the things of value that I now have. That is the challenge of effective curriculum design. So, I propose the following simple yet radical thoughts for consideration.

For the last hundred years, theological awards in Australia (as elsewhere) have been virtually universally structured on the chassis of Fields, Majors and/or Specialisations. The result has been the acquisition of a thorough, faithful and commendable knowledge of the biblical books studied, the systematic theology topics analysed, the denominational distinctives required, and some expertise in the ministry skills practised. However, what has not been attained is an integration of the fragmented compartments of knowledge and skills so presented. The major quality lauded by faculty, graduates and church leaders during the *Transforming Theology* project was the comprehensive and faithful acquisition of biblical and theological knowledge by the graduates. The major lament voiced by faculty, graduates and church leaders was the fragmentation of knowledge and its inevitable lack of integration in the person of the graduate, who all too often is confronted by a world that does not want to be addressed as the academy but wants to deal with a "real person" who not only has good theology to express but also has an integrated personhood to demonstrate. If our curriculum structures have led to theologically knowledgeable graduates, but our desired objective is a theologically informed *and integrated* person, then I suggest that we should enhance our curriculum appropriately by incorporating integrative principles and practices. By this I do not mean simply applying an overlay of pseudo-integration or some spurious thematic unification. Rather, I propose a carefully structured process of integration that permeates all the valuable knowledge and skills that we currently deliver so well.

The first thing to confront is our rigid adherence to a system of fields and majors, which are the very basis of so much of the lamented fragmentation. Not all beginning students are at the same point in their theological development, nor do they all need the same input of biblical knowledge, yet typically, all are treated as though that is the case, be that by enrolling in Introductions to the traditional fields or by a common first year program of some other kind. Such an overtly content-centred curriculum pays little heed to the development of integrated persons. If adherence to the structural concepts of fields and majors must be retained (withdrawal from entrenched habits is always difficult and often painful), then they will need to be reviewed to find a way in which integration may be effectively incorporated. If not, we will risk producing graduates who will become increasingly remote from the contemporary world and decreasingly credible within that world.[17]

A developmental curriculum, as distinct from a compartmentalised one, will feature sequenced learning rather than piecemeal units, delivered in a coordinated way not in isolation. Such sequential learning is most likely to lead to integration. However, in theological education (and arguably in other areas as well), integration needs to be understood in three dimensions. First is the integration of learnings with learnings. By that I mean that all units delivered need to be processed in relation to one another. It defeats the purpose of integration if, say, the New Testament teacher and the Theology teacher are promoting opposite views on an issue, if the learners have no opportunity to process such conflicting approaches in an open and respectful way, preferably with the engagement of both teachers. Similar observations apply to the integration of so-called academic subjects and practical subjects. Teachers need to be able to demonstrate integration among themselves and curriculum needs to facilitate such opportunities.

The second dimension of integration is that of learnings with praxis, that is, the harmonious coordination of what we know with what we do. Don Browning's Correlational Fundamental Practical Theology paradigm, with its mutual critical correlation, is worth noting in this regard. Browning's paradigm incorporates four sub-sections: descriptive theology, historical theology, systematic theology and strategic practical theology.[18] In this paradigm, the analytical observation of practice leads to the examination of normative and historical theory and then

---

17 For an illustration of a way in which this has been addressed, see the essay by Denise Goodwin, "A Practical Approach for Teaching Foundational Theology: Inquiry–Based Learning and the Matrix of Ideas Process."
18 Don S. Browning, *Equality and the Family* (Grand Rapids: Eerdmans, 2007), 10.

back to a re-formulation of theory-laden practice or truthful action.[19] Such an approach built into curriculum design has obvious application to the integration of a learner's learning and practice. Likewise, curriculum design can give teachers opportunities to demonstrate in an integrated way their commitment to life-long learning, which is more than simply producing more journal articles or monographs, and includes demonstrably growing in their knowledge and beliefs as they co-learn with students.[20]

Finally, curriculum design will need to incorporate opportunities for learners to grow in and demonstrate an integration of their learnings and their life with a moral worldview, that is, the integration of what they know, what they do and what they are. Typically this will require units of study that allow for some active expression of worldview, particularly in the closing stages of their program, which will more readily allow such demonstration. While there are numerous creative ways of achieving such integrative ends, the overarching principle is that a facilitative curriculum is needed rather than a tightly prescriptive curriculum. The teacher may well select the content to be covered; the teacher will certainly maintain overall responsibility for and control of the pedagogic process; however, the mode of engagement of content within that process needs great flexibility to allow great creativity, with the principal concern being the effectual theological development of an integrated graduate learner.

Quality Assurance or Quality Facilitation?

Whenever we venture into the realm of individualised or learner-centred education, it is not long before we encounter the legitimate dilemma of quality assurance, with its constant companions, benchmarking and assessment. If individual learners are developing their own worldview, how can we accurately measure their performance against uniform criteria or fairly compare their results with other students on a grading scale? That is, how can we assure the quality of the learning process and outcomes? My personal frustration relates

---

19 A succinct account of Browning's critical hermeneutical approach is provided in *Equality and the Family*, Chapter 1: Toward a Fundamental and Strategic Practical Theology, 3-30. This is an abridged version of his seminal work, *A Fundamental Practical Theology* (Minneapolis: Fortress, 1991).
   See also his interesting case study of Ignatius Loyola as an illustration of how spirituality and practical reason can co-exist, in *Reviving Christian Humanism* (Minneapolis: Fortress, 2012), 103-106.
20 For a further illustration of practical theology method, see the essay by Steve Taylor, "Embodiment and transformation in the context of e-learning."

to the traditional notion that *quality* is assured by reducing our performance descriptors to *quantifiable* mathematical dimensions and observable uniformity. The very question asked is that of *assurance* not *facilitation*, which I see as two quite distinct things. The following table shows the contrasting aspects of assurance *vis-à-vis* facilitation.

Quality Assurance	Quality Facilitation
Control	Flexibility
Benchmarking	Creativity
Stultifying	Liberating
Monochromatic	Kaleidoscopic
Regulations	Guiding Principles

Put simply, standard processes of quality assurance are designed to ensure that all students fit within the same parameters: of course structure, of knowledge exposure and processing and of assessment regimens. To demonstrate this fit, benchmarking processes typically demand similar course design, measure attrition and progression rates, compare grade distributions and the like. Such quantifiable data are attractive, since they give an air of mathematical precision and provide the groundwork for a level playing field across a varied spectrum of delivery. These are of course valuable and valid things to seek. However, such a regulatory approach leads to a "one size fits all" philosophy and in reality seems to have more to do with control than with facilitation of learning. It is questionable how much impact such data actually have on the learning relationships between teacher and student or on what takes place in the learning environment of the classroom.

On the other hand, quality facilitation is to do less with control and more with attainment. It is a less tidy concept, since it does not depend on the more readily manageable standardised processes of control. Facilitative processes seek opportunities rather than uniformities. They aim to assist the learner to attain the desired learning outcomes in ways that are most effectual for that learner. This is not new, being the stuff of good teaching for many years. However, I fear that creativity in learning (and associated assessment, which unfortunately has come to dominate so much of the learning activities) has become stultified by reduction to what is needed for assessment. Assessment needs to be returned to its rightful place: a facilitator of learning not a limiter of learning. Again, any evaluation of the *quality* of learning should incorporate valid *qualitative markers* and not just reduce everything to quantifiable numbers. Once that is understood, then even assessment items can be creatively constructed to be a legitimate part, rather than an inhibition, of legitimate and deep learning.[21]

Where are We Heading?

By way of conclusion, let me make some summary observations on where we as a theological education sector (particularly in Australia) are heading. We are now in a time when knowledge access is unprecedented in both its scope and its lack of controls. No longer is the academy the bastion of special knowledge— even the sacrosanct knowledge of theology. We are also in a society which is far more ruggedly self-focused and critical of institutional privilege than ever before. Thus, the learners who present for theological education are more aware of what they want, more exposed to a world of ideas and more questioning of entrenched authority than previous generations— and this is more likely to increase than to decrease. The technologically advanced nature of contemporary society has driven much of this and it also demands that educational providers adapt to such development. You may have noted that I have not addressed the topic of modes of delivery in this presentation, and that is for two reasons. First, I see the variety of modes as being not so much a challenge as the fundamental principles that underlie our learning and teaching, since many students and teachers are bringing their technological skills to bear in commendably flexible ways. Second, technical skills are developing at such a pace that whatever I might present would be at risk of immediate obsolescence. What I will say, however, is that we need to acknowledge that there is no one "best" mode of delivery and that the multi-form face of today's learning community requires a flexible approach to delivery—the challenge is to enhance the learning experience in this variety or blend of modes. The fundamental principles I have been addressing apply to all modes.

So, if the academy is to maintain relevance and to keep pace with society, it must adapt. That is not a call to abandon or compromise its mission or its

---

[21] For an examination of the issue of assessment for deep learning, see Charles De Jongh's essay, "The Contribution of Theories of Multiple Intelligences to the Promotion of Deep Learning through the Assessment of Learning."

See also the essay by Nancy Ault, "Assessing Integrative Learning and Readiness for Ministry: Can There be Common Ground?"

message. But it is a call to evolve in its pedagogical philosophy and praxis, with a focal shift away from controlled comprehensive content delivery to the facilitation of the development of the learner, through curriculum design and teaching methods which lead to that end. The academy needs to be clear about its traditional heritage, its underlying theological base, its ecclesiological mandate and its educational philosophy, and to keep these in a coherent tension. It needs to engage learners more strategically and actively in a process of relevant discovery and personal growth, and not to assume passivity or even receptivity on the part of learners: learners need to be developed not merely instructed.

It is symptomatic of contemporary Australia that there is (and I believe will continue to be) a growing difficulty for small exclusivist theological providers to sustain viability in higher education. Universities are absorbing theological colleges; small consortia are under pressure; several independent colleges have diversified their programs to extend beyond theology; and only a very small number are maintaining an independent, viable identity as a purely theological college based on a well identified "brand." This is now a theological world of greater associationalism and even federation. Such movements reflect the growing mood towards breaking down denominational or sectarian enclaves, with students having a much wider exposure to variant views and being encouraged to develop personal critical positions rather than to accept uncritically the establishment position. Hence it is imperative that the academy equip its learners to process analytically and to appropriate in deeply personal ways the information and ideas that they encounter. In a world where denominational distinctives are losing their sharpness and where institutional control of individuals is rapidly declining, theological delivery needs to embrace creatively the opportunities for deep personal learning presented by the world in which it so strategically exists.

SECTION TWO

A BIBLICAL ROAD MAP: PAUL AS A THEOLOGICAL TEACHER

1 | HIGHER EDUCATION IN THE PAULINE CHURCHES

E.A. JUDGE

Abstract

The novel metaphor of Jesus "building" his "meeting" is unexplained. Likewise how the mission was to make "students" of all nations. Teaching was not institutionalised in the "meetings." Claire Smith has analysed the wide variety of "learning" experiences that built the Pauline communities. Seven different types of Classical teacher or training are considered. Most are irrelevant to the Pauline case. Only advanced rhetorical and philosophical training stimulates Paul's attention. He rejects both in favour of practical testing for truth. Galen, the medical polymath, compares the "school of Moses and Christ" with empirical teachers who will not give logical proofs. Modern science arises not from the fixed universe of Athens, but from the temporary one of Jerusalem, open to experimental testing.

* * *

Introduction

The gospel of Matthew lays down two unusual mission statements. In either case the meaning is far from obvious. Their educational outworking has, however, been literally epoch-making.

What can it possibly mean to say "I will build" (*oikodomeso*, Matt 16:18) "my meeting" (*ekklesia*)? The metaphor is novel. Contrast the familiar image of the "meeting" as a body. Nero was head of the Roman "body," said Seneca (*On

Clemency 2.2.1). But "building my meeting" must have been utterly puzzling.[1]

What also can it mean to be sent to all the nations to "make students" (*matheteusate*) of them, "teaching"(*didaskontes*) them to "observe all the directions I gave you" (Matt 28:19-20), if there are to be no teachers? Jesus himself is often called in the gospels the "teacher" (*didaskalos*), while those who "followed" him are the "students" (*mathetai*, Latin *discipuli*).

In Acts, however, the "students" upon whom "teaching" had been enjoined turn out to be "emissaries" (*apostoloi*, 1:2). Moreover, they are not called "teachers," but "witnesses" (*martyres*, 1:8). There are new "students" (6:1), who have responded to the "teaching" (*didache*, 2:42) but these could not of course be said to have "followed" Jesus. In the epistles even the term "students" has disappeared. Whatever can have happened to the international teaching mission?

Where Have All the Teachers Gone?

In the list of diverse "gifts" (*chfarismata*, 1 Cor 5:1, cf. Eph 4:11) given in the "meeting," "emissaries" and "teachers" are separately itemised. They are all to "build" "God's house," it seems (1 Cor 3:9; 2 Cor 5:1; cf. Eph 2:22). But what can that do for "the nations"? Paul is himself once called the "teacher of nations" (1 Tim 2:7). But neither at home nor abroad was that title to be institutionalised.

With both Paul and the writer of Luke-Acts, a new and contemporary term for "being instructed" is introduced. Theophilus (Luke 1:4) and Apollos (Acts 18:25) are men already highly educated who have each now in addition "been instructed" in the new way. Paul uses the term for one "being instructed" (*catechoumenos*, Rom 2:18) in the (Mosaic) law. He would himself rather utter five words "with his mind" so as to "instruct" others than ten thousand in an ecstatic "tongue" (1 Cor 14:19, cf. Gal 6:6).

In later centuries new converts being "instructed" before baptism are called "catechumens." We have papyrus certificates stating how far the holder has reached in the curriculum of biblical study.[2] Before the time of Christ, the

---

[1] E.A. Judge, "Kultgemeinde (Kultverein)," *Reallexikon für Antike und Christentum* 22 (2007), 393-438; id., "On this rock I will build my *ekklesia*: Counter-cultic springs of multiculturalism?" *The First Christians in the Roman World: Augustan and New Testament Essays* (Tübingen: Mohr Siebeck, 2008), 619-68, at 620, 663.

[2] PSI 9.1041, P.Oxy. 36.2785, discussed by E.A. Judge, "The Interaction of Biblical and Classical Education in the Fourth Century," *Jerusalem and Athens: Cultural Transformation in Late Antiquity* (Tübingen: Mohr Siebeck, 2010), 254-63, at 256.

Roman statesman Cicero had used the Greek word *catechesis* in private for the "education" of the adolescent Octavian (*To Atticus* 15.12.2). In the late fourth century the ultra-pedantic Latin theologian Jerome boasted of having the Greek Fathers as his "catechists" in Scripture (*Ep.* 50.1). He latinised the word. Not only is this title not found in the New Testament, it is unattested even in the Greek Fathers. The formal institution of "catechists" became a feature of Western churches, but mainly in the twentieth century.

It may be that the first "students" of Jesus avoided any title to be the "teacher" or "instructor" of others. "Do not be called 'rabbi,' for you have one 'teacher' (*didaskalos*), and you are all brothers" (Matt 23:8). "And do not be called 'guides' (*kathegetai*), for you have one guide, Christ" (v. 10). "Not many of you are to become 'teachers' (*didaskaloi*), my brothers, knowing that we shall be judged more strictly" (James 3:1). "When he, the Spirit of truth comes, he will 'lead' you into all truth" (John 16:13). "All your sons will be 'taught' by the Lord" (Isaiah 54:13, cited at John 6:45). Behind these various declarations lies the age-long tension in Israel between prophet and priest or scribe. The prophet speaks directly from the Lord, denouncing scribal authority as pretentious and self-serving, or (in the novel image of Jesus) hypocritical.

The titles "apostle" ("emissary"), "prophet" and "teacher" all belong, by their primary meaning, to the communicative or didactic mission. For all three terms the initiating purpose is clear from the New Testament documents. People professing these titles continue even later to appear, for example in the *Didache* ("Teaching"). This manual was intended to set things in order for the second generation, it seems. But in the long run none of the three titles was given a permanent place in the institutional structure of the "meeting." That went instead to the "overseer" (*episkopos*), the "elder" (*presbyteros*) and the "attendant" (*diakonos*).

"Bishops," "priests" and "deacons," the anglicised forms of these Greek words, are now so inescapably suggestive, both of cultic worship and of prescriptive discipline, that one must shock oneself into recognising their different New Testament intention. The terms do not arise from ancient sacral (i.e. "religious") practice at all, but from civil life. In particular, they imply administrative responsibility in any "meeting" or other organisation.

In the Pauline pastoral epistles it is made clear that bishops, elders and deacons must be chosen on a local basis. Personal integrity and public acceptance is essential for their appointment (1 Tim 3:1-13; Titus 1:5-16). There is otherwise a major problem with adventurous "teachers" (1 Tim 1:3-7; 6:3-5, 20-21; 2 Tim 2: 14-19; 4:3-4; Titus 3: 9-11). The new administrators must themselves therefore take responsibility for the proper "message" (*logos*) and its teaching (1 Tim 5:17; Titus 1:9).

In the *Didache* the distinction is made both clear and emphatic. "Apostles," "prophets" and "teachers" are all typically on the move. So there must be limits to how much accommodation and maintenance should be supplied for such unexpected charismatic arrivals (*Didache* 11-13). Instead, local "bishops" and "deacons" of proven financial restraint should be appointed. These should be themselves respected as though they were prophets and teachers (15.1). The itinerants are not to be given priority of esteem (15.2). So the didactic mission of Christ to all the nations will be anchored in the local "meeting," "built" up there, presumably according to the Lord's "directions."

The experimental and contested character of this grand educational enterprise is itself the reason why it has been so richly documented with diverse sources. The historical implications of the New Testament corpus are intensively researched today more than ever before. No other social institution of antiquity can match its primary fascination. It combines the imprint of unique sayings, verified transcripts, a powerful interpretative framework, revelatory dogma, and especially disputed truth. This is all utterly foreign to what we mean by religion in antiquity–the scrupulous replication of inherited sanctities.[3] By sharp contrast the argumentativeness of the Pauline "meetings," and their tension over status, was taken (improbably) in 1960 to suggest their being called "scholastic communities."[4] By 1977 the social aspects of this idea were said to have contributed to "a new consensus."[5] In 2012, moreover, the historical incongruity of the term "scholastic" was systematically put to the test.[6]

There are nearly one hundred individuals mentioned in connection with the Pauline communities. We know their names. But almost always there is no title to indicate their occupation, whether civil or ecclesiastical, or their social or family status (e.g. whether married or not). Instead we are shown how they relate to others in the "meeting," or should do. Claire Smith has examined especially the verbs (as distinct from nouns) which express the purpose of the interaction (not the "teacher" but the manner of "teaching," with its converse,

---

3   E.A. Judge, 'Was Christianity a Religion?' *The First Christians in the Roman World*, 404-409.
4   "The early Christians as a scholastic community," *The First Christians in the Roman World*, 526-52.
5   A.J. Malherbe, 'Social Level and Literary Culture', in *Social Aspects of Early Christianity* (Baton Rouge: Louisiana State University, 1977) 29-59, at 31.
6   Claire S. Smith, *Pauline Communities as 'Scholastic Communities': A Study of the Vocabulary of 'Teaching' in 1 Corinthians, 1 and 2 Timothy and Titus* ((Tübingen: Mohr Siebeck, 2012).

"learning"). From only four of the letters she has identified fifty-five different terms which give effect to these personal connections and their intention. Teaching and learning may involve more than the spoken word. Mere communication would only convey data. We are concerned more for the transformation of life through understanding, attitude or belief.

Smith's chosen vocabulary is then classified into the following nine semantic groupings (for each of which there is noted here only one example):

Teaching (*didasko*)
Speaking (*lego*)
Traditioning (*grapho*)
Announcing (*kerysso*)
Revealing (*apokalypto*)
Worshipping (*propheteuo*)
Commanding (*parakaleo*)
Correcting (*paideuo*)
Reminding (*gnorizo*)

The conclusion from this rich array, each particular instance of a term being contextually explored, is that, while "scholastic" may have been heading in the right direction, we shall understand the vitality of the education that is given and received by speaking of "learning communities."

Teaching in Public Education

How do the Pauline churches measure up to the public institutions of educational practice?

The primary teacher (grammatistes)
Elementary literacy (reading and writing) was provided on an individual basis, typically for small children. The laborious process is documented by scores of papyri written by teacher or pupil at identifiable stages of competency.[7]

Paul himself (unless he had an eye-handicap) had perhaps not practised his

---

7   R. Cribiore, *Writing, Teachers, and Students in Graeco-Roman Egypt* (Atlanta: Scholars Press, 1996); *Gymnastics of the Mind: Greek Education in Hellenistic and Roman Egypt* (Princeton: Princeton University Press, 2001): alphabetical syllabification came first. P.Worp 53 has biblical words included for practice; P.Lit.Lond. 207 has a psalm marked by syllables.

writing beyond this point (Gal 6:11). As with other established figures there would have been more experienced writers available to deliver the economical, informal and swiftly readable script of his time. Professional readers were also available, later institutionalised in church.

Only in 529, however, at the second Council of Vaison (Gaul), were parishes obliged to institute elementary schooling as the public supply was failing. The alphabetic "elements" interested Paul (1 Cor 13:11, cf. Heb 5:12-14), but only as a figure of stunted growth in theological understanding, for which Paul's preferred image was the need to wean an infant off its mother's milk (1 Cor. 3:1-2).

(b) The secondary teacher (grammatikos)

Having learned to write the alphabetic characters (*grammata*), and to read a script by syllables, one went on to "grammar" school, where the meaning of "literature" was explained. Again, one had an individual teacher, the "grammarian."[8]

Literature, that is "letters" (*grammata*), was the fundamental vehicle by which the ethos of classical culture was inculcated across a thousand years. To be able to read and write was a technical skill. But the *grammaticus* (the Greek word was taken into Latin, expressing the continuity of the heritage) was proud to call himself a *scholasticus*, a gentleman of leisure (*schole*), an intellectual, entrusted with the interpretation of the "writings" of canonical authors.[9]

We know from the frequency of fragmentary texts retrieved in Egypt who the classical authors were: Homer above all, then much the same select procession of poets, dramatists, historians, orators and philosophers that is read in the modern Greek and Latin curriculum of Classics. The aim in Antiquity was not diversity, but the reinforcement of national values. The method of study with authors of any tale was by the philosophical principle of analogy: not the saga, but its ethical force. Our contemporary "English" curriculum does the same with its canonised authors. The universe is held to be rational, so educated virtue will manage life's problems.

The biblical culture basically rejected this. The universe was transient. The

---

8   H.I. Marrou, *A History of Education in Antiquity* (London: Sheed and Ward, 1956); T. Morgan, *Literate Education in the Hellenistic and Roman Worlds* (Cambridge: Cambridge University Press, 1998); M. Joyal et al. (eds), *Greek and Roman Education: A Sourcebook* (London: Routledge, 2009).

9   Lollianus, also called Homoios, son of Apolloni[us], had been voted "public *grammaticus*" by the council of the city of Oxyrhynchus (P.Oxy. 47.3366). The city was to supply his maintenance in kind, but the quality degenerated. He appeals to the imperial court itself for a better deal, since it was their concern for "virtue and education" (*paideia*) that obliged the cities to be responsible for boys: E.A. Judge, "A State Schoolteacher Makes a Salary Bid," *Jerusalem and Athens*, 130-36.

problems were internal to humanity, involving us in individual moral answerability. But the Classic intellectual principle of analogy might subsume it all. Moses, like Homer, might also be read as a book of symbols. Moses, however, had obliged the Israelites each to remind his sons of the actual events of the Exodus.

Paul may not have lingered much over the skilled techniques of reading and writing. But *paideia*, the moral training of the young in righteousness (*dikaiosyne*), was on a higher plane (2 Tim 3:15-16). Its method was the interpretation of texts (*grammata*) but not as mythical symbols (2 Tim 4:4, cf. 2 Peter 1:16). The "truth" lay in the test of actual experience. As in Israel, the "Lord's intellectual education" (*paideia kai nouthesia kyriou*) was the duty of the parents (Eph. 6:4). But the papyri show how seductive the principle of hidden meaning could be.[10]

Both Philo and Paul held to the empirical universe of Genesis against the spell of Plato's symbolic one. But there was no question of alternative schooling. An archaising fashion in the Greek language began to establish itself during their time. The contemporary vocabulary and style of the Greek Septuagint (LXX) and the New Testament had been standard (*koine*) in their day. But the growing classicism left them educationally outmoded.

It was Julian, the last heir of Constantine's house, who brought the matter to a head. Reared on the Bible, he came to hate its vulgarity. He also learned, from Jesus, to hate hypocrisy. No teacher in a public school could be a "Galilean," since he would not accept the gods of Homer. They should invent church schools, and try teaching Greek from the Bible. Only the premature death of Julian removed the threatened monstrosity.[11]

(c) The gymnastic trainer (paidotribes)

Education may be seen as a product of the three great intellectual disciplines of Greek naturalism, history, philosophy and politics. But behind it lay two disciplines that were more active, music and sport ("athletics"). Both are competitive. Unlike the contemplative life, both dancing and wrestling also

---

10 Philo, the Platonising Jewish philosopher contemporary with Paul, *On the Change of Names* 8.60: they are "symbols" of the nature-truth (*physis*) which loves concealment." The papyrus fragments P.Oxy. 36.2745 and P. Heid. 1.5 both document the alphabetical collecting of Hebrew names with their Greek etymologies. Genesis 17:5 on Abraham, with Matthew 1:21 on Jesus, perhaps stimulated this, but the earliest Christians in the papyri show no interest in giving biblically significant names to their children.

11 E.A. Judge, "Christian Innovation and its Contemporary Observers," *Jerusalem and Athens*, 232-53, for Julian 241-45; "The Interaction of Biblical and Classical Education in the Fourth Century," *Jerusalem and Athens*, 254-60.

require dedicated premises, the theatre and the stadium. Neither art was likely to appeal to Jerusalem, though singing and running may have seemed more fitting there.

Gymnastic exercise became militarily important for adolescents, especially as boys approached manhood, at eighteen. Their public trainer was responsible for their fitness as an echelon. Soldiers are dependent on each other in action. During the Hellenistic period (the three centuries before Christ) the so-called ephebic ("adolescent") gymnasium became the centre for a more comprehensive education. As the Roman hegemony took away the need for a citizen militia, enrolment in the gymnasium developed into an elite privilege. Membership became confined in Egypt to those who could prove descent from the gymnasial class across several generations (by *epikrisis* certificates, P.Oxy. 46.3276-84).

Unlike music, which seems to have had no strong attraction for Paul, his imagination was seized by the commitment and physical discipline of both the athlete and the soldier (e.g. 1 Cor 9:24-27; Phil 3:12-14; Eph 6:10-17; 1 Tim 4:7-8, cf. Heb 12:1, James 1:12, Rev 2:10). They both provide vivid models for service in Christ tested by severe ordeal, yet focused on ultimate victory, the "crown of life." But, given his upbringing, it is entirely unlikely that Paul had any relevant personal experience whether gymnastic or military.[12]

(d) The graduate secretary (grammateus)

Universally necessary in Greek civil organisations was the "secretary." As the English word implies, he had control of the records, and as minute-keeper he was also privy to the whole decision-making process. The secretary, though technically only the recorder (or "scribe"), accumulated in-house expertise. Though not the "overseer," he necessarily would tell him what to do and say. In a community with its own elaborate code of law, and long history, he was the effective manager. So it was in the Soviet Union. And so it was in first-century Jerusalem.

Every secretary (*grammateus*) who has graduated (lit. "been made a student," *matheteutheis*) in the kingdom of the heavens, is like a householder "who brings out of his strongroom things new and old" (Matt 13:52). The Lord's "meetings" were comfortable using the ordinary words for their administrative organisation, "overseers," "elders" and "assistants." Why no secretaries? Even today there is

---

12 R.P. Seesengood, *Competing Identities: The Athlete and the Gladiator in Early Christianity* (London: T. & T. Clark, 2006); A. Harnack, *Militia Christi: The Christian Religion and the Military in the First Three Centuries* (Tübingen: Mohr Siebeck, 1905; Eng. Tr. Philadelphia: Fortress, 1981).

no such established order in churches (though all the denominational bodies feel free to use such a vital *ad hoc* appointment). Perhaps no one could forget the terrible denunciations of Jesus on the "hypocrites" (Matt 23:1-36).[13]

(e) The ecumenical synods (thymelic and xystic)
Unlike the synagogues, and the hundreds of other small local associations for trade, culture, dining, or burial, that multiplied themselves across the Roman world (cf. the "Friendly Societies" of the nineteenth century, though they turned into the mutual insurance funds of the twentieth), the Lord's "meetings" formed regional networks. They took to themselves the Roman administrative terms "province" and "diocese," the very framework of the grand empire itself. But Romans were shocked by the debates that could be publicly witnessed in this imitator.

In the latter part of the third century, Aurelian is said to have castigated Rome's own senate for being contentious, "as though you were meeting in the *ekklesia* of the Christians, and not in the temple of all the gods" (*Augustan History: Aurelian* 20:5). By that stage the only other independent inter-provincial networks, the business houses of the *publicani* who took tax-collecting contracts, had largely unravelled.

But flourishing more splendidly than ever before were the semi-official "ecumenical synods of Dionysiac artists" (the "thymelic" synod, so-called from the incense altars of the tragic theatre) along with its parallel in the athletic field (the "xystic" synod, so-called from the "scraping" of the strigils after the competitors oiled themselves daily at public expense in the gymnasium).[14] These two synods ("assemblies") were also indirectly connected with the tax system, but as beneficiaries at the local level primarily. Those who were victorious in the annual festivals of their city, whether in the artistic or the athletic competition, expected to be given tax exemption there. But they might also become stars on the international theatrical circuit. Since Hellenistic times they had formed synods to protect their interests (trade unions in effect, though more glorious). The Roman imperial government strengthened its "ecumenical" control to prevent any watering-down of standards which might only increase local tax-burdens on non-winners.

---

13 C. Keith, *Jesus' Literacy: Scribal Culture and the Teacher from Galilee* (London: T. and T. Clark, 2011); C.B. Forbes, "Who was Jesus? The Historical Jesus," in M. Harding and A.M. Nobbs (eds), *The Content and Setting of the Gospel Tradition* (Grand Rapids: Eerdmans, 2010), 231-62.
14 E.A. Judge, "The Ecumenical Synod of Dionysiac Artists," *Jerusalem and Athens*, 137-39, with references to other literature, cf. *New Documents Illustrating Early Christianity* 9 (2002), 67-68.

"Synod" was itself a term always in use at a strictly local level for any kind of association. It crops up in Christian usage as early as the Protevangelium of James (second-century), but the title "ecumenical" (i.e. "world-wide") does not appear in Christian usage until after the Council of Nicaea. The late fourth-century historian Ammianus complained of the postal system being hamstrung when Constantius opened it for bishops travelling to synods.[15]

One need not, however, think of the Lord's "meetings" copying the thymelic and xystic synods. These were surely anathema to any conscientious believer, given that both theatre and stadium functioned as festival sites for the ancient and idolatrous cults denounced by ecclesiastical doctrine.[16]

(f) The public lecturer (sophistes)

A student's literary education, commenced under the *grammatikos* at secondary level, would be continued in the gymnasium. If he were to take part subsequently in the public life of his city, he would need more advanced training in the art of declamation. Given the strength needed to command attention in a crowded setting this was itself a taxing discipline. But there was also the rhetorical character of the sentences to be delivered. Audiences were educated people, alert especially to the rhythmic capacity of articulated prose and to the many elegant and studied figures of speech to be introduced within the text.

The rhetor was a professional teacher of such skills at the tertiary level. A student must negotiate personally for the strenuous training involved, and pay for it. The hazards of choice could be frustrating in a world centre like Alexandria. From Paul's time Neilus wrote about it to his father, Theon, in Oxyrhynchus (P.Oxy. 18.2190):[17]

> I was looking for a scholar (*philologos*) and Chaeremon the tutor (*kathegetes*) ... so that I, after rejecting Theon ... as possessing a completely inadequate training (*hexis*) ... on account of a shortage of sophists (*sophistai*) ... that Didymus, who, it appears, is a friend of his and has a school (*schole*), would be sailing down and would take more care than the others ... if only I had found some decent

---

15 E.A. Judge, "The Absence of Religion, even in Ammianus?" *Jerusalem and Athens*, 264-75, at 272-3.
16 T.D. Barnes, "Christians and the Theater," in W.J. Slater (ed.), *Roman Theater and Society* (Ann Arbor: University of Michigan Press, 1996), 161-68.
17 Re-edited text in B.W. Winter, *Philo and Paul among the Sophists: Alexandrian and Corinthian Responses to a Julio-Claudian Movement* (2nd ed., Grand Rapids: Eerdmans, 2002), 256-60, translated excerpts only.

teachers (*kathegetai*), I would pray never to set eyes on Didymus ... what makes me despair is that this fellow who used to be a mere provincial sees fit to compete with the rest ...

This damaged text reveals that the well-known Greek sophists of the second century already had their predecessors in the first. It confirms the impression given by Paul's letter to the Corinthians. He had fallen into a similarly competitive rhetorical scene at Corinth. His own converts looked down on him as unprofessional in speech (2 Cor 11:6, *idiotes toi logoi*). He retaliates by a self-mocking parody of the proper way to praise oneself (2 Cor 11:16-23).[18]

(g) The philosopher (philosophos)
Philosophical training was far less dramatic. The rivalry between teachers of philosophy and rhetoricians was mainly intellectual. Philosophers were certainly identified in public, but their analytical discourses were traditionally exercised within a small circle of personal devotees.[19]

Where does Paul belong between sophist and philosopher? In either case his emotional responses demonstrate that his own mission confronts education at this highest level. All the more routine stages below that are taken for granted. They may provide him with attractive figures of speech. But he is not particularly superseding the preparation they supply for adult life. Rhetoric and philosophy, however, he seems emphatically to challenge together. They are the twin pinnacles of a proud culture he sees as false (e.g. 1 Cor 1:17; 2:4; Col 2:8). Paul has not been formally trained in either. But he is familiar enough with their main terms as they are current in the general community.[20]

The unusually diverse educational outworking of this critique is demonstrated

---

18 E.A. Judge, "Paul's Boasting in Relation to Contemporary Professional Practice', *Social Distinctives of the Christians in the First Century* (Peabody, Mass.: Hendrickson, 1988), 57-71; L.L. Welborn, *An End to Enmity: Paul and the "Wrongdoer" of Second Corinthians* (Berlin: de Gruyter, 2011); R.S. Schellenberg, "Rhetorical Terminology in Paul: A Critical Reappraisal," *ZNW* 104 (2013), 177-91.

19 G.R. Stanton, "Sophists and Philosophers: Problems of Classification," *AJP* 94 (1973), 350-64; T.J. Grew, *The Rivalry between Rhetoric and Philosophy in Greek Education and Culture* (Wetherby: British Library, 1990); T. Dorandi, "The Organisation and Structure of the Philosophical Schools," *The Cambridge History of Hellenistic Philosophy* (Cambridge: Cambridge University Press, 1989), 55-62; E.A. Judge, 'What Makes a Philosophical School?' *New Documents Illustrating Early Christianity* 10 (2012), 1-5.

20 M.L. Clarke, *Higher Education in the Ancient World* (London: Routledge, 1971); E.A. Judge, "The Conflict of Educational Aims in the New Testament," *The First Christians in the Roman World*, 693-708; "The Reaction against Classical Education in the New Testament," *The First Christians in the Roman World*, 709-716; C.B. Forbes, "Paul Among the Greeks," in M. Harding and A.M. Nobbs, *All Things to All Cultures: Paul Among Jews, Greeks, and Romans* (Grand Rapids: Eerdmans, 2013), 124-142.

by Claire Smith's analysis (n. 6 above). The same applies to the New Testament corpus as a whole. It is an experimentally very unconventional combination of contentious documents. All have been processed to some extent under the force of the powerful new experiences they are driven to explain. The very rich and diverse vocabulary has been classified by Louw and Nida into 93 semantic domains. The largest is "Communication," with 56 sub-domains for 489 terms. Next comes "Attitudes and Emotions" with 24 sub-domains for 296 terms. This concentration delivers a transformative education for adult life over all.[21]

Paul's "Empirical (Fashion of) Teaching"

From the mid-second century we have for the first time several philosophically alert critiques of Christ's teaching mission. Celsus of Alexandria (?) disqualified it because its "meetings" breached the "common law" of civilised humanity (the rational universe of Plato). Origen later refuted this by appealing to a higher law of "truth" (the first assertion in our culture of the fundamental right of conscience, to think differently).[22]

Lucian of Samosata (on the Euphrates), probably of Aramaic-speaking background, wrote a satirical exposure of Peregrinus, a notorious charlatan: "... he mastered (*exemathen*) the amazing (*thaumaste*) wisdom (*sophia*) of the Christians, associating himself with their priests (*hiereis*) and instructors (*grammateis*) in Palestine." Lucian's use of the two occupational titles most pointedly avoided by Christians could reflect a knowledge of Judaism by the Syrian author, though as a satirist he was in any case "deliberately promiscuous."[23]

Galen of Pergamum, the medical polymath, however, seized the whole point:

> ... as if one had come into the school (*diatribe*) of Moses and Christ, (to) hear about laws that have not been demonstrated ... he did not consider it necessary to guide us by any logical method but adopted an empirical (fashion of) teaching...

---

21 J.P. Louw and E.A. Nida (eds), *Greek-English Lexicon of the New Testament Based on Semantic Domains* (New York: United Bible Societies, 1988).
22 E.A. Judge, "Diversity Versus the Body Corporate," *St Mark's Review* 225 (2013), 9-15, for the first public recognition of this.
23 M. Edwards, "Satire and Verisimilitude: Christianity in Lucian's Peregrinus?" *Historia* 38 (1989), 89-98.

Writing "On the Difference between the Pulses" (2.4), Galen rejected the experimental method he had himself once tried.[24]

The reason Galen rejected the experimental method is that it defied the logical proof of the Aristotelian system, "demonstration" (*apodeixis*). In 1 Cor 2:4 Paul says his own *logos* and "announcement" (*kerygma*) was not with the persuasiveness of "wisdom" (*sophia*), but by the "demonstration" (*apodeixis*) of spirit and power. This will be what Galen rejected as "empirical teaching."

Most historians agree that the modern world began with the scientific revolution of the seventeenth century. The causes of that are often left open. But the empirical method itself could only prevail once the philosophical axiom of an eternal universe ruled by inherent logic had been dislodged. Galen's retreat from experiment as an illogical method prevailed for a millennium or more.

Only when the universe was accepted as a temporary artefact did it become possible to find out by testing how it actually worked. It was the Genesis of Jerusalem that opened the way to empirical science, not the logical straitjacket of Athens. The Pauline experiment in a new kind of higher education independent of the Classical forms and open to anyone is an equally crucial stage in the making of the modern world. Today, confessional theology likewise promises to keep the tertiary sector as a whole under critical testing.

---

24 G.H.R. Horsley, with I. Johnston, Introduction to *Galen: Method of Medicine*, Books 1-4 (Cambridge, Mass.: Harvard University Press, 2011), ix-clvii, for a comprehensive overview of Galen's intellectual method.

2 | PAUL AND THE ANCIENT GYMNASIUM

RESEARCH PARADIGMS FOR "ACADEMIC CITIZENS" OF THE NEW WORLD

JAMES R. HARRISON

Abstract

The essay examines trends in the uptake of research degrees in the Australian tertiary sector from 2010-2013 and then explores the present situation in the theological sector and its implications for the future. The paper further investigates Australian discussion regarding the models of theological education and (implicitly) research: the "Athens Academy," the "Berlin University," the "Jerusalem Community," and the "Geneva Seminary." The essay brings other models into consideration ("Learning Community," "Pneumatic-missional," "Theo-cultural"), arguing that Genesis 1-11 also provides valuable insights into God's "creation" mandate for research. The ethical dimension of tertiary teaching, leadership and research is then analysed, focusing on the writings of Professor Bruce Macfarlane from 2004-2012 regarding the service of the "academic citizen" to the community, inexplicably overlooked by Christian educationists. Having established how theological research should foster and sustain professional, ecclesiastical and academic vocations for the advancement of the Kingdom of God, the remainder of the essay asks how the ethical curriculum of the ancient gymnasium compared with the teaching of the apostle Paul in his "learning communities." What agenda does the apostle establish for theological research that will empower mission and ministry inside and outside of the church in God's world?

Research in the Australian Tertiary Sector: Current Trends and Their Significance for the Theological Sector

The most recent reports on the future of innovative academic research in the Australian tertiary sector and the workplace were written, with one exception, in the period of the Gillard Government, predating Kevin Rudd's short-lived second term as Prime Minister and the subsequent election of the Abbott Government.[1] However, the social trends enunciated therein are still present and have, to some degree, been intensified by the continuing decline of manufacturing industry within Australia, along with its research base for technological innovation. A series of trends can be pinpointed which will helpfully silhouette the current debate about the future of research in theological education.

At the outset, it should be observed that Australia has a strong reputation as a world-class research destination for overseas researchers and research students, with higher education being one of the nation's leading exports.[2] In 2013, five Australian universities were ranked in the top 100 universities of the world.[3] The publishing rate of our research workforce is rated within the top 10 for OECD countries and Australian research punches well "above its weight" in molecular biology, genetics and immunology.[4] Coates and Goedegebuure observe also that higher education will prepare the future professional workforce effectively in Australia because it "fuels innovation, builds international linkages, enhances individual and social prosperity, and culturally enriches cities and the regions." Significantly, in terms of employment emanating from research degrees, Australian higher education employs 45% of graduates (2008-2009), with the business sector absorbing another 39% in the same period.[5]

Notwithstanding this overall success, the uptake of research degrees by

---

[1] H. Coates and L. Goedegebuure, "The Real Academic Briefing: Why We Need to Reconceptualise Australia's Future Academic Workforce, and Eight Possible Strategies for How to Go About This," *Research Briefing* November 2010, 1-39 (www.lhmartininstitute.edu.au/userfiles/. Accessed 1 January, 2014).

"Powering Ideas: An Innovation Agenda for the 21st Century Department of Innovation," Department of Innovation, Industry, Science and Research (DIISR), Canberra, 2009, 1-68 (sydney.edu.au/documents/about/.../20120308%20PoweringIdeas.pdf. Accessed 1 January, 2014).

"Research Skills for an Innovative Future: A Research Workforce Strategy to Cover the Decade to 2020," Department of Innovation, Industry, Science and Research (DIISR), Canberra, 2011, 1-43 (www.innovation.gov.au/research/ResearchWorkforceIssues/. Accessed 1 January, 2014).

[2] DIISR 2011, "Research Skills," XI.

[3] Center for World-Class Universities (CWCU) (2013), *Academic Ranking of World Universities*. Accessed 1 January, 2014, from www.arwu.org.

[4] DIISR 2011, "Research Skills," XI.

[5] DIISR 2011, "Research Skills," 2.

domestic students has stalled.[6] Further, although business employs a substantial number of research graduates, only one third of business firms innovate, a statistic that has remained constant for years.[7] More generally, Australia's spending on research and development lags well behind the OECD,[8] with Australia's spending growing at 8% per year since 1996-1997, as opposed to 22% in the case of our major trade partner, China.[9] More specifically, a series of demographic and social challenges now face the academic workforce: (a) in the next five years the tertiary sector will have to replace half its staff; (b) fewer academic staff are available to perform an ever increasing load of work, with staff numbers growing at a lower rate than student numbers and with the "sessional" workforce now reaching 40%; (c) the "brain drain" continues apace in Australia, with academics often preferring to work overseas or outside of the tertiary education sector; (d) roles in work and the work force have changed dramatically.[10] In the face of these challenges, it has been proposed that the PhD degree needs refreshment, with apprentice academics being given a portfolio of baseline skills in "key functional areas—research, education, integration, application, and leadership and management."[11]

While the issues outlined above certainly impact upon the theological research in the university sector, they also pose significant questions for the outcomes of theological research in the private consortia and independent colleges. Although domestic students continue to enrol in research theological degrees, they are less likely to be destined for employment in denominational theological education, the ordained and diaconal ministry, or work in parachurch and mission organisations.[12] How can we as theological educators ensure that such research students enter their non-ecclesiastical professions with sufficient reflective, collaborative, communication and leadership skills? What portfolio of skills is required for the effective grooming of such people for their vocations? To what degree do our PhD and ThD degrees have to be refreshed to ensure that these outcomes are addressed? Moreover, how do we equip their doctoral supervisors in our theological colleges, trained in the traditional disciplines, to

---

6   DIISR 2011, "Research Skills," XII.
7   DIISR 2010, "Powering Ideas," 19.
8   DIISR 2010, "Powering Ideas," 19.
9   DIISR 2010, "Powering Ideas," 20.
10 DIISR 2010, "Powering Ideas," 6-9, 39.
11 DIISR 2010, "Powering Ideas," 32.
12 Les Ball, *Transforming Theology: Student Experience and Transformative Learning in Undergraduate Theological Education* (Preston Vic: Mosaic Press, 2012), 5.

be more effective mentors in preparing such people for the professional workplace as opposed to the (increasingly less frequently chosen) ecclesiastical and academic vocations? Do the traditional research disciplines of biblical, historical, systematic and pastoral theology militate against the cross-disciplinary approaches required in this new pedagogical and pastoral situation?[13] Dare we risk neglecting to "seek the welfare of the city" (Jer 29:7) by clinging onto old paradigms in a new ministry context (Mark 2:21-22)?

Further, what missional responsibility does the church have in preparing believers, who have pursued non-theological doctoral studies at "secular" universities, for transformative leadership within their professions? This necessitates the church's moving its theological horizon from the (so-called) "service-oriented" professions such as medicine, nursing, teaching and social work into new areas of engagement (e.g. indigenous studies, visual and creative arts, media, architecture, economics, business, information technologies, science, engineering, politics and public policy, agriculture and environmental studies, etc). How can the non-theological research of believers in such diverse disciplines inform and benefit the theological research of the church and its ministries, and vice versa? In sum, the church, by means of a more holistic approach to research per se and its integration with theology, should interact with, encourage and equip believing professionals to become more "effectual agents of change and transformation in civil society."[14] Such an engagement would ultimately profit the wider "education of concerned citizens" within our churches and the advancement of the Kingdom of God within the world of work.[15]

Changing Paradigms of Theological Education: What are the "Research" Consequences for the Sector and its Paradigms of Transformation?

In an Australian context, theological education has been traditionally carried out in private denominational colleges, mostly gathered under the accreditation "umbrella" of various theological consortia (Australian College of Theology, Adelaide College of Divinity, [formerly] Melbourne College of Divinity, Sydney College of Divinity), though some colleges seek direct government accreditation

---

13 Ball, *Transforming Theology*, 21.
14 Ball, *Transforming Theology*, 18.
15 Ball, *Transforming Theology*, 15.

(e.g. Alphacrucis College, Avondale College of Higher Education, Christian Heritage College, Moore Theological College, Harvest West Bible College, Perth Bible College, Tabor Adelaide, Tabor Victoria).[16] Masters and doctoral research programs have been pursued in such contexts, in conjunction with the alternative route of higher degree studies in Departments of Religion (e.g. Sydney University, The University of Queensland). Consequently, Australian theological research is now widely known and respected overseas, no longer being confined to a handful of eminent international scholars, as was the case in the early 1970s (Leon Morris, Edwin Judge, Robert Banks). The international impact of Australian scholarship is also seen in the fact that theological scholars from Australia have held and continue to hold significant posts in seminaries and universities overseas.

With the advent of postmodernism and the renewed interest in religious perspectives in academia, theology departments have sprung up within Australian universities (Australian Catholic University, Charles Sturt University, Flinders University, Murdoch University, University of Newcastle, University of Notre Dame), including most recently the transition of the Melbourne College of Divinity to being the MCD University of Divinity and then (in 2014) to University of Divinity. In the case of the Macquarie University Ancient History Department, many of its doctoral graduates have found posts in theological colleges/seminaries and university departments across Australia and overseas. In the case of university providers, academic faculty are able to apply for federal government research grants, whereas this opportunity is not available to the private theological consortia and independently accredited providers. Notwithstanding, the theological research output of the private sector is as productive in its discipline as the university theology departments, with academic benchmarking throughout the sector being generated through the Council of Deans of Theology.[17]

Given the strength of the theological sector, it is interesting that various paradigms regarding what constitutes "transformative" theological education

---

16 Some theological consortia have disbanded (Brisbane College of Theology), while other independent colleges no longer offer suites of theology degrees (Wesley Institute).

17 For discussions of the current Australian theological scene and the history of some of their consortia, see R. Nobbs, "From Nowhere to Know How. Sydney College of Divinity: The First Twenty Years," *Pacifica* 17:2 (2004), 121-136; C. Sherlock, *Uncovering Theology: The Depth, Reach and Utility of Australian Theological Education* (Adelaide: ATF, 2009); P. Beirne, "The Melbourne College of Divinity: A Selective Historical Overview," *Pacifica* 23:2 (2010), 123-136.

have increasingly been debated for more than a decade within Australia.[18] With the exception of Banks,[19] this debate has not so far been brought into dialogue with theological research, though implications for research are implicit in the discussion. Banks has argued that the "Athens Academy" (character formation) and the "Berlin University" (vocational skills) models of theological education have to be shaped and directed by the "Jerusalem Community" model (missional focus).[20] Edgar adds a further strut to this construct by highlighting the foundational importance of knowing God with his addition of the "Geneva Seminary" model (doxological community).[21] One might also justifiably add to these models the Pauline paradigm of "Scholastic Community" (or, better, "Learning Community"), given the preponderance of "teaching" vocabulary employed by the apostle in describing his house churches.[22] In these diverse models there is accurately reflected the biblical interplay between the revealed knowledge of God ("Geneva Seminary," "Learning Community"), personal and corporate transformation through God's Word and Christ's Spirit ("Athens Academy"), and a communal call to holistic mission in the world ("Berlin University," "Jerusalem Community"). While all theological research is situated in one, several, or all of these models, both the Christian researcher and the

---

18 R. Banks, *Reenvisioning Theological Education: Exploring a Missional Alternative to Current Models* (Grand Rapids: Eerdmans, 1999); M. Frost and A. Hirsch, *The Shaping of Things to Come: Innovation and Mission for the 21st Century* (Peabody: Hendrickson, 2003); B. Edgar, "The Theology of Theological Education," *Evangelical Review of Theology* 29:3 (2005), 208-218; D. Cronshaw, *The Shaping of Things Now: Emerging Church Mission and Innovation in 21st Century Melbourne* (Saarbrücken: VDM Verlag, 2009); D. Cronshaw, "Reenvisioning Theological Education, Mission and the Local Church," *Mission Studies* 28 (2011), 91–115; D. Cronshaw, "Australian Reenvisioning of Theological Education: In Step with the Spirit?" *Australian eJournal of Theology* 18:3 (2011), 223-235; D. Cronshaw, "Reenvisioning Theological Education, Vocation and the Kingdom of God," *Zadok Papers* 195 (Summer 2012), 9-16; D. Cronshaw, "Reenvisioning Theological Education and Missional Spirituality," *Journal of Adult Theological Education* 9:1 (2012), 9-27; Ball, *Transforming Theology*.

19 Banks, *Reenvisioning Theological Education*, 237-238.

20 Banks, *Reenvisioning Theological Education*; cf. D.M. Kelsey, *Between Athens and Berlin: The Theological Education Debate* (Grand Rapids: Eerdmans, 1996). On the collision between "Jerusalem" and "Athens" in Western culture and education, see E.A. Judge, *Jerusalem and Athens: Cultural Transformation in Late Antiquity*, A. Nobbs ed. (Tübingen; Mohr Siebeck, 2010), 109-117.

21 Edgar, "Theology of Theological Education." An alternative to Edgar's "Geneva Seminary" model would be Deitrich Bonhoeffer's experiment in Christian community in his underground teaching seminary for the Confessing Church at the von Katte estate in Finkenwalde (Pomerania) in 1935, out of which grew his famous book, *Life Together: The Classic Exploration of Faith in Community*, published in 1938.

22 E.A. Judge, "The Early Christians as a Scholastic Community," in E.A. Judge, *The First Christians in the Roman World*, J.R. Harrison ed. (Tübingen: Mohr Siebeck, 2008), 526-552; C.S. Smith, *Pauline Communities as "Scholastic Communities"* (Tübingen: Mohr Siebeck, 2012), esp. 396-493 for the vocabulary of "teaching."

church—in their ministry to believers and unbelievers and as responsible stewards of God's creation—need to embrace holistically the dynamic interconnection and interaction between all of these transformative models.

In a helpful addition to the debate, Cronshaw adopts a pneumatic approach in discussing the missional model. Building on the work of Banks and Frost/Hirsch, he argues that the church has to keep in step with the missional work of the Spirit.[23] Therefore theological education, when reenvisioned by the Spirit, has pedagogic guideposts that are communal (Mark 3:14), conversational (Luke 24:15), contextual (1 Cor 9:22b), cross-cultural (Acts 1:8), character-forming (1 Cor 11:1), contemplative (Ps 46:10) and congregational (1 Cor 14:26).[24] Furthermore, Cronshaw expands the vista of the church's theological education by bringing its vocational mission into dialogue with the Kingdom of God. As Cronshaw pithily observes, "Kingdom-minded people are needed in engineering and environmental science, parenting and plumbing, indigenous health and IT."[25] Finally, although a sidelight to the Australian debate about future models of theological education in Australia, Ball has helpfully addressed the transformative principles and practices that are required in undergraduate curriculum if they are to become an intentional feature of theological education. One suspects that similar moves should be made in theological research degrees in order to address our changing ministry contexts and more diverse candidature if we are, with the Spirit's guidance, to be a truly doxological, formative, missional and vocational learning community.

More can be said, however, that is germane to this debate. Another model worthy of serious consideration by Christian researchers is the "theo-cultural" vision of the Dutch Neo-Calvinist theologian, Abraham Kuyper, along with his contemporaries (Herman Bavinck) and his intellectual heirs (e.g. Herman Dooyeweerd, Hans Rookmaaker). Well before the advent of "public theology" in the late 20th century, Kuyper (1837-1920) had served as a pastor, newspaper editor, theologian, political leader, university founder, and prime minister in Holland.[26] He adopted a Trinitarian approach to work, arguing that all gifts and talents were derived from the Father, disposed personally to their recipients

---

23 Cronshaw, "Australian Reenvisioning."
24 Cronshaw, "Reenvisioning Theological Education."
25 Cronshaw, "Vocation and the Kingdom of God," 13.
26 J.D. Bratt, *Abraham Kuyper: Modern Calvinist, Christian Democrat* (Grand Rapids: Eerdmans, 2013).

by the Son, and kindled to life in each individual through the Spirit.[27] Thus, according to Kuyper, no area of human life— including research into culture in all its various disciplines[28]— was exempt from the Lordship of Christ: "There is not a square inch in the whole domain of our human existence over which, Christ, who is sovereign over all, does not cry: 'Mine!'"[29] Kuyper argues that when believers engage the civic[30] and cultural world, they enter a sphere governed by "common" grace, but in that context they bring their own experience of special "revelatory" grace into expression in a redemptive manner.[31]

Banks, too, allows for the continuing impact of "general revelation" in creation, enabling believers to affirm in culture and creation "whatever is true" (Phil 4:8), irrespective of its pedigree and methodology.[32] The freedom of believers to conduct multidisciplinary and integrative research—freed from the constraints of intellectual fear, political correctness, and censorship—is thereby underscored. This perspective, I would add, emerges in the narrative of Genesis 1-11. Innovation in the creative arts (Gen 4:21) and industrial technology (4:22) and in the agricultural (4:3; 9:20) and livestock industries (4:4, 20), including the differences between their urban and nomadic cultures (4:20a; 10:11; 11:4),

---

27 See also R. Banks, *God the Worker: Journeys into the Mind, Heart and Imagination of God* (Valley Forge: Judson Press, 1992); D.W. Miller, *God at Work: The History and Promise of the Faith at Work Movement* (Oxford: Oxford University Press, 2007).

28 A. Kuyper, *Lectures on Calvinism* (Grand Rapids: Eerdmans, 2000), 78-109 (politics), 110-141 (science), 142-170 (art). See also H. Bavinck, *Essays on Religion, Science and Society* (Grand Rapids: Eerdmans, 2008); H. Dooyeweerd, *A New Critique of Theoretical Thought: The Necessary Presuppositions of Philosophy* (4 Vols. New York: Edwin Mellen Press, 1997); id., *In the Twilight of Western Thought: Studies in the Pretended Autonomy of Philosophical Thought* (Nutley: Craig Press, 1968); id., *Roots of Western Culture: Pagan, Secular and Christian Options* (New York: Edwin Mellen Press, 2003); H.R. Rookmaaker, *Modern Art and the Death of a Culture* (Downers Grove: IVP, 1970).

29 A. Kuyper, "Sphere Sovereignty," in id., *Abraham Kuyper: A Centennial Reader*, J.D. Bratt ed. (Grand Rapids: Eerdmans, 1998), 488.

30 Banks, *Reenvisioning Theological Education*, 151-152, 166.

31 A. Kuyper, "Common Grace," in *Abraham Kuyper: A Centennial Reader*, 194. On the transformation of culture by the early Christians, see Judge, *The First Christians*, 670-732.

32 J. Calvin, *Institutes of the Christian Religion Volume 1* (Grand Rapids: Eerdmans, 1970), Chapters 3-6; E. Brunner, *Natural Theology: Comprising "Nature and Grace" by Professor Dr. Emil Brunner and the Reply "No" by Dr. Karl Barth* (London: Geoffrey Bless and Centenary Press, 1946); id., *The Christian Doctrine of Creation and Redemption Dogmatics Vol II* (London: Lutterworth, 1952), 3-45; G.C. Berkouwer, *General Revelation* (Grand Rapids: Eerdmans, 1955); G.J. Spykman, *Reformational Theology: A New Paradigm for Doing Dogmatics* (Grand Rapids: Eerdmans, 1992), 168-170, 251-252; H. Bavinck, *Reformed Dogmatics: Prolegomena Volume 1* (Grand Rapids: Baker Academic, 2003), 301-322. For an insightful discussion of the complex methodological challenges (e.g. the limitations of evidence selection, personal bias, research ethics, among others) faced by Christian reflective practitioners in discussing human subjects, see D. Cronshaw, "A Reflective Practitioner's Methodology for Emerging Church Research," *Crucible* 3:2 (2011), 1-21.

flows from humanity's being created in the image of God (1:27; 5:1b; 9:6; cf. Jms 3:9). Clearly our ability to research and discover continues unabated, notwithstanding the all-pervasive effects of sin upon our work lives in a fallen creation (Gen 3:17-19), and our arrogant and idolatrous attempts to establish cultures independently of God (11:1-8).[33] Our "research" mandate of dominion over all creation, therefore, allows believers in particular to unlock the secrets of creation hidden there for humanity to find and to utilise them as responsible stewards who are being renewed in the image of Christ (Gen 1:28-29; 9:1-3; Rom 8:29; Col 1:15; 3:10).[34]

We turn now to Bruce Macfarlane's writings on the social intent and ethical responsibility of tertiary research, which, as far as I can discern, have been overlooked by Christian theologians and educationalists. There are intriguing resonances of Macfarlane's thought with the ethical curriculum of the ancient gymnasium and with the Pauline dynamic of service that are worth exploring.

The Social and Moral Responsibility of Research: On Being an "Academic Citizen"

During the last decade Bruce Macfarlane has published four monographs highlighting the increasing disconnect between universities and their communities, resulting in a retreat from citizenship.[35] While the American tertiary sector is deeply entrenched in local, regional and national communities, the service role of the academic has been neglected in the United Kingdom, with the result that

---

33 Dooyeweerd (*Twilight of Western Thought*, 188) states: "What is the radical, biblical sense of the revelation of creation? As Creator, God reveals Himself as the absolute Origin of all that exists outside Him. There is no power in the world that is independent of Him …. If our heart finds fully in the grip of the self-revelation of God as Creator, we can no longer imagine that there would exist a safe and neutral zone that is withdrawn from God. This is the fundamental difference between the loving God and the idols which originate from an absolutization of what only has a relative and dependent existence." Dooyeweerd points out that the traditional Greek Olympian gods "were merely deified cultural powers of Greek society" (*Twilight of Western Thought*, 188).

34 G.C. Berkouwer, *Man: The Image of God* (Grand Rapids: Eerdmans, 1962); A.A. Hoekema, *Created in God's Image* (Grand Rapids: Eerdmans, 1986); J.R. Middleton, *The Liberating Image: The Imago Dei in Genesis 1* (Grand Rapids: Brazos Press, 2005).

35 B. Macfarlane, *Teaching with Integrity: The Ethics of Higher Education Practice* (New York: RoutledgeFalmer, 2004); id., *The Academic Citizen: The Virtue of Service in University Life* (London and New York: Routledge 2007); id., *Researching with Integrity: The Ethics of Academic Enquiry* (London and New York: Routledge, 2009); id., *Intellectual Leadership in Higher Education: Renewing the Role of the University Professor* (London and New York: Routledge, 2012).

the "academic citizen" looks inward rather than outward.[36] This disconnect has occurred because of the penetration of universities by a corporate, enterprise culture, with its utilitarian values, as universities reorientated their service towards business and the economy.

Consequently, the service role of the academic has been neglected, with prestige and kudos resting solely on personal achievements in research.[37] Macfarlane sums up the social consequences of this "reward" system for staff with a series of stark questions:

> Are academics who connect to service likely to be rewarded in their achievements by university and college employers? Are professors who carry out more service than research merely treated as unappreciated workhorses? Do women, junior staff and minorities face the heaviest demands to carry out service work?[38]

Instead, as Macfarlane argues, "Institutions need to be prepared to review the way they currently recognise and reward service work to insure [sic] that academics are provided with a rational, as well as a moral, motive for being good academic citizens."[39] To facilitate this recovery of academic citizenship in the university sector, Macfarlane posits a series of moral virtues for the academic citizen instead of rational self-interest and career advancement: engagement, guardianship, loyalty, collegiality, and benevolence.[40]

Other aspects of university life are viewed through a similarly strong ethical lens in Macfarlane's thought. First, the intellectual leadership of senior academics is crucial for the future of higher education rather than the current entrepreneurial culture where academics adopt a management style of leadership at the expense of, in Macfarlane's view, academic originality and creativity.[41] The malaise is compounded by the fact that corporate sponsorship funds a vast amount of applied research in universities these days. Once again the solution for Macfarlane

---

36 Macfarlane, *The Academic Citizen*, 9-58. For essays discussing the American context, see M.B. Smith et al. (eds.), *Citizenship across the Curriculum* (Bloomington: Indiana University Press, 2010).
37 Macfarlane, *The Academic Citizen*, 59-128
38 Macfarlane, *The Academic Citizen*, 5.
39 Macfarlane, *The Academic Citizen*, 74.
40 Macfarlane, *The Academic Citizen*, 129-176. For case studies of several "academic citizens," see Macfarlane, *Intellectual Leadership*, 113-115.
41 Macfarlane, *The Academic Citizen*, 23-44, 135-136. See also B. Macfarlane and R. Chan, "The Last Judgement: Exploring Intellectual Leadership in Higher Education through Academic Obituaries," *Studies in Higher Education* 2012, 1-13 (www. *Studies in Higher Education* DOI:10.1080/03075079.2012.684679. Accessed 14 Jan 2014).

is a renewed vision of what the ethical contours of academic leadership should look like in practice: namely, the role of model, mentor, guardian, enabler and ambassador,[42] as opposed to the "rag-tag" collection of contemporary professorial roles in the tertiary sector.[43] Second, Macfarlane, drawing upon Aristotle's idea that the virtues were median points between extremes of behaviour,[44] identifies what (in his view) are the virtues (and vices) of university teaching.[45]

Third, while conceding that core principles underlie current research ethics (i.e. confidentiality, informed consent, respect for persons),[46] Macfarlane proposes an alternative list for the career path of contemporary researcher: courage, respectfulness, resoluteness, sincerity, humility and reflexivity.[47] Unlike the rule-based theories of utilitarianism and Kantianism—characteristic of the codified principles associated with modern research ethics[48]—"virtue ethics" allow people to "take personal responsibility for decisions rather than justifying actions on the basis of a de-personalised but rational rule or principle for making a judgement".[49] This perspective is crucial considering that researchers are regularly faced with complex moral decisions during the research process and afterwards in the writing up and dissemination of research results.[50] If close attention, therefore, is paid to the excellences of character and ethical values and these are brought to bear during the entire research process as much as at its beginning (i.e. the Ethics Proposal), then research will be carried out with integrity.[51]

In sum, what Macfarlane has done so successfully is to place the interplay of service and ethics once again at the centre of the debate about higher degree studies and its conduct of academic research and teaching. Although the ethical

---

42 Macfarlane, *Intellectual Leadership*, 89-103.
43 Macfarlane, *Intellectual Leadership*, 73-75.
44 Macfarlane, *Teaching with Integrity*, 35, 37-38, 39, 128.
45 Macfarlane, *Teaching with Integrity*, 128-143. The virtues mentioned are respectfulness, sensitivity, pride, courage, fairness, openness, restraint, and collegiality. Macfarlane (*ibid.*, 145) concludes: "... it is important to strike a balance between the extremes of dogmatism and moral anarchy. In terms of teaching in universities it means recognizing the importance of basic moral virtues in forming relationships with students and colleagues based on trust and mutual respect. It also means that rational virtues such as a sense of fairness or justice need to be combined successfully with affective virtues such as sensitivity." For the median virtues of research and their vice deficits and vice excesses, see Macfarlane, *Researching with Integrity*, 42, Table 3.2.
46 See I. Gregory, *Ethics in Research* (London: Continuum, 2003), 27-78. Most recently, see A. Nichols-Casebolt, *Integrity and Responsible Conduct of Research* (Oxford: Oxford University Press, 2012).
47 Macfarlane, *Researching with Integrity*, 47-136.
48 Macfarlane, *Researching with Integrity*, 22-23, 28-29.
49 Macfarlane, *Researching with Integrity*, 34.
50 Macfarlane, *Researching with Integrity*, 31.
51 *Macfarlane, Researching with Integrity*, 44-45.

paradigms of Macfarlane are drawn from Aristotelian philosophy and the "virtue ethics" of Anscombe and MacIntyre,[52] there are interesting intersections between Macfarlane's thought and the holistic vision of cultural engagement and moral transformation that Paul set before his house churches in seeking the welfare of the city for Christ.[53] Moreover, since the "tertiary" students in the ancient gymnasium were taught ethically to balance one's responsibility to the household and *polis* ("city") with a cultivation of personal indifference, we have here a useful "sounding board" against which we can assess what was pedagogically distinctive about Paul's moral, social and communal agenda for his urban Christians.[54] What light might such an investigation throw on the complex debates about the future of theological research and ministry outlined above?

The Ethical Curriculum of the Ancient Gymnasium: Balancing Self-Preservation against the Imperatives of Household and Civic Ethics

The Gymnasiarch: Selfless Pastor and Example of Civic Ethics

By the Hellenistic age, the education system had lost the aristocratic bias of the classical period because its focus had widened to include the needs of the common person. Public schools were established at Miletus, Teos, Rhodes and Delphi through the endowments of benefactors.[55] Although the trend towards free public education continued into the Roman Empire, the creation of new elementary schools mostly lay in the hands of city councils, local benefactors, and parents with the means to pay. In regard to higher education, Athens continued to be the provider *par excellence*, but the beneficence of the emperors increasingly eclipsed competitors. Vespasian, for example, endowed a chair of literature and rhetoric

---

52 *Macfarlane, Researching with Integrity*, 36. See Aristotle, *Nichomachean Ethics, passim*; G.E.M. Anscombe, "Modern Moral Philosophy," *Philosophy* 33/1 (1958): 1-19; A. MacIntyre, *After Virtue* (London: Duckworth, 1983). Macfarlane (*Researching with Integrity*, 36) also refers to Christian ethics in the thought of Aquinas.

53 See B.W. Winter, *Seek the Welfare of the City: Christians as Benefactors and Citizens* (Grand Rapids: Eerdmans, 1994).

54 See W.A. Meeks, *The First Urban Christians: The Social World of the Apostle Paul* (New Haven: Yale, 1983).

55 For decrees founding schools at Miletus (*SIG*³ 577: 200/199 BC) and Teos (*SIG*³ 578: II. cent BC), see M.M. Austin, *The Hellenistic World from Alexander to the Roman Conquest: A Selection of Ancient Sources in Translation* (Cambridge: Cambridge University, 1981), §§119-120. This section of the article draws on J.R. Harrison, "Paul and the Gymnasiarchs: Two Approaches to Pastoral Formation in Antiquity," in S.E. Porter (ed.), *Paul: Jew, Greek, and Roman. Pauline Studies: Volume V* (Leiden: Brill, 2008), 141-178.

at Rome, to which was appointed the incomparable Roman rhetorician Quintilian.

Throughout the eastern Mediterranean, Greek public education was conducted in the gymnasia, the *palaestrae* (the wrestling schools) and temples devoted to the Muses (the Museum). Visiting teachers also rented private quarters, as Paul did at Rome (Acts 28:16, 30), or hired a guild hall like that of Tyrannus in first-century Ephesus (Acts 19:9).[56] Because most cities had built at least one gymnasium, the gymnasium remained the most famous and popular educational institution in antiquity.[57] Hellenistic gymnasia offered not only physical education but also literature, philosophy and music.

There were clear-cut educational age groups. The first seven years of a Greek boy's life were spent under the tutelage of his mother. Young boys, known as *paides* ("boys"), learned the educational rudiments at elementary school under the care of male teachers up to fourteen. The sons of well-off families, called *epheboi* ("adolescents"), were sent to the gymnasia from fifteen to seventeen. Students over eighteen were called *neoi* ("youths"). There were two years of compulsory military service termed the *ephebeia* ("manhood"). Its aim was to usher the *ephebos* into the citizenship and to ensure a military reserve for the state. But by the end of the second century BC, it also included study of the humanities. Paul was well aware of the ethos of the ephebic gymnasium, appropriating its athletic curriculum in his metaphors for discipline in the Christian life (1 Cor 9:24-27; Phil 3:12-14; 1 Tim 4:7-8).

The pastoral role and ethics of the chief official at the gymnasium is worth highlighting, reminding us in our contemporary context of Macfarlane's heavy emphasis upon ethics in tertiary leadership, teaching and research. The *gymnasiarchos* (literally, "leader of the gymnasium") supervised the training of gymnasium members, directed the operations of its teaching staff, and frequently acted as a benefactor for the gymnasium. In the public inscriptions the *gymnasiarchos* was regularly honoured because he embodied the Graeco-

---

56 On the nature of Tyrannus' hall in Acts 19:9, see A.J. Malherbe, *Social Aspects of Early Christianity* (Philadelphia: Fortress, 1983), 89-91.

57 For evidence regarding the subjects taught, see the Teos decree in n. 48 above. For the workings of the gymnasium, see S.G. Miller, *Arete: Greek Sports from Ancient Sources* (Berkeley and Los Angeles 1991), §126 (*SEG* XXVII. 261). On the gymnasium, see E.N. Gardiner, *The Ancient Gymnasium* (Oxford: Clarendon Press, 1930), 72-90; J. Delorme, *Le Gymnasion: Étude sur les monuments consacrés à l'éducation en Grèce (des origines à l'Empire romain)* (Paris: E. de Boccard, 1960); O. Tzachou-Alexandri, "The Gymnasium: An Institution for Athletic and Education," in *id.* (ed.), *Mind and Body: Athletic Contests in Antiquity* (Athens: National Archeological Museum, 1989); D. Vanhove "Le gymnase," in *id.*, *Le sport dans la Grèce antique: Du jeu à la compétition* (Bruxelles: Universiteit Gent, 1992), 57-75.

Roman ideal of civic leadership. An important feature of the inscriptional portrait of the gymnasiarch is the way that he pastorally cares for and personally develops the *epheboi* and *neoi*. Perhaps one of the most moving tributes paid to a gymnasiarch is the Ephesian inscription of the gymnasiarch Mithres:

> [...] he was not neglectful, not in the case of the y[oung men] [of their ...] and good bearing, treating them with respect, [and ...] with understatement and moderation, in all respects arranging his life-style in this place, and he gave attention also to the quality of the young men, both guiding them in training and, as for love of effort both in body and soul, making much of it for the sake of the reputation of the young men being fostered both in word and deed as befitted both the place's existing inherited dignity and fame.[58]

Another example is Straton of Pergamum. Upon entering his office as gymnasiarch, he "sacrificed a steer given by himself, praying to all the gods for the safety of the people and for their unity of heart."[59] Again, the educational and pastoral impact of Menas of Sestos upon young men is summed up in this manner:

> he not only shared his sacrificial offerings with the young men but through his personal dedication he impressed upon the young men the importance of cultivating discipline and tolerance of hardship, with the result that, being thus engaged in a competition for manliness, the personalities of the younger men are directed in the development of their character towards the goal of merit.[60]

From these examples one gains a keen sense of the comprehensive pastoral care that the young boys experienced under the gymnasiarchs. There are motifs here with which Paul would have surely agreed—the convergence of "word" and "deed" in personal transformation being a conspicuous example, as well as the centrality of unity.[61]

---

58 *I. Eph.* I. 6 (II. cent BC).
59 A.R. Hands, *Charities and Social Aid in Greece and Rome* (London and Southampton: Thames and Hudson, 1968), §D54.
60 F.W. Danker, *Benefactor: Epigraphic Study of Graeco-Roman and New Testament Semantic Field* (St. Louis: Clayton Publishing House, 1982), §17.
61 Rom 13:11-14; Gal 2:14; Eph 2:8-10; 4:15-16; 4:22-24; Phil 1:9-11; 4:8-9; Col 1:9-12; 2:6-8; 3:9-10, 16-17; 1 Thess 1:3-7; 2:8; 2 Thess 2:16-17; 3:6-7, 9-10. On the centrality of unity, see P.J. Achtemeier, *The Quest for Unity in the New Testament Church* (Philadelphian 1987); D.L. Peterlin, *Paul's Letter to the Philippians in the Light of Disunity in the Church* (Leiden-New York-Köln, 1995).

However, not only is the pastoral care of the gymnasiarch for the *neoi* and *epheboi* emphasised, but also the strong ethical framework of his civic leadership is brought into sharp focus. Consider, for instance, the comments of *I. Eph.* I. 6 regarding Mithres:

> and for the remaining gymnasium affairs he took care, hating the bad and loving the good, in nothing neglectful of what relates to honour and fame for the sake of establishing as worth of memory and praise the preference he shows for the best.[62]

Another captivating vignette is found in the decree honouring Zosimos of Priene. He is described as one who strives for "eternal fame",

> rashly seeking after his own pleasure in nothing, and understanding that merit alone returns the greatest fruits and favours to those who treasure virtue in honour before foreigners and citizens'.[63]

The service ethic of Zosimos, to return to Macfarlane's discussion of tertiary educational leadership and research, is heavily underscored in the inscription: "seeking after his pleasure *in nothing.*" Finally, an insight into the corporate ethics of the gymnasiarchs can be gleaned from their oath of office, preserved for us on a large marble stele in Verroia in Macedonia. The words of the oath are as follows:

> I swear by [...] and by Heracles and by Hermes that I will be a *gymnasiarchos* in accordance with the gymnasiarchal law; and that I will do anything and everything not covered by the law in the most just manner I can; and I will not do special favours for my friends nor unjust injuries to my enemies; and from existing revenues for the young neither will I myself steal, nor will I allow anyone else to steal in any way that I might know or discover. I am true to my oath, may all be well with me; if not, may the opposite be my fate.[64]

---

62 A Pergameme inscription (*Ath. Mit.* 33 [1908] 380, No. 2) speaks of the gymnasiarch Agias: "and thinking his watchful presence in the gymnasium most desirable, he never neglected anything in his oversight of the discipline of the *epheboi* and *neoi*; with an austere loathing for evil, he made provision for the observance of good behaviour around the gymnasium."
63 *I. Priene* 112 (84 BC).
64 S.G. Miller, *Arete*, §126. As regards ethics, note the fines regarding the wrong use of money in the gymnasium (M.M. Austin, *The Hellenistic World*, §120).

The Delphic Canon: The Moral and Social Curriculum of the Ancient Gymnasium
In addition to the values espoused in the gymnasiarchal inscriptions, Paul may have noticed the ethical maxims of the seven sages—an important part of ephebic curriculum—inscribed on a stele of a local eastern Mediterranean gymnasium. He may have even listened to similar maxims expounded in the sermons of the popular philosophers at the market place, or heard them in conversations with interested inquirers or in interactions with his converts. Sosiades' collection of 147 maxims of the famous seven sages—cited *in extenso* by Stobaeus (*Eclogae* III 1.173)—was the foundational ethical curriculum taught to the *epheboi* in the Greek East. Sosiades is unknown to us, but his collection of the maxims of the seven sages is found in the fifth-century AD anthology of Stobaeus.[65] These maxims, better known to us as the Delphic canon, had been inscribed at Delphi for all to see (Plato, *Prt.* 343A-B; *Chrm.* 165A; *Hipparch.* 229A; Plutarch, *Mor.* 385D-E).

Many of the Delphic maxims have been found inscribed—with minor variations—at the gymnasium (?) at Miletopolis in the Hellespont (*I. Kyzikos* II 2 cols.1 and 2 [IV—III cent. BC]). Another version of the Delphic canon has been found at the gymnasium of the ephebes at Thera (*IG* XII[3] 1020: IV cent. BC), though the Therean version is more fragmentary. Thus the ethics of the Delphic canon had spread throughout the eastern Mediterranean gymnasia. The widespread dissemination of the Delphic maxims and the meticulous care taken in their transmission can be gauged from their presence at Egypt (*P. Ath. Univ. inv.* 2782 [I/II cent. AD]) and at Aï-Khanum on the Oxus (Afghanistan).[66]

In the ethical commands of the Delphic canon, a harmonious understanding of one's self and the gods is inculcated in the teaching of the ancient gymnasium, as well as the wide array of social relations that impacted upon the household

---

65 For the Greek text, see I. Stobaeus, *Anthologii,* C. Wachsmuth and O. Hense eds. (Berloni: Weidmannus, 1958), III 1.175 (p. 125).

66 On Egypt, see A.N. Oikonomides, "The Lost Delphic Inscription with the Commandments of the Seven and *P. Univ. Athen* 2782," *ZPE* 37 (1980), 179-183. In the case of Aï-Khanum, the Delphic maxims were inscribed on a stele (III cent. BC) erected by Clearchus (of Soli?) in the sanctuary of Cineas, the founder of the city. In the epigram on the front base of the stele, Clearchus says that the maxims on the stele came from a copy that he had *personally* transcribed while at Delphi. See L. Robert, "De Delphes à l'Oxus: inscriptions grecques nouvelles de la Bactriane," *Comptes Rendus de l'Académie des Inscriptions et Belles Lettres,* (1968): 416-457; L'Institut Fernand Courby, *Nouveau choix d'inscriptions grecques* (Paris: Société d'édition Les Belles Lettres, 1971), §37. I am indebted to E.A. Judge, "Ancient Beginnings of the Ancient World," in T.W. Hillard *et al.* (eds), *Ancient History in a Modern University. Volume II: Early Christianity, Late Antiquity, and Beyond* (Grand Rapids: Eerdmans, 1998), 468-482, esp. 473-480, for these references.

and the polis, with a view to the resolution of potential conflicts residing therein in ways that promoted social cohesion. How did one shelter oneself from the unexpected vicissitudes of Fortune ("Allow for chance" [*I. Kyzikos* II 2 col.1 No. 6]) and still cultivate the finely tuned balance of indifference and responsibility that was requisite for social order and personal happiness?[67] We will concentrate largely on the ethical commands from the list of Sosiades reproduced in the long inscription from the gymnasium (?) of Miletopolis (*I. Kyzikos* II 2 cols. 1 and 2) in the Hellespont, comprising 76 maxims of Sosiades' collection.

First, the Delphic canon places the sages' maxims in the agonistic context of the ancient gymnasium. In the inscriptions of Miletopolis and Thera, the singular form of the imperative is always used. The focus of the sages is on the self-knowledge of the individual ("Know yourself": *IG* XII 3.1020 No. 4). The overwhelming concern of Delphic ethics is self-interest ("Look after yourself": *I. Kyzikos* II 2 Col.2 No. 4; "Look after your own things": *I. Kyzikos* II 2 Col.1 No. 20; "Use your advantage": *I. Kyzikos* II 2 Col.1 No. 25), self-control ("Nothing to excess": *IG* XII 3.1020 No. 3), and self-protection ("Avoid commitment: you'll pay for it": *IG* XII 3.1020 No. 1).[68] Social attitudes are canvassed only in so far as they impinge on the individual's maintenance of harmonious relationships with others. The social agenda of the sages is intended to enable individuals to establish self-sufficiency and to preserve concord when faced with social collisions.

Second, although no organisational or thematic principle is evident in the maxims, there is an overarching direction of teaching for the ephebes, indicated by the common motifs and repetitions of terminology throughout. This undoubtedly reflects, to some extent, the widespread motifs of the popular philosophers, but the collection, inscribing, and erection of these sayings on steles in gymnasia across the eastern Mediterranean basin indicate an intentional and largely uniform curriculum. The gymnasia were aiming at an ethical product that had predefined contours. This resonates well with Macfarlane's emphasis upon a renewed ethical vision of service as opposed to economic utilitarianism in the leadership of tertiary institutions and their communities. We will therefore

---

67   See Harrison, "Paul and the Gymnasiarchs," *id.*, "The Delphic Canon and the Ephebic Ethical Curriculum: Cultivating the Self and the Gods for Harmonious Social Relations in the Household and Polis,", in H. Houge and A.W. Pitts (eds), *Ancient Education in Greco-Roman Christianity and Judaism* (T & T Clark, forthcoming).

68   E.A. Judge, "Ancient Beginnings," 476.

confine ourselves to providing a very brief overview of the social import of the 56 extant maxims from the Delphic canon found on the Miletopolis gymnasium (?) inscription, the most extensive extant inscription replicating Sosiades' collection.

Several important social attitudes are commended to the ephebes. Attention to the duties of friendship (*philia*) is a constant refrain throughout the Delphic canon (*I. Kyzikos* II 2 Col.1. Nos.1 ["Help your friends"], 9 ["Love friendship"], 15 ["Goodwill for friends"], 21 ["Favour a friend"]; *I. Kyzikos* II 2 Col.2. Nos.2 ["Look kindly on all"], 10 ["Guard friendship"]), undoubtedly because it forms a central part of the Graeco-Roman reciprocity system.[69] In this regard, Aristotle provides additional insight into the importance of *philia* ("friendship") for the civic education of the ephebes. While there are three different sources of "friendship" (i.e. goodness, pleasure, and usefulness: Aristotle, *Eth nic.* 1156a-b), *philia* remains the paramount virtue for establishing the concord (*homonoia*) and social cohesion of the city (*id.*, *Eth nic.* 1155a).[70] Consequently, the Delphic canon underscores the social importance of sticking by oaths and agreements (*I. Kyzikos* II 2 Col.1. No. 8; *I. Kyzikos* II 2 Col.2. No. 31), practising consensus (*I. Kyzikos* II 2 Col.2. Nos. 14, 22), and breaking up enmities (*I. Kyzikos* II 2 Col.2. No. 22; cf. *I. Kyzikos* II 2 Col.1 No.16 ["Hold off your enemies"]).

Other equally important social attitudes are also espoused. The centrality of the reciprocity system is affirmed (*I. Kyzikos* II 2 Col.1. No. 14 ["Return a favour"]). A cultivation of the values and aspirations of the nobility is advised for the social advancement and enlightenment of the ephebes (*I. Kyzikos* II 2 Col.1. No. 17 ["Cultivate nobility"]), as well as their continuing commitment to athletic training (*I. Kyzikos* II 2 Col.1. No. 10). In terms of household ethics, the ephebes are told in hierarchic manner to "Rule your wife" (*I. Kyzikos* II 2 Col.2. No. 3) and to "Train your sons" (*I. Kyzikos* II 2 Col.1. No. 25; cf. P. Athen.Univ. inv.2782 No. 5 ["Honour your parents"]).[71] The honorific culture of the Graeco-Roman world is strongly upheld (*I. Kyzikos* II 2 Col.1. No. 11

---

69 See J.R. Harrison, *Paul's Language of Grace in Its Graeco-Roman Context* (Tübingen: Mohr Siebeck, 2003).

70 On friendship, see D. Konstan, *Friendship in the Classical World* (Cambridge: Cambridge University Press, 1997); J.T. Fitzgerald (ed.), *Friendship, Flattery, and Frankness of Speech: Studies on Friendship in the New Testament World* (Leiden: Brill, 2003); L.S. Pangle, *Aristotle and the Philosophy of Friendship* (Cambridge: Cambridge University Press, 2003). On *homonoia*, see T.P. Lau, *The Politics of Peace: Ephesians, Dio Chrysostom and the Confucian Tradition* (Leiden: Brill, 2010).

71 For extended discussion of the maxim "Rule your wife," see Harrison, "Paul and the Gymnasiarchs," 172-177.

["Pursue glory"]; *I. Kyzikos* II 2 Col.1. No.12 ["Praise virtue"]).[72] The correct cultic attitude to the god(s) and providence is inculcated (*I. Kyzikos* II 2 Col.1. No. 20 ["Worship divinity"]; *I. Kyzikos* II 2 Col.1. No. 7 ["Honour providence"]), ensuring thereby the prosperity of the city and gymnasium. Last, patronal concern for supplicants (*I. Kyzikos* II 2 Col.1. No. 24 ["Respect/pity supplicants"]) is evinced, but it is not related to divine "pity" in any way, as in Second Temple Judaism or early Christianity. Neither are the criteria clearly articulated as to who might properly constitute a "supplicant," nor the precise extent of help to be offered, if any.[73] Indeed, is the maxim ultimately more attitudinal ("respect") in its exhortation than practical ("pity") in its outcomes for the supplicant?

Given that the Delphic canon promoted a strong interplay between the personal and social dimensions of ethical behavior on the part of the ephebes, how did Paul approach this "tertiary" curriculum of antiquity, as well as its moral paradigms (the gymnasiarchs), and what does it tell us about the apostle's "research" agenda?

Paul and the Delphic Canon: A Pedagogical Conversation across the Centuries

In establishing learning communities of God's grace across the eastern Mediterranean basin, Paul's curriculum of holistic transformation in Christ did not envisage a privatised morality for his converts. Rather the apostle expected urban believers to engage with Spirit-given discernment the values, institutions, conventions and rituals of the polis, with a view to seeking its pastoral and social welfare for the advancement of the Kingdom of God in the lives of its inhabitants. The apostle's process of civic, social, ideological and moral engagement presents

---

72 On Paul and Graeco-Roman/Jewish "glory" traditions, see J.R. Harrison, "The Brothers as the 'Glory of Christ' (2 Cor 8:23): Paul's *Doxa* Terminology in Its Ancient Benefaction Context," *NovT* 52 (2010), 156-188; id., *Paul and the Imperial Authorities at Thessalonica and Rome: A Study in the Conflict of Ideology* (Tübingen: Mohr Siebeck, 2011), 201-269. On Paul's thought in its honorific context, see R. Jewett, "Paul, Shame and Honor," in J.P. Sampley (ed.), *Paul in the Greco-Roman World* (Harrisburg: Trinity Press International, 2003), 551-574; J.R. Harrison, "Paul and Ancient Civic Ethics: Redefining the Canon of Honour in the Graeco-Roman World," in C. Breytenbach (ed.), *Paul's Graeco-Roman Context* (Leuven/Walpole: Peeters, forthcoming).

73 On pity, see respectively B.F. Harris ("The Idea of Mercy and Its Graeco-Roman Context") and E.A. Judge ("The Quest for Mercy in Late Antiquity"), in P.T. O'Brien and D.G. Peterson (eds.), *God Who is Rich in Mercy: Essays Presented to D.B. Knox* (Homebush West: Lancer, 1986), 89-105 and 107-121; D. Konstan, *Pity Transformed* (London: Duckworth, 2001).

us a useful paradigm for our research culture in the challenging times of the changing constituencies who are undertaking theological education. Paul's learning communities live out the implications of this transformation of mind in alternative lifestyles and social relations within and outside of the Body of Christ (Rom 12:1-21; 1 Cor 12:1-26). But they also embrace by their social engagement and theological thought the complexities of household relations (Eph 5:21-6:10; Col 3:18–4:1), honorific culture and the imperial ruler (Rom 13:1-7), the rituals of the reciprocity system and the expectations of friendship (Rom 13:8-10), ethnic relations (Rom 10:12; 1 Cor 12:12; Gal 3:28; Col 3:11), concern for the socially marginalised (Rom 1:14; 1 Cor 1:26-31; 12:24-25), and the extension of civic beneficence (Rom 13:3-4; Gal 6:9-10).

Paul's thinking about ministry, therefore, has intriguing social and vocational dimensions to its ecclesiastical outworking in a civic context, as much as its pastoral and evangelistic expression within the Body of Christ. While our constituencies might be changing in the theological sector and in their research focus, reflecting more the outcome of "vocation" than "ordination," Paul's thought avoids such slippery institutional dichotomies. We turn to some examples of how Paul's gospel engages the motifs of the Delphic canon, though the apostle is undoubtedly working on the wider front of popular philosophy.[74]

First, in regards to *philia*, Paul rarely uses *phil*-compounds in speaking of human love and avoids them entirely in regards to divine love.[75] Paul's overwhelming preference for *agape* ("love"), *agapetos* ("beloved") and *agapan* ("to love") is probably explained by the fact that the apostle wishes to differentiate God's love and its outworking from the operations of the Graeco-Roman reciprocity system (Rom 4:4-5; 11:5-6, 35; 13:6-10; 1 Cor 4:7). In this regard, C. Spicq observes—though he overstates the evidence—that "friendship is properly used only of a relationship between equals."[76] While this is true in most cases, Aristotle observes that there was the possibility of friendship between those who were not equals (parents and children, husbands and wives, rulers and subjects).[77] But, significantly, the friendship was proportionate to their status and not necessarily permanent. Therefore, as a description of divine and human love, *agape* was better suited to relationships involving parties of different status

---

74 A.J. Malherbe, *Paul and the Popular Philosophers* (Minneapolis: Fortress, 1989).
75 E.A. Judge, "Moral Terms in the Eulogistic Tradition," *New Docs* 2 (1982), 106.
76 C. Spicq, "agape,", in *id., Theological Lexicon of the New Testament Vol. 1* (Peabody: Hendrickson, 1999), 10-11.
77 P. Atkinson, *Friendship and the Body of Christ* (Croydon: SPCK, 2004), 19.

(inferiors/superiors). It allowed Paul to speak of enduring human relationships, founded on divine love, which—in contrast to the status-riddled operation of *philia*—did not calculate in advance the reciprocal benefits to each party.

Second, while there is clear evidence that Paul does endorse reciprocity in certain contexts,[78] his understanding of divine grace is unilateral or unconditioned in its origin, being founded on God's loving initiative, and eliciting reciprocally a response of gratitude from his dependants. Significantly, Paul redefines the dynamics of the Graeco-Roman reciprocity system in terms of love rather than indebtedness (Rom 13.8-10).

Third, in terms of the husband "ruling" his wife, Paul upends the household code of the Delphic canon. He expands considerably upon the household codes generally, supplanting the notion of "rulership" with the idea of the mutual submission of husband and wife (Eph 5:21, 22, 24, 25, 33), and infusing his argument with a theology of the Spirit (5:18b),[79] the cross (5:24b, 25-27, 29b; cf. Mk 10.35-45), the Lordship of Christ over the church (5:23-24, 25-27, 30, 32; cf. 18b-20), and the creation narrative (5:31 [Gen 2.24]). In particular, submission for each partner is motivated by reverence for Christ (Eph 5:21b): the wife submits to the husband as unto Christ (5:22) and the husband loves and serves the wife as Christ unto her (5:25). Therefore, instead of "ruling" his wife, the husband is to love her in imitation of Christ's other-centred and self-sacrificial love (Eph 5:25).

Finally, a radical social reordering, invisible to the world, had occurred in the Body of Christ. The self-promotion (Gal 5:26c: "envying one another") and heated competition of ancient culture (5:26b: "provoking one another"), with its hierarchies of esteem and obligation, were replaced by self-effacement (Gal 6:3) and mutual commitment (6:2a) as the "Law of Christ" was expressed among believers (Gal 6:2b). The new dynamic of Spirit-animated (Gal 6:8b; cf. 5:16a, 18a, 22, 25) and eschaton-oriented social relations (6:9) also differentiated the early believers' understanding of benefaction (6:10) from the patronage of the imperial ruler and the gifts of local eastern Mediterranean benefactors. The unqualified extension of benefits "to all" undermined the ancient expectation of reciprocity and stymied the patron's prior evaluation of the "worthiness" of recipients, a

---

78 See Harrison, *Paul's Language of Grace*, 324-332.
79 On the dependence of the participle *hupotassomenoi* ("being submissive": Eph 5:21) upon the verb *plerousthe* ("be filled": 5:18b), see H.W. Hoehner, *Ephesians: An Exegetical Commentary* (Grand Rapids: Eerdmans, 2003), 720; R.W. Gehring, *House Church and Mission: The Importance of Household Structures in Early Christianity* (Peabody: Hendrickson, 2004: Gmn. orig. 2000), 244.

precaution central to Graeco-Roman gift-giving rituals (Gal 6:10a). Significantly, this occurred without omitting the priority of beneficence towards the household of faith ("especially": 6:10b). Last, the "new creation" in Christ (Gal 5:6; 6:15; 2 Cor 5:17), inaugurated through the cross (6:14; cf. 1:4), set aside the religious, ethnic and cultural divisions expressed in the antinomies of "circumcision" and "uncircumcision" (6:15a) or "Greek" and "barbarian" (Rom 1:14). [80]

Conclusion

Given the changing ministry priorities of theological education in Australia, the apostle Paul provides us with a strong incentive to reconsider the needs of our research students as "academic citizens" of the new world. While Paul can endorse several commonplaces of the Delphic canon in his teaching,[81] his eschatological and apocalyptic gospel challenges many of its ideological, social and ethical premises. Alternatively, the apostle can radically redefine its rationale in various cases, or, more commonly, bypass the self-protecting concerns of the Delphic maxims for his own theological, social and ethical perspectives, with a view to empowering the Body of Christ for its mission. Paul incisively analyses the pluralistic culture of his times, bringing "new creation" perspectives to bear upon the life of church and its mission to the world in an innovative, engaged, practical and transforming way. Paul's holistic tactic in theological education is a model for the all-embracing agenda of Christian research in all its variegated expressions.

Furthermore, Paul's understanding of ethics originates with God's self-revelation in creation (Rom 1:18-32; 2:14-16) and, arising out of Israel's covenantal and messianic promises, finds its fulfilment in Christ (Rom 1:2-4; 4:1-25; 10:4) and in the outpouring of the Spirit (Rom 7:6b; 8:4; Gal 3:14). Macfarlane, as we have seen, challenges contemporary academic leadership, teaching and research in the university sector, from the framework of Aristotle's ethical median points, lived out carefully between the extremes of behavior (i.e. vice deficits and vice excesses). By contrast, Paul does not conceive of ethics as charting a judicious "middle course." Either we are being totally restored in the image of God in Christ, the second Adam (Rom 5:12-21; 1 Cor 15:45), or we are not (Rom 8:29; Eph 4:22-24; Col 3:9-11). Living under the reign of grace

---

80 See J.R. Harrison, "Paul's 'Indebtedness' to the Barbarian (Rom 1:14) in Latin West Perspective," *NovT* 55 (2013), 311-348.

81 See Harrison, "Paul and the Gymnasiarchs," 168-169.

and keeping in step with Spirit—which is inaugurated by the crucifixion of the sinful nature though the dying and rising of Christ (Rom 6:11-14; Gal 5:16-25; Eph 4:17-6:9)—unleashes ethical qualities that are personally transformative, communal in focus, non-elitist in expression, service-oriented in practice, and distinctive in social relations. However, Macfarlane's comprehensive ethical challenge to the university sector, including its research arm, should have strong resonances for believers.

No discipline of study, therefore, stands outside of the headship of Christ: his demand over its intellectual property rights and researchers is absolute. No vocation, whether ecclesiastical or professional, is more "service" oriented than any other in the Kingdom of God. Too often the talents of many believers, with substantial research degrees, are overlooked in our churches because of a blinkered understanding of what ministry is and how the Kingdom advances in its "learning" and "research" agenda. But, with a renewed openness to the Spirit and God's Word, a better appreciation of the richness and diversity of our gifting in the research disciplines can emerge once again, allowing ordained and vocational ministry to flourish with a new synergy. Paul's vision for the intellectual and pastoral leadership at Corinth remains just as pertinent for the way ahead in Australian theological education: "all things are yours, whether Paul or Apollos or Cephas or the world or life or death or the present or the future—all belong to you, and you belong to Christ, and Christ belongs to God" (1 Cor 3:21b-23).

3 | PAUL AS THEOLOGICAL EDUCATOR

HIS ORIGINAL LEGACY AND CONTINUING CHALLENGE

ROBERT BANKS

Abstract

Many aspects of Paul's life and work have received attention, among them Paul as Teacher. However, his unique contribution as a theological educator has been less closely investigated. This essay focuses particularly on: the distinctive elements in Paul's approach to communicating the faith; the specific contexts in which he undertook such communication as part of his apostolic work; and the role played by his personal character and life experience in training others.

The essay identifies elements of Paul's approach that have continuing relevance in our changed theological education environment today. Some of these will raise questions about the way we currently do theological education and challenge us to consider how much it requires change to remain consistent with its biblical roots.

• • •

Introduction

In part this essay is a response to the final question raised by Les Ball at the end of his book: "To what degree—or, probably better, in what ways—is transformative learning consistent with biblical and theological principles?"[1] This

---

[1] Les Ball, *Transforming Theology. Student Experience and Transformative Learning in Undergraduate Theological Education* (Preston Vic: Mosaic Press, 2012), 144.

echoes an earlier statement to the effect that, "This (is) not a new idea, despite the terminology and recent popularizing of concepts. Indeed, it is essentially a return to some ancient view of education (at least as old as the time of Jesus) as the transformation of lives and society".[2] This essay also springs from my long-standing interest in the foremost figure in the spread of Christianity, the apostle Paul. Interest in Paul has mainly concentrated on his theological contribution, his missionary work or, more recently, his social and cultural legacy. In comparison, his work as an educator has received little attention. In the nearly 6000 indexed periodical articles on Paul, only a few discuss his contribution as a teacher.[3]

Yet, as Joseph Grassi notes, Paul himself is our most valuable source of information on "teaching methods" in the early church.[4] He was "the teacher of teachers" among his contemporaries and was convinced that those who heard him speak should pass it on "to reliable men who will be qualified to teach others" (2 Tim 2:2). References to Paul as "teacher" or "teaching" come before us in many passages by or about him.[5] These, along with others that could be mentioned focusing on the "learning" of his hearers, build up a picture of Paul teaching publicly and privately, in religious and secular settings, and to diverse racial groups.[6] Key elements in Paul's life prepared him for this role. He was raised in a cosmopolitan city visited by popular philosophers and rhetoricians (Acts 22.30). After basic schooling in the synagogue, he undertook advanced study in Jerusalem with a well-known rabbi (Acts 22:36). Excelling in his studies, he surpassed his contemporaries in knowledge and dedication (Acts 22:4-6). He experienced a dramatic divine calling to be—among other things—a teacher of the faith (Acts 9:3-19; 22:6-21). While earlier scholars thought he was not trained in classical rhetoric, many now argue that he used a number of rhetorical devices and may have even had formal rhetorical training.[7]

Despite the differences between pedagogical practices in his time and ours

---

2   Ball, *Transforming Theology*, 30.
3   Walter F. Mills, *An Index to Periodical Literature on the Apostle Paul* (Leiden: Brill, 1933). Cf. Paul B. Zuck, *Teaching as Paul Taught* (Grand Rapids: Baker, 1998), 178.
4   Joseph Grassi, *The Secret of Paul the Apostle* (New York: Orbis, 1978), 77.
5   See Acts 11:26; 13:12; 15:35; 17:19; 18:11; 21:21, 28; 28:31; Rom 16:17; 16:17; 1 Cor 14:17; Eph 4:21; Col 1:28; 2 Thess 2:15; 1 Tim 1:10-11; 4:6; 6:1; 2 Tim 3:10; Tit 1:9; 2:10.
6   As, for example, in Rom 12:2; 1 Cor 2:12; 14:20; 2 Cor 10:5; 11:13; Phil 1:9; 2:5; 3:15; 4:8; Col.1:9-10; 2:2-4; 3:10; Eph 4:22-24; 5:6.
7   So, *contra* Rudolf Bultmann and others, Peter Marshall, *Enmity in Corinth: Social Conventions in Paul's Relations with the Corinthians* (Tübingen: J.C.B.Mohr, 1987), 393.

and a more complex approach today to curriculum design and structure, we can learn much from Paul to become more effective theological educators. Obviously the content of Paul's teaching was a vital feature in the impact he had in the first century. If I do not examine that here it is because this has received sufficient treatment in studies of Paul. What requires more emphasis is the form of his teaching, the way he actually taught. In exploring this, I do not just draw on letters to his ministry team but, since for him all believers require theological education, I take his whole corpus as relevant to our theme. I would like to identify five features of his approach from which we still have much to learn.

Others learn best when our teaching includes *story-like envisioning* as well as *didactic instruction*

Paul is not content to provide general Christian instruction or specific advice on the issues at hand. He regularly connects everything he addresses with the big picture story of God's interaction with human beings and his creation. What does this entail? According to Tom Wright, it contains three basic narratives: the stories of God, of Israel and the world, and of Jesus.[8] Ben Witherington expands this to four, each arising from the other, namely the story of creation and a world gone wrong, the story of Israel in that world, the story of Chris and, finally, the story of Christians, including Paul himself.[9] James Dunn separates the last two components, distinguishing between Paul's own story and the stories of those who believed before and after him.[10] While opinion varies on how much this set of intertwining narratives forms an explicit framework or an implicit substructure in Paul's thinking, we should not underestimate its essential role. It is never far from anything he says or writes and the central component—"the Gospel"—is a frequent reference point in his teaching (eg Gal 1:8-9; 3:1-7).

Following Paul, we ought regularly to draw students' attention to the wider context of the topics or subject areas we are examining. At times we need to do this explicitly, at times we need to weave it in as an underlying thread in our

---

8   T. Wright, *The New Testament and the People of God* (Minneapolis: Fortress, 1992), 79.
9   B. Witherington, *Paul's Narrative Thought World: The Tapestry of Triumph and Tragedy* (Louisville: Westminster John Knox, 1994), 5.
10 James D.G. Dunn, *The Theology of Paul the Apostle* (Edinburgh: T. & T. Clark, 1998), 18. On Paul's story-framed perspective more generally see the thoughtful evaluations in Bruce W. Longenecker, ed., *Narrative Dynamics in Paul: A Critical Assessment* (Louisville: Westminster John Knox, 2002).

teaching. Depending on the context, we might refer to the biblical grand narrative, to the broader history of God's mission, to core theological convictions or to an overall ethical framework. We can do this in a variety of ways:

- through spontaneous interjections in our prepared material
- through the introduction of relevant hymns and prayers
- through carefully structured "learning moments"
- through the provision of reflective exercises and assignments
- through being available to chat with students informally after class.

Others learn best when we engage with them in *discussion and conversation* as well as through *up-front presentations*

In the writings by or about Paul, the apostle asks 250 questions of his hearers or readers. While a third of these understandably appear in the letter in which he is dealing with the most practical and controversial issues (1 Corinthians), surprisingly over a hundred occur in what is regarded as his most systematic writing (Rom 3:1, 8-9). Indeed, even the accounts of Paul's more extended and structured sermons include questions and objections, such as to Jews in Antioch (Acts 13: 15, 17) and to Gentiles in Athens (Acts 17:18-20). Why, even in his writings, do we find so many questions? A close inspection reveals that they served a variety of purposes:

- seeking information
- confirming facts
- gaining attention
- procuring assent
- encouraging reflection
- eliciting a response
- stirring conscience
- pressing for an application
- pushing for a conclusion
- expressing feeling
- probing motives
- raising an alternative.[11]

---

11 So, Zuck, *Teaching as Paul Taught*, 172.

Where Paul encounters unbelievers, he frequently engages in debates with their viewpoints and objections. In the lecture hall of Tyrannus in Athens he is described as "disputing daily" over a two-year period (Acts 19:9 cf. 17:2, 17; 18:4, 20:7, 9; 24:12, 25.) When he gets together with believers, rather than giving an address, typically he "dialogued with" (not, as in some translations, "spoke" or worse "preached" to) the people (Acts 20:7), sometimes until late in the evening. On such occasions Paul then continued to "converse" with them over the Lord's Meal, occasionally "until daylight" (Acts 20:11).

In line with Paul's practice, we should make any classroom in which we are teaching a "hospitable place" where students can freely ask questions, raise objections and make comments, even if these take us outside our comfort-zone.[12] We should also develop more expertise in designing discussions and conversations within our classes that help students attain our educational goals in a way that involves more self-discovery. Strategies for implementing these include:

- intentional buzz groups
- action-reflection circles
- question-directed seminars
- interview style presentations
- conversational field exercises
- as well as more informal after-class and one-on-one individual conversations.

Others learn best when we share *ourselves* as well as our *knowledge* with our students

As Paul reminded the Thessalonians: "We were delighted to share with you not only the gospel of God but our lives as well because you had become so dear to us" (1 Thess 2:8), and also Timothy: "You know all about my teaching, my way of life, my purpose, faith, patience, love, endurance, persecutions, suffering" (2 Tim 3:10-11). While we tend to separate our knowledge and experience, ideas and character, thoughts and dispositions, for Paul they were inextricably fused. Paul's theology was not just an intellectual affair but an expression of his innermost aims, passions and struggles. This is in line with what Martin Luther

---

12   Parker J. Palmer, *To Know As We Are Known: A Spirituality of Education* (San Francisco: Harper & Row, 1983), 71-75.

said to one of his students when asked "what makes a theologian?" The Reformer replied immediately, "suffering!"[13] We view Paul's development of the most profound understanding of the atonement primarily through his reflecting on it; more likely it came to him as a result of his own experience of innocent suffering at the hands of both his opponents and even some of his churches.[14]

Paul often refers to his previous experiences when instructing his hearers (Acts 22) or readers (Rom 1, 9-11, 15-16; 2 Cor *passim*; Gal 1-2, 4-6 et al). He is also willing, where appropriate, to share what he feels as well as what he thinks about various situations, for example his yearning that others come to and grow in Christ (Rom 9:1-3; Gal 4:17) or his hurting because some of his converts are falling away or treating others unjustly (2 Cor 2:1-11; 11:28-29). In the first of the last two passages he makes reference to a wide range of emotions including pain, grief, distress, anguish, tears, joy, comfort and love.[15]

So then, along with careful thought and objective argument, we should have an eye to the personal and passionate dimensions of our teaching. As, following Parker Palmer, I have mentioned elsewhere:

> Our deeply rooted Western tendency is to externalize truth in order to communicate it to others. Yet truth is not essentially a purely objective phenomenon that we can analyze, describe, or point others towards. While it does have a real existence outside ourselves, it is more like a subject to whom we are pledged and with whom we are in relationship. The word "truth" comes from our word "troth", and embracing it is sometimes a very personal—even private—affair. Indeed the metaphor "affair" is not at all out of place. It conveys something of the intimate relationship we should have with the truth. If it is to become fully part of us, we must become "betrothed" to it. And we must share it with others—as we do best through "courting" them so that they can experience as well as hear it—we seek to "betroth" them to it as well …. In the spirit of this

---

[13] For further on experience, especially suffering, as the chief qualification for becoming a theologian see H.G. Haile, *Luther* (London: Sheldon, 1980), 304-305 and Oswald Bayer, *Martin Luther's Theology: A Contemporary Interpretation* (Grand Rapids: Eerdmans, 2008), 21-22.

[14] See further to this theme Robert Banks, "Paul: The Experience Within the Theology," *Eremos Supplement*, No. 24, 1985.

[15] The best account of Paul's emotions occurs within the wider treatment of Matthew Elliott, *Faithful Feelings: Emotion in the New Testament* (Leicester: InterVarsity Press, 2005), esp. 154-157, 172-175, 186-189, 196-197, 208-211, 219-223, 251-252.

metaphor, we could say that in offering a "course" on a subject we are actually inviting students to have "intercourse" with it.[16]

Ways in which we can bring our teaching into closer alignment with this include:

- injecting parts of our own faith journey into our instruction where these enhance and enliven it
- sharing our feelings as well as thoughts where these are naturally drawn out of us by the material
- expressing our uncertainty, vulnerability or lack of knowledge when it is appropriate to do so
- giving permission to our students for them to do any or all of these where it is relevant for them to do so
- exploring the emotional and experiential as well as the cognitive dimension of students' responses to what is taught where it seems relevant.

Others learn best when we communicate *imaginatively* as well as *informatively*

We do not tend to think of Paul as an imaginative teacher in the way Jesus was with his parables or the prophets were with their symbolic actions. With a few exceptions, he is generally regarded as a more purely cognitive and didactic communicator. Yet his speeches and writings are laden with word-pictures of various kinds. They are full of similes, metaphors, metonyms, personifications, and analogies, even on occasion allegories. In part this was a simple by-product of his being a Jew, for whom concrete thinking rooted in everyday life was dominant. In part, however, Paul demonstrates a flair for doing this in a creative way.

Paul frequently builds his instruction around a word-picture. One of the best examples of this is portraying the church as a "body." But this is no straightforward metaphor. Rather than always doing so the same way, he has two different ways of talking about it. In one, the church is the whole body (Romans and Corinthians); in the other, it is the body minus the head, which is Jesus (Ephesians and Colossians). Also, this is not his only image for the church. Depending on what he wishes to emphasise, he pictures the church also as family, a bride, a

---

16 Robert Banks, *Re-envisioning Theological Education: A Missional Alternative to Current Approaches* (Grand Rapids: Eerdmans, 1999), 174, drawing on Palmer, *To Know As We Are Known*, 31-31, 42-46.

building and a field. This enables him to throw light upon specific aspects of church from a variety of angles, drawing on the language of such diverse worlds as biology, domestic architecture and agriculture to make his point.

Indeed Paul's writings are saturated with images from the full range of human experience. For him, imagination is not just important as a means of communication but as a stimulus to ideas. Imagination is a thinking as well as an illustrative organ. As Lakoff and Johnson argue in their groundbreaking book, we work out what we think and how to live primarily through metaphors of one kind or another.[17] Proof that this is true for Paul lies in the extraordinary number and variety of such word-pictures that come before us in his writings. The Australian biblical scholar David Williams identifies all of these in his comprehensive treatment of the subject. Paul uses multiple metaphors in each of the following areas:

- the city and its neighbourhoods
- rural life and villages
- family and inheritance
- life and friendship
- physical provision
- slavery and freedom
- citizenship and politics
- law courts and justice
- manufacturing
- business and marketing
- warfare and the army
- cultic observances
- public shows and sporting events.

Over all, Williams finds more than fifty significant metaphors scattered through Paul's writings.[18]

To give an idea of how central and how creative this way of speaking and writing was for Paul, take his language of "walking." This word-picture appears more than thirty times in his letters. It is his chief way of portraying the Christian life. Since he walked so much himself—more than 15,000 kilometres in his lifetime—it is not surprising that walking appears so regularly in his letters. For

---

17   G. Lakoff and M. Johnson, *Metaphors We Live By* (Chicago: University of Chicago, 1980).
18   David Williams, *Paul's Metaphors: Their Context and Character* (Peabody, MA: Hendrickson, 1999).

Paul, like Jesus, was keenly observant of what went on around him. Everyday situations and activities were windows into or better reflections of God's truth. Since he walked so much and so often, it naturally features strongly in his writings. While sometimes he talks about walking generally, more often he focuses on the little pictures or parables drawn from preparing for, engaging in or the goal of walking. The following is a short list:

- putting shoes on your feet = taking the gospel wherever you go (Eph 6:15)
- learning to walk = beginning the Christian life (1 Thess 4:1)
- looking carefully how you walk = being conscious of your behaviour (Eph 5:15)
- walking a straight path = being honest or straightforward (Gal 2:14)
- walking in the steps of another = imitating a fellow-Christian (2 Cor 12:18)
- walking in the light = living a blameless life (Eph 5:8)
- walking too slowly = living an idle life (2 Thess 3:6)
- washing (the dust off) another's feet = performing humble duties for others (1 Tim 5:10).

The reformer Martin Luther, the philosopher Soren Kierkegaard and the apologist C.S. Lewis spoke and wrote in the same imaginative way. This is why they were such effective communicators in their own times and why they are still so popular today. We need to follow their example. This does not mean finding apt illustrations but becoming aware that the whole world is charged with God and that at any time He is constantly speaking through it. If we paid more attention to the imagery of the Bible, hymns and poetry, we would soon find ourselves thinking and speaking more vividly and evocatively. We would also learn to devise more imaginative educational experiences for our students, for example:

- in biblical studies, by encouraging them to take part in a first century type meeting
- in church history, by staging a simulation of what happened in an early church council
- in theology or ethics, by engaging in a case study of a contemporary doctrinal or moral issue
- in evangelism or mission, by playing the role of a seeker or an unbeliever responding to a Christian sharing their faith
- in pastoral ministry, by creating a dialogue, inventing a story, making a video, to share your convictions, rather than just explaining to students what each of these involved.

Others learn best when it takes place in *real-life settings* and *practical activities* as well as through *listening and thinking*

Alongside teaching in more formal and informal ways, Paul involved his learners in activities through which they learned by doing as well as by hearing. Going to church was one of these. It was not, as it generally is today, primarily a spectator exercise in which the majority form an audience who respond to what is contributed by a few up-front. Everyone brought along a contribution of some kind that created what happened in church on any particular occasion. It was a genuinely participatory event that resulted in practical theological education that built up week by week (1 Cor 16 *passim*).

Beyond this, others were encouraged by Paul or by their churches to accompany him in his wider mission. As the list of members mentioned at the end of his letter to the Romans shows, his team had a mix of genders, it incorporated cultural diversity and it crossed class lines.[19] This combination was unique among religious or philosophical groups in his time. A close reading of the early Christian documents reveals that more than thirty people were involved in this way. Significantly, Paul does not describe them as disciples or followers but as co-workers and colleagues in his enterprise (2 Cor 1:24 *et al*). All these learned not just by hearing him in public or private but by working alongside him. This group was a kind of travelling seminary engaged in mission with regular core members and others who came and went for a time.

Within that framework, as I have written elsewhere:

> ... spiritual growth and practical development, as well as substantial learning, also took place. Such learning was often in-service and non-formal in character; at other times it was more extensive and systematic. Instruction touched on matters of conduct, belief, rituals and mission ... (through) key scriptural teachings, significant historical traditions, and major theological and ethical convictions .... The point of departure for such instruction was often the life-situations of individual members, the group as a whole or the context in which they were operating.[20]

---

19 For more detail on this, see my book *Paul's Idea of Community: The Earliest House Churches in their Historical Setting* (Peabody, MA: Hendrickson, 1994), ch.15.
20 Banks, *Re-Envisioning Theological Education*, 125.

Many possibilities exist for bringing instruction and practice more closely together. The following is just a small sample of what is possible.

- a biblical studies course on the Prophets that combines an Old Testament specialist and a ministry practitioner with students working alongside local people in an urban neighbourhood, experiencing injustice and discrimination
- a church history course focusing on the Laity that includes reflection on current issues and challenges that contain some of the same tensions and opportunities
- a systematic theology course on Creation that is set it up as a camp in the outdoors where God's world can be observed and encountered, not in a room with students' backs to the windows
- an ethics course on Christian lifestyle that draws on students' experience and field-based exercises in suburbs, shopping malls and types of transport to develop a bible-based perspective on issues of busyness, mobility, consumerism and neighbourliness
- a practical theology course examining Work that gives a central place to case studies from students' own experience and visits their actual workplaces to learn more about their challenges and opportunities
- a course on apologetics or evangelism that encourages students to voice their own doubts and perplexities about Christianity as a way of opening up conversation with those they are seeking to reach.

Conclusion

I have identified five characteristics of Paul's approach to teaching from which we can learn today. We have not listened closely enough to him in this area because of the influence the University model of education has had upon us. While some aspects of this rightly shape what we do, we have accepted others too uncritically and this has weakened and compromised our efforts. One way of crystallizing the difference is to distinguish the meaning and purpose of the terms "education" and "edification." It is the latter not the former term that comes before us in the New Testament. In the ancient world, there is some overlap between the two. Education included character and skill development as well as the gaining of knowledge. Edification included the gaining of knowledge but connected this much more closely with spiritual as well as moral development and integrated understanding and living out its implications in every area of life.

Bearing this distinction in mind would act as a constant corrective to a purely schooling approach to learning as well as a creative catalyst to find the best ways of teaching others that God can use to transform students' lives as well as minds. Having "the courage to teach"[21] this way not only prepares our students for but actually ushers them into practising ministry so that it makes a decisive difference in the world around them. For, as with Paul, "turning the world upside down" (Acts 17:6) should be the ultimate aim of all our theological endeavours.

---

21 To cite the title of a further book by Parker J. Palmer, *The Courage to Teach: Exploring the Inner Landscape of a Teacher's Life* (San Francisco: Jossey-Bass, 1998).

SECTION THREE
SOME PHILOSOPHICAL BEARINGS

4 | AN ANALYSIS OF "SOUL" AS THE CENTRAL CONSTRUCT IN DIRKX'S AND RUETHER'S TRANSFORMATIVE LEARNING THEORY

NEIL HOLM

Abstract

In their 2013 paper, "A theory in progress? Issues in transformative learning theory," Taylor and Cranton were concerned that the theory of transformative learning has not progressed because there has been too much attention given to research on transformative experiences *per se* and not enough attention given to research grounded in primary sources. They identify three "central constructs": the place of experience, empathy, and the desire to change.

John Dirkx, a leading theorist in transformative learning, has focused on "soul" as a central construct. Rosemary Ruether engaged the discussion of "soul making" from a theological perspective and, while she did not use the term "transformative learning," she described soul making as "transformative metanoia," which she elaborates as a multi-dimensional transformation.

This essay enjoins a conversation with Dirkx and Ruether to examine four central constructs (experience, empathy, the desire to change, and soul) from a theological perspective in order to consider their implications for theological education.

Introduction

In their 2013 paper, Taylor and Cranton were concerned that the theory of transformative learning had not progressed because too much attention was given to research on transformative experiences per se and not enough attention given to research grounded in primary sources.[1] They suggested that a renewed exploration of the "central constructs" of transformative learning theory had the potential to provoke further discussion and research.

In this essay, I return to "soul," the central construct employed by John Dirkx, a leading theorist in transformative learning. Along with Boyd and others, Dirkx developed a transformative learning research tradition that paralleled and contrasted with Mezirow's approach to transformative learning.[2] Rather than focusing on the rational processes of critical reflection championed by Mezirow, Dirkx focused on unconscious, imaginative, and extra-rational processes.

With the exception of Ball's *Transforming Theology*, transformative learning has received little attention in Australian theological education. Although Ball noted Dirkx's contribution to transformative learning, he gave much greater prominence to Mezirow's work.[3] I have chosen to focus on Dirkx and "soul" to bring his work into the Australian discussion and because he used a distinctly theological term that has contemporary currency.

Soul in Contemporary Culture

In 2014 in Australia, "soul" has currency. *Kia Soul* is a car designed to appeal to Gen Y. *Soul* is a mobile phone and internet service provider. *Fractured Soul* is a Nintendo 3D game where play is split equally between two screens in the device as players navigate a world of hostile sci-fi robots. A push of a button allows the player's physical representation to *switch between two worlds* represented in the top and bottom screen. *Anatomy—Soul* is an ABC documentary about a young Australian fashion designer who makes beautiful shrouds. She

---

1 Edward W. Taylor and Patricia Cranton, "A theory in progress? Issues in transformative learning theory," *European Journal for Research on the Education and Learning of Adults* 4:1 (2013), 33-47, accessed September 10, 2013, doi: 10.3384/rela.2000-7426.rela5000. They identify three "central constructs": the place of experience, empathy, and the desire to change.
2 See Lisa M. Baumgartner, "Mezirow's Theory of transformative learning from 1975 to Present," in *The Handbook of Transformative Learning*. Ed. Edward W. Taylor and Patricia Cranton (San Francisco: Jossey-Bass, 2012), Kindle edition, 98-115.
3 Les Ball, *Transforming Theology* (Preston Vic: Mosaic Press, 2012), 12.

first dressed her dead grandfather and in so doing reflected on current rituals for dressing the dead. This process deeply informed her beliefs concerning the soul. *body+soul* is a newspaper magazine published by News Media. *Soul* is a Surfers Paradise apartment tower that is the third tallest residential building in Australia. *Soul*'s website shows a pinnacle-like architecture that soars from a pristine beach to the clear blue heavens:

> Unsurpassed luxury
>
> Rising up magnificently as the outstanding centrepoint of the exciting new Surfers Paradise foreshore, Soul is exceptional even by international standards. Spectacular in its grandeur and superb in its fine detail, to live in Soul is to reside in a world of refined opulence, perfectly complemented by the relaxed beachside atmosphere. With its extraordinary facilities, unbeatable lifestyle, sublime views and unrivalled location, unmatched anywhere else in the world.

Writing in *The Chronicle of Higher Education*,[4] Stephen T. Asma, Professor of Philosophy at Columbia College Chicago, reflected on "soul talk" in classes in US universities:

> No self-respecting professor of philosophy wants to discuss the soul in class. It reeks of old-time theology, or, worse, New Age quantum treacle. The soul has been a dead end in philosophy ever since the positivists unmasked its empty referential center...
>
> But make no mistake, our students are very interested in the soul. In fact, that is the main reason many of us won't raise the soul issue in our classes: the bizarre, speculative, spooky metaphysics that pours out of students, once the box has been opened, is truly chaotic and depressing. The class is a tinderbox of weird pet theories—divine vapors, God particles, reincarnation, astral projections, auras, ghosts—and mere mention of the soul is like a spark that sets off dozens of combustions.

Asma followed Wittgenstein by asking, "How is soul talk used in ordinary language?" His examples included "He is my soul mate," "She really sold her soul," "That's good soul food," "This nature hike is good for my soul," "She is

---

[4] Stephen T. Asma, "Soul Talk," *The Chronicle of Higher Education* (May 2, 2010), accessed September 16, 2013, http://chronicle.com/article/Soul-Talk/65278/.

an old soul," "James Brown has soul," "The soul reincarnates," and "Her soul is in heaven now." He noted that only two have metaphysical connotations and that the group reveals a family resemblance rather than expresses a central definition. The statements were not propositional; rather they expressed emotional attitudes and resembled other kinds of imperative or aspirational speech. Asma concluded that these expressions cohered around ideas of restoration, authenticity, expressivity, and some elements of ecstasy and naturalism. These expressions embodied an aesthetic awareness incorporated in "feelings of ecstasy, feelings for the beautiful or the sublime, poignant stirrings that might be labeled transcendent—or, negatively, feelings of horror or dread." This awareness was incorporated in "creative acts (playing music, writing poetry, handcrafting furniture, serving tea while a Zen master whacks you with a stick) as well as ethical activities (acts of altruism, self-sacrifice)."

Soul in Contemporary Theology

There may be a sense in which no self-respecting Christian professor of theology wants to discuss soul in a contemporary context. In ATLA Religion Database with ATLASerials during the period 2009-2013, most of the peer-reviewed articles published with the word "soul" in the title were by Muslim scholars or by historians or philosophers looking at "soul" in historical terms. However, soul still had currency in spiritual theology, mental health, and allied applied areas.

In a mental health paper, Gray noted, "It is no longer acceptable to speak of soul in the scientific world." She challenged this view and argued that something sets humans apart from other animals. Humans engaged in activities like philosophy and complex mathematics. This capacity, the "soul," was the seat of the will and personality that is also capable of communication with transcendent reality. The soul was not a pre-existent, immortal, spiritual substance trapped inside a body. Humans were ensouled bodies, living, breathing, holistic entities. Gray gave attention to soul because she believed that mental health professionals will develop clearer communication, better diagnosis, and more effective treatment if they recognise their underlying assumptions (and those of patients and service users) about the nature of humankind.[5]

---

5   Alison J. Gray, "Whatever happened to the soul? Some theological implications of neuroscience," *Mental Health, Religion & Culture*, 13 (6) (2010), 637-648. Accessed September 16, 2013, doi: 10.1080/13674676.2010.488424.

In the same issue of the mental health journal, Clarke was concerned that attention to spirituality in mental health tends to ignore the body in favour of soul and spirit. The paper focused more on body and spirit than soul but she described soul as "the life force that vivifies and animates the body and gives consciousness; all animals have a soul …. With our soul (also called psyche), which includes what is called 'mind,' humans engage in scientific and philosophical enquiry and analyse data that come through the senses."[6]

In 2008, a new journal began publication. Titled *Journal of Spiritual Formation and Soul Care,* it did not address the nature of "soul" in its first issue nor does it seem to have done so since then. However, in a brief article in 2005, Rowan Williams considered the nature of soul care. He emphasised that "soul" is primarily a relationship to God, and this relation shapes and is shaped by relation with other people. When we engage with others, we attend to their communicative and symbolic world. Care for souls, then, expresses care about the symbolic world of another. From this perspective, soul is the world of significance that allows the person to picture themselves by "plotting" their place in relation with other agents and with God.[7]

Williams' 2005 paper followed his more substantial treatment of soul in *Lost Icons*. In this book, Williams admitted that being deliberately provocative by conflating "self" and "soul," soul is a religious means of discussing selfhood.[8] Here we begin to encounter issues that I will explore later: Williams has drawn self, soul, and identity into the conversation. Aware that the dualistic Platonic view is "the most common concept of soul in Western societies," Williams sought to counter a similar view of self. In the dualistic view, the soul is a pre-existent, immortal, spiritual substance trapped inside a body.[9] Williams opposed contemporary fashionable ideas of self as pre-existing, self as a "true self" that is hidden or buried, a self that could be revealed by therapy, a self that is learned rather than a predetermined system of needs and desires, or a self often described as an "authentic self" (the real me, unaffected by external influences, transparent, and devoid of self-deception).[10] In *Lost Icons*, Williams argued for a self

---

6 Janice Clarke, "Body and soul in mental health care," *Mental Health, Religion & Culture* 13:6 (2010), 650. Accessed September 16, 2013, doi: 10.1080/13674676.2010.488416.
7 Rowan Williams, "The care of souls," *Advances in Psychiatric Treatment* 11 (2005), 4–5. Accessed September 19, 2013, http://apt.rcpsych.org/content/11/1/4.full.
8 Rowan Williams, *Lost Icons* (London: Continuum, 2003), 8.
9 Gray, "Whatever happened to the soul?" 638.
10 Williams had explored these issues earlier in "Interiority and Epiphany" in *On Christian Theology* (Oxford: Blackwell, 2000), 239.

constructed over time through interaction with others and with God.

Williams said that souls are the lost icons[11]. In *The Dwelling of the Light*, published about the same time, Williams explained the meaning of icons. Icons are painted as a performance accompanied by fasting and prayers that the image produced "will open a gateway for God." Created in this act of worship, they are not accurate representations but are abiding expressions of "human actions that seek to be open to God's actions." The viewer of an icon should look and pray for an openness to God's working: "to look patiently and not analytically, and allow yourself to be 'worked on'—perhaps we should say, allow yourself to be looked at by God, rather than just looking at something yourself."[12] Thus the soul as icon

> is a whole way of speaking, of presenting and "uttering" the self, that presupposes relation as the ground that gives the self room to exist, a relation developing in time, a relation with an agency which addresses and summons the self, but is in itself no part of the system of interacting and negotiating speakers in the world. In religious terms, this agency has been seen as the source of the self's life in such a way as to establish that any self's existence is a simple, unnecessary and gratuitous act on the part of the source. The self is, not because of need but because of gift.

In these terms, our soul (our self) is that part of us that is in relation to God, open to God, available to be worked on by God, or to be looked at by God. Our soul is also performative: created by God, created in prayer and worship, invested with God's self but acting, performing, in ways that invite others to look upon us and, if they are sufficiently aware and receptive, to allow God to look at them, and to allow themselves to see through us to God.

In the first volume of his spiritual theology series, Eugene Peterson also addressed self and soul. Soul is our core being.[13] Soul "signals an interiority that permeates all exteriority." The Hebrew word for soul is *nephesh*. It is also the word for neck. The neck/soul connects the head, the brain, and the nervous system

---

11 Williams, *Icons*, 196.
12 Williams, *The Dwelling of the Light* (Mulgrave, Vic: John Garrett, 2003), xvii, xviii.
13 Joel Green addresses body-soul dualism: whether humans possess a "soul" or are souls; and whether the soul is our "inner self." He concludes that soul refers to "embodied human life and especially to present, embodied human capacities for personal relatedness *vis-à-vis* the cosmos, the human family, and God." "Soul" in *The New Interpreter's Dictionary of the Bible S-Z Volume 5* (Nashville: Abingdon Press 2009), 358-9.

to the rest of the bodily functions. It connects rationality with emotion, reason with daily life. It keeps it all together. The neck is the passage by which air enters the body and comes out again as speech. The soul is the passage by which the spirit enters the body and comes out again as God-breathed life. Soul is the word that captures what it means to be uniquely and comprehensively human. Soul calls attention to "the God-origins, God-intentions, God-operations that make us what we are."[14]

Like Williams, Peterson was concerned about the way we talk about who we are. Today we use "self" to designate who we are but we use self in a way that is very different to the use that Williams believes is correct. We cannot coalesce contemporary use of self and soul. "Self is the soul minus God. Self is what is left of soul with all the transcendence and intimacy squeezed out." Soul reverberates with God relationships, human relationships, earth relationships. Self is an isolating term akin to the individual. Soul has been replaced by a self largely unconcerned about relationships. This unrelated self is a consumer who takes and does not give, a "human resource" rather than a member of staff, a client rather than a customer (derived from 16th century "a person with whom you have dealings").[15]

Soul in Dirkx's Theory of Transformative Learning

John Dirkx's engagement with transformative learning has paralleled that of Jack Mezirow, perhaps the best-known theorist of transformative learning. Rather than focusing on the rational processes of critical reflection championed by Mezirow, Dirkx focused on unconscious, imaginative, and extra-rational processes. Dirkx cited Mezirow, Boyd, Cranton as others in support of a description of transformative learning as making or remaking meaning—a learning process by which we make "a dramatic shift in how we come to know and how we understand ourselves in relation to the broader world."[16] Drawing on Jungian depth psychology, Dirkx and his colleagues used soul to mean the

---

14 Eugene Peterson, *Christ Plays in Ten Thousand Places: A Conversation in Spiritual Theology* (Grand Rapids: Eerdmans, 2005), 36-37.
15 Peterson, *Christ Plays*, 37-38.
16 John M Dirkx, "Nurturing soul work: a Jungian approach to transformative learning" in *The Handbook of Transformative Learning: Theory, Research, and Practice*. Ed. Edward W. Taylor and Patricia Cranton (San Francisco: John Wiley & Sons, 2012) Kindle edition, 115-116.

hidden inner self. The use of this language recalls Williams' concern about self as a "true self" that is hidden or buried, a self that could be revealed by therapy. However, his concept of soul or self may be more complex because he sometimes refers to "our inner selves" or "the multiplicity of selves that makes up who we are."[17] Dirkx saw transformative learning as nurturing soul or soul work. He believed that transformative learning takes place in a context that embodies deep emotions and an array of images, stories, and personal myths around which we unconsciously instruct our lives.

According to Dirkx, coming to know and understand ourselves involves "a heroic struggle to wrest consciousness and knowledge from the forces of unconsciousness and ignorance."[18] Learning through the soul involves a focus on personal, imaginative ways of knowing that draw on intuitive and emotional understandings of our experiences. He did not define soul but instead provided examples of "what is meant by soul": being awestruck by a sunset or full moon, feeling great empathy for a trapped child, or being transported to a different time and space by great music, art, or literature.[19] These descriptions suggest that Dirkx was referring to deep emotional experiences, a deep consciousness of something beyond ourselves, experiences of the "deep holiness of the world" that hint at the "unknown continuity of things." Soul expresses a relationship between the individual and his or her broader world. Soul expresses a relationship between heart and mind, between mind and emotion, and between dark and light. This reminds us of Peterson's discussion of *nephesh* but so far there is no intimation of any kind of metaphysical or spiritual relationship. When Dirkx referred to consciousness of something beyond ourselves, consciousness of the "other," he was not referring to a consciousness of a religious or deistic "other." He referred to relationship with other people, nature, or creation rather than relationship with a transcendent being: "The 'other' is anything, anyone, or any group we perceive as apart or separate from our individual natures."[20]

Transformative learning, according to Dirkx, "connects us to the immediacy of our present experience, and through this process leads us into an experience that transcends more limited ego-based views of the world." Building on the "to draw out" sense of education, Dirkx saw transformative learning as

---

17 Dirkx, "Nurturing soul work," 116; Dirkx, "Nurturing Soul in Adult Learning," *New Directions for Adult and Continuing Education* 74 (1997), 82.
18 Dirkx, *Nurturing Soul*, 79.
19 Dirkx, *Nurturing Soul*, 80.
20 Dirkx, *Nurturing Soul*, 82, 83.

"drawing out" the soul to unite with the world soul. This drawing out process fosters self knowledge by engaging with symbols, images, concrete everyday experiences, and contemplation of song, story, myth, and poetry. "Nurturing" soul is a process of recognising what is already inherent within our relationships and experiences. It involves taking account of this existing presence within the teaching-learning space and respecting its "sacred message." It provides opportunity to attend to and to consider this message and to allow it to speak.[21]

In his 2012 review of soul work, Dirkx continued to hold a similar understanding of soul although he tied it much more closely to Jungian perspectives.[22] This approach attends to emotion-laden images within our unconscious and the personal stories and myths that we use unconsciously to construct our lives. Overall, Dirkx seemed to take religious thought seriously but, like de Botton,[23] he sought to leach out any ideas that relate to duty or the supernatural. He sought to distil a kind of abstract truth lacking in particularity from the religious worldview. He may not have accepted religious truths but could see value in them as "sophisticated systems for thinking about our deepest yearnings, and experiencing and being in this weird and wonderful and endlessly perplexing thing called Life."[24] If this is the case, Dirkx's use of soul is like Peterson's use of self—God has been squeezed out. He may find a "spark of life"[25] that he seeks but it may be just that—a tiny spark rather than a mighty flash, a spluttering candle rather than a mighty sun. For instance, he did not use the religious truth of "evil" but he found it necessary to draw on negative images and influences on the inner world in all his examples of the inner life. These images include fear, anxiety, feelings of being threatened that are linked to previous behaviours of parents or teachers, and abusive relationships. Likewise, his discussion of the role of the transpersonal referred to the concept of "cultural complex" whereby our unconscious lives reflect collective dynamics as found in families, peer groups, and similar significant social groupings. He noted that from these groups we acquire defence mechanisms like denial, scapegoating, rationalisation, and intellectualisation. His discussion did not include any reference to "good" (as opposed to "evil") despite

---

21 Dirkx, *Nurturing Soul*, 83.
22 Dirkx, *Nurturing Soul Work*.
23 Alain de Botton, *Religion for Atheists: A Non-believer's Guide to the Uses of Religion* (London: Penguin, 2012).
24 Stephen Crittenden, "Review of *Religion for Atheists*," *The Global Mail*, February 24, 2012. Accessed September 18, 2013, http://www.theglobalmail.org/feature/religion-for-atheists/87/.
25 Dirkx, *Nurturing Soul*, 83.

making brief reference to a paper by Rosemary Radford Ruether.[26] Clearly, Dirkx was aware of theological ideas but, like de Botton, he sought to mine them for their instrumental value.

Ruether held a more balanced view of human nature. Humans are composed of their true nature, their *imago dei*, and their other nature with its tendency to evil (cf St Paul's discussion of the old nature and the new Christian nature). She asserted that our tendency toward evil is learned through our experience in social systems that have themselves been distorted by evil. We learn to conform to these evil systems that seek to keep us under their influence and in so doing shape us in ways that increase our alienation from each other and our alienation from ourselves. Despite the influence of these evil systems, our *imago dei* remains embedded within us. We are influenced by this image of God (and the broader society). This image persists within out "intuitive sensibilities" and its effect in the broader society and culture is seen in "good and life-giving relationships in family, friends, mentors in education, religion, work and even sometimes in politics." Ruether's term for the process of promoting growth in this "good tendency" was "soul making." We might infer that for Ruether, soul is that which is expressed in personal and social relationships characterised by love, justice, compassion, a sense of relationality and community, and a respect for ourselves and our neighbours.[27] Ruether's view of soul has elements of the views expressed by Williams and Peterson: the soul has agency, it is invested with God's self, is vulnerable to the influence of God and others but is capable of action. It has an interiority but that interiority radiates out, permeating all exteriority.

Although Ruether did not use the term "transformative learning," she described soul making as "transformative metanoia" where metanoia is

> a journey of transformed relationship, relationship to oneself, to one's immediate community, of society and of culture, finally, a transformation of our relationship to all creation, to animals and plants, air, soil and water. Reconciliation with God is within this whole process of transformation and reconciliation with others. It is what the Biblical tradition calls the "reign of God."[28]

For Ruether, transformation was multidimensional. It involves remaking our

---

26 Rosemary Radford Ruether, "Feminist Metanoia and Soul-making," *Women & Therapy* 16 (1995).
27 Ruether, "Feminist Metanoia," 34, 39.
28 Ruether, "Feminist Metanoia," 39.

understanding of ourselves, our neighbours, our society, creation, and God and allowing these "others" continually to remake and renew us.

If we accept Dirkx's definition of description of transformative learning as making or remaking meaning—a learning process by which we make "a dramatic shift in how we come to know and how we understand ourselves in relation to the broader world," we might say that Reuther argued that we can only know and understand ourselves when we reflect on what we know, reflect on what we experience, and on the basis of that reflection engage further with the world allowing the world to affect us, to remake and renew us but then to subject those new experiences to further reflection and analysis. As we will see later, praxis was an important aspect of Reuther's approach.

For Dirkx, transformation focused on understanding our inner lives and how wider forces affect them. To put it in simple terms, Dirkx's view of soul had an inner orientation while Reuther complemented the inner orientation with a more communal, engaged orientation. Dirkx did not ignore the external world but focused on its effect on the inner world while Ruether proposed a reciprocal relationship between inner and outer world. Their approach to soul making reflected these differences.

Process of Soul Work or Soul Making

Dirkx sought a model of transformative learning that takes account of our "inner worlds, of which we may be unaware." The goal of soul work is to establish a conscious relationship with our unconscious and then to elaborate and expand on this relationship. Transformative learning leads to enhanced individuation—we become more complete as a unique personality, more unified, and a more integrated person. Our inner worlds find expression in our emotions and a major focus of soul work is to recognise and address powerful emotions when they arise. However, many people learn to "modulate or control" these emotions to the extent that they lose touch with them. Soul work provides opportunity to reconnect with these emotional forces. As noted above, our inner worlds are affected by collective cultural and social influences stemming from families, schools, and other significant social groupings. Soul work responds to these collective influences and to other aspects of the inner world of each person. Taking the lead from Jung, Dirkx advised that soul work engage with the inner world mythopoetically: "imaginative engagement and elaboration of the inner stories, the private myths ... that seem to implicitly guide and inform our lives."[29]

In an educational setting, soul work proceeds through some steps. First, as a general principle and regardless of the subject matter, teachers employ image laden and image arousing processes like story, myths, poetry, music, drawing, art, journaling, dance, rituals, or performance. This strategy permits students to become "aware of and give voice to the images and unconscious dynamics that may be animating their psychic lives within the context of the subject matter and the learning process. These unconscious aspects of psyches are almost continuous." Second, teachers look for situations in which the soul becomes expressed or awakened. When the learning event is characterised by some expression of emotion, the teacher may proceed by proposing questions directed to the other than rational aspects of the learning task such as discussing why a particular learning event was lively and animated, asking what was it that aroused the excitement and engagement, and what were the associated emotions. Less successful learning events may be approached similarly with questions like, "Was there some aspect of this learning event that reminded you of a negative past experience?" Third, teachers employ the "imaginal method". This set of strategies helps students gain insight into their inner worlds that are hidden from conscious awareness but continue to influence and shape their sense of self, their interpretations of the external world, and their day-to-day actions. Steps of this process include (a) Description: students describe the event or image as clearly as they can; (b) Association: students associate the event or image with similar events and images in the past or associate the image with other aspects of our lives; (c) Amplification: students expand or amplify the meaning of the original image by connecting it with film, literature, stories, poetry, fairy tales, or myths that present similar images; and (d) Animation: students animate the image through written dialogue, role play, or other means of allowing the image to speak or to engage in other ways.[30]

In her soul making, Ruether took a somewhat different approach. As we have seen, the inner world was important to her but her focus was limited to transformed relationships for modern women. Outlining the case that women were subjugated by patriarchal social and cultural systems, she saw transform-

---

29 Dirkx, *Nurturing Soul Work*, 117- 123.
30 John M. Dirkx "Transformative Learning and the Journey of Individuation," *ERIC Digest* 223 (2000) (Clearinghouse on Adult, Career, and Vocational Education EDO-CE-00-223); *Nurturing Soul Work*, 124-125.

ation as the "process by which women's journey leads them to question these systems and embark on a process of emancipation from them to create a new self and a new society."[31] In her view of gender relationships, domination was the main factor leading to the insecure self. It was also the main factor in other exploitative relationships like race and class. In this way, she believed that her argument, although directed to women, had application to other settings. She believed that transformation in any setting depended largely on the development of alternative communities where new role models and new networks of communication were available. In these communal settings, individuals could be assisted in consciousness raising, in challenging the *status quo*, and in claiming their quest for selfhood. This new awareness often leads to feelings of anger and Ruether believed that it was important to move through this anger to a self-esteem that was sufficiently healthy to forgive oneself and others.

Ruether's emphasis on selfhood and recognition of emotions paralleled Dirkx's approach. However, her approach moved beyond the more individualistic focus on the personal to compassion for others. Transformation was possible when the individual sought to move beyond reflection to action that might involve engaging in new and relevant educational settings, working in solidarity with others (especially when these others are drawn from diverse backgrounds), seeking to ameliorate systems of exploitation of others. She advocated an engagement with praxis that was relevant to all individuals, irrespective of gender. While Dirkx focused on personal transformation and although his "animation" step could engender social action, Ruether focused on personal and social metanioa. She sought transformation and reconciliation of the whole: self, others, society, culture, and all of creation.[32] In some ways, this active soul reflects Williams' description of the soul as performative. Although she acknowledged that such a complete transformation will never be accomplished except under the reign of God, she argued that

> we must take up the task in each day, in each relationship, in each generation, in specific social and historical contexts; the struggle to enhance loving, truthful and just relationships and to curb and cure hate, fear and violence. It is the way that we also both receive and manifest the redemptive work of the Holy One.[33]

31　Ruether, "Feminist Metanoia," 33.
32　Ruether, "Feminist Metanoia," 39.
33　Ruether, "Feminist Metanoia," 44.

The primary differentiation between Ruether and Dirkx is that ultimately she recognised the presence of God behind all of creation. She recognised a transforming God able and desiring to call into existence the things that do not exist.[34] God has created a universe in which it is possible through relationships with God and through relationships with others for transformation to occur. In these ways, understanding, knowledge, imagination, compassion, empathy, self-understanding and much more that were not in existence may be called into existence.

Transformative Learning Though Praxis

Ruether's understanding of metanoia echoed Bonhoeffer's definition where metanoia was understood as "allowing oneself to be pulled into walking the path that Jesus walks" thus orienting our lives to God and others rather than "thinking of one's needs, questions, sins and fears."[35] Metanoia involved "a fundamental reorientation,"[36] engagement with the world, sharing God's pain in the world, and "living fully in the midst of life's tasks, questions, successes and failures, experiences, and perplexities."[37] Metanoia was a process of becoming fully human, becoming a Christian. This reminds us of Peterson's description of soul as the word that captures what it means to be uniquely and comprehensively human. For both Ruether and Bonhoeffer, praxis was essential to transformation. Transformation goes beyond reflection to engagement. Processes that lead to a consciousness of self remain limited without praxis. Soul work at the personal/interpersonal level is limited without praxis. Soul work must transcend the personal journey to engage in solidarity with others who are drawn from within the individual's own group and from other class and race groups. The soul needs to be actualised in action in the company of others.

According to Groome, in "contemporary literature, praxis usually refers to purposeful human activity that holds in dialectic unity both theory and practice, critical reflection and historical engagement."[38] Although he wrote more broadly

---

34 Romans 4: 17. Neil Elliott, "The Letters of Paul to the Romans" in *The New Oxford Annotated Bible New Revised Standard Version with the Apocrypha* (Oxford: Oxford University Press, 2010), 1798, suggested that "God's power to *call into existence the things that do not exist* is a key theme in the letter."
35 Dietrich Bonhoeffer, *Letters and Papers from Prison* (Minneapolis: Fortress Press, 2010), 480.
36 Bonhoeffer, *Letters and Papers from Prison*, 26.
37 Bonhoeffer, *Letters and Papers from Prison*, 486.
38 Thomas Groome, *Sharing Faith* (Eugene, OR: Wipf and Stock, 1991), 136.

about religious education, it is helpful to regard theological education as forming part of the Christian education continuum. He emphasised that the fundamental approach to religious education is "shared Christian praxis" where "share" includes mutual partnership, active participation, and dialogue with oneself, with others, with God, and with a coherent and integrated understanding of the Christian story.[39] Banks applied and extended these principles in the context of theological education.[40] He grafted work by Browning and by Dakin onto Groome's approach to develop what he called a "missional model" of theological education. In this model, he sought to go beyond other models focused on praxis to a model that placed greater emphasis on action without losing its connection with reflection. His model has the potential to provide for the kinds of outcomes sought by both Dirkx and Ruether:

> Theological education is primarily though not exclusively concerned with actual *service*—informed and transforming—of the *kingdom* and therefore primarily focuses on acquiring cognitive, spiritual-moral, and practical obedience.[41]

Like Ruether, Banks saw praxis, informed and reflective understanding and insight engaged in service of the *kingdom*, as transformative. Effective theological education built on this approach will be transformative. Although the missional model did not specifically incorporate issues of identity and soul, Banks was aware that identity issues must be dealt with in theological education. He painted a picture of numbers of theological students whose experiences before seminary were parallel to the experiences of the abused and cowed women of whom Ruether wrote or to those described by Dirkx whose lives were influenced by fear, anxiety, feelings of being threatened linked to previous behaviours of parents or teachers and abusive relationships.[42] Ruether and Dirkx have the potential to fill out some of the gaps in Banks' work in regard to identity issues.

Banks was aware of models of theological education that built on the work of Freire and Illich that enabled students to become critically aware of social structures, assisted them to devise ministry projects that transform society today and in the future, and provided learning resources and personal empowering for all kinds of ministry. He endorsed those programs that emphasised reflection

---

39   Groome, *Sharing Faith*, 138, 142.
40   Robert Banks, *Reenvisioning Theological Education* (Grand Rapids: Eerdmans, 1999), 159ff.
41   Banks, *Reenvisioning Theological Education*, 144.
42   Banks, *Reenvisioning Theological Education*, 191ff.

in ministry and life as opposed to those that emphasised reflection on ministry and life.[43] One endorsed program drew on liberation theology where theological education was conducted in the ministry or missional setting itself rather than in a distant college. Banks sought to build on this approach as he developed his missional model. This emphasis reflects Ruether's concern for social transformation through engaging in solidarity with others who are drawn from within the individual's own group and from other class and race groups. Banks discussed student selection processes designed to create a more diverse learning community and the creation of mission groups drawn from this diverse population to work in solidarity with each other and with the host community.[44]

Conclusion

This essay has analysed "soul" as a central construct in the work of John Dirkx, a leading figure in transformative learning. For Dirkx, "soul" related to a person's hidden inner self, the unconscious inner world, or self identity that was formed largely by various interpersonal negative forces. "Soul work" involved helping the person to become conscious of the forces that have shaped and damaged them. Transformative learning was a process in which teachers were aware of the importance of soul work and would take opportunities in class, when appropriate, to assist students to reflect on how their behaviour was influenced by unconscious forces and to become aware of these forces and their effect. Alternatively, teachers could be more active and use particular teaching processes that employ mythopoetic techniques. For Dirkx, transformative learning was a process that transformed the students' understanding of themselves and freed them from the negative forces that have influenced them. It was concerned largely with the individual's inner world.

Although Jung had a significant influence on Dirkx's thinking, Dirkx was also influenced by the work of Rosemary Radford Ruether. She, too, wanted to raise consciousness of forces that shape and damage but she was influenced by a notion of soul that was different to that held by Dirkx . His soul was one of interiority. Her soul was one in which interiority permeated exteriority. For Ruether, becoming fully human was a process in which the soul was actualised

---

43 Banks, *Reenvisioning Theological Education*, 137.
44 Banks, *Reenvisioning Theological Education*, 195ff.

in action in the company of others. Transformation came through praxis, where praxis involves purposeful human communal activity that holds theory and practice in dialectic unity and where there is reciprocity between critical reflection and historical engagement.

Banks' missional theological education was a form of transformative learning that was dependent on praxis. Banks wanted his students to be able to make or remake meaning and to make a dramatic shift in how they came to know and how they understood themselves in relation to the broader world. He wanted students to become critically aware of social structures and how these structures influenced them. He wanted students to acquire cognitive, spiritual-moral, and practical obedience through informed and transformative service of the kingdom. He wanted students to engage in praxis as a means of generating reciprocity between interiority and exteriority. Banks' missional approach is worth further analysis as a form of transformative learning.

Another approach that has potential benefits because it has a more complex and complete view of soul is that proposed in *Rethinking Christian Identity* by Medi Ann Volpe.[45] Volpe analyses the formation of Christian identity with reference to the theology of Gregory of Nyssa, especially his notion of soul. This view contrasts with the views in this essay but may provide a deeper and more complete understanding of formation (and possibly transformation) than that proposed by Mezirow or Dirkx. Volpe's model takes into account God, soul, desire, hope, the special difficulties of the "rationally capacious," Scripture, doctrine, liturgy, ascetic practices, the saints, and imagination work. It gives particular attention to identity, especially its relation to soul, to faith, hope and love; to discipleship and the importance of community; and to the influence of Holy Spirit and Christ. Volpe recognises the significance of praxis. Volpe presents a strong argument for the importance of the soul, formation, and the place of sin in Christian identity. Further exploration of her ideas may prove fruitful in the further development of our understanding of transformative learning.

---

45 Medi Ann Volpe, *Rethinking Christian Identity: Doctrine and Discipleship* (Oxford: Wiley-Blackwell, 2013).

5 | LEAVING HOME

A PEDAGOGY FOR THEOLOGICAL EDUCATION

DAN FLEMING AND PETER MUDGE

Abstract

This essay refers to the journey of theological education which necessarily takes one beyond one's home and into an encounter with mystery. It begins with a study of the home, which is informed by the works of David Ford and Emmanuel Levinas. Ford refers to a *cultural ecology*, which is understood as the cultural home which a community inhabits, and which we suggest can equally refer to one's own "home" worldview. Levinas is significant in his warnings about remaining within this worldview too much. In his words, this is "totalisation," understood as the damaging tendency to reduce all otherness to categories over which individual consciousness can claim control. Levinas uses the metaphor of home to illustrate this warning, noting the tendency to reduce mystery to what can be contained by the four walls of our conscious home and, in so doing, engage in a violent reductionism ill-suited to encountering what is ultimately mysterious. Arguing that this is unsuitable for theological education, we look to how pedagogies of displacement and disorientation informed by the work of Walter Brueggemann can be shown to break down the four walls of the home. In light of this, we offer for consideration a pedagogical cycle that could assist theological educators in their efforts to encourage students to "leave home."

Part One: Some Thoughts about "Home"

The cultural ecology of a "home"

What does it mean to have a home? In a number of works, David Ford refers to the "cultural ecology" of our current context, and we build on his use of this terminology here. When Ford refers to a cultural ecology, what he means is the complex intertwining of ideas, beliefs, and practices in which and through which a particular community understands itself and by which it navigates its way through life.[1] Here Ford uses ecology not in its discipline-specific sense as the study of our environment, but rather in its etymological sense as the meaning or idea (Greek *logos*) of home (Greek *ekos*). In this sense, a cultural ecology, or a cultural *home*, provides the structure by which a community makes meaning: the walls which stand strong and firm when crisis is encountered, the roof which shelters from outside forces, the windows from which one can view the world outside and, when one ventures into this world, a place to return and feel at ease when the journey ends. In this, Ford's work is congruent with recent discussions surrounding the concept of *worldview*, and in this instance this would refer to a communal worldview.[2] Ultimately, such a worldview provides a cultural home within which the community can exist. In his own work, Ford argues that a significant part of this home in most—if not all—cultures around the world is made up of religious beliefs and practices, and he uses this to found his argument for the importance of the academic discipline of theology in the current context, as that discipline which seeks to look critically at the four walls of the home, to understand their makeup, how they relate to other homes and the street on which they are positioned, and so on.[3]

From cultural ecology to individual ecology

We would like to propose that this understanding of cultural ecology may also be applied to an individual's ecology. That is, like cultures, individuals too have systems of meaning which act as homes. According to van der Kooij and others, these provide answers to ultimate concerns, meaning in life, guidance on what

---

1 David F. Ford, *Shaping Theology: Engagements in a Religious and Secular World* (Malden: Blackwell Publishing, 2007), 95, 118, 128-129.
2 Jacomijn C. van der Kooij, Doret J. de Ruyter and Siebren Miedema, "'Worldview': The Meaning and the Concept and the Impact on Religious Education," *Religious Education: The Official Journal of the Religious Education Society* 108, no. 2 (2013), 214.
3 See for example Ford, *Shaping Theology: Engagements in a Religious and Secular World*, 128-9.

to value, and guidance regarding the shape and purpose of life.[4] Just as with a cultural ecology, an individual ecology provides strength, shelter, windows through which to view the world, and a place to return home after venturing out into it. On this view, our own consciousness is our home, and it is built up in a comprehensive sense over a lifetime by our education and experiences, both explicit and implicit.

Levinas and human consciousness as being "at home with oneself"
Enter here the philosopher Emmanuel Levinas, famous for his understanding of infinite responsibility who, fascinatingly, has much to say about human consciousness—or the experience of being an "I am" as per Descartes' *cogito ergo sum*—as a home. Frequently in Levinas, being-at-home-with-one's-self is used in the same breath as the experience of being an "I" and the experience of having an "ego."[5] The idea of consciousness as being at home with one's self is a helpful metaphor, and extends on what we have outlined about the home above. For Levinas, being an "I" means becoming self-conscious and surrounding one's self within four walls, as it were, drawing into one's self what is needed for survival.[6] In his philosophy, the home is understood as that part of the human person which is concerned with obtaining and protecting the "gear consisting of things necessary" for the preservation of conscious life itself.[7]

In order to build a home for itself, the "I" of consciousness must necessarily go outside of itself and take in what is other and make it its own. For Levinas, the paradigmatic example of this is eating bread, an activity wherein the self takes something that is exterior and incorporates it into its own interiority—the "I" takes the bread home, so to speak, and uses it to build up its four walls.[8] Beyond the bare essentials of human existence, the "I" also seeks to discover and manipulate the world which is outside of itself for the purposes of its own self-referential activities.

The "I" of consciousness thus encounters objects outside of itself, brings them home, and transforms them into objects that it can "observe, handle, and

---

4   van der Kooij, de Ruyter and Miedema, "'Worldview': The Meaning and the Concept and the Impact on Religious Education,' 214-15.
5   See for example, Emmanuel Levinas, *Totality and Infinity: An Essay on Exteriority*, trans. Alphonso Lingis (Pittsburgh: Duquesne University Press, 1969), 39.
6   Roger Burggraeve, *The Wisdom of Love in the Service of Love: Emmanuel Levinas on Justice, Peace, and Human Rights* (Milwaukee: Marquette University Press, 2002), 45.
7   Levinas, *Totality and Infinity*, 152.
8   Levinas, *Totality and Infinity*, 33.

transform by labour and study within the framework of scientific theories."[9] Levinas employs the metaphor of the hand which grasps at the world and always returns to the self to explicate this idea, and he refers to this action of the "I" as *labour*.[10] Labour here is an act of *comprehension*, for which the German word *auffassen* is helpful—literally a sense of taking one's hand and grasping something. Labour should therefore be directed towards its appropriate objects which Levinas names *elements* that are independent in their being and outside of the self but are not the Other (that is, they are that for which he uses the French *l'autre*—not the Other who is mysterious). When the "I" has taken an element into itself and contained it, this element becomes "fixed between the four walls of the home" and is understood as a possession.[11] Given the anonymity of the element possessed, Levinas sees this action of drawing otherness into the self as unproblematic and states that "in the last analysis labour cannot be called violence: it is applied to what is faceless, to the resistance of nothingness."[12]

"Leaving home" as the end of authentic human existence—the trap of "totalisation"
However, the labour of the "I" of consciousness must be understood within the context of the human person as a whole. It is not the final word in human existence, but rather a necessary condition for human activity.[13] In an analogous way, the home of the child is a starting point for their existence. But they must one day *leave home* if they are to engage with the world and flourish. The home is thus not to be seen as an end in itself, but as a means to the end of authentic human existence. This leads Levinas to issue a challenge to any perspective which seeks to exalt consciousness to a level at which it is given permission to bring everything back home, to overcome it through labour, and to draw it in to the four walls of the self.[14] Any activity which falls into this trap Levinas calls a *totalisation*, and refers to it powerfully as a violence. Why? Because when I peek outside the windows of my home, or when I take a walk in the park, and I encounter mystery, ultimately what I encounter is bigger than the four walls of my home. Were I to bring it back, and attempt to fit it in, I would be compressing it into a context in which it does not—and cannot—fit, and thus do violence to it.

---

9   Adriaan Theodoor Peperzak, *Beyond: The Philosophy of Emmanuel Levinas* (Evanston: Northwestern University Press, 1997), 9.
10 Levinas, *Totality and Infinity*, 159.
11 Levinas, *Totality and Infinity*, 158.
12 Levinas, *Totality and Infinity*, 160.
13 Levinas, *Totality and Infinity*, 152.
14 Levinas, *Totality and Infinity*, 38.

Security of "the four walls" of home versus openness to what is foreign and "other"
Levinas' own concern is directed towards the mystery of the Other human person, but it is not difficult to see the theological implications of this same view. Indeed, if we return to Ford for a moment, he notes the problem that exists when religions forget about the overwhelming mystery of God and instead focus in on, and worship, their own cultural norms. When nothing but the home exists, the problem of idolatry lurks dangerously near.[15]

This presents a fascinating challenge for theological education, focused as it is on asking students to "look into the sun" as Karl Barth described it, and encounter and grapple with insatiable mystery which, by definition, resists the four walls of the home.[16] Why is this a challenge? Because it is uncomfortable and involves new and perhaps disturbing information. Our students are asked to consider critically deeply held views in light of this challenge and, as Les Ball's research shows, this is frequently noted as one of the most difficult experiences they have in theological education.[17] To put it bluntly, when we're not sure what's outside, sometimes we'd prefer to stay home and work on strengthening our doors and windows.

Leaving home, exile and displacement
So how might theological education respond to this challenge and invite students to "leave home" and encounter mystery? Levinas himself had a metaphor with which we begin. Firstly, in Levinas' musings about the encounter with mystery in the face of the Other, he lamented that the philosophy has tended to follow in the footsteps of Ulysses more than Abraham. By this he meant, picking up on his image of the home of consciousness, that human reasoning had tended to be more like Ulysses who travels the world only to return home again, than Abraham who leaves home for a journey without knowing the destination, and never to return.[18] In theological education we ask our students to leave the comforts of their homes for a journey into the wilderness, and we are the guides. These established "comforts of home" might include one or more of beliefs, unquestioned certitudes, biases, untested assumptions, or ignorance of or refusal

---

15 David F. Ford, *A Very Short Introduction to Theology* (Oxford: Oxford University Press, 2000), 77-80.
16 J.D. Smart (ed.), *Revolutionary Theology in the Making: Barth-Thurneysen Correspondence, 1914-25*, tr. J.D. Smart (London: Epworth, 1964), 92.
17 Les Ball, *Transforming Theology: Student Experience and Transformative Learning in Undergraduate Theological Education* (Preston, Vic: Mosaic Press, 2012), 87.
18 Levinas, *Totality and Infinity*, 27; 271.

to encounter the face of the neighbour or "other." So what might facilitate this leaving of home? And what pedagogy might emerge from it that could assist the teaching endeavours of theological educators? But first we turn to the work of Walter Brueggemann and a range of other biblical scholars to provide a pedagogy of displacement, and to show how such leaving home might work pedagogically in tandem with insights from the Judeo-Christian theological tradition.

Part Two: Biblical, Pedagogical and Other Perspectives on Leaving Home and Exile

> *The Greek term "theorin": a practice of travel and observation, a [person] sent by the polis to another city to witness a religious ceremony. "Theory" is a product of displacement, comprising a certain distance. To theorize, one leaves home.*[19]

In Part Two, we examine some biblical and pedagogical perspectives on the symbiotic themes of leaving home and exile. We conclude by offering links between the range of perspectives covered on these themes and some typical experiences of theological students, and finally by proposing a pedagogical cycle based on the same themes that could be helpful to theological educators.

Leaving home, exile and the pedagogical cycle within Brueggemann's three movements

Scripture scholar Walter Brueggemann proposes three movements applicable to the spiritual journey (and here applied to the pedagogical journey): from secure orientation through disturbing disorientation towards surprising reorientation. He asserts that such a transition can transpire at times in unremarkable circumstances (a feeling of dis-ease, a harsh word from another) and at other times in more traumatic contexts (a family bereavement, a child's cancer, natural disaster, or job loss).[20]

This essay focuses in particular on the experience of "disturbing disorient-

---

19 James Clifford, "Notes on travel and theory," cited in Thomas A. Tweed, *Crossing and Dwelling, a Theory of Religion* (Cambridge, MA & London: Harvard University Press, 2006), 1.
20 Walter Brueggemann, *Spirituality of the Psalms* (Minneapolis, MN: Fortress Press, 2002), 25-45; Walter Brueggemann, *Praying the Psalms: Engaging Scripture and the Life of the Spirit* (Eugene, OR: Cascade Books, 2007), 1-41. For more details on these three movements and their in-between stages refer to a commentary on Brueggemann's writings in: Peter Mudge, "Secure, Disturbed, Surprised—a proposal for theological reflection based on Walter Brueggemann's three movements" (paper presented at the EARLI Conference, Munich, Germany, August 31, 2013).

ation" and its links with "leaving home" and "exile." Brueggemann describes this middle movement as one or more of the fracturing of one's world, savage incoherence, disarray and uncertainty, a waiting upon God in order to unlearn old ways and take up new ones.[21] It is akin to the dislodgement of one's "being in the world," the dismantling of time-honoured certainties, where comfort, equilibrium, coherence and predictability for one's life disappear, and it is instead "savagely marked by incoherence, a loss of balance, and unrelieved symmetry … [a fact in our own time] that needs no argument or documentation."[22]

Brueggemann also considers this movement of disturbing disorientation within the context of "exile." He and his colleagues assert that the interconnected theme of "collapse/exile/hope" is essential for understanding both the Jewish and the Christian Scriptures.[23] In addition, he discusses "exile" not just as a dominant biblical theme, but as a personal existential metaphor for his own life journey. Reflecting on his experience of being in a seminar group wherein each person was encouraged to adopt a metaphor which disclosed their life, Brueggemann recounted, "My metaphor was exile. I can trace all that exilic business, and I think that's behind everything I do."[24] Hamilton adds to this portrait the observation that to be exiled is to be out of place, not at home, and on a journey in which one struggles with disorientation, transformation, danger, chaos, enrichment, and many other experiences.[25]

Perhaps in this section the last observations can be left understandably to Brueggemann himself, based on his fine chapter in this text on "Preaching to exiles." Whilst in this source the author is concerned with employing "the Old Testament experience of and reflection upon exile as a helpful *metaphor* for understanding [his] current faith situation in the U.S. church, and a *model* for pondering new forms of ecclesiology," here our attention is more directed towards how such metaphors as exile, leaving home and displacement can be used to develop fresh models for understanding the dynamics and challenges of theological education.[26]

---

21 Brueggemann, *Spirituality of the Psalms*, 12.
22 Brueggemann, *Spirituality of the Psalms*, 8, 25.
23 Bruce C. Birch, Walter Brueggemann, Terence E. Fretheim and David L. Petersen, "Collapse, exile, hope," in *A Theological Introduction to the Old Testament* (Nashville, TN: Abingdon Press, 2005), 327-380.
24 Walter Brueggemann with Carolyn J. Sharp, *Living Countertestimony, Conversations with Walter Brueggemann* (Louisville, KY: Westminster John Knox Press, 2012), 34.
25 Andrew Hamilton, "Exile," in *The new Westminster dictionary of Christian spirituality*, ed. P. Sheldrake (Louisville, KY: Westminster John Knox Press, 2005), 294.
26 Walter Brueggemann, *Cadences of Home: Preaching Among Exiles* (Louisville, KY: Westminster John Knox Press, 1997), 1.

Brueggemann's original observations can be applied fruitfully in this regard. For example, he helps us understand that exile is connected with "the experienced anxiety of 'deported' people,"[27] and that the ancient Jewish exiles "experienced a loss of the structured, reliable world which gave them meaning and coherence, and they found themselves in a context where their most treasured and trusted symbols of faith were mocked, trivialized, or dismissed."[28] He then concludes, "Exile is not primarily geographical, but it is social, moral, and cultural."[29]

Brueggemann also argues for certain positive interpretations of exile, such as that which emerged from the interface of the "*circumstance of exile ... and scriptural resources* that grew from and address the faith crisis of exile."[30] Such a traumatic exile led to at least one overwhelmingly affirmative outcome:

> The most remarkable observation one can make about this interface of *exilic circumstance* and *scriptural resources* is this: Exile did not lead the Jews in the Old Testament to abandon faith or to settle for abdicating despair, nor to retreat to privatistic religion. On the contrary, exile evoked the most brilliant literature and the most daring theological articulation in the Old Testament.[31]

Finally, Brueggemann makes a number of other comments on the deeper significance of exile that can only be stated here and left elsewhere for later, more substantial elaboration and application. Here we mention only five. First, "Exiles must grieve their loss and express their resentful sadness about what was and now is not and will never be again."[32] Second, association of certain words with "exile" such as "forgotten, forsaken" suggests that "the exiles are like 'a motherless child,' that is, an abandoned, vulnerable orphan.... There is no sure home, no old family place, no recognizable family food. I suggest the theme of *rootlessness,* as though we do not belong anywhere."[33] Third, "The most obvious reality and greatest threat to exiles is the *power of despair.*"[34] Fourth, "Exile is an experience of *profaned absence.* The 'absence of God' is not only a personal, emotional sense, but a public, institutional awareness that

---

27 Brueggemann, *Cadences of Home*, 1.
28 Brueggemann, *Cadences of Home*, 2.
29 Brueggemann, *Cadences of Home*, 2.
30 Brueggemann, *Cadences of Home*, 3 (italics in original).
31 Brueggemann, *Cadences of Home*, 3.
32 Brueggemann, *Cadences of Home*, 4.
33 Brueggemann, *Cadences of Home*, 5.
34 Brueggemann, *Cadences of Home*, 6.

'the glory has departed'… [and it becomes clear] that what have long been treasured symbols are treated lightly or with contempt."[35] Fifth and finally, Brueggemann sums up his consideration of exile, deportation and leaving home in the one word "danger." This composite experience is at the same time one marked by danger and opportunity, but an experience nonetheless that evokes dangerous memories, dangerous criticism, dangerous promises, dangerous songs, dangerous bread, and dangerous departures and journeys.[36]

Perhaps these five dimensions of "exile" point to one of the more challenging and "dangerous" tasks to be attempted in the relationship between teachers and their students—to understand a student's experience of leaving home and exile, the teacher needs in some way to encounter and reflect upon that type of experience him/herself.[37] This is considered in more detail in the next section.

One final point requires articulation for Part Two of this essay. There are numerous other areas of research and related scholars that could be discussed here but space prevents a fuller articulation of these links, which must be left to future consideration. But suffice to say that the following ideas and links provide fertile ground in which the seeds of "exile" and "leaving home" could be planted in order to reap further insights in this field. This includes the following authors and their fields of investigation. Leaving home involves absorption of "threshold concepts" which lead to deeper knowing, transformation and connected knowing within a topic;[38] leaving one's cherished home and concepts can provoke "blurred encounters" where unexpected boundaries are crossed and fresh judgments need to be made about new decisions and directions[39]; for teachers and learners alike, teaching is a subversive activity that sometimes stretches them towards uncomfortable ideas and concepts, and the need to question and critique is at the heart of transformative pedagogy[40]; de Bono,

---

35 Brueggemann, *Cadences of Home*, 7. See also apophatic darkness and absence in Owen Davies & Denys Turner (eds.), *Silence and the Word: Negative Theology and Incarnation* (Cambridge: Cambridge University Press, 2002).
36 Brueggemann, *Cadences of Home*, 134.
37 Brueggemann, *Cadences of Home*, 110-134; see also Hamilton, "Exile," 294-295.
38 Ray Land, Jan H. F. Meyer & Jan Smith (eds), *Threshold Concepts within the Disciplines* (Rotterdam, NL: Sense Publishers, 2008); Jan H. F. Meyer, Ray Land & Caroline Baillie (eds), *Threshold Concepts and Transformational Learning* (Rotterdam, NL: Sense Publishers, 2010).
39 Helen Cameron, John Reader, Victoria Slater, with Chris Rowland, *Theological Reflection for Human Flourishing* (London: SCM Press, 2012), 17-18.
40 Neil Postman & Charles Weingartner, *Teaching as a Subversive Activity* (New York: Delta, 1971).

Medina and Berns,[41] among many, assert that the brain is a conservative, self-patterning system that delights in pre-existing patterns but which, in order to leave home and embrace transformation, needs to be "shocked out of" these into new patterns, and out of its lack of perception, imagination, and fear of change via such techniques as "lateral thinking" and CoRT thinking skills. Similar arguments can be traced in the writings of Claxton, Claxton & Lucas, Armstrong, and Vardy.[42]

A brief pedagogical excursus—some implications for theological students
In a reflection on exile and homecoming that we would suggest is particularly redolent for theological teachers and their students, Frederick Buechner avers that each of us carries inside us "a vision of wholeness that we sense is our true home and that beckons us." [43] He further asserts that to be homeless is equivalent to having "homes all over the place but not to be really at home in any of them. To be really at home is to be really at peace … there can be no real peace for any of us until there is peace for all of us."[44]

With reference to Buechner's valuable insight, what then might be the experience of our theological teachers and students in relation to this proposed pedagogy of "leaving home," feeling lost, "exile," disturbing disorientation, and searching for the path homewards? Could these aspects be manifested in their lives as one or more of confusion about theological concepts; exile as a social, moral or cultural experience; an inability to connect theory with concrete praxis; an unwillingness or inability to consider new concepts or new interpretations, or to engage in dialogue/conversation with those "different from me;" as an experience of paralysis and confusion between kataphatic and apophatic knowing; as compassion for those who feel "orphaned" or a sense of

---

41 Edward de Bono, *Serious Creativity, Using the Power of Lateral Thinking to Create New Ideas* (London: Fontana, 1993); John Medina, *Brain Rules, 12 Principles for Surviving at Work, Home and School* (Melbourne: Scribe, 2012); Gregory Berns, *Iconoclast, A Neuroscientist Reveals how to Think Differently* (New York, NY: Harvard Business Review Press, 2010).
42 Guy Claxton, *Hare Brain Tortoise Mind. How Intelligence Increases When You Think Less* (New York: HarperPerennial, 2000); Guy Claxton & Bill Lucas, *Be Creative. Essential Steps to Revitalize Your Work and Life* (London: BBC Books, 2004); Karen Armstrong, *A Short History of Myth* (Melbourne: Canongate/Text Publishing Company, 2005a), 161ff; Peter Vardy, *Dialogue Australasia—The 5 Strand Approach to Religious and Values Education* (2007). Accessed 7 January, 2008. www.dialogueaustralasia.org/REVALUES3.html
43 Frederick Buechner, *The Longing for Home: Recollections and Reflections* (San Francisco, CA: HarperSanFrancisco, 1996), 110.
44 Buechner, *The Longing for Home*, 140.

"rootlessness"—that their trusted symbols of faith no longer have relevance; or in extreme circumstances, they might experience a crisis of faith, belief or ethical commitment? Equally, a student might be prevented from leaving home by those security mindsets that operate when one feels threatened; by distance and online course complexities; by more complex ways of knowing presented by Habermas, or by higher-order skills from Bloom's taxonomy. Moreover, one might ask, is it possible to achieve Buechner's sense of "peace" while one is also enduring "exile" or "leaving home" as a teacher or student?

It is proposed that the above research and the ensuing pedagogical cycle could assist theological teachers and students in addressing some of the above issues, in employing a model that illuminates the journey of those "leaving home" or cocooned in "exile," and perhaps even by providing a compass for pinpointing where one is generally situated in relation to that overall journey.

Part Three: A proposal for a pedagogy of displacement in theological education

> *Exile is, of course, not simply a change of address. It is also a spiritual dislocation. Anthropologists and psychologists tell us that displaced people feel lost in a universe that has suddenly become alien. Once the fixed point of "home" is gone, there is a fundamental lack of orientation that makes everything seem relative and aimless .... Their "world"—inextricably linked with their unique place in the cosmos—has literally come to an end.*[45]

Towards a proposed pedagogy of displacement embracing home–exile–homecoming

The foregoing reflections suggest valuable elements that could inform a pedagogical cycle applicable to many aspects of theological education. Here the term "pedagogical cycle" is taken to mean a way of operating in any theological teaching context, a framework used by the theological educator, and insinuating a series of verbs or operations (desired framework or series of movements) used by the teacher in a cyclical and repetitive fashion.[46]

---

45 Karen Armstrong, *The Spiral Staircase* (London: Harper Perennial, 2005b), 41.
46 Thomas H. Groome, *Sharing Faith: The Way of Shared Christian Praxis* (New York: Wipf & Stock, 1999), 2.

The pedagogical cycle envisaged here has five general verb-based movements that could be applied constructively to student and teacher interaction concerned with aspects of theological education such as readings, topics, online discussions, face-to-face forums, assessment tasks, field placements, course design and meta-approaches, or even entire courses. These five movements are:

1. *Subsisting with "business as usual" manifested as secure orientation.* The person is at home, secure, not challenged by anything discomforting, but still aware that "all is not as it should be." They have adopted a stance of totalisation, or a damaging tendency to reduce all otherness to an objectivity over which individual consciousness can claim control. They are "stuck within the four walls of their [self-constructed and self-defended] house," maintained through reinforced positions of pattern creation and reinforcement. There is a lack of openness to what is foreign or "other" and a rejection of poetic and prophetic imagination. Their dominant theological stance is kataphatic.
2. *Encountering the "other" and "Other".* This challenging encounter is often experienced via dialogue and encounter with the "other" as neighbour, alien or stranger. As a result of this confronting and risky encounter, the "four walls of their house" begin to break down as, at the same time, new worlds begin to open up. This occurs hand in hand with the next movement.
3. *Experiencing disturbing disorientation.* This movement can also manifest as displacement or dissonance. As the person's four walls collapse and disintegrate, they are challenged to adopt dispositions of openness, risk and intellectual empathy in their personal pedagogy and in theological education in general. Their house experiences continual cycles of deconstruction and disintegration. They are being drawn into a theological stance balanced between the kataphatic and the apophatic.
4. *Confronting surprising re-orientation or re-formation.* The person re-engages with awe, wonder and imagination in a revitalised journey homewards. There begins to emerge, notwithstanding ongoing challenges, an improved ambience within the theological classroom and a more engaging quality of relationship between student and educator. The person, their ideas and paradigms are being re-shaped in preparation for the journey home. Typically, there occurs an inpouring of critical poetic and prophetic imagination. A new house is being rebuilt from the ashes of the old—one more appropriate and sufficiently flexible for this next stage of the journey.

5. *Being called to transformation.* The person is challenged to move towards transformation.[47] Their house continues to be redesigned, rebuilt, refurbished, with rooms added on (or demolished) as required. The person begins to achieve a more equitable balance between kataphatic and apophatic knowing and theology. He or she is now resilient enough to repeat the cycle as many times as necessary, in direct proportion to how many times they are called to "leave home," to go into exile, and experience disturbing disorientation, dissonance or displacement. One adage that could be adopted for this movement is: "To live is to change, and to live long is to change often." Or, as Charles Winquist expresses it, "Homecoming is not a return to the past but it is a becoming into the future."[48]

These five movements could be summarised diagrammatically as follows:

---

47 Ball, *Transforming Theology*, passim.
48 Charles Winquist. *Homecoming: Interpretation, Transformation and Individuation* (Missoula, Montana: Scholars Press, 1978), 9.

Returning from exile: to "know the place for the first time"
Finally, it could be argued that the experiences considered in this essay—those of "being at home," "leaving home," "exile" and "returning and recognising home"—are perhaps most famously echoed within the literary domain by T. S. Eliot's poem "Little Gidding."[49] Here, Eliot declares that beginnings and endings interweave, that we will not cease from exploration [and exile], and most importantly, after crossing many unremembered gates, we will ultimately return home to the place from where we commenced the journey, and "know the place for the first time." Raine notes ways in which Eliot throughout his writings images this inability to return home and to know self and place for the first time as "the buried life" or the failure to live consistently to one's full potential. This could transpire when "the *business of living* supplants the *cultivation of the inner life*," or when due to our "rationed heart … self-ignorance [and] … occluded selves,"[50] one prefers to "remain at home" and stay in one's comfort zone, rather than "leave home" decisively and at times, irrevocably.

We conclude by asserting that this passage, accompanied by the weight of other arguments, scholars and pedagogies in this essay, lays a compelling claim that the paradigm of "leaving home" can provide a useful and transformative pedagogy for theological education:

> What we call the beginning is often the end
> And to make an end is to make a beginning.
> The end is where we start from …
>
> We shall not cease from exploration
> And the end of all our exploring
> Will be to arrive where we started
> And know the place for the first time.
> Through the unknown, unremembered gate
> When the last of earth left to discover
> Is that which was the beginning …

---

49 T.S. Eliot, "Little Gidding, Four Quartets," in *T. S. Eliot: Collected poems, 1909-1962* (London: Faber & Faber, 1974), 201-209.
50 Craig Raine, *T. S. Eliot* (Oxford: Oxford University Press, 2006), xx. Italics ours combined with author's own which is "the business of living."

And all shall be well and
All manner of thing shall be well
When the tongues of flames are in-folded
Into the crowned knot of fire
And the fire and the rose are one.[51]

---

[51] Eliot, "Little Gidding," stanza 5, lines 1-3, 26-32, 42-46, pages 208-209.

6 | ASSESSING INTEGRATIVE LEARNING AND READINESS FOR MINISTRY

CAN THERE BE COMMON GROUND?

NANCY AULT

Abstract

This essay explores the intuitive component in the assessment of integrative learning. When students, educators and, more widely, the stakeholders in theological education attempt to evaluate the extent and quality of integrative learning, they may rely heavily upon intuition and some form of subjective feeling of rightness. Although comprehensive rubrics of assessment can be developed to make explicit implicit criteria, accumulative intuition and matching intuition can play a significant but unacknowledged role in assessment. It is suggested that one of the factors being intuitively assessed is resiliency. Diversity in theological traditions can influence what is considered valid criteria so that the integrative learning of a student could be commended in one institution and found wanting in another. Resiliency may provide a point of commonality.

Introduction

How do you know what you know? The answer to this question is often unclear in the assessment of integrative learning and readiness for ministry. A student may successfully complete the academic curriculum, may demonstrate his or her capacity to integrate theory with practice and may have shown his or her competence in field placements and yet those involved in the overall assessment of integrative and formational learning may deem the student unready or unsuitable for ministry. The student may request feedback, wanting to know by what criteria he or she has been judged, and the formational/assessment team is left trying to explain their intuitions, how they know what they claim to know.

In this essay, I will explore some aspects of integrative learning and assessment. Second, I will focus upon the intuitive component of assessment, particularly in connection with readiness for ministry. Finally, I will address the question, "Can there be a common ground?"

Integrative Learning

Aspirations for integrative and transformative learning are not unique to theology. Disciplines such as nursing, teaching and social work will describe their courses and shape their assessments with the purpose of enabling the student to integrate theoretical learning (knowledge) with experience (life). In relation to theology, Klimoski, O'Neil and Schuth define integration as "a formative process that engages students in traditions of theological knowledge, pastoral practice, and Christian identity as they examine, re-interpret, and commit themselves to a worldview that bears the deep imprint of those traditions."[1] Foster *et al.* suggest that through integration a student is able to make connections which might otherwise remain hidden.[2] Thus, through the process of integration, a student's horizon can be transformed. However, without a degree of openness to engage in the process, a student may complete his or her theological education with "little more than an ability to argue more strongly why he or she was right in the first place."[3] Hence, the process of integrative

---

1 Victor J. Klimoski, Kevin J. O'Neil and Katarina M. Schuth, *Educating Leaders for Ministry: Issues and Responses* (Collegeville, Minn: Liturgical Press, 2005), 50. (Italics in original)
2 Charles R. Foster *et al.*, *Educating Clergy. Teaching Practices and Pastoral Imagination* (San Francisco, CA: Jossey-Bass, 2006), 25.
3 Klimoski, O'Neil and Schuth, *Educating Leaders for Ministry,* 50.

learning may be undermined and subverted by a student's attitude to learning, as well as by his or her underlying beliefs and biases.

Three Educational Orders

Education can be seen through three lenses or orders: that of information, that of formation and that of transformation. In first order education, information is transmitted to the students. Learning in this paradigm is passive; the learner is a vessel into which learning is poured. The interest is with factual knowledge and the student's intellect is valued. In second order learning, or formation, reflection is introduced. Here, discussion, negotiation and exploration occur. Questions are encouraged. Imagination and intuition are nurtured. The horizon of a student's awareness is extended, values and motives are critiqued. However, formation suggests an ideal into which a student is moulded. Third order learning, transformation, is related to change. Transformational learning requires a change in a student's perceptions, conceptions and actions. According to Stephen Sterling, we "need to 'see' differently if we are to know and act differently."[4] When such an existential change occurs, a student perceives and engages in the world in a new way. Les Ball suggests the phrase "integrative learning" as a way in which "all the positive ideals of formative and transformative learning" can be brought together and embraced as a whole.[5]

Three Apprenticeships

There is an old saying that one can lead a horse to water but one cannot make the horse drink. So too, with integrative learning, students may be exposed to curriculums, teaching methods and assessments which promote integration, but they cannot be forced to integrate what they are learning with their life experience. Referencing William Sullivan, Foster *et al.* identify three apprenticeships involved in professional education which are relevant to theological education: cognitive (theology), practical (practice and skills) and normative

---

4   Stephen Sterling, *Sustainable Education. Re-Visioning Learning and Change*, Schumacher Briefings (Foxhole, Devon: Green Books Ltd, 2001), 52.
5   Les Ball, *Transforming Theology. Student Experience and Transformative Learning in Undergraduate Theological Education* (Preston Vic: Mosaic Press, 2012), 123.

(identity).⁶ Each of these apprenticeships interacts with and influences the others in the integrative process. According to Foster et al., the ability of students to engage in integrative learning will depend on their internal freedom to engage in a critique of personal beliefs and values, their spirituality, their prior knowledge and their understanding of the theological and ministerial enterprise.⁷

Some students may be natural reflectors and integrators for which the process of integration is second nature. Their integrative writing moves beyond mere description to explore processes, assumptions and feelings. They write or express themselves from a position of openness, looking at their experience from multiple perspectives. They test and link new ideas to their understanding of God, self and others and show an inner change as they modify their assumptions.

Other students may be non-reflectors and integrators. Their integrative writing is like a travelogue. It meanders around the countryside of their experience with occasional reference to theological discourse. There is a basic description of the scenery and the places that have been visited/activities undertaken and, here and there, a Bible verse is inserted. There is little or no evidence of reflection and self-awareness. Non-reflectors tend to write or express themselves from a position of certitude or self-assurance.⁸ Integrative learning involves a process which is different for each student. Whereas some students may make connections almost automatically, it may take other students years to comprehend the reflective-integrative enterprise and some students may never be able to master the art of reflection and integration at any level.

Integrative learning is not only a process but also a product, in the sense of the development of the student. The cognitive apprenticeship (knowledge) and the practical apprenticeship (skills) may be assessed by certain well defined criteria. However, the normative apprenticeship involves personal being and by what criteria is a person to be assessed? Assessing integrative learning across all apprenticeships becomes complex and multi-dimensional.

---

6   Foster et al., *Educating Clergy*. 25-26.
7   Klimoski, O'Neil and Schuth, *Educating Leaders for Ministry*, 53.
8   Patricia O'Connell Killen and John de Beer, *The Art of Theological Reflection* (New York: Crossroad, 1994), 4-16.

Assessing Integration

Integrative learning is influenced by both the methods used in teaching and the quality of the assessment processes. Many assessment methods that encourage integrative learning such as journals, portfolios and theological reflections are often difficult to evaluate for two reasons. First, evidence of integrative learning is cumulative and taking a snapshot at any one time may misrepresent the learning which has occurred. Therefore, many snapshots need to be taken over a sustained period of time. Second, such assessments involve subjective material which can be difficult to quantify. Although these assessment methods are labour intensive, they move beyond asking a student for the reiteration of facts (first order learning) to supporting the exploration of ideas and concepts with the potential outcome that a student's horizon of understanding may be widened and transformed (second and third order learning).

Understanding

Foster *et al.* argue that integrative learning involves increasing the depth and breadth of a student's understanding.[9] Although *knowing* and *understanding* may be used interchangeably, they are not synonymous. Knowledge involves facts, whereas understanding requires engaging with the meaning of the facts and the concepts that underlie the meaning. Understanding discerns constructs and patterns.

Wiggins and McTighe observe that *understanding* can be used in different ways. They suggest that there are six types of understanding: explanation, interpretation, application, perspective, empathy and self-knowledge. They say that we truly understand when we:

> *Can explain*—via generalizations or principles, providing justified and systematic accounts of phenomena, facts, and data; make insightful connections and provide illuminating examples or illustrations.
>
> *Can interpret*—tell meaningful stories; offer apt translations; provide a revealing historical or personal dimension to ideas and events; make the object of understanding personal or accessible through images, anecdotes, analogies, and models.

---

9   Foster et al., *Educating Clergy*, 25.

Can apply—effectively use and adapt what we know in diverse and real contexts—we can "do" the subject.

Have perspective—see and hear points of view through critical eyes and ears; see the big picture.

Can empathize—find value in what others might find odd, alien, or implausible; perceive sensitively on the basis of prior direct experience.

Have self-knowledge—show metacognitive awareness; perceive the personal style, prejudices, projections, and habits of mind that both shape and impede our own understanding; are aware of what we do not understand; reflect on the meaning of learning and experience.[10]

Understanding has several dimensions. Thus, in integrative learning, the "depth and breadth" of understanding will involve many nuances.

6 Facet Rubric

As it has been observed, one of the difficulties in assessing integrative learning is its subjective nature. The question of criteria was raised. Wiggins and McTighe argue that "understanding requires performance tasks" and in response developed the 6 Facet Rubric which traces how each type of understanding might develop over a continuum ranging from the naïve to the sophisticated. The six types of understanding (explanation, interpretation, application, perspective, empathy and self-knowledge) are inherent in the cognitive, practical and normative apprenticeships. For example, interpretation is significant in the cognitive endeavour. Interpretation asks the questions: What does it mean? Why does it matter? What does it illustrate in human experience? What makes sense?[11] Interpretation may extend from the profound to the literal:

Profound: a powerful and illuminating interpretation and analysis of the importance /meaning/ significance; tells a rich and insightful story; provides a rich history or context; sees deeply and incisively any ironies in the different interpretations.

---

10 Grant Wiggins and Jay McTighe, *Understanding by Design* (Alexandria, VA: Association for Supervision and Curriculum Development, 2005), 82. (Italics in original)
11 Wiggins and McTighe, *Understanding by Design*, 178-179.

Revealing: a nuanced interpretation and analysis of the importance/ meaning/ significance; tells an insightful story; provides a telling history or con text; sees subtle differences, levels, and ironies in diverse interpretations.

Perceptive: a helpful interpretation or analysis of the importance/ meaning/ significance; tells a clear and instructive story; provides a useful history or con- text; sees different levels of interpretation.

Interpreted: a plausible interpretation or analysis of the importance/ meaning/ significance; makes sense of a story; provides a history or context.

Literal: a simplistic or superficial reading; mechanical translation; a decoding with little or no interpretation; no sense of wider importance or significance; a restatement of what was taught or read.[12]

Practically, empathy is necessary in pastoral relationships. Understanding as empathy asks the questions: How does it seem to you? What do they see that I don't? What do I need to experience if I am to understand?[13] Empathy may range from the mature to the egocentric:

Mature: disposed and able to see and feel what others see and feel; unusually open to and willing to seek out the odd, alien, or different.

Sensitive: disposed to see and feel what others see and feel; open to the unfamiliar or different.

Aware: knows and feels that others see and feel differently; somewhat able to empathize with others; has difficulty making sense of odd or alien views.

Developing: has some capacity and self-discipline to "walk in another's shoes" but is still primarily limited to one's own reactions and attitudes; puzzled or put off by different feeling.

Egocentric: has little or no empathy beyond intellectual awareness of others; sees things through own ideas and feelings; ignores or is threatened or puzzled by different feelings, attitudes, or views. [14]

Self-knowledge is fundamental in the normative apprenticeship. Understanding as self-knowledge asks the questions: How does who I am shape my views? What are limits to my understanding? My blind spots? What might I

---

12 Wiggins and McTighe, *Understanding by Design*, 178-179.
13 Wiggins and McTighe, *Understanding by Design*, 178-179.
14 Wiggins and McTighe, *Understanding by Design*, 178-179.

misunderstand because of habit, prejudice, or style?[15] Self-knowledge may stretch between wise and innocent:

> *Wise:* deeply aware of the boundaries of one's own and others' understanding; able to recognize his prejudice and projections; has integrity–able and willing to act on what one understands.
>
> *Circumspect:* aware of one's ignorance and that of others; aware of one's prejudices; knows the strengths and limits of one's understanding.
>
> *Thoughtful:* generally aware of what is and is not understood; aware of how prejudice and projection can occur without awareness and shape one's views.
>
> *Unreflective:* generally unaware of one's specific ignorance; generally unaware of how subjective prejudgments color understandings.
>
> *Innocent:* completely unaware of the bounds of one's understanding and of the role of projection and prejudice in opinions and attempts to understand.[16]

Wiggins and McTighe argue that to achieve the criteria of understanding at each level, learning experiences need to be designed from the desired outcome backwards, that is, through backwards design. Backwards design may be a useful principle for those involved in developing theological and formational programs. However, in the context of assessment, the 6 Facet Rubric of understanding articulates some of the subjective criteria involved in evaluating the three apprenticeships. As such, it and similar classifications can provide the criteria that will enable specific feedback to be given to students. At the same time, rubrics may disintegrate into compartmentalisation by the student and of the student. Les Ball observes that integrative learning in Christian theology

> …embraces and promotes the characteristics of the holistic congruence of all fields of learning, imbuing life practices with theologically formed principles, and the cultivation of a holistically consistent person whose values and relationships embody the ideals of the Christian heritage.[17]

Assessing integrative learning involves a holistic overview. Klimoski, O'Neil and Schuth suggest wisdom, balance, purity of heart, wholeness, discipline, humility,

---

15 Wiggins and McTighe, *Understanding by Design*, 178-179.
16 Wiggins and McTighe, *Understanding by Design*, 178-179.
17 Ball, *Transforming Theology*, 124.

love of learning, willingness to risk, honesty, self-possession, self-reflection, capacity for change, tolerance for complexity and selflessness as "virtues for integration."[18] Qualities such as these add additional depth to the criteria associated with the different types of understanding. Looking at a student with a longer and wider perspective, seeing the student holistically with all the complexity and ambiguity which this implies, is challenging and assessors are forced to move beyond tick-box criteria which they may consciously or unconsciously be using.

Challenges

A student can successfully complete the three apprenticeships involved in integrative learning and yet those involved in the overall assessment process may deem the student unready or unsuitable for ministry. If asked to name the criteria by which the student has been evaluated, the assessors are left trying to explain themselves and how they know what they know. The challenges which arise include making explicit that which is implicit; measuring growth; and verbalising and qualifying the personal and subjective.

As it has been suggested, the product of integrative learning is more than the sum of its parts. Formational teams, lecturers, supervisors and professionals bring different perspectives with different criteria to the task of assessment. Matrices such as Wiggins and McTighe's 6 Facet Rubric for understanding can be helpful. Nevertheless, the assessment of integration and readiness for ministry is something more than academic achievement, the ability to perform certain skills or the ability to write thoughtful reflections. When educators and, more widely, the stakeholders in theological education attempt to evaluate the extent and quality of integrative learning and that elusive "something more," they may rely heavily upon intuition.

Intuition

Although some criteria used in assessing integration and readiness for ministry may be made explicit and systematically mapped, there is often a dimension of evaluation in which the criteria are implicit and reasoning is intuitive. Assessors experience a sense of knowing which is automatic, unconscious and associated with a *felt* sense of rightness. Criteria embedded in intuitive evaluation remain

---

18   Klimoski, O'Neil and Schuth, *Educating Leaders for Ministry*, 62-64.

unnamed. Thus, assessment of integrative learning reflects two different cognitive systems related to reasoning, making judgements and choices.[19] The idea that there are two different processes in reasoning is not a new concept and can be traced back to Aristotle.[20] Although several Dual Process Theories have been proposed, there is a general consensus that System 1, intuition, describes those processes which are automatic and unconscious and System 2, rule-based reasoning, describes those processes which are conscious and use abstract concepts.[21]

There is a lack of consensus about the definition of intuition. It has been defined as a "judgment for a given course of action that comes to mind with an aura or conviction of rightness or plausibility, but without clearly articulated reasons or justifications essentially 'knowing' but without knowing why."[22] There is often a feeling of rightness associated with intuition.[23] Intuition involves the emotions as in the expression "gut feeling" and feeling is complemented by experience.[24]

Glöckner and Witteman suggest four types of intuition which may overlap. Associated intuition involves a simple learning-retrieval process that is connected to conditioning and social types of learning. Associated intuition is also linked with feelings of like and dislike or the emotions. Matching intuition involves a learning-retrieval process based upon a model. In matching intuition a comparison is made with exemplars, prototypes, images and schemas which have been previously learnt. Accumulative intuition involves a learning-retrieval process connected to the accumulation of information. In the intuitive process, this information is automatically scanned and weighed according to importance. Constructive intuition involves a learning-retrieval process based upon the automatic construction of mental representations. These constructions may go beyond existing information and exemplars. With constructive intuition,

---

19 Steven A. Sloman, "Two Systems of Reasoning," in *Heuristics and Biases. The Psychology of Intuitive Judgment*, ed. Thomas Gilovich, Dale Griffin, and Daniel Kahneman (New York and Cambridge: Cambridge University Press, 2002), 383.
20 Sloman, "Two Systems of Reasoning," 380.
21 Andreas Glöckner and Cilia Witteman, "Beyond Dual-Process Models: A Categorisation of Processes Underying Intuitive Judgement and Decision Making," *Thinking & Reasoning* 16, no. 1 (2010), 4-5.
22 Gerard P. Hodgkinson *et al.*, "Intuition in Organizations: Implications for Strategic Management," *Long Range Panning* 42 (2009), 279.
23 Valerie A. Thompson, Jamie A. Prowse Turner and Gordon Pennycook, "Intuituition, Reason, and Metacognition," *Cognitive Psychology* 63 (2011), 134.
24 Thompson, Prowse Turner and Pennycook, "Intuituition, Reason, and Metacognition." 134; Eugene Sadler-Smith, "Intuition in Decision-Making: Friend or Foe?" *Training Journal* (2007), 135; Hodgkinson et al., "Intuition in Organizations: Implications for Strategic Management," 282.

something new may be created and enter conscious awareness.[25] Although all these forms of intuition may be involved in the assessment of integrative learning, matching intuition and accumulative intuition are especially worth noting.

Assessors who are involved in teaching and formation programs work alongside students and over time they may consciously and unconsciously observe a student's pattern of behaviours and depth of reflection. These observations form part of the input to the intuitive process of assessment and provide the content which is scanned in accumulative intuition. Many snapshots need to be taken over time to assess integration in the assessments and tasks which are set for students. Assessors who regularly interact with students may unconsciously be taking snapshots which contribute to their intuitive evaluations.

In matching intuition, comparisons are made with exemplars, prototypes or schemas. It has been observed that fire-fighters and nurses often make intuitive judgements which they follow through rather than stopping and weighing up alternatives. Hodgkinson and his colleagues observe that:

> As a result of accumulated expertise, domain experts develop complex, domain-relevant mental representations (known as schemas) and associated action scripts, which afford them not only a highly-tuned awareness of the situation, but also the capability to pattern match, in order to sense when something is "out-of-kilter" and intuitively know what actions to perform.[26]

The creation of "domain-relevant mental representations" may occur in the assessment of integrative learning. Those involved in assessment are both intuitively looking back over incremental observations as well as forward into the ministerial context. The forward looking component can involve a specific mental image of what a minister or priest looks like and it is against this exemplar that a student is evaluated. It is conceivable that one of the qualities of the exemplar is the capacity of the minister or priest to flourish in the vicissitudes of ministry. In matching intuition, the forward looking dimension may not only correlate the coherence between image and student but also indirectly appraise whether the student will thrive. Thus, one of the hidden, implicit criteria by which assessors evaluate integrative learning and readiness for ministry may be the student's resilience.

---

25 Glöckner and Witteman, "Beyond Dual-Process Models," 7-13.
26 Hodgkinson et al., "Intuition in Organizations: Implications for Strategic Management," 283.

Resilience

Like intuition, there is no accepted definition of resilience. Resilience can be viewed simply as the capacity to bounce back from difficult situations. Resilience is also conceived as that capacity that allows "not only reactive recovery but also proactive learning and growth through conquering challenges."[27] Resilience is important for both health and well-being. Steven Southwick and Dennis Charney observe that, "More than education, more than experience, more than training, a person's level of resilience will determine who succeeds and who fails. That's true in the cancer ward, it's true in the Olympics, and it's true in the boardroom."[28] A review of literature on ministerial burnout shows that ministry can be added to this list.[29]

Resilience is multidimensional, involving biological, psychological, social and spiritual dynamics.[30] Southwick and Charney name 10 factors influencing resilience: realistic optimism, facing fear, moral compass, religion and spirituality, social support, resilient role models, physical fitness, brain fitness (mentally sharp), cognitive and emotional flexibility and meaning and purpose.[31] Online, the "i-resilience" tool delineates the components of resilience as adaptability, confidence, social support and a sense of purpose.[32] In this scheme, religion and spirituality are subsumed under "sense of purpose."

Spirituality has been seen as at the heart of wellness.[33] Spirituality/religion is

---

27 Youssef and Luthans quoted by Ivan Robertson and Cary L. Cooper, "Resilience," *Stress and Health* 29 (2013), 175.
28 Steven M. Southwick and Dennis S. Charney, *Resilience. The Science of Mastering Life's Greatest Challenges* (Cambridge: Cambridge University Press, 2012), 12.
29 Elizabeth Ann Jackson-Jordon, "Clergy Burnour and Resilience: A Review of the Literature," *The Journal of Pastoral Care & Counseling* 67, no. 1 (2013), 3.
    Cameron Lee, "Dispositional Resiliency and Adjustment in Protestant Pastors: A Pilot Study," *Pastoral Psychology* 59 (2010).
    Maureen H. Miner, Martin Dowson and Sam Sterlan, "Ministry Orientation and Ministr Outcomes: Evaluation of a New Multidimensional Model of Clergy Burnout and Job Satisfaction," *Journal of Occupational and Organizational Psychology* 83, no. 1 (2010).
    Douglas W. Turton and Leslie J. Francis, "The Relationship between Attitude toward Prayer and Professional Burnout among Anglican Parochial Clergy in England: Are Praying Clergy Healthier Clergy?" *Mental Helath, Religion & Culture* 10, no. 1 (2007).
30 Robertson and Cooper, "Resilience," 175-176.
    Roberta R. Greene, Colleen Galambos and Youjung Lee, "Resilience Theory," *Journal of Human Behavior in the Social Environment* 8, no. 4 (2004), 78.
31 Southwick and Charney, *Resilience. The Science of Mastering Life's Greatest Challenges*, 11.
32 robertsoncooper, "*I-Resilience* Report," http://www.robertsoncooper.com/iresilience/#.UjVxqX9UYg8.
33 Jane E. Myers, Thomas J. Sweeney and J. Melvin Witmer, "The Wheel of Wellness Counseling for Wellness: A Holistic Model for Treatment Planning," *Journal of Counseling and Development* 78, no. 3 (2000), 252-253.

a component which emerges as significant in resilience along with attitude, interpersonal connections and education. It has been observed that ministers with a strong spiritual life are more likely to be resilient under stressful conditions.[34] Resiliency may be influenced by personality. For example, Cameron Lee found, in a pilot study of Protestant pastors, that gratitude was positively associated with resiliency.[35]

In addition to the behavioural and psychological factors linked with resiliency the environment, past and present, and personal experience are also important. Although the capacity for resiliency can be influenced by past traumatic events, these events may have a positive or negative effect on a person depending on the person, the intensity of the trauma/s and the networks of support available.[36] Whatever the components and influences, a person's capacity for resiliency is not static or fixed. Research has shown that resiliency can be developed.[37]

If the qualities necessary for integrative learning and the "virtues for integration" are examined, there are overlaps with some of the factors which are associated with developing and sustaining resiliency.[38] Integrative learning presupposes that students have the ability to examine their presuppositions with respect to their spirituality, theology, ministry and their beliefs and values. It also assumes the capacity for growth and development within all three apprenticeships: cognitive, skill and normative. The implications of these assumptions are that students will have some degree of cognitive, emotional and spiritual flexibility as well as the openness to and the capacity for continual learning. Internal flexibility, openness and the capacity for ongoing learning are among the factors important in resiliency. It has been suggested that backward looking accumulative intuition and forward looking matching intuition may be functioning in the assessment of integrative learning with respect to readiness

---

34 Miner, Dowson and Sterlan, "Ministry Orientation and Ministry Outcomes: Evaluation of a New Multidimensional Model of Clergy Burnout and Job Satisfaction," 183.
   Jackson-Jordon, "Clergy Burnour and Resilience: A Review of the Literature," 3.
   Turton and Francis, "The Relationship between Attitude toward Prayer and Professional Burnout among Anglican Parochial Clergy in England," 70-72.
   Katheryn Rhoads Meek et al., "Maintaining Personal Resiliency: Lessons Learned from Evangelical Protestant Clery," *Journal of Psychology and Theology* 31, no. 4 (2003), 343-344.
35 Lee, "Dispositional Resiliency and Adjustment in Protestant Pastors," 631.
36 Robertson and Cooper, "Resilience," 175.
37 Robertson and Cooper, "Resilience," 175.
   Mary Lynn Pulley and Michael Wakefield, "Building Resiliency: How to Thrive in Times of Change" (Greensboro, N.C.: Center for Creative Leadership, 2001), 9-21.
38 Klimoski, O'Neil and Schuth, *Educating Leaders for Ministry*, 62-64.

for ministry. Assessors could be both looking backward at a student's capacity for transformational change during the years of study and formation and looking forward to see if the qualities which have been perceived overlap with those deemed important in a future environment. However, as it has been observed, matching intuition is domain specific and this leads to the question of whether there can be a common ground in assessment.

Can there be a common ground?

Implicit and explicit criteria may be used in the process of evaluating integration. Often the explicit criteria are comprised of specific abilities or skills against which a student is measured along a sliding scale such as poor, fair, good and excellent. Other criteria which initially may be implicit can be made explicit through matrixes such as Wiggins and McTighe's 6 Facet Rubric. A dimension of evaluation may be based on a feeling of rightness in which it is difficult to articulate the criteria used and the internal processes which have led to a particular decision. This knowing without knowing suggests intuition. There may be an inner looking back at past observations and there may be a matching against a model. Whether criteria are explicit or implicit or whether choices are made consciously or unconsciously, assessors do select specific criteria to evaluate integrative learning and readiness for ministry.

Klimoski, O'Neil and Schuth ask, "What do integrated students look like? What can we expect from them in terms of how they respond to new ideas, pastoral dilemmas, in discussions that involve more than linking the right answer to the right question?"[39] What students are expected to look like and how they are expected to respond suggest that they are being measured against a particular exemplar or schema. Within the Australian context, there is a diversity of theological traditions and theological perspectives and each will influence and shape the criteria selected and the exemplars or schemas used in theological education and formation for ministry. Hence, it is conceivable that a student could be commended in one institution and not in another because those involved in assessment carry different images and use different criteria against which they measure the student.

With integrative learning, there is a formative dimension involving, in varying

---

39 Klimoski, O'Neil and Schuth, *Educating Leaders for Ministry*, 52.

degrees, all three apprenticeships. Recognising that there will be nuances and overlaps, for some traditions such as the Roman Catholic and Anglican, formation will be measured against the exemplar of the ideal priest and for other traditions such as the Baptist and Pentecostal, formation will be measured against schemas of what is appropriate behaviour for a disciple of Christ.[40] If the six types of understandings are revisited, what is considered acceptable criteria for sophisticated explanation, profound interpretation, masterful application, insightful perspective, mature empathy and wise self-knowledge may vary according to tradition. Similarly, with intuitive forward matching, there may be different exemplars and schemas. Although criteria for assessing integrative learning and readiness for ministry may intersect and certain commonalities be shared across the different traditions, there is likely to be a divergence from a common ground according to perspective.

To find a common ground in the assessment of integrative learning and readiness for ministry, it is necessary to revisit backward design and ask for what end the educative and formational enterprise is undertaken. If discipleship and ministry are conceived as core, then integrative learning may be seen as a process to prepare students for future discipleship, service and ministry (lay or ordained) in which they thrive and grow. Although how each tradition envisions the future can differ, it is possible there will be the singular hope that students will flourish. In this way, resiliency could be an unacknowledged common factor in the assessment of integrative learning, particularly with respect to readiness for ministry.

A backward design which takes into account what an integrated student looks like will be dependent on the "domain-relevant mental representations" of a particular theological perspective, whether denominationally based or not. Theologically, there is more than one exemplar or schema for those in ministry. If assessment of integrative learning is governed by and limited to the constraints of a tradition and theological perspective, then it is likely that there will not be a common ground. However, if a common objective is that students will have resiliency to witness in a changing and often hostile environment, then resiliency could be a shared, although implicit, component in assessment across theological perspectives and diverse traditions.

---

40 Ball, *Transforming Theology*, 122-123.

Conclusion

Integrative learning involves the integration of the cognitive, the practical and the normative but it is greater than the sum of its parts. The assessment of integrative learning involves the evaluation of both objective and subjective factors. The criteria used in assessment may be explicit and measurable. Criteria can also be implicit and difficult to quantify and only accessed through the processes of intuition. In so far as traditions and theological perspectives differ, it is conceivable that there will not be a common ground for assessing integrative learning because the exemplars and schemas that represent what integration and transformation look like are different. If, however, through the forward looking component of intuition, the capacity of a student to continue to grow even under adverse conditions is being evaluated, then it is possible that resiliency provides an unacknowledged common ground.

7 | THE CONTRIBUTION OF THEORIES OF MULTIPLE INTELLIGENCES TO THE PROMOTION OF DEEP LEARNING THROUGH THE ASSESSMENT OF LEARNING

CHARLES DE JONGH

Abstract

The overwhelming consensus is that the assessment of learning is a key factor influencing whether students adopt a deep approach to learning, with the students' experience and perception of assessment a determinative factor. While theories of multiple intelligences have been widely applied to teaching, they have not been meaningfully applied to the assessment of learning or to the promotion of deep learning. This essay considers the contribution of theories of multiple intelligences to the promotion of deep learning through the assessment of learning by considering the development of principles for Multiple Intelligences Based Assessment for Deep Learning, followed by the design of an instrument for use in its application.

Deep Learning and Multiple Intelligences

Deep Learning

Deep learning is one of three main approaches to learning, the other two being surface and strategy learning, and is concerned with the quality of the relationship between student and learning.[1] As Biggs explains, "Approaches to learning describe the way students relate to a teaching/learning environment; they are not fixed characteristics of students…."[2] Deep learning is that learning which occurs when it is essentially motivated from within the student, resulting in learning that has *deep* consequences and significance. Ramsden argues that "the process is internal: the students are concerned with integrating the new material with their personal experiences, knowledge and interests;"[3] while Rhem suggests that a deep learning approach "embraces a sense of the student's *intention* in taking up a learning task as well as *how* he goes about the task (processing it)."[4]

Surface and deep learning contrast in that "the essential distinction between them is that a surface approach focuses on what can be called the *sign* [the object of study] while a deep approach focuses on what is signified [the significance of what is studied]."[5] Additionally, Biggs argues that "the surface approach arises from an intention to get the task out of the way with minimum trouble."[6] Strategy learning, also referred to as achieving learning, is learning which is adopted by students with a strategic motivation, and may be deep or surface. Fry, Ketteridge and Marshall suggest that, in this approach, the student organizes "learning specifically to obtain a high examination grade … a learner who often uses a deep approach may adopt some of the techniques of a surface approach to meet the requirements of a specific activity."[7]

A choice for deep learning is influenced by internal and external factors. Firstly, considering that the motivation comes from within, it is apparent that

---

1. John Bowden and Ference Marton, *The University of Learning – Beyond Quality and Competence* (London: RoutledgeFalmer, 1998), 61.
2. John Biggs, *Teaching for Quality Learning at University*, 2nd ed. (Maidenhead: Open University, 2003), 17.
3. Paul Ramsden, *Learning to Teach in Higher Education*, 2nd ed. (London: RoutledgeFalmer, 2003), 48-49.
4. James Rhem, "Deep/Surface Approaches to Learning: An Introduction," *The National Teaching and Learning Forum* 5:1 (1995), 2.
5. Bowden and Marton, *The University of Learning*, 49.
6. Biggs, *Teaching for Quality Learning at University*, 14.
7. Heather Fry, Steve Ketteridge and Stephanie Marshall, "Understanding Student Learning," in *A Handbook for Teaching and Learning in Higher Education*, eds. Heather Fry, Steve Ketteridge and Stephanie Marshall (London: Kogan Page, 2003), 19.

deep learning is an approach that is internal or intrinsic to the student.[8] In other words, while external factors influence the choice for deep learning, the greater impetus comes from within. Among the factors motivating deep learning, Entwistle has identified interest in a subject aside from academic requirements and personal self-confidence;[9] while a key motivation is the belief that studies are an opportunity to learn about reality and to develop one's thinking about reality.[10]

Nightingale *et al.* comment that deep learning "describe[s] a situation in which a student is motivated intrinsically to satisfy curiosity about a topic;"[11] while Prosser and Trigwell observe that the student has "an intrinsic interest in the task and an expectation of enjoyment in carrying it out."[12] Further to this, the student is often willing to work *beyond* the essential requirements of the particular learning experience, to the extent that deep learning will often encourage "[reading] widely, discuss[ing] issues and [reflecting] on what has been heard and read, integrating details into broad, over-arching (or high-level) ideas which she or he is constantly trying to develop."[13] As a result, the student will, amongst other things, integrate new learning into existing knowledge; critically interact with existing and new knowledge; work at higher cognitive levels; restructure existing knowledge where appropriate; and vigorously interact with the material.[14]

The overwhelming consensus amongst scholars is that the assessment of learning is one of the most important influencing factors in relation to the approach students take to their learning.[15] Biggs argues that students who incline to a

---

[8] Biggs, *Teaching for Quality Learning at University*, 16-17; Ference Marton and Roger Säljö, "Approaches to Learning," in *The Experience of Learning*, ed. Ference Marton (Edinburgh: Scottish Academic, 1984), 44; Michael Prosser and Keith Trigwell, *Understanding Learning and Teaching: The Experience in Higher Education* (Buckingham: SRHE and Open University, 1999), 3.

[9] Noel Entwistle, "Learning and Studying: Contrasts and Influences." *Creating the Future: Perspectives on Educational Change*. Accessed December 16, 2007, http://www.newhorizins.org/future/Creating_the_Future/crfut_entwistle.html, 9.

[10] Marton and Säljö, "Approaches to Learning," 45.

[11] Peggy Nightingale *et al*, "Assessment Project Glossary," in *Assessing Learning in Universities*, eds Peggy Nightingale *et al* (Sydney: UNSW, 1996), 267.

[12] Prosser and Trigwell, *Understanding Learning and Teaching: The Experience in Higher Education*, 3.

[13] Nightingale *et al*, "Assessment Project Glossary," 267.

[14] Denise Chalmers and Richard Fuller, *Teaching for Learning at University* (London: Kogan Page, 1996), 7; Fry, Ketteridge and Marshall, "Understanding Student Learning," 18; David Lambert and David Lines, *Understanding Assessment: Purposes, Perceptions, Practice* (London: RoutledgeFalmer, 2000), 152.

[15] Biggs, *Teaching for Quality Learning at University*, 15-16; David Boud, "Assessment and Learning: Contradictory or Complementary?" in *Assessment for Learning in Higher Education*, ed. Peter Knight (London: Kogan Page, 1995), 37; Bowden and Marton, *The University of Learning – Beyond Quality and Competence*, 61-66; Entwistle, "Learning and Studying: Contrasts and Influences," 6; Catherine Haines, *Assessing Students' Written Work* (London: RoutledgeFalmer, 2004), 3; Ramsden, *Learning to Teach in Higher Education*, 45; Rhem, "Deep/Surface Approaches to Learning: An Introduction," 4.

surface approach to learning are most commonly influenced by assessment,[16] while Bowden and Marton emphasise that students are further influenced by their subjective experience of assessment.[17] Consequently, students' experience and perception of assessment will impact on their approach to learning.[18] In practice, students are inclined to evaluate the required assessment and then make a choice regarding their approach to learning.[19] Educators are, therefore, to understand that assessment sends coded messages to students that will influence their approach to learning.[20]

Multiple Intelligences

In an endeavour to promote deep learning through the assessment of learning, the proposal is that theories of multiple intelligences provide a valuable contribution to the endeavour. Historically, *intelligence* was a term used to describe a person's particular or unusual ability, without specifically defining the extent or range of what may be regarded as intelligent. Around 1900, Alfred Binet and his colleagues carried out work that gave rise to the IQ (intelligence quotient) test, which was understood to be testing a unitary trait referred to as intelligence;[21] over time, this gave rise to IQ tests and standardised testing.[22] Consequently, *intelligence* was reduced to a single overarching construct;[23] an acceptance which prompted Sternberg to observe that "among scientific disciplines the field of intelligence has not been notable for rapid progress, either in theory or in practical application."[24]

---

16   Biggs, *Teaching for Quality Learning at University*, 36.
17   Bowden and Marton, *The University of Learning*, 8.
18   Bowden and Marton, *The University of Learning*, 9; Chalmers and Fuller, *Teaching for Learning at University*, 42; George Madaus, "The Influence of Testing on the Curriculum," in *Understanding Outcomes-Based Education: Teaching and Assessment in South Africa – A Reader*, eds John Gultig et al. (Cape Town: SAIDE/Oxford, 1998), 40; Marton and Säljö, "Approaches to Learning," 45; Rhem, "Deep/Surface Approaches to Learning: An Introduction," 2.
19   Biggs, *Teaching for Quality Learning at University*, 140-144; Chalmers and Fuller, *Teaching for Learning at University*, 42.
20   Boud, "Assessment and Learning: Contradictory or Complementary?" 37.
21   Daniel T. Willingham, "Reframing the Mind: A Response to Howard Gardner." Accessed August 2, 2006, http://www.educationnext.org/unabridged/20043/willingham.pdf, 7.
22   Howard Gardner, *Multiple Intelligences: The Theory in Practice – A Reader* (New York: Basic, 1993), 163-166.
23   Stephen Denig, "Multiple Intelligences and Learning Styles: Two Complementary Dimensions," *Teachers College Record*, 106:1 (2004), 4.
24   Robert J. Sternberg, *Beyond IQ: A Triarchic Theory of Human Intelligence* (Cambridge: University, 1985), 4.

The later part of the twentieth century saw questions being asked regarding the orthodox understanding of intelligence. Rather than viewing intelligence as a *uni*-dimensional phenomenon, certain scholars have come to regard intelligence as a *multi*-dimensional phenomenon. For example, Kuhn argues that "intelligence is a multidimensional phenomenon that is present at multiple levels of our brain/mind/body system."[25] Within this debate, Gardner and Sternberg investigated the possible broader extent and nature of human intelligence.[26] At the time of writing his ground breaking book, *Frames of Mind: The Theory of Multiple Intelligences*, Gardner observed, "I was claiming that all human beings possess not just a single intelligence (often called "g" for general intelligence). Rather, as a species we human beings are better described as have a set of relatively autonomous intelligences."[27] Similarly, Sternberg argued for and supported the understanding of multiplicity, but without the autonomy of Gardner;[28] as such, "[Multiple Intelligence] theory represents a pluralistic view of intelligences."[29]

This essay will consider the contribution of theories of multiple intelligences to the promotion of deep learning through the assessment of learning by considering the development of principles for Multiple Intelligences Based Assessment for Deep Learning (MIBADL), followed by the design of an instrument for use in the application of MIBADL. In particular, reference will be made to the eight intelligences proposed by Gardner (linguistic, musical, logical-mathematical, spatial, bodily-kinesthetic, intrapersonal, interpersonal and naturalistic)[30] and three abilities proposed by Robert Sternberg (analytical, creative and practical).[31]

---

25 David Lazear, *Multiple Intelligence Approaches to Assessment – Solving the Assessment Conundrum (Revised)* (Chicago: Zephyr, 1999), 3.
26 Howard Gardner, *Frames of Mind: The Theory of Multiple Intelligences*, 20th anniversary ed. (New York: Basic, 1983); Sternberg, *Beyond IQ: A Triarchic Theory of Human Intelligence*.
27 Howard Gardner, "Multiple Intelligences After Twenty Years," Paper presented at the meeting of the American Educational Research Association, Chicago, 2004, 4.
28 Robert J. Sternberg, *The Triarchic Mind: A New Theory of Human Intelligence* (New York: Penguin, 1988), 11.
29 Karen Goodnough, "Enhancing Professional Knowledge: A Case Study of an Elementary Teacher," *Canadian Journal of Education*, 26:2 (2001), 218-236.
30 Gardner, *Frames of Mind: The Theory of Multiple Intelligences*; Gardner, *Multiple Intelligences: The Theory in Practice – A Reader*, 73-227; Howard Garner, *Intelligence Reframed: Multiple Intelligences for the 21st Century* (New York: Basic, 1999), 47.
31 Sternberg, *Beyond IQ: A Triarchic Theory of Human Intelligence*; Sternberg, *The Triarchic Mind: A New Theory of Human Intelligence*; Robert J. Sternberg, "Applying the Triarchic Theory of Human Intelligence in the Classroom," in *Intelligence, Instruction, and Assessment: Theory into Practice*, eds Robert J. Sternberg and Wendy M. Williams (London: Lawrence Erlbaum, 1998), 2-3.

Principles for Multiple Intelligences Based Assessment for Deep Learning

The development of principles for MIBADL involves three stages: the derivation of principles for Deep Learning Assessment (DLA); the derivation of principles for multiple intelligences based assessment (MIBA); and synthesizing the two sets of principles into those for MIBADL.

(a) Deriving principles for Deep Learning Assessment

Improved assessment practice contributes to improved learning, as well as the promotion of deep learning.[32] This is particularly important in relation to the "backwash effect," in which the approach to learning is shaped by student expectations of assessment;[33] therefore, the imperative is to align assessment to the desired approach to learning.[34] However, it should be observed that certain scholars have reservations regarding the promotion of deep learning through assessment; for example, Atherton argues that efforts to promote deep learning may simply contribute to more complex surface learning.[35] The challenge is how assessment can promote deep learning with proposals including good preparatory guidance and teaching, teacher support, setting of high expectations, clearly defined assessment requirements, a choice of tasks, appropriate resourcing and time, emphasising principles and structures, teaching to elicit a response, building on existing knowledge, emphasising depth, assessment demanding integration, assessment supporting explicit aims and objectives, and meaningful and timeous feedback.[36]

---

32 Boud, "Assessment and Learning: Contradictory or Complementary?" 37; Bowden and Marton, *The University of Learning*, 8 & 62; Chalmers and Fuller, *Teaching for Learning at University*, 41; Entwistle, "Learning and Studying: Contrasts and Influences," 6; Haines, *Assessing Students' Written Work*, 3.

33 Biggs, *Teaching for Quality Learning at University*, 140-141; Boud, "Assessment and Learning: Contradictory or Complementary?" 37; Chalmers and Fuller, *Teaching for Learning at University*, 42; Madaus, "The Influence of Testing on the Curriculum," 40.

34 Biggs, *Teaching for Quality Learning at University*, 140-141.

35 James S. Atherton, "Learning and Teaching: Approaches to Study 'Deep' and 'Surface.'" Accessed September 15, 2005, http://www.learningandteaching.info/learning/deepsurf.htm, 5.

36 Biggs, *Teaching for Quality Learning at University*, 16-17; Elizabeth Campbell, "Teaching Strategies to Foster 'Deep' Versus 'Surface' Learning," *Teaching Options*, November (1998), accessed September 15, 2005, http://www.uottawa.ca/academic/cut/options/Nov_98/Teaching Strategies_en.htm 6; Engineering Subject Centre, "Deep and Surface Approaches to Learning." Accessed September 15, 2005, http://www.engsc.ac.uk/er/theory/learning.asp, 8; Haines, *Assessing Students' Written Work*, 10; D. Logan, "Students' Views on Assessment," in *Conference on Assessment of Learning and Teaching*, ed. ULIE (London: ULIE, 1971), 9; Barbara E. Walvoord and Virginia J. Anderson, *Effective Grading* (San Francisco: Jossey-Bass, 1998), 116.

Accepting a relationship between assessment and approaches to learning, principles for assessment that will increase the probability of deep learning may be derived:[37]

1. Assessment is integral to course design and should be centred on the students' envisaged achievement;
2. Assessment requirements focus on the significant principles and structures of the course;
3. Assessment is based on clear and stated objectives and outcomes, which are directly associated with the aims and purpose of the course;
4. Assessment for deep learning makes use of a wide variety of methods and types;
5. Assessment requirements and criteria are clearly and explicitly stated;
6. Assessment for deep learning is supported by good preparatory guidance, material and personal support, and appropriate resourcing;
7. Assessment gives early and comprehensive feedback, with the intention of addressing weaknesses and improving learning.

1. Assessment is integral to course design and should be centred on the students' envisaged achievement

While assessment is often regarded as an addendum to a course, it needs to be viewed as integral if it is to make a deliberate and purposive contribution to the intended development of the student (associated with principle seven).[38] Practically, this means that the educator should be able to explain the rationale behind all assessment, and what role it plays in relation to the overall objectives and outcomes of the given course (see principle three). This approach promotes deep

---

[37] Thomas A. Angelo and K Patricia Cross, *Classroom Assessment Techniques: A Handbook for College Teachers* (San Francisco: Jossey-Bass, 1993), 4-11; Entwistle, "Learning and Studying: Contrasts and Influences;" Qualifications and Curriculum Authority, "The Ten Principles." Accessed March 17, 2006, http://www.qca.org.uk/907.html; Phil Race, "What Has Assessment Done for Us – and To Us?" in *Assessment for Learning in Higher Education*, ed. Peter Knight (London: Kogan Page, 1995), 67-68; Rhem, "Deep/Surface Approaches to Learning: An Introduction;" Robert J. Sternberg, "Assessing What Matters," *Educational Leadership*, 65:4 (2007), 20-26; Keith Trigwell and Michael Prosser, "Towards an Understanding of Individual Acts of Teaching." Accessed December 10, 2009, http://www.herdsa.org.au/confs/1996/trigwell1.html; Keith Trigwell, Michael Prosser and Fiona Waterhouse, "Relations Between Teachers' Approaches to Teaching and Students' Approaches to Learning," *Higher Education*, 37 (1999), 57-70; Walvoord and Anderson, *Effective Grading*, 2-3 & 189-191.

[38] Entwistle, "Learning and Studying: Contrasts and Influences," 14; Engineering Subject Centre, "Deep and Surface Approaches to Learning," 11-12; Kathy Luckett and Lee Sutherland, "Assessment Practices that Improve Teaching and Learning," in *Improving Teaching and Learning in Higher Education: A Handbook for Southern Africa*, ed. Sinfree B. Makoni (Johannesburg: WITS, 2000), 10.

learning in that it purposely contributes to the students' growing understanding in accordance with the envisaged achievement of the student (see principle five).

2. Assessment requirements focus on the significant principles and structures of the course

This principle is best considered in negative terms, namely, that assessment requirements that focus on insignificant or peripheral aspects will not (see principles three and five), by their very nature, promote deep learning and will tend towards surface learning. Positively, assessment that focuses on principles and structures is more likely to promote deep learning.[39] This is achieved in that students will be required to focus on the important aspects of what is being studied and to integrate that into their broader spectrum of knowledge and learning, all of which can contribute to the promotion of deep learning.

3. Assessment is based on clear and stated objectives and outcomes, which are directly associated with the aims and purpose of the course

To promote deep learning, assessment needs to be linked to clear and stated objectives and outcomes;[40] in other words, it must be clear to the student what the course objectives and outcomes are, and how the assessment items relate to them (see principles five and six). In practical terms, every educator should be able to demonstrate the relationship between the assessment items and the purpose or outcomes of the given course. This promotes a deep approach to learning; as such, assessment would demand that the student come to terms with that which is essential and fundamental to the course.

4. Assessment for deep learning makes use of a wide variety of methods and types

One of the greatest challenges to assessment for deep learning is the common preference for assessment that is predominantly focused on *reading and writing, reproduction and examination,* in which assignments and examinations remain the dominant assessment forms. While they can promote deep learning, the possibilities for assessment go way beyond these limited forms. A range of appropriate methods and types of assessment can promote deep learning, where expect-

---

[39] Engineering Subject Centre, "Deep and Surface Approaches to Learning," 8; Entwistle, "Learning and Studying: Contrasts and Influences," 8.
[40] Campbell, "Teaching Strategies to Foster 'Deep' Versus 'Surface' Learning," 6.

ations are clearly stated (see principle five).[41] When students are free to choose their preferred assessment form, it is more likely that they will be encouraged to work at a deeper level, promoting a deep approach to learning.[42]

5. Assessment requirements and criteria are clearly and explicitly stated

A significant problem with assessment, for many students, lies in uncertainty regarding assessment requirements, especially the specific criteria (associated with principle six). Students often encounter assessment items, with little or no indication of what is expected of them; in other words, without clear criteria. Practically, this principle demands that students are given the best possible academic and technical guidance in relation to assessment (see principle seven). With respect to deep learning, this principle will contribute in that students will be more likely to work in the intended direction and with the intended emphasis (associated with principle three).

6. Assessment for deep learning is supported by good preparatory guidance, material and personal support, and appropriate resourcing

This principle is arguably a statement of a key aspect of good teaching practice; however, when students do not receive the necessary guidance, support and resourcing they will often be unable to meet expectations, which will impact on their approach to learning (associated with principles three and five). This principle requires that students be given the guidance and support required for the meaningful completion of assessment items (including the concern of principle seven). This provides students with the backing that they need to respond appropriately and meaningfully to any assessment items.

7. Assessment gives early and comprehensive feedback, with the intention of addressing weaknesses and improving learning

This principle relates to the responsibility of the educator to the students following the submission of assessment items.[43] The first is constructive feedback, considering that such feedback is a valuable part of learning. Secondly, feedback needs to be given early and comprehensively; the longer the delay in

---

41 Ramsden, *Learning to Teach in Higher Education*, 68-72.
42 Campbell, "Teaching Strategies to Foster 'Deep' Versus 'Surface' Learning," 6-8.
43 Chew Fook Tim, "Encouraging Deep Learning." Accessed September 15, 2005, http://www.cdtl.nus.edu.sg/link/mar2004/learn1.htm, 5.

giving feedback, the less the impact of such feedback (associated with principle five). Finally, the intention of the feedback is to help the student address their areas of weakness, which become growth points, further developing what has been submitted by the student.

(b) Deriving principles for Multiple Intelligences Based Assessment

Based on the study of Gardner and Sternberg's understandings of multiple intelligences, consequent principles are derived for the assessment of learning. By their very nature, such principles are premised on an acceptance of theories of multiple intelligences. While Gardner refers to *intelligences* and Sternberg to *abilities*, for the sake of simplicity, the term *intelligences* will be used in this essay, acknowledging that not all scholars agree on the use of the term.[44] It is to be appreciated that these are not all-encompassing principles for assessment, but only those deriving from theories of multiple intelligences.

1. Acknowledge that students have different intelligence strengths;
2. Acknowledge that students achieve differently;
3. Assessment options should acknowledge different intelligences and be characterized by variety;
4. Variety and choice apply in the specific assessment of all objectives and outcomes;
5. The variety in assessment is to be based on different intelligences.

1. Acknowledge that students have different intelligence strengths

Gardner argues that various intelligences are to be considered in assessment, because students differ with respect to their intelligence strengths (and weaknesses).[45] Sternberg has similarly argued the case, especially in the context of research into different cultural and national settings.[46] Based on the multifaceted nature of intelligence, this first principle argues that the educator must acknowledge intelligence differences between students. This means that different

---

44 Gardner, *Intelligence Reframed: Multiple Intelligences for the 21st Century*, 33-34&41-44; Sternberg, "Applying the Triarchic Theory of Human Intelligence in the Classroom," 2-3; Amy C. Brualdi, *Multiple Intelligences: Gardner's Theory*, ERIC Identifier ED410226 (Washington: ERIC Clearinghouse on Assessment and Evaluation). Accessed September 13, 2004, http://www.ericfacility.net/ericdigests/ed410226.html, 15; Robert J. Sternberg and Elena L. Grigorenko, "Teaching for Successful Intelligence: Principles, Procedures, and Practices," *Journal for the Education of the Gifted*, 27:2-3 (2003), 207-208.
45 Gardner, *Multiple Intelligences: The Theory in Practice – A Reader*, 177.
46 Robert J. Sternberg, "Recognizing Neglected Strengths," *Educational Leadership*, 64:1 (2006), 30-35.

students may be better able to express themselves in different ways, thereby achieving differently (as expressed in principle two).

2. Acknowledge that students achieve differently

Premised on principle one, the logical implication is that students will achieve differently. For example, a student who is stronger in Gardner's linguistic intelligence may find the writing of essays and examinations a rewarding option for assessment, while struggling with assessment that demands musical or spatial intelligence. Similarly, a student strong in Sternberg's practical abilities may find assessment requiring practical ability more stimulating than assessment focusing on analytical abilities. This principle requires educators to acknowledge that students achieve differently, based on the differences between intelligences; Gardner refers to assessment instruments that are "intelligence fair."[47] With respect to the assessment of learning, this principle requires the educator to ensure variety in assessment based on differences in student achievement.

3. Assessment options should acknowledge different intelligences and be characterized by variety

Based on principles one and two, assessment options should acknowledge the different intelligences, which is more than giving options between topics that still expect the same form of presentation. In the light of students' different intelligence strengths and the acknowledgement of those differences in the assessment of learning, it follows that assessment options should be the norm.[48] Assessment options should be characterized by variety across the assessment experience. In practice, this principle calls for intelligence-based variety in assessment across the assessment experience of the student.

4. Variety and choice apply in the specific assessment of all objectives and outcomes

Principle four requires variety and choice within specific assessment items, based on the acknowledgement that students vary in terms of intelligence strengths. The previous principle argues that across the entire assessment experience (the macro-context) there needs to be variety, while this principle

---

47 Gardner, *Multiple Intelligences: The Theory in Practice – A Reader*, 176.
48 Sternberg and Grigorenko, "Teaching for Successful Intelligence: Principles, Procedures, and Practices," 208.

argues that within each assessment item (the micro-context) there needs to be both variety and choice. In the context of theories of multiple intelligences and the acknowledgment of different intelligence strengths, that variety of assessment items should be shaped by the varieties of intelligence as variously expressed.[49]

5. The variety in assessment is to be based on different intelligences

Principle one requires the acknowledgement of different intelligence strengths and principle two calls for the acknowledgement that students achieve differently. This gives rise to principle three, that assessment should be characterised by variety across the assessment experience. All this logically culminates in principle five which requires that variety in assessment is to be based on different intelligences.[50] If the differences between students lie in their intelligence strengths, then the variety in assessment should be based on the various intelligences. This principle requires that variety in assessment is aligned with the various intelligences, giving rise to what may be referred to as "intelligence based assessment items."

(c) Deriving Principles for Multiple Intelligences Based Assessment for Deep Learning

The final stage is to bring together the relevant principles for DLA (excluding principles four to seven which relate to good practice in all assessment) and the principles for MIBA into the principles for MIBADL. This stage initially considers the interrelationship between the initial sets of principles, then derives the principles for Multiple Intelligences Based Assessment for Deep Learning. The diagram in Figure A demonstrates the associations and links between the first two sets of principles.

The two sets of principles reflect significant association, which indicates that theories of multiple intelligences do have a contribution to make to the promotion of a deep approach to learning through assessment. Based on the association, four principles are derived for MIBADL:

---

49 Sternberg and Grigorenko, "Teaching for Successful Intelligence: Principles, Procedures, and Practices," 211-212.
50 Sternberg, "Applying the Triarchic Theory of Human Intelligence in the Classroom," 10-11.

1. The student's envisaged achievement is integral to course design, acknowledging that students have different intelligence strengths and achieve differently;
2. The focus is on the significant principles and structures of the course material; therefore, allowance is made for different intelligence strengths, different ways of achieving, and for variety and choice;
3. Variety and choice in assessment is based on clear and stated objectives and outcomes, which are directly associated with the aims and purpose of the course;
4. A wide variety of methods and types of assessment is utilized, based on an intentional consideration of different intelligences.

1. The student's envisaged achievement is integral to course design, acknowledging that students have different intelligence strengths and achieve differently

It has already been argued that the student's envisaged achievement is to be the central concern of assessment and that, in terms of theories of multiple intelligences, students are different in terms of their intelligence strengths, which means that they achieve differently. If the intention is to assess students and their envisaged achievement, then multiple intelligences based assessment requires allowance to be made for the differences between students with respect to their intelligence strengths and the ways in which they may achieve. The first principle, therefore, retains the emphasis that the student's envisaged achievement is paramount in course design and assessment; but adds that the way in which that achievement is to be assessed commences with the acknowledgement of the differences in intelligence strengths, and with that the reality that students will achieve differently.

Figure A: Associations and Links between DLA and MIBA Principles

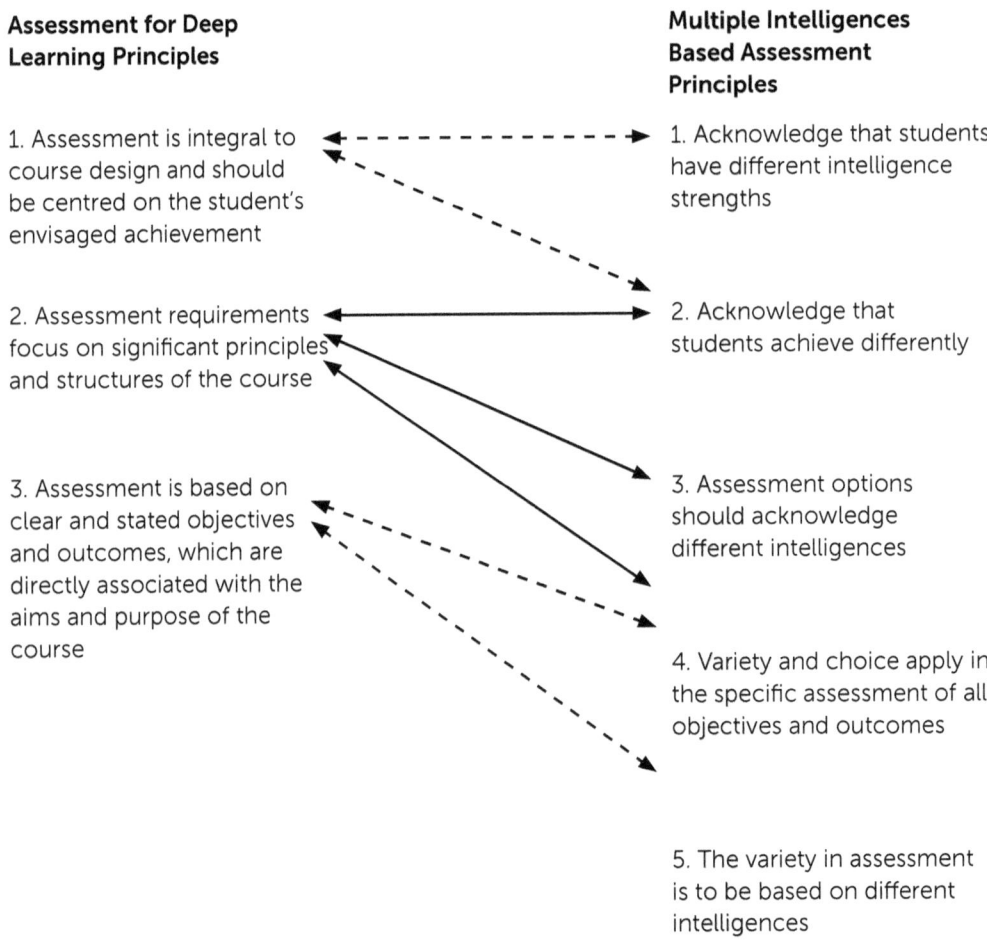

2. *The focus is on the significant principles and structures of the course material; therefore, allowance is made for different intelligence strengths, different ways of achieving, and for variety and choice*

The principles for deep learning assessment call for a focus on the significant principles and structures of course material; consequently, as for the first principle, differences between students should not be an unduly advantageous or inhibiting factor. The theory of multiple intelligences contributes an understanding that, if significant principles and structures are to be the focus of assessment, differences between students should not be permitted to have an undue impact on the ability to demonstrate their achievement in relation to those significant principles and structures. Therefore, this second principle requires that significant principles and structures are the focus of assessment and that allowance is made for different intelligence strengths, different ways of achieving, and for variety and choice in the given assessment.

3. Variety and choice in assessment is based on clear and stated objectives and outcomes, which are directly associated with the aims and purpose of the course
As has been indicated in principles one and two, one of the most basic ways in which deep learning can be promoted and the desired focus maintained lies in the acknowledgement of intelligence differences between students. The starting point for the application of these principles lies in this principle which, though not directly referring to theories of multiple intelligences, in part bases the call for variety and choice on the acceptance of the intelligence differences between students. Variety and choice in assessment is to be directly linked to clear and stated objectives and outcomes which are directly linked to the aims and purpose of the course. However, it needs to be understood that the choice-aspect of these principles is required because of the intelligence differences between students, which is best catered for those differences in intentional variety with respect to assessment.

4. A wide variety of methods and types of assessment is utilized, based on an intentional consideration of different intelligences
This principle argues that the choice-aspect of assessment should be based on the intentional consideration of different intelligences. It is proposed that the variety of methods and types of assessment utilised should be based on the intentional consideration of different intelligences, as expressed in theories of multiple intelligences. The use of an intentional theoretical foundation meaningfully contributes to the design of assessment that is deliberate, rather than the random determination of variety in and for assessment. The main point of this principle is that the theories of multiple intelligences be utilised for the intentional development of variety in the assessment of learning.

Conclusion: An Instrument for the Application of MIBADL

Having derived the principles for MIBADL, the final step is to operationalise the principles in an instrument for the development of assessment items. Gardner's intelligences are arguably too cumbersome and impractical for most academic contexts, while Sternberg's three abilities are more manageable, but exclude the personal/relational aspects of Gardner's intelligences. Equivalences between the two are as in Figure B below.

Figure B: Gardner's Intelligences and Sternberg's Abilities

Gardner's Eight Intelligences	Sternberg's Three Abilities
Linguistic	Componential — analytical/ academic
Logical-mathematical	
Musical	Experiential — creative
Spatial	
Bodily-kinesthetic	Contextual — practical
Naturalistic	
Interpersonal	*No intentional parallel*
Intrapersonal	

Working with this comparison, four intelligence emphases may be derived — essentially Sternberg's abilities plus a fourth encapsulating Gardner's personal intelligences. These emphases are *linguistic, creative, practical* and *relational*, which relate to Gardner's intelligences and Sternberg's abilities as below in Figure C.

Figure C: Intelligence Emphases

Emphases	Gardner	Sternberg
Linguistic	Linguistic Logical-mathematical	Analytical/ academic
Creative	Musical Spatial	Creative
Practical	Bodily-kinesthetic Naturalistic	Practical
Relational	Interpersonal Interpersonal	No intentional parallel

These four intelligence emphases are the foundation for the assessment options, each having a matching assessment emphasis, as in Figure D.

Figure D: Intelligences Based Assessment Options

Intelligence emphases	Intelligence emphases	Essential emphases
Linguistic	Written work	Write about
Creative	Creative work	Create afresh
Practical	Practical task	Make anew
Relational	Relational task	Relate amongst

These options are then applied to the development of assessment requirements, which may be completed by utilising the instrument presented below in Figure E.

Figure E: Application to the Assessment of Learning

Outcome/s statement	Intelligence emphasis	Assessment item	Assessment criteria
	→	→	
Clear statement of intended or required outcome/s	Linguistic	Assessment item in *linguistic* form; for example, an assignment or examination.	
	Creative	Assessment item in *creative* form; for example, an artwork or inventive solution.	
	Practical	Assessment item in *practical* form; for example, a practical task or situational application.	
	Relational	Assessment item in *relational* form; for example, reporting on a relationship or reflective evaluation.	

Two examples illustrate the manner in which this construct could be applied. The first example applies to the field of Religious Studies, in which the students are required to reflect on the character and nature of God. Typically, students would be expected either to write an assignment or to be examined on the topic. In terms of MIBADL, the following process would be followed: clearly state the intended outcome, construct assessment items related to each of the intelligence emphases, and determine the relevant assessment criteria. Focusing on the first two steps, the result could be as in the following example in Figure F.

Figure F: Example 1 – Religious Studies

Outcome statement
The student will be able to demonstrate an awareness and understanding of the various dimensions of the character and nature of God.
Intelligence emphasis and assessment item
Linguistic: The student is to write an assignment that clearly delineates and discusses the various dimensions of the character and nature of God. The final assessment item is a written assignment.   *Creative:*   The student is to produce an artistic, musical or dramatic work that reflects the various dimensions of the character and nature of God. The final assessment item is the artwork, musical score or dramatic script.   *Practical:*   The student is to demonstrate practically eight dimensions of the character and nature of God, in the context of a local community of faith, recording their experiences in a journal. The final assessment item is a detailed workbook.   *Relational:*   The student is to establish a relationship with a person, previously unknown to them, and in that relationship they are to deliberately live out the relational consequences of the character and nature of God. The final assessment item is a reflective journal.

The second example demonstrates how this approach may be used within a more typical approach to assessment in the subject of Art History, where students are being assessed on their understanding of key influences on art through history. Typically, an examination would ask a question such as, "Discuss, with examples, how the following have influenced art through history...." In terms of MIBADL, a second alternative may read, "By means of a drawing of a chair and a dog, illustrate how each of the following has influenced art through history...." This would afford the student the option of demonstrating the influences by means of illustration, as indicated in Figure G.

Figure G: Example 2 – Art History

Outcome statement

The student will be able to demonstrate an understanding of key influences on art through history.

Intelligence emphasis and assessment item

Linguistic:

The student is to answer the following question:

Discuss, with examples, how the following have influenced art through history...

  OR

Creative / Practical:

The student is to respond to the following requirement:

By means of a drawing of a chair and a dog, illustrate how each of the following has influenced art through history...

SECTION FOUR
SOME DIFFERENT DIRECTIONS

8 | ADDRESSING THE NEED FOR BETTER INTEGRATION IN THEOLOGICAL EDUCATION

PROPOSALS, PROGRESS, AND POSSIBILITIES FROM THE MEDICAL EDUCATION MODEL

RICHARD HIBBERT AND EVELYN HIBBERT

Abstract

This essay assumes that the key to enhancing theological education is intentionally integrating knowing with being and doing, theory with practice, and theology with life and ministry. After outlining the longstanding call for better integration, it analyses evidence of a continuing need in this area, outlines recent proposals designed to address it, and highlights several signs of recent progress. Building on this analysis, the essay explores the potential of medical training in Australia to serve as a foil for reflection on ways of strengthening the relationship between knowing, being, and doing in theological education.

Introduction

Life is an integrated whole. We experience life not as fragmented bits, but as a unified whole in which every part affects every other part. Events and circumstances affect our emotions, our motivation and our thoughts. Sickness, for example, influences every part of our lives -our feelings, motivation, and ability to work or study, and the events that occur in our relationships with other people influence everything else that is happening in our lives.

Since every aspect of life is interconnected, the process of learning in theological colleges should continuously be related to students' lives. Theological education cannot focus only on understanding God and his ways, but must help people grow in Christlikeness and develop skills for ministry. It must foster the formation of Christian leaders whose lives are marked by the fruit of the Holy Spirit and who are able to help others grow in Christ. Theological educator David Wells writes:

> The church, at least in its better moments, has known that its ministers need to be people of godly character, knowledgeable of the Word, competent in its proclamation and application, and people who have the requisite skills to be shepherds of God's flock.[1]

This essay argues that the key to enhancing theological education is the intentional integration of knowing with being and doing, of theory with practice, and of theology with life and ministry. Enabling thoroughgoing integration to occur requires theological educators to rethink aspects of the design and methodology of theological education.[2]

There have been many recent calls for better integration of knowing, being and doing in theological education. This essay outlines several calls for integration that have been made over the past few decades, and analyses evidence both that there is a continuing need to keep working on this area and that some progress has been made on it. Building on this, several proposals for addressing the lack of integration are evaluated. Finally, the current model of medical education in Australia is analysed for its potential to provide insights into how better integration in theological education might be achieved.

---

1 David Wells, "Educating for a Counter-Cultural Spirituality," in *Theological Education in the Evangelical Tradition*, ed. D.G. Hart and Albert Mohler (Grand Rapids, MI: Baker, 1996), 291.
2 Robert Banks, *Reenvisioning Theological Education: Exploring a Missional Alternative to Current Models* (Grand Rapids, MI: Eerdmans, 1999), 8-11; Robert Ferris, *Renewal in Theological Education: Strategies for Change* (Wheaton, IL: Billy Graham Center, 1990), 27.

The Call for Integration

Recent writing about theological education has highlighted the need to strengthen the relationships among knowing, being and doing. This concern is evident in book titles such as *Integral Ministry Training*, *A Guide to an Integrated Approach to Theological Education*, and *Beyond Fragmentation: Integrating Mission and Theological Education*.[3] It is a concern shared by many evangelical theological educators. The International Council for Evangelical Theological Education's (ICETE) Manifesto on the Renewal of Theological Education, for example, highlights gaps in current theological education and calls for reform to address them.[4] One of these gaps, according to this document, is in the area of integration:

> Our programmes of theological education must combine spiritual and practical with academic objectives in one holistic integrated educational approach. We are at fault that we so often focus educational requirements narrowly on cognitive attainments, while we hope for student growth in other dimensions but leave it largely to chance. Our programmes must be designed to attend to the growth and equipping of the whole man of God.[5]

A recent survey of theological educators and church leaders from all major Christian traditions in every part of the world confirms that integration continues to be a major concern. This survey of more than 1500 such leaders asked, "What are the most important elements in the program of preparation and/or formation for Christian ministry?" Responses stressed that experiential learning in the location of ministry (in both churches and communities) must be integrated with spiritual formation and academic programs.[6]

Calls for integration are not new. As far back as 1967, the Director of the Theological Education Fund lamented that theological students around the

---

3   Robert Brynjolfson and Jonathan Lewis (eds), *Integral Ministry Training: Design and Evaluation* (Pasadena, CA: William Carey Library, 2006); Paul Mohan Raj, *A Guide to an Integrated Approach to Theological Education* (Bangalore, India: Theological Book Trust 2008); Bernhard Ott, *Beyond Fragmentation: Integrating Mission and Theological Education* (Oxford: Regnum, 2001).
4   "ICETE Manifesto on the Renewal of Evangelical Theological Education," ICETE (International Council for Evangelical Theological Education), accessed 3 October, 2013, http://www.icete-edu.org/manifesto/index.htm.
5   ICETE, "ICETE Manifesto."
6   "Global Survey on Theological Education," GlobeTheoLib, accessed 9 October, 2013, http://www.globethics.net/web/gtl/research/global-survey, 5.

world, rather than being allowed to stay in real life and integrate their learning with it, were being extracted away from it into artificial communities.[7] The Theological Education by Extension (TEE) movement that also started in the 1960s was driven in part by the need for more integration between cognitive inputs, life and ministry.[8]

Calls for integration were intensified in 1983 with the publication of Edward Farley's book *Theologia: The Fragmentation and Unity of Theological Education*. Farley diagnosed the fundamental problem in current theological education as a lack of integration in the curriculum due to confusion about the central goal of theological education. He argued that the central goal of theological education—the development of theological wisdom—had been obscured by the fragmentation of the curriculum into separate subject areas. Instead of developing heartfelt knowledge of God, theological schools have focused on developing scholarly knowledge.[9] There is little doubt that the specialisation of faculty into distinct subject areas can mean that students experience learning in a fragmented and disjointed way.

While it is true that developing theological wisdom should be a central goal of theological education, Farley seems to portray the development of theological wisdom as a largely individualistic enterprise that takes place in the mind of the theological student and that takes place in isolation from the lives of other people and the church's mission.[10] His proposal needs to be extended so that students' theological reflection enables them not only to think theologically but also to participate in God's mission in the world and help other Christians do the same. Integration should be fostered by creating a learning environment in which theological studies and missional engagement with the world are brought into dynamic dialogue.[11]

---

7   James Hopewell, "Mission and the Seminary Structure," *International Review of Mission* 56 (1967), 158-163.
8   Lois McKinney, "Why Renewal is Needed in Theological Education," *Evangelical Missions Quarterly* 18 (1982), 85-96; Ferris, *Renewal*, 13-15.
9   Farley, *Theologia*, 136-137; 152-153.
10 Christopher Duraisingh, "Ministerial Formation for Mission," *International Review of Mission* 81(1992), 39.
11 Steve de Gruchy, "Theological Education and Missional Practice: A Vital Dialogue," in *Handbook of Theological Education in World Christianity: Theological Perspectives, Ecumenical Trends, Regional Surveys* (Eugene, OR: Wipf and Stock, 2010).

The Need for Better Integration: Evidence from Australia and Overseas

There is evidence from both Australia and overseas of a continuing need for effort to be directed towards improving integration. A recent survey of church leaders in Australia found that church and mission leaders are concerned about deficiencies in the personal qualities of graduates and ministry skills. They would like to see personal growth and the development of ministry skills to be addressed more intentionally.[12]

It is not only church leaders who see room for improvement in theological training. Les Ball's recent study of theological education in Australia discovered a "disconnect" between theological education and life and ministry, and found that theological education does not sufficiently result in personal transformation and ministry preparedness.[13] Despite a widely held assumption that the study of theology should involve significant personal transformation, and the expectation that theological colleges should facilitate spiritual formation, his study suggests there is little evidence to show that theological colleges actually produce transformation.[14]

Two main areas are highlighted by Ball's study: the personal formation of students and the development of ministry skills. Students surveyed in Ball's study reported little personal change over the course of their college education, and the changes they did report were primarily intellectual.[15] More than a tenth of final year students felt that their college experience reflected an "over-intellectual approach to theology" and a "lack of practical connection to life or ministry, with virtually no connection with the secular world which is a large part of the context of lived Christianity."[16] This was echoed by interviews with recent graduates, who said that any connections that were made between their lives and their studies were informal and *ad hoc*.[17] While there was a common recognition in the colleges of the value of the diversity of students' life experiences and backgrounds, there is an equally common exclusion of those experiences and backgrounds from the teaching/learning enterprise.

---

12 Charles Sherlock, *Uncovering Theology: The Depth, Reach, and Utility of Australian Theological Education* (Adelaide: ATF Press, 2009), 81-82.
13 Les Ball, *Transforming Theology. Student Experience and Transformative Learning in Undergraduate Theological Education* (Preston, Vic: Mosaic Press, 2012).
14 Ball, *Transforming Theology*, 5.
15 Ball, *Transforming Theology*, 67-69.
16 Ball, *Transforming Theology*, 55.
17 Ball, *Transforming Theology*, 57.

Ball's study also raises a question mark over how formative the college community is on students' lives. Most theological institutions in Australia rely on their relatively unstructured extracurricular campus life to provide transformation. He found that while faculty strongly emphasised the college community as a major element in students' development, and students did find the community worthwhile and enjoyable, none of the graduates who were surveyed mentioned its formative influence in terms of personal growth or developing ministry skills.[18]

Ball found that when ministry skills are taught in theological colleges and Bible schools, they tend to be talked about in classrooms rather than being developed through practice, modelling and mentoring.[19] Although colleges sometimes run extracurricular programs focused on ministry skills, these are not usually integrated with the academic program, and structured or intentional connections between students' life experience are very rarely made.[20] Field placements are rarely integrated with classroom curriculum. Connections that are made tend to be incidental and at the students' initiative. In Ball's assessment, this is an area where "faculty generally seem to have a lack of either capacity to initiate or confidence to implement."[21]

The current need for better integration between theological studies, life, and ministry is not restricted to Australia. Observers of global theological education report that seminary curricula are "unrelated to life" and that graduates are "ill prepared for ministry."[22] In Canada, for example, a regional director for theological education lamented that most pastors "feel unprepared by their seminary education for the demands of pastoral ministry" and are, as new graduates, "functionally incompetent."[23] Church leaders in India complain about declining commitment, lack of vision for people, and shallow understanding of both Scripture and society among theologically trained students. One Indian theological educator explains that a major part of the problem is the lack of spiritual

---

18 Ball, *Transforming Theology*, 74.
19 Ball, *Transforming Theology*, 38.
20 Ball, *Transforming Theology*, 61, 64.
21 Ball, *Transforming Theology*, 65.
22 Ferris, *Renewal in Theological Education*, 7.
23 Tim Dearborn, "Preparing New Leaders for the Church of the Future: Transforming Theological Education through Multi-Institutional Partnerships," *Transformation: An International Journal of Holistic Mission Studies* 12 (1995), 7.

formation in the way they are trained.[24] In East and Central Africa there is also growing dissatisfaction with theological education expressed by both churches and graduates. Seminaries are seen as irrelevant in training people for church ministry, faculty have been accused of being too theoretical in their approach to training, and graduates feel their training institutions do not adequately prepare them to deal with life issues that they encounter in ministry.[25]

Proposals for Better Integration

Several recent proposals for redesigning theological education hold particular promise for integrating knowing God's Word with life and ministry. The three that will be outlined here all involve teachers and students engaged in life and ministry together. John Frame's model, for example, sees faculty, students, and their families living in community, living, eating and working together, learning from the example of faculty and older students. Faculty live among, supervise and serve alongside students in a broad variety of ministries including evangelism, discipling, teaching Bible classes, visitation and preaching while they also teach biblical studies, theology, church history and practical theology. Frame particularly emphasises community among teachers and learners.[26]

Writing from India, Jesudason Jeyaraj suggests a similar model but places the emphasis on both teachers' and students' involvement in society, basing this on the ministry training pattern of Jesus who "made [his] training contextual and people-oriented."[27] Involvement in society, for Jeyaraj, includes things like being involved for a whole subject in a village or a slum and helping the community get basic facilities, and having students involved at weekends or for short-term blocks in prison ministry, village adult education, and development work.

Robert Banks' model takes Frame's emphasis on community and Jeyaraj's concern for involvement in society and combines them by focusing on praxis

---

24 Jesudason Jeyaraj, *Christian Ministry: Models of Ministry and Training* (Bangalore: Theological Book Trust, 2002), 264-265.

25 J.K. Mwangi, J.K. & B.J. De Klerk, "An Integrated Competency-Based Training Model for theological training," *HTS Teologiese Studies/Theological Studies* 67 (2011), accessed 12 October, 2013, http://dx.doi.org/10.4102/hts.v67i2.1036.

26 John Frame, "Proposals for a New North American Model," in *Missions and Theological Education in World Perspective*, ed. Harvie Conn and Samuel Rowen, (Farmington, MI: Associates of Urbana, 1984), 379-380.

27 Jeyaraj, *Christian Ministry*, 266.

(reflection on ministry practice) that is wholly or partly field-based. Students and teachers in this model become a learning community in which they share their lives, are involved in ministry and reflect on that ministry in the light of the Bible and theology.[28]

In each of these models, faculty are holistic examples of Christian life and ministry. To be able to do this effectively, teachers need to have a vital, personal relationship with God, communicate their subject matter with passion so that it connects with real life and the lives of their students, and share not only knowledge but their lives (cf. 1 Thess. 1:5-6).[29] They are involved in ministry alongside students, functioning as models and mentors, and following the pattern of Jesus' training of the twelve, and Paul's training of Timothy, Titus, Aquila and Priscilla.

None of these models is perfect, and all of them are costly in terms of the demands they put on faculty. They demand that lecturers put at least as strong a focus on the formation of students as on academic work and publishing. Faculty would need to spend significant time with students outside classes over meals, in their homes, and doing ministry together.

Recent Progress towards Better Integration

Two recent studies—from North America and Australia—provide encouraging signs that progress is being made in some theological institutions to address the need for integration. In the North American *Educating Clergy* study, completed in 2005, faculty, students and graduates were surveyed and interviewed, focus groups were conducted, and classes and other aspects of campus life were observed at ten North American seminaries. This detailed qualitative study addressed the question of how seminary educators enable their students to integrate knowledge and skill, moral integrity, and religious commitment. Researchers discovered that the seminary educators they observed and interviewed were intentionally enabling students to reflect dynamically on issues from life and ministry in the light of the Bible and theology in their classes and through the broader curriculum.[30]

One seminary in this study, for example, had designed a series of required

---

28 Banks, *Reenvisioning Theological Education*, 126, 142, 144, 146.
29 Banks, *Reenvisioning Theological Education*, 171-175.
30 Charles Foster, Lisa Dahill, Lawrence Golemon, and Barbara Tolentino, *Educating Clergy: Teaching Practices and Pastoral Imagination* (San Francisco, CA: Jossey-Bass, 2006), 329-354.

units in which students met in small groups to reflect on the issues they were experiencing in life and ministry and to reflect on these in the light of the class inputs. Another seminary had established formal procedures to track and link student experience across chapel, field, and classroom throughout their course.[31] The researchers also found that field education in several seminaries was well developed. Particularly encouraging developments in some seminaries included the following: ministry supervisors and sites were carefully selected, some faculty were involved in field work, learning contracts were drawn up in which progress was regularly reviewed, and reflection groups had been instituted in which students doing a practicum met weekly with a faculty member to reflect on their ministry experiences.[32]

A second sign that progress is being made in addressing the need for integration can be found in Darren Cronshaw's overview of the changes that two Australian theological colleges have made to their programs over the past decade.[33] The Australian College of Ministries (ACOM), a merger of two Churches of Christ theological colleges, decentralised its training in the early 2000s in order to allow students to remain in their ministry contexts and still access training. Training is now done through a combination of distance education, individual mentoring, small group face-to-face intensives that facilitate learning by discussion in each subject area, formation groups, and practical ministry reflection. The whole syllabus has been "redesigned around developing not just knowledge but spiritual formation and practical ministry skills."[34] The college's basic philosophy is that practice and thinking must continuously be connected by reflection on action. This approach supports contextually engaged thinking and practice and is clearly directed at facilitating integration.

Whitley College, the Baptist College of Victoria, provides another Australian example of progress towards integration. While the changes they have made are not as far-reaching in terms of educational format as those made by ACOM, Cronshaw reports that the college is "giving fresh priority to opportunities for action-reflection, helping students integrate faith and life, pursuing interdisciplinary studies, and engaging the life of local churches."[35] Interdisciplinary

---

31 Foster et al., *Educating Clergy*, 349.
32 Foster et al., *Educating Clergy*, 300-321.
33 Darren Cronshaw, "Reenvisioning Theological Education, Mission, and the Local Church," *Mission Studies* 28 (2011), 91-115.
34 Cronshaw, "Reenvisioning Theological Education," 93.
35 Cronshaw, "Reenvisioning Theological Education," 94.

subjects and team teaching are common, as are subjects that revolve around practical issues in ministry, such as the subjects "Exploring Ministry through Case Studies" and "Facing Crisis and Transition."[36] Subjects like these bring Scripture, cultural and contextual insights, and personal experience into conversation with one another.

The Medical Model of Training as a Foil for Reflection

Graduates of theological education serve as pastors, church elders, missionaries, chaplains, or as Christians in the secular workforce. In these roles they are expected to have qualities and skills that enable them to engage with the complex world they encounter. Theological education must develop in graduates these cognitive, practical and affective qualities and abilities in an integrated way so that they can serve as effective Christian leaders. This task is a daunting challenge and responsibility.

> We have entrusted to our seminaries and theological schools a daunting responsibility. They are expected to prepare wise, compassionate, theologically astute and pastorally proficient servants who can lead the Church and our societies through the crises of the twenty-first century.[37]

Theological schools have compared themselves for generations to medical schools, and many strive to produce "the divinity equivalent of the physician-scientist."[38] But unlike doctors, who see real patients and diseases during their medical training, many students of theological colleges face ministry situations after graduation that they had never experienced during their training. One Christian leader illustrates this from his own experience:

> The first memorial service I ever attended in my life was as the officiant. The first time I had ever seen someone die in the hospital was as their pastor .... The first couple in marriage crisis I ever encountered was as their supposed therapist .... I may have been able to write 20-page papers on heaven, prepare brilliant strategies

---

36   Cronshaw, "Reenvisioning Theological Education," 99.
37   Dearborn, "Preparing New Leaders," 7.
38   Farley, *Theologia*, 4.

for church growth and articulate a clear understanding of marriage
.... However, no one had ever guided me in how to live out these
truths.[39]

The education of both doctors and Christian leaders can be seen as an apprenticeship that has three dimensions: "a cognitive or intellectual apprenticeship, a practical apprenticeship of skill, and an apprenticeship of identity formation."[40] The current model of training medical practitioners in Australia is designed to address each of these dimensions—cognitive, practical, and attitudinal—and it provides clues that may help theological educators strengthen the relationship between the development of character qualities, ministry skills, and biblical and theological knowledge. Medical training serves as a particularly helpful foil for reflection because it shares with theological education the need to ensure that its graduates have mastered a large body of knowledge. In addition to providing knowledge, medical training is responsible for developing clinical skills and appropriate attitudes in trainee doctors.

Just as doctors are trained in the context of clinical practice, theological education that aims to help people to apply the eternal Word of God to their changing contexts must expose them to the "clinical practice" of ministry and guide them in reflecting on that practice in the light of Scripture with the help of theological, historical, and social scientific insights. Ministry and missional practice should be the contextual laboratory for theological reflection and the commitment of theological educators "to being on the cutting edge of responding to life, should be as profound as that of medical educators."[41]

Four Elements of the Medical Model that Support Integration

Just as a doctor's ability to apply his or her knowledge to illness is critical for people's life and health, the Christian minister's ability to apply knowledge to life is critical for people's wellbeing in this life and in eternity. The medical model of training suggests several directions that theological education should continue to pursue in order to make further progress in helping students

---

[39] Dearborn, "Preparing New Leaders," 7.
[40] Foster et al., Educating Clergy, 5.
[41] de Gruchy, "Theological Education,"43.

integrate knowledge with life and ministry. While each of these directions is being pursued to some extent by some theological training programs, there is room for further development, refining of methods, and broader implementation in more colleges.

Incorporating practical ministry experience into every semester
The best way to help students learn the skills and attitudes needed for ministry is for them to engage in ministry. Practical skills are best acquired by practice and reflection on that practice in the light of theory. Medical training requires that students spend specified amounts of time in in-context learning for the development of their professional skills. Beginning in the first weeks of their course, students spend days in hospital or other clinical settings. Periods of experiential training are incorporated throughout their degree and become longer placements as the degree progresses. Theological colleges could adopt a similar model by incorporating student exposure to various ministry contexts in the early semesters and gradually transitioning to longer placements by the time of the final semester. Doing this would also help students to feel connected to their chosen ministry during the time they are studying.

Practical experience can be incorporated into theological training in several ways. One of these is to include ministry experience days throughout the entire degree. These could be timetabled, for example, as one day a week or as one-week blocks embedded in each semester. Doing this would ensure a constant exposure to ministry practice and provide a foil for reflection during on-campus learning. It would also help teachers to keep content relevant as students bring questions and issues back to classes.

Developing learning communities with graduates
The medical model of education has developed a network of learning communities outside the medical schools that are still vitally connected with those schools. These communities are, to use Etienne Wenger's term, "communities of practice" in that they engage in a common practice and learn how to do it better as they interact regularly.[42] Medical communities of practice consist of groups of doctors who meet together regularly to learn from one another through presentations and discussions of medical cases, sharing research findings, and

---

42 Etienne Wenger-Trayner, "Communities of Practice: A Brief Introduction," accessed 25 November, 2013, http://wenger-trayner.com/theory/.

engaging in focused training courses. Medical learning communities are vitally connected to medical schools because every teacher in a medical training program is also a member of one or more of these communities. Many of these communities are also open to students. Doctors in these communities feel a duty of care for the learning of more junior doctors and this fosters in medical students the same attitude of wanting to pass on their learning to others.

Theological colleges and their graduates would benefit from the development of learning communities. Through meetings of lecturers and graduates, lecturers would sharpen their understanding of current ministry challenges faced by graduates as they listen to them share their experiences, and they in turn would share insights with those graduates to help them reflect on and enhance their ministry practice. Secondly, these communities could go some way to addressing the isolation that graduates of theological colleges often feel. Sharing the challenges they are facing in ministry and interacting with faculty is likely not only to be deeply encouraging to graduates but also to be a catalyst for continuing learning and growth as they reflect biblically, theologically, and missiologically on the things that are happening in their ministries.

Developing learning communities of graduates would also provide a pool of mentors and trainers for students and new graduates. One of the major challenges of helping students develop ministry skills is finding enough ministry trainers or supervisors who can invest sufficient time in students. If students are enabled to become trainers by embedding the desire to train others and the development of training skills into the curriculum, a large and self-perpetuating pool of trainers of future generations of students is likely to emerge.

Faculty intentionally serving as holistic role models
Medical students not only learn medical and scientific knowledge and how to perform procedures; they learn how to think and act like doctors. They learn how *doctors* approach the problems they face, how *doctors* talk to patients, and how *doctors* talk to colleagues. They learn doctors' attitudes towards work and the people they encounter, and what they consider acceptable, ethical and appropriate. Senior doctors become role models for medical students and students are actively enculturated into being doctors through a process of modelling and giving feedback.

In the same way that doctors learn how to be doctors, theological students learn how to be Christian leaders by observing the examples of Christian leaders whom they admire and by interacting with them. In order for people to grow in their relationship with Christ, they need to see what it means in the lives of others and receive feedback from others. In other words, they need to have good role models. In theological education, lecturers are students' primary role models and students will imitate faculty, whether or not this is planned. A well-designed theological education curriculum should intentionally consider which elements of Christian character are most important for faculty to model, and ensure that students have sufficient exposure to faculty to see these elements in their lives.

For faculty to be able to mentor students and be effective role models, they must be able and willing to spend significant time with students outside classes. The demands of teaching and writing can make faculty reticent to do this. The dean of a Bible college in North America recently tried to recruit faculty members to meet with a small group of students twice a week to mentor them over coffee or a meal, but discovered very few faculty members who were willing to do this.[43] To overcome this reticence so that the formative benefits of role modelling by faculty can become a reality, colleges and faculty will need to create, value, and pursue opportunities for faculty and students to interact informally.

Adopt a problem-based approach to learning
Of the four elements of medical training discussed here, the first three have been employed for centuries,[44] but the fourth is a relatively recent innovation. Over the past 35 years, the majority of medical schools in Australia have shifted from a fact-based approach to learning to a problem-based approach.[45] Courses based on problem-based learning (PBL) are constructed around clinical problems. Students are confronted with case studies of people with medical problems. They learn how to solve these problems, think critically, evaluate knowledge and relate to people compassionately as they work on these cases in small

---

43 Grant Lovejoy, "Epilogue," in *Beyond Literate Western Models: Contextualizing Theological Education in Oral Contexts*, ed. Samuel Chiang and Grant Lovejoy (Hong Kong: International Orality Network, 2013), 183-197.

44 Each of these elements of medical training is evident in medical training programs from at least the 17th century onwards. For details, see Charles O'Malley, *A History of Medical Education: An International Symposium Held February 5-9, 1968* (Berkeley, CA: University of California Press, 1970).

45 Australian Medical Council, *Assessment and Accreditation of Medical Schools: Standards and Procedures* (Canberra: Australian Medical Council, 2002); "Celebrating 30 Years: The Newcastle Medical Program 2008," University of Newcastle, accessed 12 October 2013, http://www.newcastle.edu.au/Resources/Divisions/Vice-Chancellor/Corporate%20Development%20and%20Community%20Partnerships/Alumni%20unit/Documents/Medicine-Alumni-2009.pdf.

groups facilitated by a teacher. Problems are first discussed in the small group and later researched individually by each student and finally discussed again in the group.[46] The process centres around "active, collaborative, contextual and facilitated learning of core content triggered by carefully designed problems for group study."[47] Interaction in these small groups also helps students learn how to work with and relate to fellow students.

Shifting to a problem-based approach has meant designing the curriculum around major body systems such as the cardiovascular system or the nervous system rather than around fragmented disciplines such as anatomy, physiology, and pathology.[48] This approach suggests possibilities for theological education: courses could be integrated around issues and problems faced in life and ministry rather than around traditional disciplines such as systematic theology or church history. As an example, students could be presented with the challenge of effectively communicating a Christian understanding of God to Muslims. Addressing this problem might involve students visiting a mosque, listening to a talk given by an imam, and engaging in conversations with Muslims. Students would also engage with relevant insights from theology, biblical studies, church history, cultural anthropology, world religions, and intercultural communication. Using this approach, multiple learning outcomes related to several disciplines in the current theological curriculum could be worked on and assessed simultaneously.

PBL has been effective in supporting the integration of medical knowledge with the development of skills and dispositions, but it is not a panacea. Studies that compare programs oriented around PBL with courses based on traditional, fact-based approach to acquiring medical knowledge have shown little overall difference in students' acquisition of medical knowledge, but some studies have found that the traditional approach does result in slightly higher levels of science-based medical knowledge.[49] PBL, though, tends to result in better ability to apply medical knowledge to real-life situations, is associated with better student motivation, satisfaction, engagement with learning, and leads to higher

---

46   Diana Dolman and David Gijbels, "Research on Problem-Based Learning: Future Challenges," *Medical Education* 47 (2013), 214-218.
47   Neville Chiavaroli, Stephen Trumble and Geoffrey McColl, "The Principles of Problem-Based Learning Are More Important than the Method," *Medical Journal of Australia* 199 (2013), 589.
48   Chiavaroli et al., "The Principles of Problem-Based Learning," 588.
49   Chiavaroli et al., "The Principles of Problem-Based Learning," 589; Gerald Choon-Huat Koh, Hoon Eng Khoo, Mee Lian Wong and David Koh, "The Effects of Problem-Based Learning during Medical School on Physician Competency: A Systematic Review," *Canadian Medical Association Journal* 178 (2008), 34-41.

levels of skill in teamwork, communication, and the capacity to deal with uncertainty.[50]

Medical training programs have faced two key challenges in implementing PBL that theological educators need to be aware of. First, no definitive guide to its practice has been produced. As a result, differing interpretations of how to implement it have developed.[51] Recent discussion of PBL in the medical education literature has navigated through these ambiguities by recommending that the essential philosophy of PBL should be adopted rather than a prescriptive set of teaching practices.[52] Theological education programs that are considering adopting PBL would do well to apply its philosophy in a flexible way that is sensitive to their contexts.

A second challenge faced by medical schools in implementing PBL has been the adequate preparation and training of a sufficient number of tutors for the small group facilitation of learning that is central to this approach. In comparison to traditional lecture-based approaches, PBL requires more manpower and hours of face-to-face contact with students.[53] Theological colleges considering this approach need to take this into account.

There are encouraging precedents for the use of an approach similar to that of PBL in theological education. Much of the theologising done by the apostle Paul was developed in response to situations in the early church. Bruce Kaye points out that many of the great theological works of Christian history were developed in response to issues in society. He points out that Augustine's *City of God* is essentially an applied theological analysis of the Roman Empire, that Anselm's work on the incarnation is a missionary tract, that Richard Hooker's work on ecclesiastical polity is an articulation of how Christian life could be lived in the framework of Elizabethan politics, and that Calvin's *Institutes* are arranged not around traditional theological topics but around how to live the Christian life.[54]

---

50 Dolman and Gijbels, "Research on Problem-Based Learning," 214; Filip Dochy, Mien Segers, Piet Van den Bossche and David Gijbels, "Effects of Problem-Based Learning: A Meta-Analysis," *Learning and Instruction* 13 (2003), 533-568; Geoffrey Norman and Henk Schmidt, "Effectiveness of Problem-Based Learning Curricula: Theory, Practice and Paper Darts," *Medical Education* 34 (2000), 721-728; Chiavaroli *et al.*, "The Principles of Problem-Based Learning," 589.
51 David Taylor and Barbara Miflin, "Problem-Based Learning: Where Are We Now?" *Medical Teacher* 30 (2008), 742-63.
52 Chiavaroli *et al.*, "The Principles of Problem-Based Learning," 589.
53 Koh *et al.*, "The Effects of Problem-Based Learning," 34.
54 Bruce Kaye, "Theology for Life in a Plural Society," in *The Furtherance of Religious Beliefs: Essays on the History of Theological Education in Australia*, ed. Geoff Treloar (Sydney: Centre for the Study of Australian Christianity, 1997), 203-215.

Harvie Conn echoes this reality in his observation that "theology has always been done in serious life-situations and not as a mere intellectual enquiry."[55]

Conclusion

The need for better integration of knowing, being and doing in theological education has been discussed for decades and helpful proposals about how to do this have been put forward. Encouraging signs of progress in this direction are evident in some theological colleges, but there is still more work to be done. One way that theological education could work towards strengthening integration is to consider four directions suggested by the medical model of training. This approach could be trialled in an existing college and its impact on learning and ministry effectiveness evaluated. Moving to a problem-based approach to learning and combining this with ongoing ministry experience, interaction with communities of church and mission leaders, and intentional holistic modelling by faculty could have the effect of re-invigorating theological education and forming a new generation of teachers and students for more effective missional engagement with the world.

---

55 Harvie Conn, "Theological Education and the Search for Excellence," *Westminster Theological Journal* 41(1979), 326.

9 | RESPONDING TO COMPLEXITY

MOVING FROM COMPETENCE TO CAPABILITY

STEPHEN SMITH AND LEON O'FLYNN

Abstract

This essay seeks to add insights to the discussion on transformational learning in theological education by acknowledging the difference between *learning for competence* (what individuals know or do in terms of skills and knowledge) and *learning for capability* (individuals adapting to change and generating new, useful knowledge for improved practice). *Learning for capability* is discussed through a complexity framework where developing effective spiritual leaders within a rapidly changing world may require educational institutions to shift from a teaching culture that is focused on instruction to a learning culture that is focused on inquiry.

Background

This essay seeks to add knowledge to the discussion on transformational learning in theological education through insights gained during research in the fields of hermeneutics, knowledge management and health science. The crossover and integration of disciplines has provided a creative opportunity for mutual learning. Both authors have conducted extensive research within the framework of Churches of Christ in Australia, New Zealand, the Pacific and the United States.[1] This essay shares their current best thinking as they continue to explore an emerging pedagogical practice within the Australian College of Ministries—an experiment for mutual learning and critical review.

Previous Research

Smith's previous research provided "proof of concept" for processes conducive to transformational learning in health promotion practice using the framework of complex living systems.[2] Complexity theory was found to be useful in improving health services in aged care,[3] healthcare management,[4] medical education,[5] mental health,[6] health promotion,[7] nurse management[8] and a general application to managing change in healthcare organisations.[9] This knowledge was applied to establish processes for transformational learning in the development of healthy and effective spiritual leaders within Churches of Christ in New South Wales.[10]

O'Flynn's previous research explored the psyche of Churches of Christ through their historical approach to understanding and interpreting Scripture.[11] He analysed what had been a predominantly Baconian inductive methodology

---

1. Leon O'Flynn, "Hermeneutics and the Churches of Christ: A Possible Direction" (DMin thesis, Australian College of Theology, 2012); Stephen Smith, "Connecting People: Improving Knowledge Sharing and Collaboration" (DMgt thesis, Southern Cross University, 2002); Stephen Smith, "Savouring Life: The Leader's Journey to Health and Effectiveness" (PhD thesis, University of Sydney, 2012a).
2. Smith, "Savouring Life: The Leader's Journey to Health and Effectiveness."
3. Edward Henriksen and Ulv Rosenqvist, "Contradictions in Elderly Care: A Descriptive Study of Politicians' and Managers' Understanding of Elderly Care," *Health and Social Care in the Community* 11 (2003), 27–35.
4. Reuben R. McDaniel and Dean J. Driebe, "Complexity Science and Health Care Management," in *Advances in Health Care Management*, ed. John D. Blair, Myron D. Fottler and Grant T. Savage (Sydney, NSW: Elsevier, 2001), 11–36.
5. Sarah W. Fraser and Trisha Greenhalgh, "Coping with Complexity: Educating for Capability," *British Medical Journal* 323 (2001), 799–803.
6. Harry Minas, "Leadership for Change in Complex Systems," *Australasian Psychiatry* 13 (2005), 33–39.
7. Tim Wilson and Tim Holt, "Complexity and Clinical Care," *British Medical Journal* 323 (2001), 685–688.
8. Thomas R. Clancy and Connie-White Delaney, "Complex Nursing Systems," *Journal of Nursing Management* 13 (2005), 192–201.
9. Sally Redfern, "Achieving Change in Health Care Practice," *Journal of Evaluation in Clinical Practice* 9 (2003), 225–238.
10. Stephen Smith, "Savouring Life: The Leader's Journey to Health, Resilience and Effectiveness," in *Spirituality and Human Flourishing*, ed. M. Dowson, M. Miner and S. Devenish (Charlotte, NC: Information Age Press, 2012b).
11. O'Flynn, "Hermeneutics.".

that reduced Scripture to a scientific, lifeless legal document.[12] To move forward he proposed a hermeneutic model that provided a more suitable framework for transformational change, where the study of Scripture in context results in living differently and wholeheartedly belonging to Jesus.[13]

This essay is framed in response to the growing need within the Churches of Christ movement for the development of effective spiritual leaders.[14] After a brief discussion on complexity, it will detail leverage points for transformative learning being tested within the context of the Australian College of Ministries (ACOM). A key concept is that a hermeneutical lens of transformative learning is the process through which students' way of knowing (epistemology) enriches the way they understand the world (ontology) to the extent that it results in holistic change. As such, transformation occurs through *sensemaking*, which leads to new whole-of-life behaviours.

Question to be Considered

The core research question is: "How can we prepare students to be effective ministry practitioners in a world that is rapidly changing?" Of vital importance in this inquiry is an understanding that the ACOM is developing leaders to live in, cope with and thrive in contexts that are *uncertain* (not enough credible information), *complex* (more information than can be processed), *ambiguous* (lack of a value/conceptual framework) and *incongruous* (competing value/conceptual frameworks). The aim is to improve pedagogical practice within the ACOM in ways that can be measured in the quality of transformational student outcomes.

In the education of medical practitioners, the use of simple cause-and-effect modelling was no longer an accurate predictor of outcomes due to reliance on a system to be "constant, predictable and independent."[15] This was consistent with a changing understanding of human and organisational systems that, for

---

12 Leon O'Flynn, "Jude and the Ministry of Churches of Christ" (MTh thesis, Tyndale-Carey Graduate School, 2008); M. Eugene Boring, *Disciples and the Bible* (St Louis, MO: Chalice Press, 1997).
13 O'Flynn, "Hermeneutics."
14 Andrew P. Ball, "Stimulating Emotional, Spiritual, and Systemic Leadership Awareness: An Urgent Priority for Australian Church Leaders" (DMin thesis, Fuller Theological Seminary, 2012).
15 Paul E. Plsek and Trisha Greenhalgh, "The Challenge of Complexity in Health Care," *British Medical Journal* 323 (2001), 625–628, at 625.

the most part, was built on Newtonian assumptions of a "clockwork universe."[16] Newton described the universe as a great clock-like machine, and his thinking had an enormous effect on the emerging worldview of the time. When applied to organisations, the metaphor compares organisational charts to the blueprints of a great machine, where managers produce outcomes by manipulating people as moving parts to be ordered, controlled and replaced, only to be benchmarked when worn and re-engineered when broken.

The deliberate change from a focus on competence to capability requires the development of a new hermeneutical lens.[17] Without methodological deep change, a new lens is not adopted; rather, the current lens is modified—often only temporarily. This hermeneutical lens must also fit the cultural DNA of the organisation ensuring that the organisation is not subject to "whims" or the latest fad.

Medical practitioners and educators are now seeing the benefits of approaching the human body as such a system.[18] Meanwhile, in organisational theory, the journey to appreciating complex living systems involves a new way of thinking[19]—that is, standing back from a detailed analysis of system "parts" and taking "a crude look at the whole,"[20] from analysis to synthesis. Complex systems are non-linear,[21] with cause and effect often distant in time and space.[22] While a detailed explanation of complexity theory is outside the scope of this essay, Smith described complexity as a domain of knowledge that:

> contains many unknown unknowns . . . (where) cause and effect are discoverable in retrospect but not knowable in advance, and do not necessarily repeat. A metaphor for this is the rainforest, where signifi-

---

16 Edwin E. Olson and Glenda H. Eoyang, *Facilitating Organisational Change: Lessons from Complexity Science* (San Francisco, CA: Jossey-Bass, 2001); Margaret J. Wheatley, *Leadership and the New Science: Discovering Order in a Chaotic World* (San Francisco, CA: Berrett-Koehler, 1999).
17 Perry W.H. Shaw, "Towards a Multidimensional Approach to Theological Education," *International Congregational Journal* 6.1 (2006), 53–63.
18 Fraser and Greenhalgh, "Coping with Complexity;" Wilson and Holt, "Complexity and Clinical Care."
19 Miguel Pina e Cunha, João Vieira da Cunha and Ken Kamoche, "The Age of Emergence: Toward a New Organisational Mindset," *S.A.M. Advanced Management Journal* 66 (2001), 25–29.
20 Murray Gell-Mann, *The Quark and the Jaguar: Adventures in the Simple and the Complex* (New York, NY: Freeman, 1994).
21 Kevin J. Dooley, "A Complex Adaptive Systems Model of Organisation Change," *Nonlinear Dynamics, Psychology, and Life Sciences* 1 (1997), 69–97.
22 Robert J. Brodnick and Larry J. Krafft, "'Chaos and Complexity Theory: Implications for Research and Planning" (paper presented at the 37th Annual Forum of the Association for Institutional Research, Orlando, FL, 1997).

cant variables are knowable, but only in hindsight. The possible ramifications of any change is unpredictable, as there are living systems within living systems, within living systems—all interconnected and influencing each other. Effective leadership in this domain is to experiment. Collaboration and co-creation work well in this domain of emergent practice. Small, leveraging changes may affect the system in unpredictable ways in a web of responding actions and interactions. Experiment, assess, nudge, do more, do less and experiment again. The most effective learning culture is one of inquiry.[23]

Smith found the Churches of Christ to be a complex system—a diverse, decentralised movement of autonomous but interdependent communities.[24] Like a human body, the health of the movement and the leaders within it are woven together with ever-shifting complexity—each affecting, and being affected by, the other. When applied to theological education, an understanding of complexity is helpful in the preparation of leaders for a world that is quickly changing. In essence, this means that educational institutions are preparing leaders for a world of uncertainties and unknowns. Equipping leaders who can effectively navigate this changing environment will require educational institutions to do more than simply transfer programmed knowledge from experts to students.

The natural tendency of an organisation that has made the change from competence to capability is to drift back towards the familiar competence space. The development and implementation of a new hermeneutical lens is not the end of the process. O'Flynn noted that the key to the successful change of a hermeneutical lens is the continual refreshing of the organisation's vision.[25]

Smith noted the distinction between competence and capability in preparing effective practitioners in areas of clinical practice such as medicine and nursing, as well as in the training of management professionals.[26] The growing understanding of complexity in medicine has pushed the profession from *learning for competence* (what individuals know or do in terms of skills and knowledge)

---

[23] Smith, "Savouring Life: The Leader's Journey to Health and Effectiveness," 147.
[24] Smith, "Savouring Life: The Leader's Journey to Health and Effectiveness."
[25] O'Flynn, "Hermeneutics."
[26] Smith, "Savouring Life: The Leader's Journey to Health and Effectiveness." See also Fraser and Greenhalgh, "Coping with Complexity;" Anne Gardner, Stewart Hase, Glenn Gardner, Jenny Carryer and Sandra Dunn, "From Competence to Capability: A Study of Nurse Practitioners in Clinical Practice," *Journal of Clinical Nursing* 17 (2008), 250–258; Robert Brown and Sandra McCartney, "A Capability Approach to the MBA," *Capability* 1 (1994), 33–45.

into *learning for capability* (individuals adapting to change and generating new, useful knowledge for improved practice). Essentially, capability is a holistic attribute; it is more than competence. While the two ideas may at times be used interchangeably, they are used hierarchically here. *Competence* is about being trained to have the skills to do a job. *Capability* is about knowing what jobs to do. Capable people know how to learn and can apply competencies to new and unfamiliar situations. Capability is the inner resources that people use to learn and adapt to the challenges they face.

Traditionally, ministry practitioners have been equipped through education and training that focused on enhancing competence (skills, knowledge and attitudes). However, in a world where complexity is now normative, equipping leaders for competency does not appear to be enough to generate new knowledge and the continuous improvement of professional practice. Previous approaches to learning prepared students for known roles in known professions within known sets of parameters. In contrast, leaders are now being equipped to lead in a constantly changing, uncertain environment.

Smith found that competency may be enough in simple environments where knowledge is predictable and knowable in advance.[27] In this context, the learner follows the well-worn path of those who have gone before. Experts know the way forward and students can benchmark their progress like points on a map to reach the desired, and clearly known, destination. As long as the leader knows how to read and interpret the map, the arrival at a predetermined destination is almost inevitable because the risk of variables is diminished by the past practice of those who have gone before. The competent leader flourishes in a learning culture that values instruction.

In contrast, capable leaders thrive as explorers. Navigating in uncharted waters and making their own maps—where knowledge is unpredictable and only knowable in retrospect—requires capable leaders who navigate the unknown with an internal compass, hoping for a destination that is valued but is yet only imagined. Capable leaders flourish in a learning culture that values inquiry. This is shown in Figure 1.

---

27 Smith, "Savouring Life: The Leader's Journey to Health and Effectiveness."

Figure 1: Moving from competence to capability.

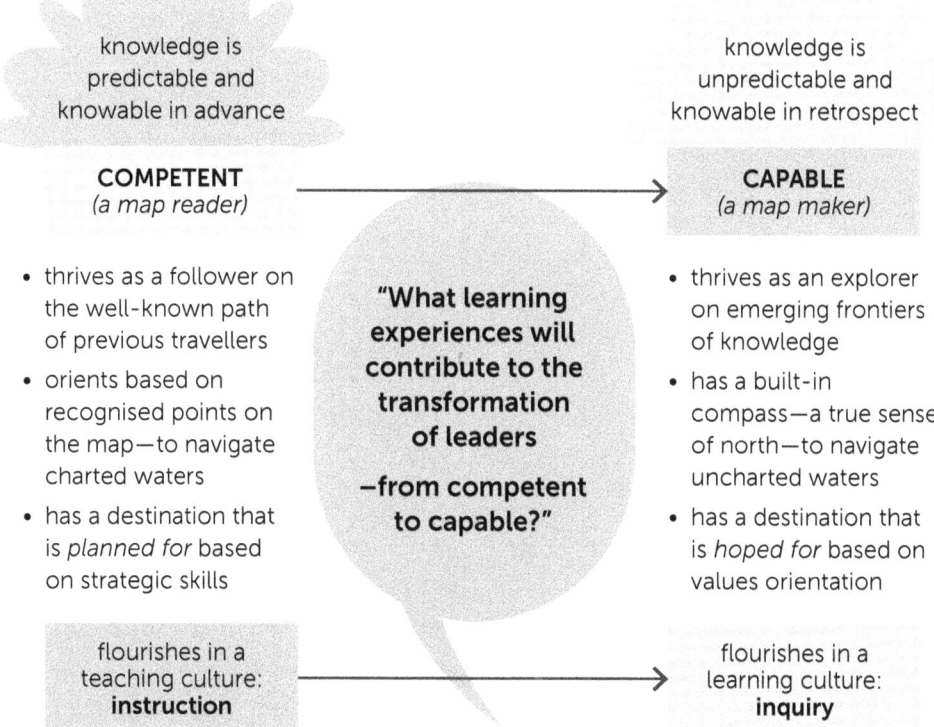

Capable leaders intuitively generate their own personal theories of practice. In sensemaking, they observe what they do and reflect on it. They will gather data, challenge assumptions, create new theories and generate evidence to support their claims, which will be tested for validity through the critical analysis of others. In short, they make sense of what they are doing through inquiry for both personal and organisational transformation. This is not merely about acquiring knowledge; it is a process in which we make and remake ourselves as whole people.

What does this look like in practice? In the literature, transformative learning requires a personal journey that includes: (1) the introduction of challenging ideas—a "disorienting dilemma;"[28] (2) testing taken-for-granted assumptions; (3) self-examination; (4) awareness of a gap in knowledge and/or behaviour; and

---

28 Jack Mezirow and Edward W. Taylor, *Learning as Transformation* (San Francisco, CA: Jossey-Bass, 2009), 19.

(5) an integration of new knowledge (cognitive, behavioural and affective) into their whole-of-life. For each learner, this process is emergent and personal. In an attempt to nudge systemic change, the authors asked: "What learning experiences may contribute to the transformation of leaders (from competent to capable)?"[29] Through research and the review of the literature relating to complexity theory,[30] we identified some learning approaches we were testing, in our organisational context, to explore deep transformational learning in the student inquirer:

Orienting inquiry around the question, "How do I improve my practice?"
This emphasis grounds theoretical knowledge into *learning at work* and *learning for work*. It links theory and practice, as per Lewin's well-known adage, "There is nothing so practical as a good theory."[31]

Helping the learner to remain curious.
Staying poised as the learner rather than the expert creates a learning culture conducive to adaptive thinking and behaviour.[32]

Asking provocative questions.
Asking questions that challenge basic thinking assumptions and patterns of behaviour.[33] Seek the big picture and align small goals with the most significant value priorities. Question the big, undiscussable sacred cows (what Argyris calls double-loop learning),[34] such as "Should this organisation even exist?"

---

29 Smith, "Savouring Life: The Leader's Journey to Health and Effectiveness," 227.
30 Robert Axelrod and Michael D. Cohen, *Harnessing Complexity: Organisational Implications of a Scientific Frontier* (New York, NY: Free Press, 2000); C.K. Prahalad and Venkat Ramaswamy, *The Future of Competition: Co-creating Unique Value for Customers* (Boston, MA: Harvard Business School Press, 2004); Otto Scharmer, *Theory U: Leading from the Future as it Emerges* (San Francisco, CA: Berrett-Koehler, 2009); Peter Senge, *The Fifth Discipline* (New York, NY: Doubleday, 1990); Peter Senge, Art Kleiner, Charlotte Roberts, Richard Ross and Bryan Smith, *The Fifth Discipline Fieldbook: Strategies and Tools for Building a Learning Organization* (London: Nicholas Brealey, 2004); David J. Snowden and Mary E. Boone, "A Leader's Framework for Decision Making," *Harvard Business Review* 85 (2007), 61–68; Ralph D. Stacey, *Strategic Management and Organizational Dynamics: The Challenge of Complexity* (London: Pearson, 2003); Yoland Wadsworth, *Building in Research and Evaluation: Human Inquiry for Living Systems* (Hawthorn, Vic: Action Research Press, 2010); Wilson and Holt, "Complexity and Clinical Care;" Brenda Zimmerman, Curt Lindberg and Paul E. Plsek, *Edgeware: Insights from Complexity Science for Health Care Leaders* (Irving, TX: VHA Press, 1998).
31 Kurt Lewin, *Field Theory in Social Science: Selected Theoretical Papers*, ed. Dorwin Cartwright (New York, NY: Harper and Row, 1951), 169.
32 Scharmer, *Theory U*.
33 Wadsworth, *Building in Research and Evaluation*.
34 Chris Argyris, *Overcoming Organisational Defences* (London: Prentice Hall, 1990).

4. Encouraging learners to incorporate different ways of knowing into their inquiries.

(a) *Experiential knowing*—personal perceptions, observations, feelings and intuitions that may be tacit and pre-verbal and embedded in the relationships within the situation.

(b) *Presentational knowing*—participants share their experience (the tacit) with others for mutual learning through exhibits in the form of words, images or multimedia in order to generate sharing and mutual discovery.

(c) *Propositional knowing*—sensemaking is developed into statements, theories and concepts. Challenging these models through rigorous review is vital in order to add depth to the learning. The propositions are carried by exhibits (handouts, guides, reflections and articles) to articulate the learning propositions.

(d) *Practical knowing*—being aware of ways to improve what is being done. It is about competency and skill, which is grounded in know-how.[35]

5. Using intuition.

Recognise and record decision-making processes based on deeper experiences and spiritual insights rather than merely gathering measurable data.[36] Through critical reflection and peer feedback, this recognises and tests the role and process of being a spiritual leader rather than merely an operational manager.

6. Gathering stories for mutual sensemaking.

Personal narratives capture the tacit experiences of individuals and group processes; as such, they are powerful zdata-gathering tools.[37] Sharing stories facilitates group sensemaking—especially the responses to stories. These responses may take the form of a reply (a storyteller's reaction to other stories), an echo (a personal story reflecting the theme in another story), a re-creation (a remoulded version of another person's story) and/or a reflection (ponderings on deeper meanings or applications). Gathering, recording and sharing stories can significantly contribute to the co-creation of new knowledge for improved practice. Lave and Wenger described stories as "packages of situated knowledge"

---

[35] John Heron, *Co-operative Inquiry: Research into the Human Condition* (London: Sage, 1996), 238–239; John Heron and Peter Reason, "Extending Epistemology within a Co-operative Inquiry," in *The Sage Handbook of Action Research: Participative Inquiry and Practice (Second Edition)*, ed. Peter Reason and Hilary Bradbury (London: Sage, 2008), 199–210, 367.

[36] Scharmer, *Theory U*.

[37] Stacey, *Strategic Management*.

and cited examples of the power of stories in Alcoholics Anonymous, saying that "talk is a central medium of transformation."[38] The role of stories in sensemaking has been given considerable attention by researchers such as Weick, who observed that "telling stories about remarkable experiences is one of the ways in which people try to make the unexpected expectable, hence manageable."[39]

7. Creating metaphors to learn and adapt.

Common language, stories and images help to create shared meanings. By clothing their intuition in metaphors, students are able to make sense of the reality they are experiencing and thus build collaborative behaviours to enhance deep change.[40]

8. Developing heuristic models.

Gathering ideas in the form of "rule of thumb" diagrams (developed individually or in groups using whiteboards or collaborative technologies) serves to ignite further sensemaking discussions and to develop deeper group understanding.[41] Theoretical models can become a toolkit for individual and organisational transformation, as ideas are used, discussed and tested repeatedly by practitioners.[42]

9. Initiating co-operative inquiry.

Group learning is a way that can bring about organisational transformation. Change management efforts are more effective when participants co-create change.[43] Co-operative inquiry is not research about people; rather, it is research with people. All participants collaborate on a research challenge to engage in the design, management, experience, observation and analysis of the project as co-researchers.

10. Experimenting to nudge change.

Testing, trying and piloting are all ways to explore what might work and what might not. Small, well-focused actions can produce a ripple effect (leverage)

---

38 Jean Lave and Etienne Wenger, *Situated Learning: Legitimate Peripheral Participation* (Cambridge: Cambridge University Press, 1991), 108, 85.
39 Karl E. Weick, *Sensemaking in Organizations* (London: Sage, 1995), 127.
40 Axelrod and Cohen, *Harnessing Complexity*.
41 Wadsworth, *Building in Research and Evaluation*.
42 Smith, "Savouring Life: The Leader's Journey to Health and Effectiveness."
43 Prahalad and Ramaswamy, *Future of Competition*.

that may produce enduring improvements. If it works, do more of it; if it does not work, stop doing it, as *failure* is merely *data* for learning.[44]

11. Learning while taking action.

Action learning is a process of collaborative transformation in which members of a social system transform themselves and their organisationthrough iterative cycles of planning, acting, observing and reflecting.[45] Each cycle of *inquiry-driven action* leads to enriched human encounters that shape conceptual models that can inform improved professional practice.[46]

12. Emphasising holistic learning.

This is more about *being* than *doing*. The whole person is engaged—head (cognitive, thinking), heart (emotional, feeling) and hands (physical, doing)—and he or she learns to pursue wholeheartedly his or her vocational interests and to be fully absorbed in the learning journey.

13. Researching the action.

Action research is a disciplined inquiry process designed to improve professional practice conducted by and for those undertaking the action.[47] The approach researches reality in order to transform it[48] and equally transforms reality in order to research it.[49] Action research is an effective approach to transformational learning because it requires three areas of development from the researcher when conducting the inquiry: (1) theoretical development (making a contribution to the body of knowledge); (2) organisational development (improving professional practice at work); and (3) personal development (being personally transformed in the process).[50]

---

44   Snowden and Boone, "Leader's Framework;" Wilson and Holt, "Complexity and Clinical Care."
45   Ron Passfield, "Action Learning for Professional and Organisational Development: An Action Research Case Study in Higher Education." (PhD thesis, Griffith University, 1996).
46   Heron and Reason, "Extending Epistemology."
47   Danny Burns, *Systemic Action Research* (Bristol: Policy Press, 2010); S. Goff, J. Gregg and K. May, "Participatory Action Research: Change Management in the 'No Go' Zone," in *Effective Change Management using Action Learning and Action Research*, ed. S. Sankaran, B. Dick, Ron Passfield and P. Swepson (Lismore, NSW: Southern Cross University Press, 2001), 83–94.
48   Orlando Fals Borda, "Investigating Reality in Order to Transform it: The Colombian Experience," *Dialectical Anthropology* 4 (1979), 33–55.
49   Stephen Kemmis, "Critical Theory and Participatory Action Research," in *The Sage Handbook of Action Research: Participative Inquiry and Practice*, ed. Peter Reason and Hilary Bradbury (London: Sage, 2008), 199–210.
50   Jean McNiff and Jack Whitehead, *You and Your Action Research Project*. 3rd ed. (London: Routledge, 2010); Smith, "Savouring Life: The Leader's Journey to Health and Effectiveness."

14. Inquiring appreciatively.

Appreciative Inquiry is a method of generating theory and improving practice by asking positive questions, seeking and sharing success stories, collaborating to identify exemplars of positive behaviours and values,[51] and seeking to orient around "telling it like it might become" rather than "telling it like it is."[52]

15. Building a lifelong pattern of reflective practice.

This is a way of recording, sharing and verifying real-world data, particularly as reflection-on-action, which focuses on the past,[53] reflection-in-action, which focuses on the present,[54] and reflection-for-action, which focuses on the future.[55]

16. Creating immersion experiences.

Mezirow's early work on transformative learning highlighted the importance of a "disorienting dilemma" as a catalyst for a student beginning a transformational journey.[56] Immersion experiences such as mission trips, study tours, field placements, walking where Jesus walked, sleeping with the homeless, working with the disadvantaged, volunteering as a ministry intern and starting a new ministry are a few of the possibilities for holistic learning in which the student's entrenched worldview may be radically challenged.

A high standard of academic rigour is required in this kind of holistic learning.[57] It is a vehicle through which the tacit must be made explicit and students are expected to generate their own contributions to theory to improve their practice. Smith suggested a quality framework (figure 2) for testing rigour in this kind of inquiry,[58] where the student is required to produce evidence of:

- generating new knowledge (knowledge quality)

---

51 David Cooperrider and Suresh Srivastva, "Appreciative Inquiry into Organizational Life," in *Research in Organizational Change and Development*, ed. William A. Pasmore and Richard W. Woodman. Vol. 1 (Greenwich: JAI Press, 1987), 129–169.
52 Kenneth J. Gergen and Tojo J. Thatchenkery, "Organisation Science as Social Construction: Postmodern Potentials," *Journal of Applied Behavioural Science* 32 (1996), 356–377, at 370.
53 Donald A. Schon, *The Reflective Practitioner: How Professionals Think in Action* (Cambridge: Basic Books, 1983).
54 Schon, *Reflective Practitioner*.
55 Joellen P. Killion and Guy R. Todnem, "A Process of Personal Theory Building," *Educational Leadership* 48 (1991), 14–17.
56 Jack Mezirow, "Perspective Transformation," *Adult Education* 28 (1978), 100–110.
57 Yvonna S. Lincoln and Egon G. Guba, *Fourth Generation Evaluation* (London: Sage, 1989).
58 Smith, "Savouring Life: The Leader's Journey to Health and Effectiveness."

- achieving action-oriented outcomes (outcome quality)
- transforming researcher, participants and organisation (change quality)
- testing of research value and applicability by participants in organisation (practice quality)
- co-creating and sharing knowledge owned by stakeholders (democratic quality)
- confirming rigorous and appropriate research method (process quality).

Conclusion

In summary, the ACOM's approach to learning utilises online learning supplemented by face-to-face experiences and on-the-job inquiry. These practical tools are the natural output of a hermeneutical lens that seeks capability. Each tool has three core elements, which are built into every unit of learning:

- *hot-house experiences*, which create engaging temporary learning communities (workshops, peer gatherings or residentials), where the basic assumptions of life are challenged through disorienting experiences conducive to discovering new knowledge
- *action learning experiences*, with challenging on-the-job projects used to ground the learning experience in everyday practice and to integrate the discovery and testing of theoretical knowledge
- ties for deep personal formation form the foundation for ethical, well-grounded and self-differentiated leader development.

For the authors, this continues to be a journey of personal and organisational discovery. This essay reveals their reflections as they test and explore ways to shift the ACOM from a teaching culture focused on instruction to a learning culture focused on inquiry. It is a hopeful experiment in showing students how to learn for themselves by continuously inquiring, adapting and inquiring again in order to thrive in an increasingly complex world.

Figure 2: Learning Experiences

Testing Learning Experience that May Contribute to Transformational Learning:

Searching for New Knowledge:
1. Orienting inquiry around the question, 'How do I improve my practice?'
2. Helping to learning to remain curious
3. Asking provactive queations
4. Encounraging learners to incorporate different ways of knowing into their inquires
5. Using intuition
6. Gathering stories for mutual sensemaking
7. Creating metaphors to learn and adapt
8. Developing heuristic models
9. Initiating co-operative inquiry
10. Experimenting to nudge change
11. Learning while taking action
12. Emphasising holistic learning
13. Researching the action
14. Inquiring appreciatively
15. Building a lifelong pattern of relective practice
16. Creating immersion experiences

Evidence of Rigour (Quality Framework):
- generating new knowledge *(knowledge qualty)*
- achieving action-oriented outcomes *(outcome quality)*
- transforming researcher, participants and organisation *(change quality)*
- testing of researc value and applicability by participants in organisation *(practice quality)*
- co-creating and sharing knowledge owned by stakeholders *(democratic quality)*
- confirming rigorous and appropriate research method *(process quality)*

SECTION FIVE

DRIVING THE TECHNOLOGY

10 | MAKING THE IMPLICIT EXPLICIT

EXPLORING THE ROLE OF LEARNING DESIGN IN IMPROVING FORMATIONAL LEARNING OUTCOMES

DIANE HOCKRIDGE

Abstract

This essay explores how insights from research and practice in the field of Learning Design might offer a way forward for the particular theological educational challenge of how to design learning to encourage "formation" of learners. It provides an overview of the challenges of designing for formational learning and a summary of relevant research in this area to date. It suggests that the field of Learning Design, through its stated aim of distilling and sharing effective teaching methods, may offer a means to: (i) conceptualise the practice of designing learning; (ii) approach specific educational issues (such as formational learning); (iii) develop templates, patterns, visualisations or generic learning designs which can be used across many different disciplines; and (iv) enhance educators' pedagogical understanding and thus improve educators' design practice. In particular, the essay offers a preliminary consideration of whether the *Learning Design Conceptual Map*[1] may provide a means of developing principles, practices and learning designs for formational learning.

⋯

---

[1] J. Dalziel *et al.*, "The Larnaca Declaration on Learning Design – 2013," (2013), Available at www.larnacadeclaration.org.

Introduction

The learning and teaching environments of today present educators with an ever-broadening range of pedagogical challenges and choices. As traditional classrooms incorporate the use of new technologies and greater proportions of courses are offered in blended or distance mode, there has been a renewed focus on the need to *design* learning and teaching experiences. Recent research in the Australian theological education sector, which provides higher education degrees preparing people for leadership in Christian churches and organisations, specifically noted the need for careful design of learning for the sector.[2]

A particular challenge for theological educators is designing learning experiences that are effective for "formation". Formation refers to desired outcomes relating to personal spiritual growth, character development, and capacity for lifelong Christian ministry, and tends to be considered an integral part of theological education. Despite its integral place in theological education, theological institutions and educators often struggle to deal adequately with formation in formal higher education programs, particularly in non-campus-based learning.[3] Most theological education programs to date have been primarily campus-based and it appears to be commonly assumed by theological educators that formation happens around the edges of formal learning, or as a result of students' participation in a campus community. Ball's research noted that approaches to formation in Australian theological institutions tend to be somewhat *ad hoc* and focused on extracurricular activities.[4] As theological education increasingly adopts more flexible teaching approaches, often not based on campus, and as the proportion of students studying part time and by distance continues to increase, theological educators need to reconsider their approaches to encouraging student formation.

There has in recent years been extensive discussion in the theological education literature and community around the suitability and possibility of encouraging student formation through distance and online learning.[5] Alongside this discussion some theological educators are exploring how they might use

---

2   Les Ball, *Transforming Theology: Student Experience and Transformative Learning in Undergraduate Theological Education* (Preston Vic: Mosaic Press, 2012).
3   Ball, *Transforming Theology*.
    Diane Hockridge, "Challenges for Educators Using Distance and Online Education to Prepare Students for Relational Professions," *Distance Education* 34, no. 2 (2013).
4   Ball, *Transforming Theology*, 19.
5   Hockridge, "Challenges for Educators Using Distance and Online Education."

new pedagogies and technologies to prepare students effectively for the demands of their future profession. This essay provides an overview of the challenges of designing for formational learning and a summary of relevant research in this area to date. It suggests that, if formation is considered to be an integral part of theological education, then theological educators need to take a more strategic, intentional and explicit approach to designing learning principles and practices that contribute to the formation of students across multiple modes of study including non-campus based learning contexts.

The field of *Learning Design*[6] may provide a way to conceptualise and approach the challenges facing theological educators who wish to design courses and learning experiences that improve formational outcomes. Researchers and practitioners in the field of Learning Design are attempting to develop ways to make Learning Design more explicit by representing learning designs visually which enables sharing and re-use of good learning practice. As Conole & Wills point out, most educators' design practice tends to be implicit and practice-based.[7] In the case of theological educators, while a variety of campus-based teaching and learning approaches and practices that contribute to formation have been developed, much of this remains implicit, within the heads of individual educators, or perhaps shared within individual institutions. This essay considers how to draw out the implicit knowledge and experience of theological educators, make it more explicit, and build on it to develop meaningful and formational learning outcomes for students, in not only campus-based but also non-face-to-face learning contexts. It suggests that the field of Learning Design, through its stated aim of distilling and sharing effective teaching methods, may offer a means to: (i) conceptualise the practice of designing learning; (ii) approach specific educational issues (such as formational learning); (iii) develop templates, patterns, visualisations or generic learning designs which can be used across many different disciplines; and (iv) enhance educators' pedagogical understanding and thus improve educator's design practice. In particular, the essay offers a preliminary consideration of whether the *Learning Design Conceptual Map* may provide a means of developing principles, practices

---

6 "Learning design" can be used to refer to either the broad field of educational research and practice, or a specific instance of "a learning design" or sequence of learning and teaching activities. This essay follows the recommended usage of capitalisation to refer to the field "Learning Design", and lower case "learning design" to refer to instances. (Dalziel *et al.*, "Larnaca Declaration," 12).

7 Gráinne Conole and Sandra Wills, "Representing Learning Designs – Making Design Explicit and Shareable," *Educational Media International* 50, no. 1 (2013), 1.

and learning designs for formational learning.[8] In doing so, it lays the groundwork for further design-based research into developing learning designs that improve formational learning outcomes in theological education.[9]

Do We Need to Design Learning?

The use of the term "design" in relation to education is growing. This is partly a result of the increasing use of technology in education. Goodyear & Retalis suggest that education needs to become more design-savvy if it is to improve outcomes for learners: "Using technology to help other people learn is complex. It needs to be approached in a planful spirit. That is why we speak of design."[10] The widespread shift to outcomes-based education and push towards more student-centred learning which is occurring across all educational sectors adds to the need for educators to come to grips with designing learning. In Australia, an increasingly regulated higher education sector is expected to demonstrate effectiveness in teaching practice, which further drives more careful and explicit design of learning.

Somewhat surprisingly, however, educators as a profession have not yet developed generally accepted ways of designing learning, nor is there an agreed descriptive language for teaching and learning activities. Goodyear & Retalis note that while the work of "teaching-as-design" is growing in importance, it is not yet adequately supported with time, tools or intellectual resources.[11] Faculty members with teaching roles in higher education institutions do not necessarily have backgrounds in education and may not be familiar or comfortable with educational design.[12] Moreover, in many educational institutions there is not a

---

8   Dalziel et al., "Larnaca Declaration."
9   Design-based research is a methodology increasingly being used for educational research. E.g. Johannes Cronje, "What Is This Thing Called 'Design' in Design Research and Instructional Design," *Educational Media International* 50, no. 1 (2013). G. Conole, *Designing for Learning in an Open World* (New York: Springer, 2013). doi:DOI 10.1007/978-1-4419-8517-0. Thomas C. Reeves, Jan Herrington and Ron Oliver, "Design Research: A Socially Responsible Approach to Instructional Technology Research in Higher Education," *Journal of Computing in Higher Education* 16, no. 2 (2005).
10 P. Goodyear and S. Retalis, "Learning, Technology & Design," in *Technology-Enhanced Learning. Design Patterns and Pattern Languages,* eds. P. Goodyear and S. Retalis (Rotterdam: Sense Publishing, 2010), 10.
11 L. Fink, *Creating Significant Learning Experiences: An Integrated Approach to Designing College Courses* (San Francisco: Jossey-Bass, 2003).
12 Leanne Cameron, "Planner Tools - Sharing and Reusing Good Practice," in *LAMS and Learning Design*, ed. J. Dalziel, C. Alexander and K. Jaroslaw (Cyprus: University of Nicosia Press, 2010).

culture of sharing good teaching ideas and practice. As a result, good teaching practices tend to remain private and implicit, rather than explicit and shared.[13] This is not a new problem. Shulman pointed out in 1987 that teaching, unlike other fields, is a profession devoid of a history of practice: "One of the frustrations of teaching as an occupation and profession is its extensive individual and collective amnesia, the consistency with which the best creations of its practitioners are lost to both contemporary and future peers."[14]

The increasing use of technologies in education has further highlighted this issue. In a sense, educational technologies both reveal the problem and offer a potential solution. Current practice in higher education, including theological institutions, tends to follow a traditional teaching model in which individual academics teach a particular set of individual subjects. As institutions offer courses using online technologies, the individual faculty member is often expected to translate or redevelop the classroom-based subject for the online environment. However, many faculty members are not experienced in educational design and adequate support and resources may not be available to assist educators to make effective use of technologies. The effort involved in such a process raises the question of whether this teaching model is the most effective. At the same time, the online learning materials that are developed in this process are potentially re-usable by both the designing academic and by others. This has led some researchers to ask whether there might be ways in which educators could establish (i) a culture of talking about designing learning and (ii) a language for talking about it and/or a way of representing or visualising teaching and learning activities.

Other disciplines and professions such as architecture and information technology have developed such languages and means of representation. In these professions, "design patterns" are widely and effectively used to enable professionals in these fields to communicate cogently and meaningfully with one another about complex concepts and practices.[15] In recent years, some researchers and practitioners in the field of Learning Design have been exploring whether there might be ways of representing educational designs and means of

---

13   Dalziel *et al.*, "Larnaca Declaration."
14   Lee Shulman, *The Wisdom of Practice* (San Francisco: Jossey-Bass, 2004), 232.
15   C. Alexander, S. Ishikawa, M. Silversteirn, M. Jacobson, I. Fiksdahl-King and S. Angel, *A Pattern Language: Towns, Buildings, Construction* (New York: Oxford University Press, 1977). Richard Helm Erich Gamma, Ralph Johnson and John Vlissides, *Design Patterns. Elements of Reusable Object-Oriented Software* (Boston: Addison-Wesley, 1995; repr., 21st printing, November 2000).

communicating and sharing these among educators. This paper explores whether this area of Learning Design research might hold potential for helping theological educators to come to grips with some of the particular design challenges of theological education. Before exploring the potential of Learning Design, let us examine the challenges of designing learning for formational outcomes.

Challenges of designing learning for formational outcomes

How to design and provide effective formational learning, particularly in non-face-to-face teaching contexts, presents a significant and complex challenge for theological educators. Here we note four aspects of this challenge.

Complexity of formation

Formation is a term which, while widely used in theological education, remains ill-defined and resonates with complexity. The term "formation" encompasses many aspects with different Christian traditions placing emphasis on varying aspects. It relates to deep issues of identity, personal spiritual growth, character, and capacity for lifelong Christian ministry. Previous research explored Australian theological educators' understandings of formation.[16] This research found that formation could be described in general terms as a holistic process of growth and change in an individual. It involves addressing and shaping the whole person, not just the mind. It is a process in which growth in character and spiritual development is expected and one which is expected to continue throughout a student's life. It involves change, challenge, and transformation, sometimes through disequilibrium or disorienting experiences. Some of these occur in the process of students coming to grips with their own beliefs or being challenged by others' beliefs.

Through interviews with educators the research identified several categories of formation:

- *Personal or spiritual formation*: involves growth in personal knowledge, love and service of God, in spiritual understanding and maturity

---

16   Hockridge, "Challenges for Educators Using Distance and Online Education."

- *Ministry or pastoral formation*: involves the development and practice of ministry and pastoral skills and the development of a ministerial identity
- *Intellectual or Academic formation*: involves intellectual engagement with content, particularly the Scriptures, as part of the intellectual formation process
- *Enculturation*: involves the taking on of an ethos, or a way of thinking, acting and behaving.

Participants emphasised that formation has both an *applied or practical* element and a *communal or relational* element. Students are expected to apply what they are learning in their personal lives and ministry contexts. As one educator put it: "We expect their theological learning to shape the way they live."[17] Moreover, while the formational process of growth and change happens within the individual, it is necessarily expressed or evidenced in relationships and in community. The term "formation" or "formational learning" in this essay should be understood to include all these elements.

Formation is thus long term in nature referring to the personal, spiritual and ministerial journey of individuals, not only during their formal theological training, but throughout their entire lives, in a rich variety of contexts. The depth and complexity of what theological educators mean when they refer to formation makes it an educationally challenging concept to come to grips with.

Sidelining of formation

The difficulty of coming to grips with how to approach formation educationally is demonstrated in the ways in which formation has been "sidelined" in theological education. Ball notes that of the three types of learning apprenticeships in theological education identified by Foster *et al.*, that is, cognitive or intellectual, practical or skills-based, and normative or identity formation, the normative apprenticeship relating to formation was most neglected, often being left to "non-academy" or "extracurricular activities."[18] Recent research in Australia similarly noted that current approaches to formation tend to be *ad hoc* and focused on extracurricular activities.[19] Where formational learning is

---

17   Hockridge, "Challenges for Educators Using Distance and Online Education."
18   Charles R Foster, Lisa E Dahill, Lawrence A Golemon and Barbara Wang Tolentino, *Educating Clergy: Teaching Practices and Pastoral Imagination* (San Francisco: Jossey-Bass, 2006), cited in Ball, *Transforming Theology*, 19.
19   Ball, *Transforming Theology*; Hockridge, "Challenges for Educators Using Distance and Online Education."

formally incorporated in theological degrees it tends to be directed towards students preparing for ordination and, as Ball points out, a substantial number of theological students on a "non-ordination" track therefore miss out.[20] As noted in the introduction, if formation is considered to be an integral part of theological education, then theological educators need to be more intentional and explicit in defining formational learning outcomes and appropriate educational practices to achieve formation, across multiple modes of study.

The shape and structure of theological programs of study
Ball's report on the Transforming Theology project noted considerable similarity in theological degree programs around the country with little change since the 1970s in a curriculum which is based around three main fields of biblical studies, Christian thought and Christian practice. He identified a lack of integration between these fields and a skewed focus in theological education programs toward "covering content." He also noted a lack of connection with the student's prior learning and current life experience outside the theological college. He suggests that the focus on content rather than connection is one of the contributing factors to the production of graduates who are not well prepared for life and ministry.

Ball's report suggested that theological educators need to design the curriculum strategically to promote the development of an integrated person. He envisages this would involve the preservation of the high value placed on the historical and creedal basis of theological education while at the same time developing practical skills of students and expanding pedagogical horizons to take seriously the formation of people and the transformation of individuals and society.[21] Given the complex, multi-faceted, long-term nature of formation, it is important that theological institutions consider how to design curricula that integrate formation at all levels.

Formational learning at a distance
Designing courses for student formation is particularly challenging where there is little or no face-to-face contact among lecturers and students. There has been considerable discussion in the literature and on the ground in theological institutions about the suitability of distance and online education for theological

---

20 Ball, *Transforming Theology*.
21 Ball, *Transforming Theology*, 88.

education and whether it is possible to encourage formation at a distance using online educational technologies.[22] Recently, however, there has been a shift in the focus of the literature from addressing questions around suitability to considering how learning technologies can be used for theological education and exploring new pedagogies. For example, research grants were recently offered by the Wabash Centre for Teaching & Learning in Theology and Religion for educators wishing to explore "expanding ministry formation into new pedagogical contexts."[23] Projects such as these are evidence of a genuine interest in working through how theological education might adapt to new teaching and learning environments and use new pedagogies and technologies to prepare students effectively for the demands of their future profession.

In Australia, restrictions on distance theological education offerings which had been in place have recently been lifted and some theological institutions that previously did not offer distance education are exploring the opportunities to do so. Other colleges with experience in offering distance and online theological education are continuing to develop and expand such programs. Educators from these colleges are keen to share their experiences, as demonstrated by the recent organisation of colloquiums on e-learning, the establishment of an online interest group for Australian distance and online theological educators, and conferences on learning and teaching.[24]

In summary, the Australian theological education sector is experiencing a growing awareness of the need for designing learning. It has, through the Transforming Theology project report, received a call to redesign theological curricula strategically and intentionally. It is beginning to grapple with the challenges of using technologies in learning and also with the challenge of how to address formational learning across all modes of study. How then can theological educators effectively address these challenges?

Some recent research in the theological sector offers insight into designing for formational learning. Nichols' doctoral research in distance education and spiritual formation points out the potential for using the life context of students for formation. His research shows that distance theological education students tend to be involved in a local church community. He argues that theological

---

22 For an overview of this discussion see Hockridge, "Challenges for Educators Using Distance and Online Education."
23 "Expanding Ministry Formation into New Pedagogical Contexts," Wabash Center, accessed 23 January, 2014, http://www.wabashcenter.wabash.edu/grants/article.aspx?id=25323.
24 Eg Online community: https://www.facebook.com/groups/137933413017312/.

educators should explore ways to incorporate distance learners' real-life church and work contexts into their formal studies to complement the formation that is already taking place.[25]

Ball proposes "integrative learning" as a solution to the skewed focus he identified in theological education programs. The kind of integrative learning that Ball envisions cultivates the development of a holistically consistent person through cognitive, practical and personal formation, the integration of learning across the curriculum, and integration of learning with life, work and a coherent worldview. He suggests that this will require strategic integration of supervised field education into programs; development of student-centred learning methods; inclusion of opportunities for first year students to review critically their existing frameworks in the light of new knowledge; and creation of better connections with student's current life context.[26]

The author's previous research explored educators' concerns and issues around formation in distance and online theological education.[27] It concluded that the issues relating to distance theological education are primarily *pedagogical* rather than *formational*. It argued that rather than assuming that it is not possible to do formation at a distance, theological educators need to be more strategic and intentional about how to approach formation, in ways that are appropriate to the learning and teaching contexts in which they operate. In other words, the ways in which theological educators have traditionally approached formation may not work so well at a distance and new pedagogical approaches need to be developed. This research was able to offer preliminary suggestions as to how identified categories of formation practices might be used to assist educators to intentionally design for formation in theological education. What is needed now is a means of identifying and designing effective educational principles, practices and environments for formation. Since formation of students is a multi-layered and ongoing holistic process, educators will need to design for formation at multiple levels (lesson, unit, course, and curriculum), and in multiple contexts (individual learner, peer-peer, teacher-learner, church /community /workplace).

---

25 Mark Nichols, "The *Akadameia* as Paradigm for Online Community in Theological Distance Education," *Journal of Christian Education* 54, no. 1 (May, 2011), 5-23.
26 Ball, *Transforming Theology*, 102, 124.
27 Hockridge, "Challenges for Educators Using Distance and Online Education," 17.

Exploring Learning Design as a Means of improving Formational Outcomes

The field of Learning Design research and practice may assist theological educators to approach the challenges of designing for formational learning. The remainder of this essay offers an introduction to Learning Design and its potential for conceptualising and approaching the design challenges of formational learning.

Within the broader area of evidence-based research into educational design, a specific field of research has focused in recent years on the problem of how to represent and share effective educational practices. This field of Learning Design initially grew out of the work of Rob Koper and others at Open University of Netherlands on the Educational Modelling Language which evolved into the IMS Learning Design specification. A variety of different approaches, initiatives and tools which aimed to find ways to represent and share learning designs has been developed. Some of these focused on the development of computational languages (such as the IMS LD, 2003) or the development of executable or "runnable" sequences, such as the Learning Activity Management System (LAMS), 2003. Others have included the SoURCE project at the UK Open University (2002), the AUTC Learning Design project in Australia (2003), the Open University Learning Design Initiative (OULDI) commencing in 2007, and the LDSE Project (Learning Design Support Environment) at the University of London (2009).[28]

Learning Design research has focused at different levels, from design principles at the whole of curriculum level to individual sequences of learning activities. The core concepts of Learning Design are: representing and/or visualising teaching and learning activities; sharing these; and providing guidance to educators. Although Learning Design uses and acknowledges the value of technology, its focus is not exclusively or primarily on technology. Rather, its focus is on pedagogy and the explicit and precise description of technology-enhanced pedagogical processes.[29]

Researchers and practitioners in the field of Learning Design tend to have two general aims. The first is to provide a means for educators to document and

---

28   An overview of Learning Design initiatives and tools can be found at the Learning Design Timeline website: http://learningdesigntimeline.wordpress.com/.
29   Eva Dobozy, "Learning Design Research: Advancing Pedagogies in the Digital Age," *Educational Media International* 50, no. 1 (2013).

work with their designs for planning and implementation; the second is to provide a way of sharing, adapting and re-using designs.[30] In order to share and re-use designs it is necessary to develop ways to generalise across cases and thus streamline the process of future design by offering general principles of application, or perhaps even universal patterns.[31] This has led to a great deal of development, experimentation and discussion around the possibility of developing an educational notation or language and generated a degree of tension within the field about whether Learning Design is primarily about pedagogical meta-models or the search for principles for effective learning and teaching.[32]

This field of Learning Design research, through its stated aim of distilling and sharing effective teaching methods, appears to have the potential to:

- conceptualise the practice of designing learning;
- offer a means of approaching specific educational issues (such as formational learning);
- develop templates, patterns, visualisations or generic learning designs which can be used across many different disciplines; and
- offer a way to enhance educators' pedagogical understanding.

These aspects of Learning Design suggest a way forward for theological educators in designing courses and learning experiences to improve formational outcomes in the following ways.

Conceptualising the practice of designing learning

Learning Design is still working out its position in wider educational theory and practice. The relationship of Learning Design to educational theory is of particular concern in the literature. Dobozy suggested the need for Learning Design researchers to work on developing ontological and epistemological clarity.[33] Such clarity may be in the process of being worked through. In

---

30 Sue Bennett et al., "Researching Learning Design in Open, Distance, and Flexible Learning: Investigating Approaches to Supporting Design Processes and Practices," *Distance Education* 30, no. 2 (2009).
31 Helen Beetham and Rhona Sharpe, "An Introduction to Rethinking Pedagogy for a Digital Age," in *Rethinking Pedagogy for a Digital Age*, ed. Helen Beetham and Rhona Sharpe (Oxford: Routledge, 2007), 1-10.
32 Dalziel et al., "Larnaca Declaration." While these issues are of interest, they are beyond the scope of this chapter.
33 Dobozy, "Learning Design Research: Advancing Pedagogies in the Digital Age."

September 2012, a group of Learning Design researchers met in Cyprus to develop an agreed conceptual basis for Learning Design. The result was the *Larnaca Declaration on Learning Design*.[34] The Larnaca Declaration explains that Learning Design "is trying to develop a general descriptive framework that could describe many different types of teaching and learning activities (which themselves may have been based on different underlying pedagogical theories)."[35] Thus, Learning Design can be seen as a layer of abstraction above traditional learning theories. It is not a theory about how learners learn, nor does it make claims about how teachers "should" teach; instead, Learning Design aims to provide a descriptive framework for the sequence and kind of activities that occur in the classroom or online.[36]

The question of whether it is possible, or even desirable, to develop a "pedagogically neutral" framework has been raised.[37] Dobozy notes a common tendency for Learning Design to be broadly equated with social constructivist learning theory, which is not consistent with pedagogical neutrality.[38] The Larnaca Declaration suggests that the aim of a Learning Design framework is not absolute pedagogical neutrality, which is not possible, but the goal is "a framework of sufficient accuracy and expressiveness that it can describe many different examples of teaching and learning activities (which are themselves based on different pedagogical theories."[39] The Larnaca Declaration moves beyond the constraints of Learning Design being connected with a specific learning theory or pedagogical approach. Its inclusive and pluralist design enables learning designers working out of different educational paradigms to work with the model. Dobozy suggests this has the potential to provide clear guidance for future Learning Design research. At this early stage, the declaration offers both a distillation of research in Learning Design to date and a potential means of conceptualising and framing future research and practice. In particular, it describes the *Learning Design Conceptual Map* (Figure 1) which maps the wider educational landscape as it relates to core Learning Design concepts.

---

34 Dalziel *et al.*, "Larnaca Declaration."
35 Dalziel *et al.*, "Larnaca Declaration," 13.
36 Dalziel *et al.*, "Larnaca Declaration,"
37 F. Chatteur, L. Carvalho and A. Dong, "Embedding Pedagogical Principles and Theories into Design Patterns," in *Technology-Enhanced Learning. Design Patterns and Pattern Languages*. Ron Oliver *et al.*, "Describing ICT Based Learning Designs That Promote Quality Learning Outcomes," in *Rethinking Pedagogy for a Digital Age.*.
38 Dobozy, "Learning Design Research: Advancing Pedagogies in the Digital Age."
39 Dalziel *et al.*, "Larnaca Declaration," 13.

Figure 1. The Learning Design Conceptual Map

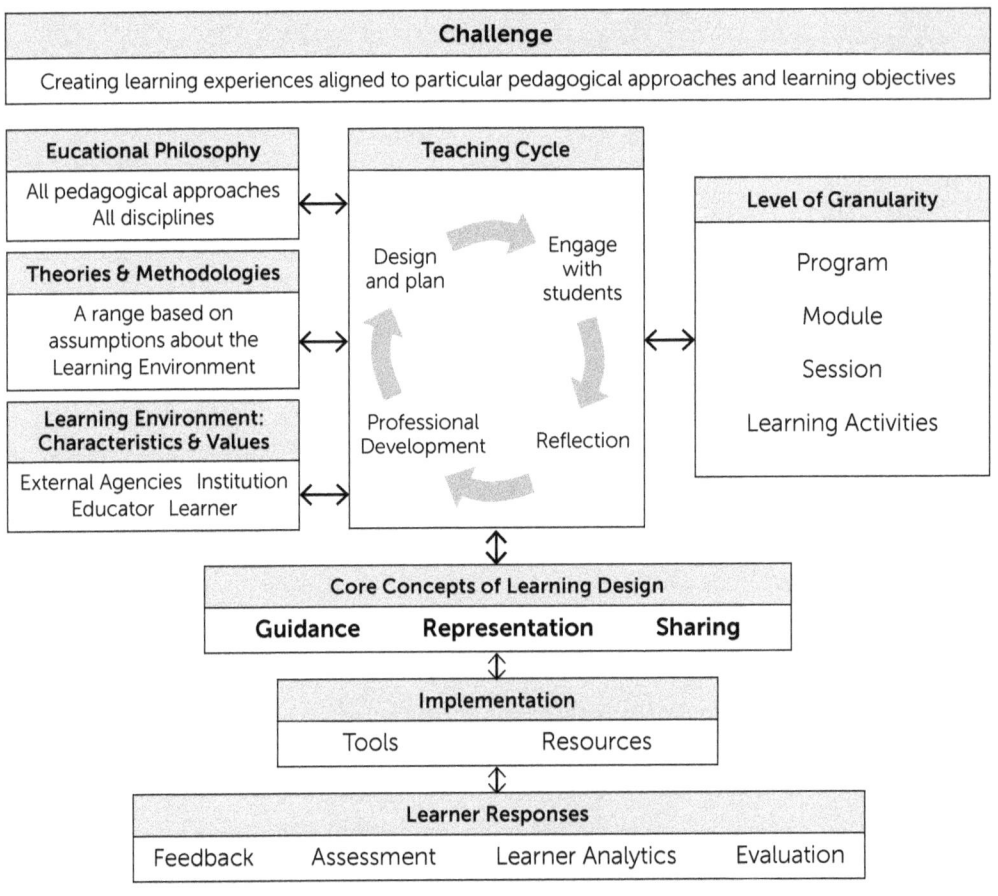

The conceptual map addresses the overall challenge of "creating learning experiences aligned to particular pedagogical values and objectives." The conceptual map has at its centre the three core Learning Design concepts of guidance, representation, and sharing. It attempts to provide a way of conceptualising the connections among all key components of learning and teaching design and practice including:

- relevant educational philosophies, theories and methodologies;
- the characteristics and values of the learning environment that provide the context for Learning Design;
- the impact of various stages in the teaching cycle on Learning Design;
- the granularity or level of the Learning Design; and
- factors relating to implementation, evaluation and learner responses to learning designs.

The Learning Design Conceptual Map (LD-CM) may provide a helpful framework to guide research on Learning Design relating to formation, as described in the following section. Any research undertaken in the theological education sector that draws on the conceptual map may test its potential usefulness and applicability and perhaps contribute to the ongoing development of the map itself.

A means of approaching specific educational issues

How might Learning Design and the LD-CM be used to guide theological educators in the development of appropriate learning designs, particularly learning designs that support and encourage desired formational learning outcomes? At this stage it appears that the LD-CM could be used in two ways to assist theological educators in learning design for formation.

The first is in providing a way to develop and assess the educational effectiveness and coherence of a particular approach to an educational challenge at a "macro" level. The top box of the conceptual map provides a place for educators to describe the educational challenge to be addressed. For theological educators the particular challenge is to create learning experiences that are aligned to *formational* values and objectives. As already suggested, theological educators need to define formational learning outcomes more clearly, and then identify appropriate educational principles and practices for formation. The Learning Design Conceptual Map sets out the key components of educational design and practice that need consideration. It prompts the consideration of the underlying educational philosophy of the institution or educator and the educational theory or methodologies that inform it. What is the educational theoretical base for formation and is it consistent with the desired formational values and objectives and the teaching and learning methods we use? Dalziel and Ball have both suggested that theological educators need to consider how to align their methods of learning and teaching with the ultimate goals of theological education.[40] The Conceptual Map might be a useful tool for considering formational design at a macro level and assessing alignment of theory, values, outcomes and practice. As another example, we have already noted that the educational challenge of designing for formational learning is one which needs to be addressed at a number of educational levels. The LD-CM

---

40 Ball, *Transforming Theology*. J. Dalziel, "Learning Design, LAMS, and Christian Education," *Journal of Christian Education* 54, no. 1 (2011).

provides a conceptual "place" that allows different levels of "granularity" to be addressed and may therefore provide a basis for designing for formational learning at various levels: from incorporating an individual learning activity with formational goals, to integrating an explicit approach to formation at the broader levels of granularity such as unit or whole program.

The second way the LD-CM could be used is to analyse existing or planned learning designs for formational learning which could be further refined and shared with other educators. As the Larnaca Declaration points out, the conceptual map offers a means of exploring the relationships among the "moving parts" of how an educator comes to teach in a particular way at a particular moment, and it provides a way of approaching this that draws attention to related issues that affect educator decision making.[41] By offering a means of depicting connections between the relevant elements in learning and teaching (such as the characteristics and values of institutions, educators and learners, the nature of the teaching cycle, or the response of learners), the LD-CM may help educators to clarify decision-making about teaching, promote effective learning design and ultimately effective student learning.

Developing templates, patterns, visualisations or generic learning designs which can be used across many different disciplines

The attempt to represent or visualise learning designs so they can be communicated to others offers a way for educators to connect with and benefit from the insights of educators in other disciplines with which they may not naturally come into contact. The Learning Activity Management System (LAMS) is an example of a Learning Design system that enables educators to create sequences of learning activities using an online interface that are simultaneously a representation of the learning activity and also provides a "runnable" instance that can be used by students. These are then stored on the LAMS repository and can be accessed and re-used. Many educators are already sharing learning designs online via the LAMS community (lamscommunity.org). The developer of LAMS, James Dalziel, suggests that LAMS might be used to develop learning designs for theological education.[42] Figures 2 and 3 present two examples of learning designs at the learning activity level from the LAMS repository that may be of relevance to theological education.

---

41 Dalziel *et al.*, "Larnaca Declaration," 29.
42 Dalziel, "Learning Design, LAMS, and Christian Education."

Figure 2: Preaching in Acts Sequence

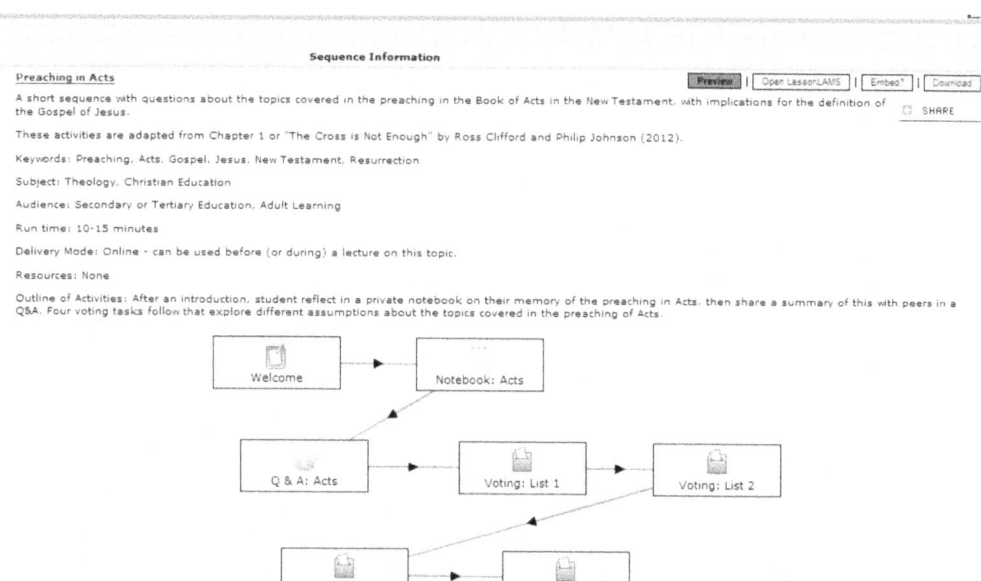

This is a simple learning sequence, intended to be used as a pre-lecture preparation exercise, which asks students to engage in reflection and analysis of the Book of Acts.

A learning design such as that in Figure 3 shows a potential cross-disciplinary use of learning designs which could be used in theological field work or practical learning contexts. The emphasis on practical experience, interaction with others, and the opportunity for reflection and analysis of experience are all learning activities that could contribute to formational learning. The learning designs and approaches of other disciplines which face similar challenges in preparing students for relational professions, such as teaching, counselling, business, and medicine, may have potential for reuse in theological education contexts.

In attempting to represent the basic building blocks and the individual elements of learning and teaching practice, such learning designs are deceptively simple. As yet, while a number of different methods or "proto" examples have been developed for creating and sharing learning designs, it is acknowledged that there is room for improvement and the search for a widely accepted learning and teaching descriptive language remains unfulfilled.[43] Despite this, it may be possible for theological educators to use systems like LAMS, or others such as

---

43 Dalziel *et al.*, "Larnaca Declaration."

the Pedagogical Pattern Collector from the Learning Design Grid, the LD Compendium,[44] or perhaps others not yet created, to develop learning designs that encapsulate practices that are effective for formational learning and become examples that can be used by others.

Figure 3: Bedside Manner – Medical Training

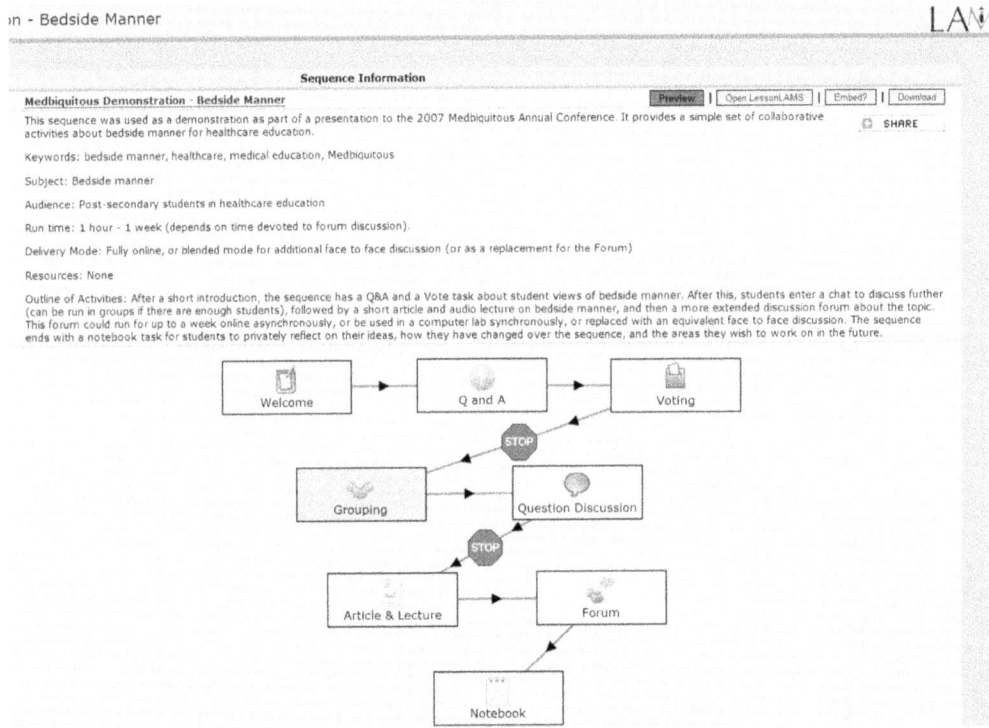

The work on "design patterns" by researchers such as Goodyear may also be a fruitful area to explore for its relevance to the educational challenges faced by theological educators. As Goodyear & Retalis point out, the search for design patterns often involves the search for what is "good."[45] Design patterns originated in the field of architecture with the work of Christopher Alexander who sought to understand what it is about spaces that helps people feel most alive and complete. His design approach had a moral component in the sense that his designs aimed to make life better in some way. For Alexander, patterns are not just neat formats for communicating solutions: they are intended to make a

---

44 Learning Design Grid: http://www.ld-grid.org/resources/tools/pedagogical-pattern-collector. LD Compendium: http://compendiumld.open.ac.uk/.
45 Peter Goodyear and Symeon Retalis, "Learning, Technology & Design."

difference, to empower people to enhance coherence in the things and places they create. Goodyear and Retalis would like to see this applied to education: "Good technology enhanced learning (TEL) design is characterised by a commitment to helping people create circumstances in which learning can be experienced as coherent with what is most deeply valued in the rest of life, as a source of pleasure, growth and transformation."[46] These sentiments are particularly relevant to the theological education context that has a clear moral basis and intentionally seeks to connect values, practice and learning. Such an approach to design offers a way for educators to address the underlying motivations and aims of teaching and learning and to explore ways of designing learning so that it is coherent with these. It may help to address the skewed focus on content that was identified by Ball to address theological educators' concerns over the use of technology in learning and to aid them in designing courses in ways that help meaningful learning and contribute to the formation of students.

Enhancing educators' pedagogical understanding and thus improving educators' design practice

One of the core concepts of Learning Design is providing guidance to educators. Many Learning Design researchers are interested in developing ways of providing design guidance and support for educators, as a means to making learning design more explicit: "Practitioners should be encouraged to interrogate and engage with their own understanding in order to externalize and make explicit the 'knowing how,' so that it can be shared and learnt from."[47] Conole & Wills suggest that representations of learning designs can both help guide educator' design practice and help educators to think beyond content to focus on the learner experience and thus offer a way of enhancing educators' pedagogical understanding.[48] Similarly Bennett et al. suggest: "The aim is not to prescribe a particular design to be copied but to extend a teacher's pedagogical repertoire through the process of modifying someone else's design."[49]

An important component of the author's further research into formational learning design will be working with educators to provide ongoing support and guidance for their design practice. The following three learning design projects,

---

[46] Peter Goodyear and Symeon Retalis, "Learning, Technology & Design," 45.
[47] Rhona Sharpe and Martin Oliver, "Supporting Practitioners' Design for Learning: Principles of Effective Resources and Interventions," in *Rethinking Pedagogy for a Digital Age*, 47.
[48] Conole and Wills, "Representing Learning Designs – Making Design Explicit and Shareable."
[49] Bennett et al., "Researching Learning Design in Open, Distance, and Flexible Learning," 155.

undertaken in other contexts, present as potential models for working with theological educators to develop formational learning designs.

HEART (HEaring And Realising Teaching voice) Project[50]

This project, based at Auckland University, aims to help educators and designers select and work with existing learning designs, by helping them reflect on and articulate the educational beliefs underlying their own and others' teaching and learning design practice. It is based on the assumption that an ability to articulate, defend, or modify one's pedagogical standpoint is fundamental to success in adapting learning design to different contexts. Interestingly, in the context of theological education, this project specifically references Parker Palmer's writing on teaching as a vocation which is based on the premise that "good teaching comes from the identity and integrity of the teacher."[51] The goal of this project was to provoke and support "good talk about good teaching."[52] It attempted to find a way of dealing adequately with the value and professionalism of educators and to approach design as far more than a set of tips or techniques.

Viewpoints Project, University of Ulster[53]

This project aimed to develop a set of practical tools to support academics in curriculum design processes and to identify ways that institutional policies, processes and procedures might help support the embedding of new modes of curriculum engagement. It involved a series of carefully designed workshops or interventions that were intended to seed and support the emergence of a new educational discourse among faculty and decision makers in the university. The evaluation report of this project concluded that the Viewpoints process is an especially efficient and powerful way of engaging academics in curriculum redesign activities and could usefully inform other institutions wishing to implement transformational change in their own educational context.

---

50 Claire Donald, Adam Blake, Isabelle Girault, Ashwini Datt and Elizabeth Ramsay, "Approaches to learning design: past the head and the hands to the HEART of the matter," *Distance Education* 30, no. 2 (2009), 179-199.
51 P. J. Palmer, *The Courage to Teach: Exploring the Inner Landscape of the Teacher's Life*, 10th anniversary ed.(San Francisco: Jossey-Bass, 2007), 10, cited in Donald et al, "Approaches to learning design."
52 Palmer, *The Courage to Teach*, 149.
53 David Nicol, "Transformational Change in Teaching and Learning: Recasting the Educational Discourse. Evaluation of the Viewpoints Project at the University of Ulster" (University of Strathclyde, 2012).

OULDI-JISC Project, Open University of the UK[54]

This project gathered evidence about how educators "design" and aimed to develop theoretically informed ways to visualise designs, to produce effective tools to guide and support design and explore how practitioners share and communicate teaching and learning plans and experiences. While most Learning Design projects tend to focus at the learning activity and collection of learning activities levels of granularity, this project had a special emphasis on design at a module or session (unit) level.

It is suggested that future research on learning design in theological education could build on such projects to develop an appropriate model to design and share effective learning designs that focus on formational learning.

The Way Ahead?

This essay has suggested that a number of factors have led to a degree of readiness within the Australian theological education sector to engage with questions around pedagogy and course design, particularly relating to formational learning. It has also suggested that the field of Learning Design, with its developments to date in representing and sharing learning designs in a variety of teaching and learning contexts, may be of relevance to theological educators in designing formational learning experiences.

Further research is planned to explore how formational learning outcomes may be improved in theological education institutions by using a design-based methodology and drawing on insights and experience from the field of Learning Design. This will involve working collaboratively with theological educators to identify a sound theoretical base for formation, to identify formational learning outcomes and to develop design principles and educational practices for formation. These will then be used as the basis for developing "good" learning designs for formational learning which will be trialed and refined with a view to developing an overall approach for improving formational learning outcomes in theological education and developing re-usable designs, tools and resources that can be shared. Throughout, the focus will be on finding effective ways to support educators in the design process.

---

54 "Open University Learning Design Initiative," accessed 24 January, 2014, http://www.open.ac.uk/blogs/OULDI/

11 | THEOLOGY FOR THE IGENERATION

KARA MARTIN

Abstract

Twelve years ago, Mark Prensky stated: "Today's students are no longer the people our educational system was designed to teach."[1] The issue for theological institutions is that the generation of students he was referring to is now ready for higher education. These students have spent their entire learning lives in a digital world, with an emphasis on visual inputs, and have flow-on expectations of the educational experience. One response to this challenge is to develop a fully online educational experience, including video inputs. The Ridley Certificate is an example of an educational experience designed for this iGeneration: it is portable, accessible and engaging. Its significant feature is that the learner fully controls the learning experience: *when* learning takes place, *where* it takes place, *how deeply* material is studied, as well as *the pace* at which learning is undertaken. This essay reflects on what has been learnt in the development of this innovative educational resource, and also gives some broader suggestions for educational strategies to meet the needs of the iGeneration.

* * *

---

[1] M. Prensky, "Digital Natives, Digital Immigrants," *On the Horizon* Vol. 9 No. 5 (October 2001), 1/6.

Introduction

A famous YouTube clip shows a one year old child playing with an iPad. She effortlessly uses the device. Then she is handed a magazine, and struggles to come to terms with what to do with it. She tries swiping the pages, and then throws it down in exasperation. In on-screen titles, her father comments that for her a magazine is "an iPad that is broken."[2]

That clip has now been incorporated into an Apple advertising campaign that illustrates the generation we are seeking to teach. While IBM's slogan was "Think," suggesting that its technology, the computer, was an extension of the brain, Apple's slogan that cracked the market, "Think Different," suggests that Apple products are an extension of the user's creativity, of their very being.[3]

The generation we are seeking to teach is a digital generation, whose very ways of thinking are influenced by the technology they use. This calls for new approaches by educators.

The Digital Generation (iGeneration)

A recent Pew Research Report in the US found that 78% of teens own a mobile phone, with almost half being smartphones, and with a rapidly growing number using them as their primary Internet access device. Interestingly, this offsets economic disadvantage, since there is roughly the same percentage of teens owning mobile phones whether in the lowest-earning bracket or the highest-earning bracket.[4]

Tablet ownership is also growing quickly, with a quarter of teens owning them. The report also indicated that babies as young as six months are already playing with their parents' electronic devices, while 50% of children 5–8 years old use tablets regularly for educational purposes.

---

2   YouTube clip, http://www.youtube.com/watch?v=aXV-yaFmQNk, accessed 20 March 2014.
3   R. Siltanen, "The Real Story Behind Apple's Think Different Campaign, 14 December, 2011," http://www.forbes.com/sites/onmarketing/2011/12/14/the-real-story-behind-apples-think-different-campaign/, accessed 20 March 2014.
4   March 2013 report, as reported in *PCMag.com*: S. Milot, "More Teens Accessing the Web from Phones rather than PCs," http://www.pcmag.com/article2/0,2817,2416548,00.asp, accessed 20 March 2014.

In Australia, 90% of children (5–14) have accessed the Internet.[5] In terms of duration of screen time, a study of children (aged 5–14 years) by the Australian Bureau of Statistics found that 46% of children spent more than 10 hours a week on screen-based activities (TV, DVD, computers, games consoles, etc.), far outranking any sporting activity. The ABS study did not specify hours above 10 hours a week, but a 2010 US study of 8–18 year olds suggested that total screen time is probably closer to *10 hours a day* with more than 7.5 hours being purely for entertainment: texting, social media, games, YouTube and so on.[6]

The research into the impact of such significant screen time is ongoing. Shirley Keegan has summarised the research and found both positive and negative effects:

> On the positive side these include improved complex reasoning and problem solving …. On the negative side they encompass difficulty in concentrating on books or long articles, becoming more easily distracted, impulsiveness … and lack of concentration in general.[7]

Keegan quotes Professor Susan Greenfield who believes that teens' brains have been "rewired."[8] While Greenfield is very cautionary about the impact, perhaps the only consensus on impact is summarised by Jonathan Carr: "Dozens of studies by psychologists, neurobiologists, educators and web designers point to the same conclusion: when we go online, we enter an environment that promotes cursory reading, hurried and distracted thinking, and superficial learning."[9]

Notwithstanding the possible negative effects of their digital consumption, the iGeneration,[10] or "digital natives" as Prensky referred to them, have developed a series of behaviours that have further been encouraged by their learning experiences. Prensky summarises those behaviours in the following quote from his 2001 article:

---

5 ABS, "Square Eyes and Couch Potatoes," June 2013, accessed 17 December, 2013, http://www.abs.gov.au/ausstats/abs@.nsf/Products/4156.0.55.001~June+2013~Main+Features~Square+eyes+and+couch+potatoes:+Children's+participation+in+physical+activity+and+screen-based+activities?OpenDocument.

6 The January 2010 study was released by the Kaiser Family Foundation, http://kff.org/other/event/generation-m2-media-in-the-lives-of/, accessed 20 March 2014.

7 S. Keegan, "Digital Technologies are Re-shaping our Brains," *Qualitative Market Research: An International Journal*, Vol. 5, No. 3 (2012), 328–346, at 330.

8 Greenfield, quoted in Keegan, "Digital Technologies are Re-shaping our Brains," 330.

9 Carr, quoted in Keegan, "Digital Technologies are Re-shaping our Brains," 335.

10 Other terms for those born since 1980 include Millennials, Net Generation, Net Gen, Gen N, Gen Y, Dot-Coms, Echo-Boomers, Me Generation, Generation D (Digital), Nexters; compiled in J. Feiertag and Z. Berge, "Training Generation N: How Educators Should Approach the Net Generation," *Education + Training*, Vol. 50 No. 6 (2008), 457–464, at 457. A Google search delivered another term: Screenagers!

Digital Natives are used to receiving information really fast. They like to parallel process and multi-task. They prefer their graphics *before* their text rather than the opposite. They prefer random access (like hypertext). They function best when networked. They thrive on instant gratification and frequent rewards.[11]

Characteristics of the iGeneration

This essay focuses on several characteristics of the iGeneration that have consequences for the way we educate students. The characteristics I will be focusing on and analysing are:[12]

- Multitasking (often identified in its negative terms as "distracting"). This is characterised by doing multiple activities at once. In an oft-cited *New York Times* article "Growing up Digital, Wired for Distraction", Matt Richtel quoted research from the Kaiser Family Foundation in the US that half of students aged 8–18 are "using the Internet, watching TV or using some other form of media, while doing their homework."[13]
- Using multiple inputs. Ron Berk points out that students like to access multiple interactive inputs, moving seamlessly between real and virtual worlds.[14]
- Sourcing own information. Students like to use search engines to source their own information, and make their own decisions about the credibility of the information received. An Online Computer Library Center (OCLC) study of 394 undergraduates and graduates in 2006 found that 89% begin with a search engine, and prefer search engines to online or physical libraries.[15]
- Controlling their learning: time and depth. Berk notes that this generation like instantaneous access and instant gratification. Rather than traditional courses where students have to wait for an enrolment, and are set tasks to complete at weekly intervals, this generation of students prefers to study

---

11 Prensky, "Digital Natives, Digital Immigrants," 2/6.
12 This is synthesised material from Ron Berk's excellent article, "Teaching Strategies for the Net Generation," originally published in *Transformative Dialogues: Teaching and Learning Journal*, November 2009, http://www.ronberk.com/articles/2009_strategies.pdf, accessed 20 March 2014.
13 M. Richtel, "Growing up Digital, Wired for Distraction," *New York Times* (2010), http://www.nytimes.com/2010/11/21/technology/21brain.html?pagewanted=all&_r=0, accessed 20 March 2014.
14 Berk, "Teaching Strategies for the Net Generation," 10.
15 Quoted in Berk, "Teaching Strategies for the Net Generation," 9–10.

at their own pace, and to the depth that they want, to achieve the results that they need.[16]
- Preferring short spurts of information, followed by reflection and use. These students have shorter attention spans, noted by Berk and Richtel, who quotes Harvard Medical School Associate Professor Michael Rich reporting that this generation has brains less able to sustain attention: "Their brains are rewarded not for staying on task but for jumping to the next thing."[17]
- Desiring to combine learning with other pursuits. For this generation, lifestyle is more important than discrete endeavours. Berk notes that most undergraduates want to combine study with work and other lifestyle choices. This means that they like flexibility in their schedule, as well as the opportunity to stop and start their study, depending on their lifestyle.[18]
- Preferring formative to summative assessment. Berk notes that these students tend to learn by trial and error, as well as by inductive study. "They are kinaesthetic, experiential, hands-on learners."[19]

As an example of the educational consequences of such characteristics, Peggy Johnson, a Digital Education Consultant, has said in reference to school students, "We now have the opportunity and the responsibility to redefine the way young people learn, making the experience more immersive and interactive, and extending learning outside the boundaries of the classroom."[20]

The Challenge Facing Traditional Education

The following table demonstrates the issues facing traditional educational approaches in light of the characteristics of the iGeneration, and the initiatives that have been considered as part of the Ridley Certificate design process:

---

16 Berk, "Teaching Strategies for the Net Generation," 10 and 13.
17 Berk, "Teaching Strategies for the Net Generation," 11. Richtel, "Growing up Digital, Wired for Distraction," 1/11.
18 Berk, "Teaching Strategies for the Net Generation," 12.
19 Berk, "Teaching Strategies for the Net Generation," 10–11.
20 P. Johnson, "Now is the Time for Digital Tech to Transform K–12 Learning," *Huffington Post*, 1 August, 2013, http://www.huffingtonpost.com/peggy-johnson/now-is-the-time-for-digit_b_3685085.html, accessed 20 March 2014.

Characteristic	Traditional Education	Initiatives
Multitasking	Lecture-style, content-heavy approaches militate against the desire of students to do multiple activities.	• Opportunity to do a variety of interactive activities.
Using multiple inputs	A lecture alone will not satisfy desire for multiple, especially visual, inputs.	• Combine a variety of inputs: visual, lecture, small group, participatory. It is important that all inputs are linked to learning outcomes, and are relevant.
Sourcing own information	The lecturer as the subject expert and source of all information may be resented by the iGeneration.	• Introduce students to good sources of information, including online access to library resources as well as reputable websites. • Demonstrate to students how to evaluate and critique sources of information.
Controlling their learning: time and depth	Subject choice and semester timing tend to be controlled by the institution. Students are restricted in their choice. Prescribed learning outcomes and assessment tasks are predicated on all work being completed.	• More variety of subject offerings; the ability to study when and where they want. • A minimum level of content to be accessed for assessment; with options of further study at greater depth by individual choice.
Preferring short spurts of information, then reflection and use	Typically in Australia, theological education is delivered in blocks of lectures and tutorials. Often the material is focused on knowledge rather than skills.	• iGeneration students prefer a variety of shorter inputs. • They need time to reflect on knowledge. • They are more motivated by the ability to apply knowledge quickly, or at least to test its relevance.
Desiring to combine learning with other pursuits	Although the model of residential seminary is rapidly changing in Australia (often due to financial constraints rather than pedagogical considerations), there is still generally a belief that full-time face-to-face study is preferable for theological study.	• Students will tend to combine study with work and other pursuits, so need to have the opportunity for flexibility in their learning program through online subjects, intensives, evening classes and the opportunity to apply what they are learning to work and their lifestyle activities.
Preferring formative to summative assessment	Traditionally, theological education has preferred summative assessments, such as exams and essays, as the best means of assessing learning. This is partly due to issues of ease (exams are quicker to mark and easier to administer; essays allow testing of critical thinking).	• The ability to test ideas with the teacher and class and to scaffold learning is much preferred by the iGeneration. • They also want assessments that allow participation and expression of practical learning, rather than being focused on knowledge.

Feiertag and Berge summarise: "This generation, for better or for worse, does not respond well to the lecture and has become accustomed to interactivity."[21] They suggest that the appropriate response to educating this generation is not *pedagogy* (from the Greek meaning "to lead the child") but *andragogy* (from the Greek meaning "to lead the man/adult"). We need to use adult learning techniques, a shift toward "a practical approach to education; students must see the end goal and understand how the steps toward it fit into the big picture."[22]

The Concerns about Technology from Theological Educators

However, such a shift in educational approach is often faced by theological educators with a great deal of fear, as expressed by Stephen Haar in his inaugural lecture as Academic Dean of the Australian Lutheran College (ALC):

> Worldwide, theological educators have been among the slowest to adopt new instructional technologies and new forms of communication. This tardiness is not simply due to the challenges of learning how to use digital technology and equipment. Rather, some teachers have deep concerns about the theological appropriateness and pedagogical effectiveness of technology. These concerns reflect deeper convictions about the nature of theology, the embodied character of learning, and the standards of intellectual, pastoral, and spiritual development expected of those preparing for ministry in the church.[23]

Haar points out that there are sound biblical reasons for concerns about changes to theological pedagogy, such as the model of master and pupil exemplified by Jesus and his disciples. However, such a model matches neither the modern teaching world nor the learning preferences of contemporary adults. In this lecture, Haar was articulating his vision for the ALC of a review of program and pedagogy, and the implementation of a "bricks and clicks" model.[24]

Some of the usual opposition to distance learning has been challenged. Steve

---

21 Feiertag and Berge, "Training Generation N," 461.
22 Feiertag and Berge, "Training Generation N," 462.
23 S. Haar, "e-Constructing Theological Education for Ministry in a www World" (2008), 3/10, http://www.alc.edu.au/assets/education/about/academic-publications/opening-lecture/2008-e-Constructing-theological-education.pdf, accessed 20 March 2014.
24 Haar, "e-Constructing Theological Education for Ministry in a www World," 4/10.

Delamarter has said, "Daniel Ulrich, who was our dean of distance learning and also a New Testament scholar, came up with an idea regarding the Apostle Paul, which others have since discovered on their own. Paul might be viewed as a prototypical distance educator."[25] This is because Paul often taught through letters, by distance, and even describes, being "absent in body, but present in spirit" (1 Cor 5:3).[26]

Professor Russell Haitch of Bethany Theological Seminary concurs with this description, pointing out that Paul sometimes preferred distance learning, as it were. For example in 2 Corinthians 1:23-2:9, Paul wrote, "I made up my mind not to make you another painful visit." Later, in 10:10, he described his detractors who complained, "his letters are weighty and strong, but his bodily presence is weak, and his speech is contemptible." It appears Paul agreed with that view.[27]

Roger White's seminal paper, "Promoting Spiritual Formation in Distance Education," gives a detailed analysis of the relationship-building techniques that Paul was able to utilise through his letters which can be replicated in online education, including: addressing people by name, inclusion of personal references and encouragements, incorporation of prayers and requests for prayers, goal for learning, questions to generate reflection, contemporary illustrations, use of exhortation, and a reliance on the Holy Spirit.[28] However, Rovai, Baker & Cox went so far as to suggest that Paul's extensive travelling would not have been necessary if all spiritual formation and education could have been achieved at a distance.[29]

The halfway point for many theological educators includes forms of hybrid learning. For example, Fuller Seminary in California is conducting an exercise looking at "The Seminary of the Future."[30] One author of the report, Andy Crouch, has described an extreme view of distance learning, as "'gnostic technologies' -

---

25 S. Delamarter et al., "Technology, Pedagogy, and Transformation in Theological Education: Five Case Studies," *Teaching Theology and Religion*, Vol. 10 No. 2 (2007), 64–79, at 74.
26 Indeed in Colossians 4:16 it is clear that Paul wrote letters for a general audience and circular distribution.
27 R. Haitch, "Absent in Body, Present in Spirit: A Theological Anthropology of Distance Education," http://www.napce.org/documents/!pdfs/papers-2013/haitch.pdf, accessed 17 March, 2014.
28 R. White, "Promoting Spiritual Formation in Distance Education," *Christian Education Journal*, Fall, 3:2 (2006), 308–309.
29 A. Rovai , J. Baker and W. Cox, "How Christianly is Christian Distance Higher Education?" *Christian Higher Education*, 7:1 (2008), 4.
30 For more information, see: http://future.fuller.edu/About_the_Conversation/Why_is_it_important_/, accessed 20 March 2014.

technologies that allow people to pretend that bodies do not matter".[31] The Fuller report recommends a combination of face-to-face and online learning that it describes as "augmented reality." It supports this approach theologically: "Augmented reality recognizes that the most meaningful experiences and relationships in human beings' lives take place in the created world .... Technology's role, including information technology, is not to replace this world but unearth its latent wealth of potential."[32]

Concerns versus Adoption of Technology in Education

In the wider educational environment there have also been some concerns about too much enthusiasm for technology. Bennett & Maton have surveyed research and concluded, "The lack of evidence for the existence of an entire generation of digital natives seriously undermines arguments made for radical change to education because of a disjuncture between the needs of young people and their educational institutions."[33]

However, the reality is that students who present to tertiary institutions have been through schools that have embraced technology and different educational strategies. An article about "Funky School" in *The Australian* claimed that "of Australia's 9,529 schools, thousands of state and private schools have adopted the [technology-enhanced flexible education] model, with more agile learning spaces opening every day."[34] Agile learning, also called "personalised" or "self-directed" learning, involves at a minimum students taking responsibility for their learning, and at its extremes, involves learning spaces of up to 200 children with up to six teachers.

So, whatever the reluctance or suspicion of the extent of change in this generation, expectations have been created for these iGeneraton students about the nature of the education that they will receive.

---

31 See: http://future.fuller.edu/Discussion_Points/Discussion_Point_6__Augmented_Reality__Technology_and_Personal_Presence/, accessed 20 March 2014.
32 See: http://future.fuller.edu/Discussion_Points/Discussion_Point_6__Augmented_Reality__Technology_and_Personal_Presence/, accessed 20 March 2014.
33 S. Bennett and K. Maton, "Beyond the 'Digital Natives' Debate," originally published in *Journal of Computer Assisted Learning*, 26 (S, 2010), 321–331, at 10/24.
34 C. Overington, "Funky School," *The Australian*, 10/09/2011 (2011), 1/6, http://www.theaustralian.com.au/news/features/funky-school-story-e6frg8h6-1226130668112, accessed March 2014.

The Ridley Certificate as a Means of Connecting with the iGeneration

In March 2013, Ridley Melbourne commenced delivery of the Ridley Certificate, a new online teaching resource. The Certificate is not accredited, but is prepared by highly trained academics, mostly sourced from Ridley Melbourne Mission and Ministry College. The Ridley Certificate was initiated as a partnership between the theological college and the local church. The concept was to deliver solid theological teaching in local church contexts through innovative delivery techniques. The decision was made that an enhanced visual delivery technique would be more effective than either static video (video recording of a lecture in front of a class) or text content. A Visual Design Manager was recruited to oversee the recording and production of the material.

The course will eventually allow students to choose 12 subjects from 20 options. Each subject consists of six lessons, with each lesson including two 20-minute video lectures. The video lectures are intentionally recorded for the Certificate, not static videos, as is often the case. This choice is driven by the belief that educational experiences should be directed at the specific learning audience. The experience of receiving learning in an online context is different from the embodied lecture experience. The videos are edited to include on-screen text and supplementary visuals to enhance the verbal content. The videos are supported with discussion/reflection questions, including reference to a textbook and homework. Progress with learning is measured via a multiple-choice questionnaire.

Students access all the material online. They can sign in and study in an individual context, or study as part of a small group, or watch the material projected on a screen in a congregational setting.

How the Ridley Certificate Meets the Needs of the iGeneration

In terms of the characteristics identified earlier, there is much evidence of a positive response to the features of the Certificate. **Student Comments**[35]

---

35 Feedback on the certificate is collected via online surveys at the completion of the course, which uses a mixture of quantitative and qualitative measures. In addition, feedback from unsolicited qualitative responses has been used.

Characteristic	Ridley Certificate	Student Comments
Multitasking	• The material can be accessed in the domestic environment or in a group setting. • With mobile devices the material can be accessed wherever the person is. • Lectures can be paused and/or reviewed if required. • There are links from discussion questions to other documents.	"I can do it lying on my couch, at my desk, go back and do it again if I want." [This student uses a mobile device so he is able to access the material between other tasks.]
Using multiple inputs	• There are visual inputs, discussion questions, links to a text, additional readings, and an interactive multiple choice quiz.	"There are video lectures, questionnaires, handouts…" "[The quiz feedback was] very helpful in guiding the way I should be thinking in regards to the questions asked."
Sourcing own information	• The student has a sense of being in control of the information through the online interface.	[The lessons encouraged me to think for myself:] "I think this has been one of the biggest challenges for me as I tend to read and accept what others say if I think they have more knowledge than me."
Controlling their learning: time and depth	• Students are able to login anytime. They are not restricted to semesters or class times. • There is a base level of learning: watching the video lectures, which is assessed. • Discussion/Reflection questions and Taking it Further options allow students to study at greater depth.	"I can do it anywhere, anytime." "It is very flexible." "The further learning was a great benefit in supplementing the course."
Preferring short spurts of information, then reflection and use	• Short lectures allow focus on key material. • Questions lead reflection. • There is a focus on application of the material.	"It is good content, broken up." "20 minute video lectures suit me fine."
Desiring to combine learning with other pursuits	• The structure of the certificate means that study can be fitted in alongside work commitments and other activities.	"With my work schedule [as an obstetrician] it is not possible for me to take the time to be in class in person." "I have joined the Board of [a Christian aid organisation] and need to improve in my understanding." "It is helping me find my place in all of this."
Preferring formative to summative assessment	• Traditionally, theological education has preferred summative assessments, such as exams and essays, as the best means of assessing learning. • The Ridley Certificate uses multiple-choice questionnaires which can be completed multiple times until the student achieves the grade they want. Feedback to wrong answers guides the student toward the correct answer.	"The [lesson] quizzes were a great insight and a help for the final quiz." "[The quiz feedback was a] good way to make you think about your answer without actually giving you the correct answer."

Pedagogical/Andragogical Shortcomings of the Ridley Certificate

Having summarised and analysed the Certificate, and the way it addresses the needs of the iGeneration, it is also important to recognise the shortcomings of the Certificate.

First, there are shortcomings in the Assessment procedures. The Ridley Certificate uses an online multiple-choice questionnaire as the only form of assessment. As a standard statement on assessment, the *Australian Higher Education Threshold Standards* document includes Assessment in *Course Standards*, but mentions only that "Assessment tasks for the course of study and its units provide opportunities for students to demonstrate achievement of the expected student learning outcomes for the course of study."[36] The American Association for Higher Education has issued "Nine Principles of Good Practice for Assessing Student Learning," which is more definitive. Principle 2 suggests assessment should employ "a diverse array of methods, including those that call for actual performance, using them over time so as to reveal change, growth, and increasing degrees of integration."[37] These examples show that assessment can be for a number of reasons including accreditation and determining whether learning goals have been met. The Ridley Certificate, however, has chosen its single assessment method to minimise administrative costs, thus ensuring that students are able to receive high quality theological education at a fraction of the usual price. This self-assessment is aimed at giving a sense of progress and encouraging further learning, rather than testing competency.

Second, one major characteristic of the iGeneration not included in the analysis is their need to participate and belong.[38] While most online education can provide capacity for community, this is not facilitated in the Ridley Certificate. However, 70% of subjects delivered so far have been to students studying in group situations: small groups, church educational programs, or other congregational settings. Learning in this context is more likely to provide a more supportive and relevant learning environment and to enhance community.

---

36 *Higher Education Standards Framework (Threshold Standards) 2011*, Section 5.1, http://www.comlaw.gov.au/Details/F2013C00169/Html/Text#_Toc330548951, accessed 20 March 2014.
37 AAHE, "Nine Principles of Good Practice for Assessing Student Learning," 1996, https://teaching.uncc.edu/sites/teaching.uncc.edu/files/media/files/file/AssessmentAndGrading/9Principles.pdf, accessed 20 March 2014.
38 For an excellent discussion of the implications of this characteristic, see Neil Holm's paper, "Educating the Net Generation for Transformation and Transcendence," originally published in *Journal of Christian Education*, Vol. 54, No. 2 (2011), 5–18.

Third, there is no interaction between the teacher and the student. In the appropriately named "The Importance of Still Teaching the iGeneration: New Technologies and the Centrality of Pedagogy," Philip and Garcia emphasise the role of the teacher to facilitate understanding and promote classroom discourse.[39] While this is again ameliorated in group settings, where there is typically a facilitator present, the lack of guided learning is particularly an issue for the solo online learner in the Ridley Certificate.

Beyond Online: Further Teaching Strategies for the iGeneration

While the Ridley Certificate has been designed for a specific purpose and is filling a niche, there are some further teaching strategies suggested from the research for this essay about the characteristics of the iGeneration that build on the initiatives listed above. These would be significant for incorporation into theological education, particularly where there is greater flexibility in terms of modes of study and/or assessment. The following material addresses classroom as well as online experiences.

While up to now there has been a focus on the on-line iGeneration learner, it is also useful to point out that there are challenges for the teacher when faced with a class of iGeneration students. Venne and Coleman warn that students in this cohort may need to be more coddled than previous generations, and may come across as arrogant. They need detailed instructions and will tend to be conservative. They also have difficulty recognising plagiarism, have weaker verbal skills and may have difficulty with critical thinking.[40]

The Teacher

Long and Coldren identify a number of features of lecturers' interpersonal style that would enhance their teaching. These include:

- Explaining thinking behind, not just giving answers
- Laughing at mistakes and using them as opportunities for learning

---

[39] T. Philip and A. Garcia, "The Importance of Still Teaching the iGeneration: New Technologies and the Centrality of Pedagogy," *Harvard Educational Review*, Vol. 83, No. 2 (Summer 2013), 314.

[40] V. Venne and D. Coleman, "Training the Millennial Learner Through Experiential Evolutionary Scaffolding," *Journal of Genetic Counselors*, 19 (2010), 554–569, at 557.

- Creating a team atmosphere
- Using personal anecdotes that are professionally relevant
- Using engaging nonverbal cues (in a face-to-face or a video context)
- Talking with (not at) students
- Getting excited.[41]

In a follow-up study, Moss *et al.* identified that the three key aspects of teaching style that undergraduates and postgraduates respond to are:

Being interesting/entertaining
Showing passion for the subject
Explaining well.[42]

In terms of their personality characteristics, the top three are:

Willing to help students
Love of the subject
Sense of humour.[43]

The Learner

Moss *et al.* also identified "behaviour required from students" to enhance the learning experience. The top three behaviours include:

Willing to be challenged
Engagement/Critical Thinking
Participation.[44]

The Techniques

Ron Berk, Professor Emeritus at Johns Hopkins University, has identified a number of useful techniques specifically for the iGeneration including:

- Incorporate technology into lectures and assessments, in a meaningful way, utilising a range of inputs including music, video clips, video games, search engines and research databases, with a focus on those things that are animated, image-based and interactive

---

41 H. Long and J. Coldren, "Interpersonal Influences in Large Lecture-Based Classes," *College Training*, Vol. 54 No. 2 (2006), 237–243, at 241–242.
42 G. Moss, J. Dyson and A. Flosi, "Impact Teaching: Lead or be Left Behind," *Journal of International Education Research*, Vol. 7 No. 2 (2011), 7–12, at 10–11.
43 Moss *et al.*, "Impact Teaching," 10–11.
44 Moss *et al*, "Impact Teaching," 10–11.

- Allow students to operate at their own speed, with a focus on engagement and participation
- Shorten lecture content and increase group discussion and learner-centred activities such as simulations, improvisations and problem-solving exercises
- Permit multitasking in class
- Include visual prompts in presentations
- Be available for face-to-face meeting with students
- Use live and online methods to encourage interaction and sharing of opinions including Q&A, debates, comments, blogging
- Be sensitive to the work and family demands of students when planning workloads and activities
- Provide regular and prompt and constructive feedback in class and on assessments, and in response to emails.[45]

Moss *et al.* included, as an essential feature for graduates and undergraduates, the need for students to be assisted by the lecturer to relate teaching to real world contexts.[46]

Conclusion

The iGeneration is being exposed to more digital input that anyone could have imagined even 10 years ago. The impact on brains is being researched, the impact on learning and the resultant changes to educational environments are being assessed, but hard data of the full impact on growing brains is still years away. We simply do not fully understand how the use of technology is impacting the way students think and perceive their world, and on the sense of identity of learners.

This essay has briefly summarised the evidence to date and presented a new way of delivering theological education, as demonstrated in the Ridley Certificate. The effectiveness of the Certificate for increasing biblical literacy and transforming the spiritual lives of students is a topic for further research in three to five years' time, when the first students have completed training and there is evidence of the application of their learning. Yet even now, there does seem to be agreement that the expectations of effective education for the iGeneration

---

45 Berk, "Teaching Strategies for the Net Generation," 14–16.
46 Moss *et al.*, "Impact Teaching," 10–11.

will include guided use of technology, greater freedom in learning, and an increased focus on visual input. These are the elements most appreciated by users of the Ridley Certificate.

An implicit assumption of this essay is that the characteristics of learners should drive the approach to teaching in theological education. However, this needs to be balanced with the changing expectations of teachers, as well as the requirements of stakeholders, and by the vision of theological educators of what a graduate of their institution will look like. These are issues for prayer and further consideration.

12 | VIDEO GAME DESIGN AND THE THEOLOGICAL CLASSROOM

GAMIFICATION AS A TOOL FOR STUDENT-CENTRED LEARNING

ISAAC SOON

Abstract

Gamification, the use of video game mechanics and design in the classroom, is an educational framework gaining traction worldwide. Though the results of gamification have been positive, there has been little engagement between it and the theological higher education sector. The intention here is to explore the mechanics of gamification with the most potential to help educators align with their twenty-first century stakeholders and to help theological education move beyond the lecture-based (and thus lecturer-oriented) classroom that has long monopolised learning practices in the humanities. This essay will argue that, despite some methodological and ethical cautions, gamification is a viable option for theological educators to transform their courses into interactive and vibrant student-centred experiences.

Introduction

In the field of education, new digital frontiers are often seen as harbingers of inexorable change. Proponents of advancing technologies often expect that their systems will inevitably supplant traditional methods of teaching.¹ Obversely, as digital learning tools increase, a large number of educators (theological and non-theological) remain sceptical and/or cautious at the efficacy of using non-traditional elements, technology or otherwise, in contemporary pedagogy.² For a variety of reasons, the tendency has been to avoid the new in favour of the established.³ Theological training in many places around the world has for too long reflected this hesitant attitude. It is certainly not that the older way of teaching and learning in the humanities has been wholly bad; it has served many generations of scholarship and research and has produced those of us who are already successful within the guild. But, there has been little development to refine the system despite the arrival of twenty-first century students who are fundamentally different learners from those for whom the system was originally designed.⁴ Additionally, the task of facilitating learning is for theological educators not simply a social vocation but a theological one as well. We affirm that humanity is called to participate in God's creative agency, most especially in education. Scholarship therefore needs to take seriously the potential of new creative methods in optimising learning environments. It is therefore the aim here to stimulate innovation and ingenuity amongst theological educators by examining one framework gaining traction worldwide known as gamification. Gamification is the use of video game mechanics and design in the classroom. Though the results of gamification have been positive there has been little engagement between it and theological higher education.

Of all the digital resources teachers have at their disposal, what is it about video games that makes them so applicable for the educational sector? The fact is that this current generation of digital natives is already well versed with video games.⁵ While the typical classroom mainly involves the cognitive aspect of

---

1 Thomas Edison's famous overstatement applies here: "I believe that the motion picture is destined to revolutionize [sic] our educational system and that in a few years it will supplant largely, if not entirely, the use of textbooks." Cited in L. Cuban, *Teachers and Machines: The Classroom Use of Technology Since 1920* (New York: Teachers College Press, 1986), 9.
2 cf. D.J.A. Clines, "Learning, Teaching, and Researching Biblical Studies, Today and Tomorrow," *JBL* 129, no. 1 (2010), 5–29.
3 See M.E. Hess, *Engaging Technology in Theological Education: All That We Can't Leave Behind*, Communication, Culture, and Religion Series (Lanham: Rowman & Littlefield Publishers, 2005).
4 M. Prensky, "Digital Natives, Digital Immigrants Part 1," *On The Horizon* 9.5 (2001), 1–6; M. Prensky, "Digital Natives, Digital Immigrants Part 2," *On The Horizon* 9.6 (2001), 1–6; C.M. Steiner, M.D. Kickmeier-Rust and D. Albert, "Little Big Difference: Gender Aspects and Gender-Based Adaptation in Educational Games," in *Learning by Playing: Game-based Education System Design and Development*, ed. M. Chang et al., (Heidelberg: Springer, 2009), 150.
5 Steiner, Kickmeier-Rust and Albert, "Little Big Difference," 150.

learning, many games have been shown to create meaningful and effective learning systems that combine cognitive, emotional, and social elements.[6] Video game mechanics, dynamics, and aesthetics can actually assist teachers in understanding how their students learn today and how their pedagogical practices can accommodate their learning.[7] Barab stresses:

> There are many reasons that educators should care about video games, including their noted discursive richness, depth of collaborative inquiry, complexity of game play, opportunities for consequentiality, rich perception-action cycles, exploration of situated identities, and the complex forms of learning and participation that can occur during game play.[8]

Though there are many different aspects that researchers focus on, this essay delineates a student-centred form of gamification.[9] Aspects of gamification sketched in this essay have been chosen because of their immediate relevance to some of the issues brought up by theological educational research in Australia.[10] One such issue we seek to address here is the level of independence and "broad thinking" that a student is able to demonstrate beyond the tertiary institution.[11] First, a brief history of video games in education as well as the current status of gaming research will be considered in order to show its cogency for the sector. Next, pertinent gamification principles of design will be explored in relation to three key relationships in a student-centred learning environment: (1) student to content, (2) student to student, (3) and student to teacher.[12] Potential implications and ethical reservations that arise with the use of gamification, such as motivation, quality, addiction and gender-bias will be weighed and considered. The intention here is to explore the mechanics of gamification which have the

---

6   J.J. Lee and J. Hammer, "Gamification in Education: What, How, Why Bother?" *Academic Exchange Quarterly* 15.2 (2011), 146–151.
7   G. Zichermann, *Gamification by Design: Implementing Game Mechanics in Web and Mobile Apps* (Sebastopol, CA: O'Reilly Media, 2011), 35–6.
8   S.A. Barab, "Introduction to Section III," in *Games, Learning, and Society: Learning and Meaning in the Digital Age*, ed. C. Steinkuehler, K. Squire and S.A. Barab, Learning in Doing (Cambridge: CUP, 2012), 271.
9   The type of gamification outlined here is essentially a type of blended learning environment. See H. Singh, "Building Effective Blended Learning Programs," *Educational Technology* 43.6 (2003), 51–54.
10 See Les Ball, *Transforming Theology: Student Experience and Transformative Learning in Undergraduate Theological Education* (Preston Vic: Mosaic Press, 2012) esp. 23–28.
11 Ball, *Transforming Theology*, 14.
12 These are what Ball states are "the important arenas of interactive learning." Ball, *Transforming Theology*, 24.

most potential to help educators align with their twenty-first century stakeholders and to help theological education move beyond the lecture-based (and thus lecturer-oriented) classroom that has long monopolised learning practices in the humanities. This essay will argue that, despite some cautions, gamification is a viable option for theological educators to transform their courses into interactive and vibrant student-centred experiences.

A Brief History of Video Games in Education

Since the invention of the computer, gaming software has been used in the classroom as an educational aid. The purpose of this type of software was to integrate learning and play using digital media. The creation of meaningful play is essentially "the goal of successful game design."[13] However, many of these early games were built with an emphasis on the learning aspect over and above the aspect of play. Consequently, they began to feel less like games and more like work. Thus by the turn of the millennium, educational games, known affectionately as "edutainment software," were largely abandoned and the market culled.[14] Still, in the late 1990s and early 2000s, research surged forward continuously emphasising the pedagogical potential of video games and what they have to teach us about the way this generation of learners learns.[15] Today, in the field of ludology (or "game studies"), there is a thriving discussion amongst game developers and educators as to the future of video games in education.[16] The 2013 New Media Consortium Horizon Report (a report "that helps education leaders, trustees, policy makers, and others easily understand the impact of key

---

13 A. Polaine, "Developing a Language of Interactivity Through the Theory of Play" (PhD Thesis, University of Technology Sydney, 2010), 86; See also C. Steinkuehler, K. Squire and S.A. Barab (eds), *Games, Learning, and Society: Learning and Meaning in the Digital Age*, Learning in Doing (Cambridge: CUP, 2012), xvii.

14 L. Sheldon, *The Multiplayer Classroom: Designing Coursework As A Game* (Boston, MA: Course Technology/Cengage Learning, 2012), 15.

15 J.P. Gee, *What Video Games Have to Teach Us About Learning and Literacy* (New York, NY: Palgrave MacMillan, 2003); See also S. Egenfeldt-Nielsen, "Beyond Edutainment: Exploring the Educational Potential of Computer Games" (IT University of Copenhagen, 2005).

16 G. Frasca, "Ludology Meets Narratology: Similitude and Differences Between (Video)games and Narrative," *Parnasso* 3 (1999), 265–71; See also Polaine, "Developing a Language of Interactivity Through the Theory of Play," 82; K. Squire, *Video Games and Learning: Teaching and Participatory Culture in the Digital Age*, TEC (New York: Teachers College Press, 2011); Steinkuehler, Squire and Barab, *Games, Learning, and Society*.

emerging technologies on education")[17] affirms the significance of video games in learning today:

> Research has long indicated that video games help stimulate the production of dopamine, a chemical that provokes learning by reinforcing neuronal connections and communications. Furthermore, educational gameplay has proven to increase soft skills in learners, such as critical thinking, creative problem-solving, and teamwork. By exploring the way people engage with games – their behaviors [sic], mindsets, and motivations – researchers are getting better at designing adaptive games and effective game frameworks that transform learning experiences.[18]

As the above denotes, researchers have begun to move away from video games themselves and towards game frameworks.[19] Often the terms "gamification" and "game-based learning" are used synonymously; however, there is a subtle difference. Game-based learning is what de Freitas classifies as "topic specific gamification," which uses video games in a course as a didactic tool catered to a specific subject.[20] Gamification proper, however, is understood to be "classroom gamification" which endeavours to replicate and integrate gaming experience in the traditional classroom.[21] These are what Chris Heard alternatively calls "content gamification" and "curricular gamification."[22] It is this latter form of gamification that interests us here.

Unlike edutainment software and game-based learning, gamification is not the use of video games in curriculum. Instead, gamification involves using game mechanics and design in order to turn the classroom and the whole curriculum into a gaming experience.[23] More broadly, it is "the application of game mechanics to non-game activities."[24] Using discourse theory and design ethno-

---

17 L. Johnson et al., *NMC Horizon Report 2013 Higher Education Edition* (Austin, TX: The New Media Consortium, 2013).
18 Johnson et al., *NMC Horizon Report*, 21.
19 Sheldon, *The Multiplayer Classroom*; Gee, *What Video Games Have to Teach Us About Learning and Literacy*; Lee and Hammer, "Gamification in Education."
20 A.A. de Freitas and M.M. de Freitas, "Classroom Live: a Software-assisted Gamification Tool," *Computer Science Education* 23.2 (2013), 189.
21 de Freitas and de Freitas, "Classroom Live," 190.
22 C. Heard, "Gamifying Higher Education: a Useful Distinction," Blog, *Higgaion: Musings on the Bible and Christianity*, October 17, 2013, http://drchris.me/higgaion/?p=1239.
23 Sheldon, *The Multiplayer Classroom*, xiv.
24 Sheldon, *The Multiplayer Classroom*, 75.

graphy, game researchers have examined the social interactions and community that help people to assign meaning to and learn from the huge amount of information found in video games.[25] In recent years, educators around the world from different scholastic levels (primary, secondary, tertiary) have taken up the challenge to "gamify" their classrooms with favourable results.

Before educators realised gamification's potential for learning, the application of game mechanics to non-game contexts first gained popularity amongst international billion dollar companies as a way to develop motivation and initiative within their workforce and strategically to market their own brands and products. Recent analysis has shown that the gamification market worldwide is set to be a multi-billion dollar industry in the next three to five years.[26] While in the business world, the benefit of extrinsic rewards in gamification is largely questioned (as will be discussed below), it is significant to note that many major companies around the world have seen the results of gamification and are investing accordingly. However, the mentality of the corporate brand of gamification is self-centred and is not the type of gamification that this essay seeks to justify.[27] The type that this essay demonstrates is one that is client-focused. With student-centred gamification, the student's needs and benefits are situated at the forefront of all designs and decisions.

Student to Content

At a foundational level, the most basic relationship in a learning environment is between the student and the content. At face value, course curriculum may simply seem like information that learners need to know and understand. However, inherent in higher education is the particular expectation that students will not only grasp such skills but eventually employ them as well. The three gamification mechanisms explored here can help learners to understand, retain, and apply their knowledge while directing their efforts towards their own personal aspirations.

---

25 See Gee, *What Video Games Have to Teach Us About Learning and Literacy*; C. Steinkuehler, "Massively Multiplayer Online Video Gaming as Participation in A Discourse," *Mind, Culture, and Activity* 13.1 (2006), 39; S.A. Barab *et al.*, "Our Designs and the Social Agendas They Carry," *The Journal of the Learning Sciences* 16.2 (2007), 263–305.

26 A. Gaskell, "Gamification Market to Be Worth $5.5 Billion by 2018," *Technorati*, June 5, 2013, http://technorati.com/social-media/article/gamification-market-to-be-worth-55/.

27 Zichermann, *Gamification by Design*, 13.

Video games utilise continual cycles of feedback and criticism in order to inform the participant of the level of his or her progress. This provides a stark contrast when applied to the typical systems used by educators to assess student comprehension. In undergraduate education, learners usually receive their largest portion of feedback at the conclusion of a semester once exam marks and/or essay papers have been graded and returned. Other than questions in lectures or mid-term papers, there is little opportunity for students to gauge the health of their knowledge base throughout the semester. As a result, students are forced to rely on personal levels of motivation and drive in order to establish better patterns of study and research. This consequently increases anxiety as well as the pressure of failure. However, in games there is almost always immediate feedback for the participant.[28] Known as "feedback loops," they are effective because they continuously give players information on how they are progressing.[29] Interestingly, whereas the everyday classroom assumes self-motivation and impetus, the result of feedback loops is that participants actually begin to foster more of these qualities in themselves.[30] As far as what this would look like in an actual classroom, it might be an automated quiz or immediate questionnaire after a class reading or at various points in a lecture, like an immediate review. Learners would be able to repeat these quizzes as many times as needed until they get 100%. Feedback loops are a low-stakes way to help students learn from their mistakes while reducing the fear of failure.[31] Allowing students to repeat quizzes with the knowledge that they can run through them again and again until they have reproduced all concepts is just one way of applying feedback loops to increase retention. Consistent implementation of these miniature reviews into the activities, assessments, and examinations in a course can provide students with more opportunities to learn from their mistakes, thereby increasing a student's comprehension and confidence in his or her ability.

When assessing a participant's ability to apply their knowledge of a subject, games emphasise achievement through the use of attrition. In the classroom, every student starts off with full marks and, as his or her assignments are handed in and marked, that percentage slowly decreases. The mechanism involved here

---

28 Sheldon, *The Multiplayer Classroom*, 95.
29 Zichermann, *Gamification by Design*, 77.
30 Zichermann, *Gamification by Design*, 77.
31 Sheldon, *The Multiplayer Classroom*, xv.

is subtraction. Letter grades are "penalties for failure."[32] In games, however, every player starts off with a score of zero; what would be a failing status in academia.[33] Players then perform different challenges and quests (what in the classroom we might call assignments and tests) in order to achieve experience points, or course marks. Along the way students might receive badges or move up in rank based on their achievement. The use of these small competitive indicators serves as a motivator for learning.[34] If a player misses a challenge he/she can always make it up on another quest, though for fewer experience points than the original assessment. The mechanism involved here is attrition. Applied in a biblical languages course, for example, if students do poorly in a short translation assignment they can make it up by doing one or two other minor translations, each worth fewer marks than the original but together may make up a similar score as that attained had they done the previous assessment perfectly.[35] Mathematically, the difference between attrition in gamification and subtraction in the traditional grading system is exactly the same.[36] However, the perspectival difference is significant for the student. Whereas in a traditional system the student is constantly pressured to maintain 100%, with the use of gamification, a student's achievement is focused on upward progression.[37] A student's viewpoint may actually shift away from maintaining grades towards the idea of becoming an expert in the content of the course. With attrition, a student's grade reflects how much of the course they have mastered and been able to successfully apply not how much they have missed.[38]

One of the most important foci in gaming is the integration of the identity of the player into the game itself. Successful games are known for their use of strong narratives and stories. In fact, one major element that characterises the playing of video games is their first person narrative perspective. This point of

32 Sheldon, *The Multiplayer Classroom*, 43.
33 Sheldon, *The Multiplayer Classroom*, 5.
34 Badges have come into common use as simple digital animations, which indicate completion of skills, topics, and other accomplishments in educational contexts. The use of levels and ranks imitates the gameplay of video games where the level of players increases as they gain more experience and ability.
35 Of course the assessments should be of relatively the same difficulty and level, though perhaps smaller in terms of length and breadth.
36 Sheldon, *The Multiplayer Classroom*, 58.
37 Gee, *What Video Games Have to Teach Us About Learning and Literacy*, 64.
38 Arguably, one could propose that using this achievement-based grading system will not change every student's perspective on his or her grade. However, when this system is used in conjunction with other elements proposed in this essay, it is likely that students will be more able to view their grade in terms of how competent they are in the particular field as opposed to how competent they are not.

view effectively connects the identity of the player with the worldview of the game and has important implications for the classroom. Typically, a classroom is divided into two roles: student and teacher. It can be construed that, based on the structure and delivery of the traditional classroom, the teacher is the principal character and the students play secondary roles. In a game, however, a player plays as the main character. He/she is the protagonist in the story not a supporting subject.[39] When a player enters into the world of a game and takes on the identity of the character in the story, it is known as "virtual identity."[40] This concept can be used to bridge a student's real world identity and their intended or ideal identity goal, i.e. who they want to be once they have completed their studies. Virtual identity employed in the theological classroom involves enabling the students to take roles based on their ideal identity goals as scholars/pastors (or others) and not just scholars in training, which is their real world identity. This element of gamification empowers the participant to take on a purposeful role in the classroom other than just as a "student." As a result, students begin to see their learning endeavours as actual scholarly research and not just preparation. The outcome of virtual identity is ownership that helps to create an environment where students are involved in transformational play. The classroom becomes a place where their actions have significant real world weight.[41] Using virtual identity to incorporate the life goals that students have invites a new sense of imagination in and amongst their study. Such an environment allows students to engage with the content on an emotional level, not just on a cognitive one. A class, then, becomes a designed experience, a place that integrates content and context, where the student's learning has a legitimate and meaningful effect on their personhood and future.[42]

---

39 S.A. Barab, M. Gresalfi and A. Ingram-Goble, "Transformational Play: Using Games to Position Person, Content, and Context," *Educational Researcher* 39, no. 7 (2010), 527; Gee, *What Video Games Have to Teach Us About Learning and Literacy*, 51; cf. Hans-Georg Gadamer, *Truth and Method* (London: Sheed and Ward Ltd., 1975), 132.
40 Gee, *What Video Games Have to Teach Us About Learning and Literacy*, 60.
41 Barab, Gresalfi and Ingram-Goble, "Transformational Play," 526.
42 E.R. Halverson, "Participatory Media Spaces: A Design Perspective on Learning with Media and Technology in the Twenty-First Century," in *Games, Learning, and Society: Learning and Meaning in the Digital Age*, ed. C. Steinkuehler, K. Squire and S.A. Barab, Learning in Doing (Cambridge: CUP, 2012), 247; Barab, Gresalfi and Ingram-Goble, "Transformational Play," 526.

Student to Student

The next significant dynamic in a classroom is the relationship from peer to peer. This relation can be characterised by the idea of competitiveness. Some learners naturally compare their work to the work of their peers in order to motivate and/or challenge themselves further. However, the student-to-student dynamic in theological education may also be characterised by disconnection. Because of the format of classes, students are not frequently able to engage with their peers in order to share strengths and bolster weaknesses. Furthermore, with competition as an added element, students who perform on a lower level, seeing the difference in quality between their work and those at the top of the class, are less motivated to work harder. The use of the following mechanics of gamification can amend some of these gaps and promote higher levels of student-to-student collaboration and learning.

A phenomenon that has arisen in the social fabric of many online video games is what researchers have called "nurturing affinity spaces."[43] These spaces exist outside of the game and are where players go in order to seek advice and help for problems that arise in the game.[44] Games use these affinity spaces as "knowledge communities," self-sustaining ecosystems that promote collaboration amongst those who share the same ambitions.[45] In games, proactively seeking help from other players is a commonplace behaviour. When a player is having trouble working through a solution for a quest he/she consults other more experienced players first before going to the game makers for a solution, if at all. In contrast, Marquis has noted that, "While the traditional college campus and the virtual classroom are relatively good at providing a social life for students, those social interactions are seldom centered [sic] on truly meaningful problems."[46] Online class discussion boards are often for grades or troubleshooting rather than collaborative engagement on a key problem or issue. Nurturing affinity space in the theological classroom would mean that if students have a problem with an assessment, task or idea, they would first exhaust the community knowledge of their peers, whether online or

---

43 J.P. Gee and E. Hayes, "Nurturing Affinity Spaces and Game-Based Learning," in *Games, Learning, and Society: Learning and Meaning in the Digital Age*, ed. C. Steinkuehler, K. Squire and S.A. Barab, Learning in Doing (Cambridge: CUP, 2012), 129.
44 Gee and Hayes, "Nurturing Affinity Spaces and Game-Based Learning," 146-147.
45 Gee, *What Video Games Have to Teach Us About Learning and Literacy*, 197.
46 J. Marquis, "What Does Game-based Learning Offer Higher Education?," *Online Universities Blog*, October 14, 2011, http://www.onlineuniversities.com/blog/2011/10/what-does-game-based-learning-offer-higher-education/.

face-to-face, before approaching teachers and even texts for information.[47] Though students are asking for help amongst their peers, it should not be automatically "seen as replacing a person's responsibility for his or her own learning."[48] This is not about the student finding the easy answer, but merely about guidance and direction for them to seek out sources and avenues of research through networking. It is about nurturing a healthy behaviour, which draws on peers who are more experienced and uses that information to guide research and learning. Neither does it mean that a teacher's role in the classroom becomes redundant, only that collaboration with other students is encouraged as a primary option.

As students begin to collaborate more with one another, learning from one another's strengths and building skills together, a greater sense of community arises. As that community matures, there is the potential for students to "move beyond simplistic conceptions of the 'right answer'—a notion that is an unfortunate by-product of too much testing."[49] In the gaming world this maturation is called "theorycrafting".[50] Theorycrafting is the use of methodological analysis and advanced levels of interpretation in order to experiment and critically assess alternative solutions to problems.[51] Students using theorycrafting are expected not just to regurgitate information but to know how to apply it in a variety of situations and circumstances in collaboration with others. This further reinforces their understanding and comprehension of the course subject matter and creates a stronger more potent affinity space for them to learn. In a class on exegesis, theorycrafting might look like group of students looking at ways to interpret 1 Corinthians 6:9-10 with an emphasis on the word *arsenokoitēs*. Each might represent a different hermeneutical approach: one group might us reader-response theory, another social-scientific, another historical-critical, and another liberation theology. Basically, theorycrafting is advanced problem solving. It allows students to experiment collaboratively with various issues in their proper context rather than in abstract theoretical discussions (i.e. a lecture), encouraging more in-depth understanding of both the problem and the problem solving methods.

---

47 Gee and Hayes, "Nurturing Affinity Spaces and Game-Based Learning," 144.
48 Gee and Hayes, "Nurturing Affinity Spaces and Game-Based Learning," 144.
49 T. Choontanom and B. Nardi, "Theorycrafting: The Art and Science of Using Numbers to Interpret the World," in *Games, Learning, and Society: Learning and Meaning in the Digital Age*, ed. C. Steinkuehler, K. Squire and S.A. Barab, Learning in Doing (Cambridge: CUP, 2012), 205.
50 Choontanom and Nardi, "Theorycrafting."
51 Choontanom and Nardi, "Theorycrafting," 185-186.

Student to Teacher

Gamification mechanics recast the traditional student-teacher relationship. Normally, a student is the object of a teacher's ideas and knowledge. The teacher lectures and shares ideas and the student listens. In this passive learning environment, the student is then expected to imitate the teacher's ability to interact and apply ideas and concepts without much guidance. However, the importance of mentorship, or in student-centred terms, apprenticeship, is key in video game design. This is what gamification researchers have called "cognitive apprenticeship," where experts apprentice newcomers.[52] But it is not simply a matter of disseminating information from one person to the other. It is about a creative and effective mentorship between student and teacher, stimulating patterns of guidance and continued nurturing (affinity spaces, theorycrafting, feedback loops). A theological classroom which takes cognitive apprenticeship seriously starts by having students complete quests (i.e. assessments), gain problem-solving skills, and engage in collaboration with their peers in complex tasks in context rather than in abstraction. Class time is therefore devoted to these activities rather than being solely focused on the absorption of knowledge. Lectures and information are for the most part moved on to an external platform such as video lectures on an online learning management system, and class time is therefore utilised for lecture reviews, questions, and/or further information that a teacher deems necessary. Teachers as expert scholars are then able to come alongside students as novice scholars in order to work through problems together.[53] Any extra information that teachers provide during a quest or activity challenge is provided within the actual context of use, allowing students to accommodate the new information into knowledge that has already been grounded, an important factor in learning and retention.[54] Furthermore, since teachers and students are working alongside on the same sets of problems, students are able to view the teacher's actions and decisions, his/her methodology,

---

52 K. Squire, "Designed Cultures," in *Games, Learning, and Society: Learning and Meaning in the Digital Age*, ed. C. Steinkuehler, K. Squire and S.A. Barab, Learning in Doing (Cambridge: CUP, 2012), 18; See A. Collins, J.S. Brown and S.E. Newman, *Cognitive Apprenticeship: Teaching the Craft of Reading, Writing and Mathematics* (Cambridge, MA: Centre for the Study of Reading, University of Illinois, 1987).

53 Squire, "Designed Cultures," 18.

54 C. Steinkuehler and Y. Oh, "Apprenticeship in Massively Multiplayer Online Games," in *Games, Learning, and Society: Learning and Meaning in the Digital Age*, ed. C. Steinkuehler, K. Squire and S.A. Barab, Learning in Doing (Cambridge: CUP, 2012), 158.

as a clear model of the skills necessary to complete the challenge.[55] Teachers are then more able to help students to understand the content as well as the behaviours, habits, and critical methods with which they approach that content.[56]

Implications and Cautions

Are these mechanics practical for the theological classroom? Based on the research above, they are clearly potent tools for learning. However, there are some considerations that must be weighed before one goes about gamifying a whole course. First is the issue of time. If one decides to take the proposition of cognitive apprenticeship seriously by moving lectures online and having classroom time focused on theorycrafting, the preparation time needed for a course has now doubled. A large portion of time is spent creating the video lectures themselves. Next, time that would normally have gone to preparing for a lecture has to be devoted to planning and creating different classroom activities and quizzes in order to challenge students in a variety of different ways. This involves a serious time investment. Obviously with the number of students in a class, teachers are not always able to be the ones giving feedback. It therefore requires teachers to be well acquainted with their Learning Management System and its capabilities in order to create "passive" forms of feedback such as online quizzes and tests in order to give students an opportunity to apply their knowledge.

Second is the issue of quality. The cognitive, emotional, and social aspects of game mechanics must be integrated well with course content. It is not a matter of a simple semester outline, a website and a class plan. Each and every activity inside and outside of the class must be carefully considered and constructed, aligned with the course and student outcomes, and delivered in a way that does not emphasise knowledge above its relevance to the student's life and future. One of the reasons why gamification is not successful in many areas, corporate and educational, is its poor delivery and execution.[57]

---

55 Steinkuehler and Y. Oh, "Apprenticeship in Massively Multiplayer Online Games," 177.
56 See Clines, "Learning, Teaching, and Researching Biblical Studies, Today and Tomorrow," 7, 15–17; Steinkuehler and Oh, "Apprenticeship in Massively Multiplayer Online Games," 157.
57 Sheldon, *The Multiplayer Classroom*, 10.

Third is the issue of extrinsic versus intrinsic motivation.[58] A criticism of gamification is that game mechanics provide only extrinsic motivations (through the use of badges, levelling, point systems, and so on) that do not have long-term effects and actually in some cases reduce performance.[59] If the process of learning starts off with an extrinsic incentive, it is very possible that in order for learning to continue this "reward loop" must be maintained indefinitely.[60] However, through the use of these relatively intangible means, learners will likely "remain engaged over the long term because their daily performance contributes to their cumulative classroom standing."[61] These extrinsic rewards help to motivate the students and help to track their progress and if done well the extrinsic rewards might actually become intrinsic outcomes, as students begin to appreciate becoming an expert in the field. For example, when a student makes an investment into studying Greek, even though a temporary reward of success may be a badge or a higher rank along the way, because the end focus of the course has been geared towards the learner's passion and desired outcome, the transformative reward and the meaningful experience is actually that they become better Greek scholars. The full reward is the realisation that they have a better understanding and appreciation for the Greek language and its various applications and the use of minor extrinsic motivators helps to serve that telos.

Fourth is the issue of addiction. One concern with the use of gamification is the possibility that its mechanics may arouse addictive behaviour. Many studies, while investigating "pathological gaming"[62] and its relationship to other addictive behaviours, have been reluctant to diagnose "video game addiction" as a disorder. This is because there is surprisingly no consensus amongst researchers as to standardised criteria for discerning addiction itself.[63] Recently, however, numerous studies have questioned whether video games are inherently addictive

---

58 For "intrinsic" and "extrinsic" rewards see Sheldon, *The Multiplayer Classroom*, 75-79; Zichermann, *Gamification by Design*, 26-27.
59 S. Nicholson, "Strategies for Meaningful Gamification: Concepts Behind Transformative Play and Participatory Museums" (presented at the Meaningful Play 2012, Lansing, Michigan, 2012), 1, http://scottnicholson.com/pubs/meaningfulstrategies.pdf.
60 Zichermann, *Gamification by Design*, 27.
61 de Freitas and de Freitas, "Classroom Live: a Software-assisted Gamification Tool," 186-187.
62 D. A. Gentile *et al.*, "Pathological Video Game Use Among Youths: A Two-Year Longitudinal Study," *Pediatrics* 127/2 (2011), e319–e329.
63 see M.D. Griffiths, "Videogame Addiction: Further Thoughts and Observations," *International Journal of Mental Health and Addiction* 6/2 (2007), 184; M.M. Skoric, L.L.C. Teo and R.L. Neo, "Children and Video Games: Addiction, Engagement, and Scholastic Achievement," *CyberPsychology & Behavior* 12/5 (2009), 568.

or whether "addiction concerns the interaction between the individual, their culture and their environment."[64] The work of Wood is most convincing, particularly his reluctance to adhere to a reductionist typology of addiction, making allowance for complexity.[65] None the less, the potential for addiction to occur in a gamified classroom on a similar level as with regular video games is low. This is because, though gamification uses and implements various game elements and mechanics, it does not replicate the gaming experience verbatim. Additionally, it is not game-based learning, as mentioned above, which uses video games in the classroom for specific topics. Gamification merely draws on key elements that are successful within games and applies them to a classroom. The idea that gamification turns the classroom into an exact replica of the game environment is really an oversimplification of the way that the methods that are applied in a course. If anything, gamification mechanics allows space for students to develop a desire for lifelong learning.

Finally, there is the issue of gender bias. An ethical concern is that gamification methods are predisposed towards male students, presumably because video games are seen to be stereotypically popular amongst young men. A study done by the Pew Research Center in 2008 found that, amongst Americans, 65% of gamers were male and 35% were female.[66] The female percentage in the last two years has increased to 45-47%.[67] This research demonstrates that the methods used in games are effective in engaging both male and female players significantly. Additionally, some of the gamification methods, such as the nurturing affinity spaces, function as inclusive havens for learning, regardless of ethnicity, social standing, or gender.[68] Rather than engender sexism in the classroom, gamification methods may actually promote a learning environment where both male and female learners have an equal amount of support in

---

64 R.T.A. Wood, "Problems with the Concept of Video Game 'Addiction': Some Case Study Examples," *International Journal of Mental Health and Addiction* 6/2 (2007), 176.
65 R.T.A. Wood, "A Response to Blaszczynski, Griffiths and Turners' Comments on the Paper 'Problems with the Concept of Video Game "Addiction": Some Case Study Examples' (this Issue)," *International Journal of Mental Health and Addiction* 6/2 (2008), 193.
66 A. Lenhart *et al.*, *Teens, Video Games, and Civics* (Washington: Pew Internet and American Life Project, 2008), http://www.pewinternet.org/files/old-media//Files/Reports/2008/PIP_Teens_Games_and_Civics_Report_FINAL.pdf.pdf.
67 *2012 Sales, Demographic and Usage Date: Essential Facts About the Computer and Video Game Industry* (Entertainment Software Association, 2012), http://www.theesa.com/facts/pdfs/esa_ef_2012.pdf; *2013 Sales, Demographic and Usage Date: Essential Facts About the Computer and Video Game Industry* (Entertainment Software Association, 2013), http://www.theesa.com/facts/pdfs/esa_ef_2013.pdf.
68 Gee and Hayes, "Nurturing Affinity Spaces and Game-Based Learning," 134.

pursuing whatever kind of professional career they desire, despite institutional, denominational, and departmental discriminations.[69]

Conclusion

Gamification, the use of video game mechanics and design in the classroom, has a lot of potential for bringing transformational learning and meaningful play into the theological classroom. The ability of its methods to revitalise key relationships in a classroom setting (student-content, student-student, student-teacher) makes it a versatile instrument in improving the experience of learners. It is an innovative answer to a traditional education system in need of reanimation.[70] However, it is not a panacea for teaching in the humanities; it is not without its own cautions and it would be a mistake to gamify the whole system.

An important element of videos games is their ability to immerse a player into a narrative world in which they can interact and exercise volition. Using these game design methods in order to shape learning experiences can help provide a realistic narrative context for theological students to study. Rather than learning in a hypothetical setting exterior to the main story where the real research and scholarly activity happens, their study happens within the narrative of the scholars and pastors and teachers in the field. As a result, they are exposed to higher levels of independence and broad thinking. Gamification opens possibilities for students to flourish, helping them to see themselves as novice professionals rather than just students, and nurturing a higher level of ownership, responsibility, and motivation.

---

69 See M. Guest, S. Sharma and R. Song, *Gender and Career Progression in Theology and Religious Studies* (Durham, UK: Durham University, 2013).
70 Gee, *What Video Games Have to Teach Us About Learning and Literacy*, 22.

13 | EMBODIMENT AND TRANSFORMATION IN THE CONTEXT OF E-LEARNING

STEVE TAYLOR

Abstract

This essay argues that e-learning is a theological necessity. Four themes—of theological teaching as embodied in "living libraries," as nurturing hospitable space, as verbal driven in pedagogy and as cultivating communities of inquiry—are outlined. Within each of these themes, a dialogue is conducted between Luke 5:1-11, *Transforming Theology* and e-learning literature. The argument is then applied specifically to the task of teaching and learning, with three categories of pedagogical design grounded in a case study of a recent Introduction to Theology class. Finally, a theological note is made regarding the implications when the Incarnate One is read as the Ascended One. This suggests that the move from "face to face" to "digital at distance" is actually a following of the trajectory of Jesus, the miracle of Resurrection and Ascension in which both place and space are redefined—or, in the words of this project, transformed theologically.

• • •

Introduction

One place that any theologian might begin to reflect on teaching and learning is in a New Testament call story. One of the best known is the first encounter of Jesus with Simon Peter and John by the Lake of Gennesaret in Luke 5:1-11. As a way of introducing transformation in the context of e-learning, I will begin by contemporising this call narrative. While my approach might at first glance be considered as too casually playful for something as significant as transformation, I hope that, as this essay unfolds, a more thoughtful and intellectually rigorous interaction will become evident.

Luke 5:1-11: The e-Learning Version[1]

One day as Jesus was standing by the Lake of Gennesaret, the people were crowding around him checking their Facebook status and live tweeting updates as they were *listening to the Word of God.*

[Jesus] got into one of the boats ... Then he sat down and taught the people by handing the disciples a Kindle, on which had been loaded core theology texts, including the Dead Sea Scrolls and the latest translation of the First Testament.

Then Jesus said to Simon, "Don't be afraid; from now on you will fish for people." So he gave the disciples their Moodle login and automated password, which gave them access to a core topic—Discipleship. The course came complete with topic outlines for the next three years, along with hyperlinks to Vimeo video of the Sermon on the Mount. Assessment for this topic included the completion of weekly forums and a number of compulsory "doing contemporary theology" case studies. One involved a written response to a question asked by a rich young ruler, another an exercise in going ahead of Jesus looking for a donkey.

Jesus had toyed with the idea of offering a MOOCS, a Massive Open Online Course. This would have meant a focus on the crowds rather than the disciples, through open access and large-scale interactive participation.

Sadly his treasurer had resisted, pointing out that it was better to give the money to the poor rather than fund the video lecture style pedagogy which, it was argued, would increase student retention of texts from the Apocrypha.

Transforming Theology: 2012

At first glance such a contemporisation of a Lukan call story and the implicit assumption that transformational processes around Jesus might involve e-learning sound incongruous. We are shaped by a set of expectations regarding

---

1 Italics are from the *New International Version*, specifically Luke 5:1, 3, 10.

embodiment that privilege face to face interaction. However, this essay will, by taking four themes prominent in the e-learning literature, argue that in fact transforming theology must involve online technologies. In offering this argument, the goal will be to be theological, rather than pragmatic and technical, regarding embodiment, transformation and e-learning.

With regard to an overview of theology in Australia today, the best resource is Les Ball's *Transforming Theology*. It tests "the claims made by various theological colleges that they provide a transformative education."[2] The results demonstrate that, despite a wide range of cultural changes, including contextual theologies, inter-cultural awareness, feminist critiques and understanding of adult learning principles, theology curriculum has, for the last 35 years, remained remarkably uniform, with very limited development in areas of content, aims and structure.

> A fundamental premise of transformative learning is that it connects with and forms part of the stage of life of the learner, who comes to the educative program with significant life experience and established character and learning styles ... the research showed that, despite recent developments in experiential learning in field placements or other practical learning exercises, connection with a student's prior or concurrent life experience was generally not strategically structured within a curriculum.[3]

In sum, his claim is that in Australia our theological talk of transformation strides far ahead of our transformative walk. His analysis should be of deep concern to all those involved in teaching in the theological sector.

What is intriguing with regard to the theme of this essay is the very limited focus in *Transforming Theology* on e-learning. It is mentioned on only five pages, covering some 4% of the book's content. One reference is to the setting of the classroom, in which it is noted that whether physical or digital, the classroom space can be formational.[4] A second reference is to the slow adoption of e-learning and the fact that, at the time of research, of all the higher education providers of undergraduate theological degrees in Australia, when asked about improvements, only a couple of schools were considering "the adoption of

---

2 Les Ball, *Transforming Theology. Student Experience and Transformative Learning in Undergraduate Theological Education* (Preston Vic: Mosaic Press, 2012), 1.
3 Ball, *Transforming Theology*, 1.
4 Ball, *Transforming Theology*, 23-4.

online learning."[5] A third reference was to research that suggested a theological community of trust, so essential to the facilitation of transformative learning, "applies to online learning just as much as to classroom-based learning, with many successful accounts offered of the formation of strong on-line communities."[6] A fourth reference noted that "the very question of online curriculum design has not been given much attention."[7] A number of design possibilities were then positively noted, including community building forums and multi-learner activities. A fifth reference was an encouragement to consider the potential provided by electronic means to distribute lecture content prior. It was argued that such a move would free the student from "enslavement to time-poor content delivery" and make possible a "teacher-led program that adds value to that content by various creative means."[8]

Ball called this the "inside-out classroom." Another term now more prevalent is that of "flipped classroom."[9] Let me provide an illustration. During 2013, in my undergraduate first year Introduction to Theology class, taught at the Adelaide College of Divinity, all lecture notes and readings were placed online. The timetabled classroom time became, by negotiation with students, not a lecture, but a space for discussion of readings, for providing feedback on student progress and for working with each student on an individual "doing theology" project. This experience will, toward the conclusion of this essay, become a case study against which to test the four e-learning themes I wish to unfold.

2012: The Year of the MOOC

In sum, *Transforming Theology*, with regard to e-learning, offers five references, over seven pages, some 4% of its total content. By way of contrast, in the same year as *Transforming Theology* was published, *The New York Times* dubbed 2012 "The Year of the MOOC."[10] This contrast is not made to be critical of what is a fine book. It is rather to provide another perspective against which to test the

---

5   Ball, *Transforming Theology*, 93.
6   Ball, *Transforming Theology*, 101.
7   Ball, *Transforming Theology*, 111.
8   Ball, *Transforming Theology*, 131, 130.
9   See for example http://www.uq.edu.au/tediteach/flipped-classroom/what-is-fc.html, accessed March 13, 2014.
10 Laura Pappano, http://www.nytimes.com/2012/11/04/education/edlife/massive-open-online-courses-are-multiplying-at-a-rapid-pace.html?pagewanted=all&_r=0, accessed September 23, 2013.

Australian reality noted by Ball that, while only a "couple of [theological] schools [were] considering … the adoption of online learning", the world of higher education was caught in a tsunami of technological change.[11] Such is the pace of change that has affected the stable state that is theological education in Australia.

To be fair, despite the initial hype regarding MOOCS, more recent commentary has been muted. Some critics' commentary is worth pondering. One is the observation regarding the very low completion rates. In the course Bioelectricity, offered in 2012 at Duke University, while 12,725 students enrolled, only 7,761 ever watched a video. Even fewer (only 3,658) students attempted a quiz, while only 345, some 2.7%, attempted the final exam.[12] Other critics' claims, when examined more closely, hold little logic. For example, one concern is that 80% of communication is non-verbal, and thus face-to-face communication is superior to modes offered in the e-learning environment. Yet written texts remain for most scholars essential tools of the pedagogical trade, all of which are themselves non-verbal. So face-to-face communication is deemed to be privileged, while bibliographies and set weekly readings remain essential learning tools. Despite the flow and ebb around MOOCS, the questions of the relationship between theology and e-learning, the place of transformation in a digital world, remain important.

Pragmatic reasons for contemplating e-learning include access. To summarise a conversation with a student during a Distance Review, conducted at Uniting College for Leadership and Theology in 2012, "Without distance I couldn't have studied to be a minister. It was simply impossible for me to move to a State capital." This is a narrative in which the provision of distance education makes possible learning for those bounded by their physical location.

Economic reasons for contemplating e-learning centre around the pressure to remain viable in what is essentially a competitive theological market. With distance education, a theological school might reach more students. Simultaneously other providers, in other States and countries, can reach students in my State. Thus the realities of changes in global technology, mixed with the essentially capitalist model that underpins the multiplicity of theological schools, drives much interest in e-learning.

My interest is neither pragmatic nor economic. It is theological. To return to

---

11 Ball, *Transforming Theology*, 93.
12 See Dayna Catropa, "Big (MOOC) Data". *Inside Higher Ed*, February 24, 2013, accessed September 23, 2013, http://www.insidehighered.com/blogs/stratedgy/big-mooc-data.

my initial story, what type of ministerial formation might Jesus offer today? Would he privilege face-to-face engagement with his disciples? Or would he encourage online access, digital forums and the use of open source content?

Transforming Theology Online

Given this brief survey of theological teaching today, in what follows four themes will be outlined and then applied to e-learning. Each theme—embodiment, participation, praxis and community—will be integrated with my introduction, teasing out the implications of the call narrative as embodied in the words, deeds and person of Jesus the Christ. My argument is that when considered in light of concepts of these themes, of embodiment, participation, praxis and community, such an integration may provide a frame by which to understand e-learning as deeply theological.

The first theme begins with the notion of "living libraries." At the heart of Christian theology is a belief in Incarnation. The Word becomes flesh and dwelt among us. The invitation from Jesus, whether in John 1 or in the call narrative of Luke 5, is an invitation to participate in embodiment. "Come, Follow me" (John 1:43; Luke 5:11) is an invitation to relationship, as is the invitation to be children born of God (John 1:12), in "closest relationship" (1:18), with the One in whom you will see "heaven open and the angels of God descending and ascending on the Son of Man" (John 1:51).

One way to understand the particularity of embodiment offered in this transformative approach to theology is the concept of "living libraries." This approach to community learning began in Denmark in 2000. Rather than produce a written resource for libraries, a youth movement provided people. Rather than read a written resource, the community could book a person, and through conversation explore the perspective of another. In this Danish example, rather than write a resource on violence toward migrants, people who had experienced violence made themselves available for conversations. An independent audit of "living libraries" has recorded benefits including new learning and improved levels of community cohesion and engagement.[13]

This provides a way to understand e-learning, as opening up "living libraries."

---

13 Kevin Harris and Linda Constable, "'Light a light going on.' The Report on the Local Living Library Project," accessed February 4, 2013, http:www.local-level.org.uk/uploads/8/2/1/0/8210988/locallivinglibraryreport.pdf.

This can be applied in three ways to the task of theological education. The first "living library" is the lecturer who, with training and research, enables students to have a conversation with the Christian tradition. What has been read previously by the lecturer is thus synthesised, integrated and made accessible through the person of the lecturer.

A second area is invited guests. A particularly rich recent learning experience in e-learning at Uniting College has been an on-line cohort which used video-conferencing to allow the participation of overseas guests. Titled "Church Re-think," it involved interviewing individuals, including from New Zealand, Canada and Australia, whom the class had identified as thinking courageously and creatively about the church in mission today. In that sense, each visitor was a "living library," an embodiment via digital technologies of wisdom for this cohort of students.

A third area is the student. Everyone brings both a set of life experiences, as well as a context. These experiences and contexts add individual colour to every theological encounter. Incarnational embodiment expects us to take this seriously. It suggests that alongside content design, transformative e-learning needs to include the planning for experiential design, ways in which the student experience and context are intentionally drawn into the teaching of theology.

In this regard, is it challenging to note that one hypothesis being generated in the e-learning arena is that the closer a student is to their context, the more likely they are to begin to experience transforming theology, as they seek to integrate content with their current lived experience. Ruth has observed that online learning made more likely engagement with context, in noting the "importance of the individual student's context when taking the course."[14] In other words, the face-to-face class removes a student from their context, while e-learning allows them to stay in context, increasing their range of connections they as a "living library" are likely to make.

Similarly, in *Transforming Theology*, Ball noted that while some colleges held that residential community was more effective in transformation, among students "the perception is of a sometimes contrived college community, which can be remote from other significant elements of life."[15] Ball argued the focus should not be a community defined by local residence but by a sense of "theological cohort," a "community of trust."[16] Such communities were as likely online as in

---

14 Lester Ruth, "Converting My Course Converted Me: How Reinventing an On-campus Course for an Online Environment Reinvigorated My Teaching," *Teaching Theology and Religion*, 9/4 (2006), 241.
15 Ball, *Transforming Theology*, 100.
16 Ball, *Transforming Theology*, 100.

a classroom.[17] The work of Ruth and Ball not only provides a focus on lecturer, guest, student as "living libraries" of Incarnational embodiment. It also assumes a second theme in e-learning, that of the nurture of hospitable space.

Second, then, is the nurture of hospitable space. One of the themes recurring in recent theology is that of hospitality. This often includes discussion of Jesus as offering "table fellowship." The phrase is evident in the work of Jacob Neusner, who noted that of the 341 rulings that go back to the Pharisees, 229 relate to table fellowship.[18] It helps us understand the radical nature of Jesus' embodiment and the way his words and deeds are a participation in hospitality. What are the implications of Jesus' invitation to come follow him into hospitable space? What does it mean for e-learning in theology?

Richard Ascough has referred to the often heard, "But, of course, online learning cannot replicate the community building that goes on in the classroom."[19] He responded that the failure to create community is due not to the technology that is e-learning, but to the instructional design. In other words, do not blame the tools but the user, in this case the theology teacher. Ascough drew on Palloff and Pratt, who had argued that there are six elements critical to successful distance learning: honesty, responsiveness, relevance, respect, openness, and empowerment.[20] For Ascough, "It is striking that not one of these is a technological issue."[21]

Brent Hege outlined how safe and vibrant virtual community and sustained, lively engagement with that community of learners can be created online.[22] Perry and Edwards have argued for three types of educational presence—social presence, cognitive presence, and teaching presence. Each is the result of course design, how the tools are used. Perry and Edwards presented the need to pay attention to social presence in the learning environment.[23] The literature thus

---

17 Ball, *Transforming Theology*, 111.
18 See Jacob Neusner, *From Politics to Piety: The Emergence of Pharisaic Judaism* (Englewood Cliffs, NJ: Prentice Hall, 1973).
19 Richard S. Ascough "Welcoming Design—Hosting a Hospitable Online Course," *Teaching Theology and Religion*, 10/3 (2007), 131.
20 See Rena M. Palloff and Keith Pratt, *Building Learning Communities in Cyberspace: Effective Strategies for the Online Classroom* (San Francisco: Jossey-Bass, 1999), 160.
21 Ascough, *Teaching Theology and Religion*, 131.
22 Brent A. R. Hege "The Online Theology Classroom: Strategies for Engaging a Community of Distance Learners in a Hybrid Model of Online Education," *Teaching Theology and Religion* 14/1 (January 2011), 13-20.
23 Beth Perry and Margaret Edwards, "Exemplary Online Educators: Creating a Community of Inquiry," *Turkish Online Journal of Distance Education* 6/2 (2005, accessed March 13, 2014, http://tojde.anadolu.edu.tr/tojde18/articles/article6.htm.

suggests that alongside content and experiential design, transformative e-learning also needs to include the planning for interactional design.

In a traditional face-to-face class, two key locations for interaction are the class and the cup of tea. It is important to note that both of these are synchronous. In contrast, interaction in an e-learning context can occur in many diverse ways. These include quiz, forum, blog, wiki, general discussion, threaded discussion. What is instructive is the realisation that each of these can be either synchronous or asynchronous. In other words, the opportunities for social presence in an e-learning context are expanded. Hospitality can occur not only during a set "lecture time", but 24/7 as social presence is encouraged in the design of e-learning and in the active facilitation of safe space.

This brings us to our third theme in e-learning, that of verb-driven pedagogies. It is instructive to note how the call narrative of Luke 5 is shaped around the verbs—follow, make, fishers. The commission of the twelve in Luke 6 and the 70/72 in Luke 10 is similarly verb driven—sent, proclaim, heal. This suggests a theology that is verb-driven, that invites a doing, in the context of the practice of ministry.

It could be argued that this is the trajectory envisaged in *Transforming Theology*, given its plea that the learning experience of adult students, who bring significant life experience, be integrated into their learning. This, it is suggested, will require a shift from information transmission to a "holistic and potentially transformative development of the person within an authentic community."[24] To quote from Mezirow:

> the process of becoming critically aware of how and why our assumptions have come to constrain the way we perceive, understand, and feel about our world; changing these structures or habitual expectation to make possible a more inclusive, discriminating, and integrative perspective; and finally making choices or otherwise acting on these new understandings.[25]

Challenging assumptions becomes possible as hospitable space is created and as the diversity that is student stories is shared. But the goal is transformation. The creation of hospitality must result in "choices," in verb-driven actions. This is reinforced when *Transforming Theology* cites the 2011 UNESCO Curriculum

---

24 Ball, *Transforming Theology*, 17.
25 Ball, *Transforming Theology*, 11-12, citing Mezirow, *Transformative Dimensions of Adult Learning* (San Francisco: Jossey-Bass, 1991), 167.

Reform Manifesto and the eleven principles for undergraduate curricula worldwide. Seven of these are verb driven, including "seminars devoted to complex real life problems," "highlight the challenges, open questions and uncertainties," "awareness of the great problems humanity is facing," "demonstrate and rigorously practice," "examine critically," "engage with the world's complexity and messiness," "practice and application."[26]

With regard to e-learning, it is intriguing that Lester Ruth describes his pedagogical journey into e-learning as requiring from him a shift from noun driven to verb driven. "My original on-campus course had been noun-driven (my time with students was about transferring information, i.e. nouns), but becoming an online teacher has resulted in my courses being verb-driven (my time with students is about various uses of course content, i.e. verbs)."[27] In other words, e-learning can make possible the transformative vision being cast in *Transforming Theology*. A verb-driven pedagogy involves a focus on words like assess, collaborate, experiment, imagine, inquire, perform, simulate, reflect, describe, identify, review, examine, distinguish, practise, design.[28] Returning to my initial example, my undergraduate first year Introduction to Theology class, with all the learning resources placed online, the interaction, whether face-to-face or online, could shift from information transfer to the utilisation of the course content. Verb-driven words like collaborate, inquire, reflect, review became a far more accurate description of our time together.

Such a verb-driven approach must by necessity involve not only the individual, but the class as a community of inquiry. Hence we lead to a fourth (and final) element, the cultivation of communities of inquiry. The entire process of discipleship around Jesus revolved around a community of inquiry. Central to the Gospel narratives is a gathering of disciples. In this community, Jesus takes the lead, asking questions: Who do you say that I am? Who among you should cast the first stone? Do you love me, Peter?

With regard to e-learning, the term "communities of inquiry" is helpfully explored in the work of Richard Ascough.[29] He brings together two concepts.

---

26 Ball, *Transforming Theology*, 15, drawing on UNESCO, "Curriculum Reform Manifesto: *Principles for Rethinking Undergraduate Curricula for the 21st Century*," 15 August 2011, accessed September 23, 2012, http://curriculumreform.org/curriculum-reform-manifesto/.
27 Ruth, *Teaching Theology and Religion*, 239.
28 See Kathleen Taylor, Catherine Marienau and Morris Fiddler, *Developing Adult Learners: Strategies for Teachers and Trainers* (San Francisco: Jossey-Bass, 2000) and Jane Vella, *Learning to Listen, Learning to Teach: The Power of Dialogue in Educating Adult,* (San Francisco: Jossey-Bass, 2002).
29 Ascough, *Teaching Theology and Religion*, 132.

First is that of "communities of practice," defined as a group of people "who share a concern, a set of problems, or a passion about a topic, and who deepen their knowledge and expertise in this area by interacting on an ongoing basis."[30] This aligns with the notion of verb-driven pedagogies, in which the focus for the e-learning community is on "practice." Second, he deals with "bounded learning communities"—"groups that form within a structured teaching or training setting, typically a course," that develop "in direct response to guidance provided by an instructor, supported by a cumulative resource base."[31]

Applying the lens of transforming theology, we can envisage Jesus' calling of disciples into a "community of inquiry," one that assumes a "community of practice" in the invitation to come, follow, make, fish. This is a community that is gathered around the Messianic inquiry, from "Who do you say that I am?" through to "Do you love me, Peter?" These are identity-forming, verb-driven questions. In so doing, e-learning becomes an explicitly theological task, the transformative, communal encounter with the questions asked by us of the Living Word. Adaptation and deployment would be driven not by technological or economic reasons, but by the desire to participate in the possibility of profoundly transformative change in identity and behaviour.

Pushing this argument further, there is evidence in the literature that e-learning might actually enhance ministerial formation. Ball noted how online technologies allow "multi-learner activities rather than a reliance on the standard (and isolating) individual learning tasks."[32] Palloff and Pratt documented how many workplace skills are gained through participation in the online learning community and are transferable to the world of work.[33] Randy Garrison has argued that asynchronous online learning—because of its emphasis on "reflective collaboration"—can be more conducive to cognitive development than a

---

30 Etienne Wenger, *Communities of Practice: Learning, Meaning, and Identity* (Cambridge: Cambridge University Press, 1998).
31 Brent G. Wilson, Stacey Ludwig-Hardman, Christine L. Thornam and Joanna C. Dunlap, "Bounded Community: Designing and Facilitating Learning Communities in Formal Courses," *International Review of Research in Open and Distance Learning* 5/3 (2004), accessed February 9, 2007, http://www.irrodl.org/index.php/irrodl/article/view/204/286.
32 Ball, *Transforming Theology*, 111.
33 Palloff and Pratt. *Building Learning Communities in Cyberspace*.

traditional classroom environment.[34] In other words, asynchronous learning is more likely to cultivate a reflective practitioner.

This might seem counter-intuitive, given the implicit (and at times explicit) privileging in theological discourse of the face-to-face. However, consider by way of example, skills essential to the ministerial role, those of consensus building and group work. These can be easily incorporated into online courses, given the technology, with the assumption that students will collaborate with distant colleagues. In so doing, they are being expected to engage cooperatively with diverse individuals in diverse contexts.

Thus in one of the introductory courses I teach (Reading Cultures), the assessment criteria include to "enable students to see ministry and ministers from a sociological perspective and to develop greater social sensitivity about the ministry process" and to "engage collaboratively with set readings, and various forms of media in order to explore social, economic, political, religious, ecological and educational perspectives in Australian society." Both of these invite a focus on being in community and engaging in collaboration. To achieve these outcomes, a group learning task is set. Students are invited to become consultants, preparing a report for a local leadership team on ministry options. A set of case studies, based on real world scenarios, is provided. In other words, there is created a "community of inquiry" around a "verb-driven" application of class learnings made to real world complexity.

Invariably there is resistance, often shaped by students' prior experience of being placed in a somewhat arbitrary fashion in groups of varying ability and dedication. In response, I draw attention to the fact that the nature of ministry assumes a placement in a role in which the group is arbitrary and in which participants have different abilities and commitments. This is thus preparing them for real life ministry. To support the learning, I offer resources to enhance the development of a "community of inquiry." A further set of resistances to group activities is posed by those who enrol by distance. They wonder how they will become a group, given their sense of isolation. Again, I draw attention to the fact that ministry by definition expects an ability to build relationships, no matter how isolated the context. This is thus preparing them for real life ministry.

---

34 In Richard A. Pruitt, "The Application of Cognitive-Developmental or Mediated Cognitive Learning Strategies in Online College Coursework," *Teaching Theology and Religion*, 14/3 (July 2011), 226-246, citing Randy Garrison, "Cognitive Presence for Effective Asynchronous Online Learning," in *Elements of Quality Online Education: Practice and Direction*, ed. John R. Bourne and Janet C. Moore (Needham, MA: Sloan., 2003), 47–58 at 48, 50.

Experience shows that while the class Moodle site is used initially to allow contact, a range of other technologies is employed, including Skype, email and conference calls. Thus Ball's "multi-learner activity is experienced."[35] The setting of a verb-driven project builds a community of inquiry around the transformative question of how to relate faith to real world problems. I referred earlier to the distant student who, in a Distance Review conducted earlier this year, highlighted the way that e-learning gave her access to ministry. During the review, she also drew attention to this very assignment. She described how it turned her educational experience with our distance offerings from individual to community. What had been a "one-to-one" relationship with a marker now became a "one-to-many" relationship with students throughout Australia. She felt a greater sense of connection to a community of learners. To use a theological term, it enabled her to experience more fully the catholicity of the church as she engaged with other students and learnt from their diversity.

One further dimension of this "community of inquiry" is worth teasing out as it relates to e-learning. Ball, in *Transforming Theology*, noted the argument of Winkelmes that the classroom is the most feasible location for formation. Ball then described how e-learning can make this formational space asynchronous.[36]

> Even when the classroom is the virtual space of online learning, instructional strategies need to be designed to enhance personal and formational learning by focusing on the affective domain, especially encouraging relational interaction and promoting a sense of community, and incorporating the important arenas of interactive learning: student-to-student, student-to-teacher, and student-to-content.[37]

This begins to weave together the four themes I have developed to date. It takes note of the multiplicity of learnings present when lecturers, guests and students are understood affectively, as "living libraries." It reminds us of the necessity of hospitable space, in order to encourage relational interaction. It points us to verb-driven pedagogies in the search for interactive learning. It seeks community, specifically, community of inquiry.

---

35 Ball, *Transforming Theology*, 111.
36 Mary Ann Winkelmes, "The Classroom as a Place of Formation: Purposefully Creating a Transformative Environment for Today's Diverse Seminary Population," *Teaching Theology & Religion* 7, 4 (October 2004), 213.
37 Ball, *Transforming Theology*, 24.

A Classroom Case Study

What this suggests is a three-fold task in the teaching of theology.

The first task is content design. This has, as *Transforming Theology* reminds us, been the historic focus of undergraduate theological education. Given my argument above, the dialogue between Jesus' call narratives and literature on e-learning, I want to suggest that theological educators consider two further intentional design tasks.

One is interactional design. This incorporates the theological themes already advanced, of hospitable space and community of inquiry. Interactional design will involve the intentional processes by which as much time is spent designing ways for interaction to occur as is spent considering information to be disseminated. To quote Ruth, "Discussions were not some by-product intruding into my agenda for the course. They were the course. I had to manage them well."[38]

Another is experiential design. This incorporates the theological themes of "living libraries" and verb-driven pedagogies. Interactional design will involve the intentional processes in which time is spent not only designing ways for interaction to occur or gathering information to be disseminated, but also charting processes by which experience can be named, affirmed and processed. To quote Jude Long, the theological teacher's role is thus seen more as a learning facilitator than as a lecturer.[39]

Let me illustrate these three designs with a return to my original example, the undergraduate first year core unit, Introduction to theology. In introducing the class on the first morning face-to-face, I asked if anyone did not have access to the internet. Everyone did. I then asked if anyone did not have access to a printer. Again, everyone did. This ensured there would be no access issues for what I was about to propose. I then suggested that, given theology is best done in community, that we might spend our class doing, rather than hearing, theology. Each student would identify a theological question and work, during class time, on this topic (student-centred). Each week, I would introduce (becoming a "living library") the tools they might need to do (verb-driven) the theological work to address their question. Framing this using the Wesleyan quadrilateral, we would together (as a "community of inquiry") explore how to use the library to access the tradition, how to employ the Bible in response to questions of faith, how to integrate experience into our thinking and, finally, in

---

38 Ruth, *Teaching Theology and Religion*, 237.
39 Long, in Ball, *Transforming Theology*, 24.

ways that valued imaginative reason. This enabled a bringing together of resources that could serve students both face-to-face and at a distance. Both access the same resources on Moodle. A specific part of the established site is dedicated to the doing of theology. This includes a contemporary example, which I as lecturer undertake, building a wiki of my "doing theology" in order to model the process.

So, let me analyse this example of a "flipped classroom," made possible by e-learning, against the three design tasks I have advanced.

	Content	Interactional	Experiential
My (current) theological question is …		Learner driven, with each participant identifying a theological question they will work on. Verb driven, in that theology is an activity, an action of questioning.	
I'm curious about this because ….			Names curiosity as important. Validates lived experience. Helps clarify how individual experience shapes doing of theology. The class example provided by the lecturer ensures the lecturer's experience is also named.
The theological frame I'm going to use is …	Draws on a range of theological models introduced in initial lecture material.	Expects application of lecture material.	
My conversation partners will need to include ….	Invites participants into the library, to find conversational partners. Research skills learnt by induction.		Model of dinner party (imagine six people you would like to invite to discuss your doing theology question with you) provides way of seeing theology within their practice and experience.
I'd like to express my findings by …..	Draws on the diversity of ways theology can be expressed, introduced in initial lecture material.		Provides a way to link the production of theological resource with the gifts and context brought by a student. In one case, a student with a passion for drama labours for hours over a script, thus integrating their passions with theological production.

The depth of engagement has surprised us all. I saw far more evidence of students in the library reading more widely in the tradition than I had previously experienced. Each "doing theology" question identified by the students related in some way to a core theological issue, yet was asked in a way that I would have been unlikely to address. In other ways, their questions were taking them into the theological tradition, yet in a student-centred manner.

Student feedback was overwhelmingly positive. One hundred per cent strongly agreed that it was a worthwhile learning experience. One commented: "The creative lesson style was very effective and helped me to integrate the readings into other thoughts in different ways." Another noted the value of "time in the library," a comment that pointed to the value of freeing class time for them to pursue their own theological questions. A third noted: "The emphasis on learning of theology ourselves was refreshing. Other theologians—the tradition—were examined to this end of building one's own theology."

In sum, this type of "flipped classroom learning experience" has been made possible first because of e-learning and the opportunity to shift content into another mode of access. Second, it arose from an intentional design process, which included consideration of interaction and experiential design, in order to enhance student engagement with content.

Incarnation and Ascension

As a theologian, I want to make one final note in this exploration of embodiment and transformation in e-learning. My starting point by way of introduction was Luke 5, a Gospel call narrative. It provides a theological ground, of Incarnation, the Word made flesh grounded in the particularity of place. My argument then proceeded to outline four themes. Each theme was related to the Gospel narratives, to the Incarnate One who is visible in embodiment, participation, praxis and community.

In making this argument, I want now to make explicit a potential theological danger, that this Incarnate One is pressed into a place. I am referring to the argument that face-to-face teaching is somehow, in some way, more Incarnational because it allows face-to-face interaction. By extension, this Incarnational face-to-face move privileges one classroom and marginalises another. It turns distance into a poor cousin. More worryingly, it runs the danger of asserting that digital is in fact a second hand degree. (Not that I am aware of any theological school charging less, or that gaining a degree by distance is stated as somehow "second class".)

My concern is that this application of Incarnation as face-to-face is in fact a theological mis-step. It overlooks the reality of Resurrection and Ascension. It is commonly theological to assert that the Resurrected Jesus redefines embodiment. We understand the body in the life to come as mysteriously synchronous with the Resurrected Jesus who occupies a different time and space continuum, as he appears and disappears from among them.

There is also the Creedal affirmation that Jesus ascended into Heaven. The Ascended One is the Resurrected One who is the Incarnate One. Now we have a One who is visible in embodiment, participation, praxis and community, seated at the right hand of the Father. Once again, our notions of place and space are re-defined. The claims of Ascension maintain that despite physical separation, relationship remains possible, in ways that are different, but nevertheless are embodied, participative, verb-driven and communal. And no theologian would claim that the Resurrected and Ascended One is somehow a poor cousin, that relationship is now "second class."

So, when I begin with a call narrative of the Incarnate One in Luke 5, I am asking that themes of embodiment, participation, praxis and community be read in ways that are continuous with Resurrection and Ascension. By application, I am thus suggesting that e-learning is theological, that physical absence does not mean a loss of embodiment. Instead connection continues, as prayer at the right hand of the Father. This theological reality, in which Incarnation is Ascension, seems to me to provide yet further encouragement in the search for a transforming theology in the context of e-learning.

Conclusion

In sum, I began by contemporising Luke 5:1-11. While somewhat playful, the suggestion of an e-learning version was made in order to allow a more a serious argument to be unfurled. The argument has been that the Incarnate One, visible in embodiment, participation, praxis and community, must encourage understandings of theological teaching as embodied in "living libraries," as nurturing hospitable space, as verb-driven in pedagogy and as cultivating communities of inquiry. In outlining these four themes, I have sought to conduct a dialogue between Luke 5:1-11, *Transforming Theology* and some e-learning literature. I have also, since this is about teaching and learning, sought to be practical in offering a number of examples of e-learning practice.

I have then argued that, in light of these four themes, transforming theology needs to prioritise three categories of pedagogical design, not only seeking content, but with a similar intentionality, mapping interaction and experiential design into our teaching and learning. This has been grounded in a case study of a recent Introduction to Theology class.

Finally, I have noted that this Incarnate One is also an Ascended One. I am thus suggesting that the move, from face-to-face to digital at distance, is actually a following of the trajectory of Jesus, the miracle of Resurrection and Ascension in which both place and space are redefined—or, in the words of this project, transformed theologically.

The argument has thus woven together these Incarnational themes, that e-learning is a theological necessity. I am suggesting that Jesus would have used e-learning—not for pragmatic or economic reasons, but for theological reasons, as an expression of Incarnation, as an act of transforming theology, for theology's sake.

This then suggests a hypothesis that one way to enhance the transforming of theology in Australia will be through the embrace of e-learning. While I have pursued this as a theological claim, I conclude by noting it is suggested in some of the e-learning literature. Lester Ruth, currently Liturgy lecturer at Duke, has described how "online teaching has revolutionized all my teaching ... it was in an online environment that I first stumbled upon sound pedagogy."[40] Or to quote Ball, "Effective online design has developed the sense of community as a formative dimension ... in ways that strategically and more intentionally embrace the aspects of context and activity rather than simply content and absorption."[41] If Ball in *Transforming Theology* is right, then e-learning is indeed transformation. Considering teaching as not only the design of content but as the design of interaction and experience will change us, improve our teaching and learning. For the goal, surely, is theological transformation, not theological information.

---

40   Ruth, *Teaching Theology and Religion*, 237.
41   Ball, *Transforming Theology*, 111.

SECTION SIX

GOING AHEAD: IDEAS FROM THE FIELD

14 | A PRACTICAL APPROACH FOR TEACHING FOUNDATIONAL THEOLOGY

INQUIRY-BASED LEARNING AND THE MATRIX OF IDEAS PROCESS

DENISE GOODWIN

Abstract

Delivering foundational theology units to practising teachers seeking accreditation to teach in Catholic schools in Melbourne offered an opportunity to engage them in their own learning. In the following *Inquiry-Based Learning* (IBL) module, a constructivist learning approach engaged students' worldviews, thus assisting them in the identification and analysis of Christological thought through strategic group discussion, collaborative learning and construction of a matrix of ideas. Details of the methodology, examples of students' work, and outcomes of the method are provided. The matrix of ideas process offers a practical learning technique for students and has a wide educational application where critical thought and strategy are needed to analyse theological writings. This essay articulates one strand of matrix application to teaching foundational theology.

* * *

Rationale

The purpose of this essay is to offer a study in the form of a practical example for an inquiry-based method of learning in a Christological topic in theology at a foundational level. Inquiry-based learning has a part to play in transformative learning because pedagogically they are both underpinned by a constructivist learning model that is person-centred and acknowledges the importance of life experiences as an integral part of the person's learning.[1] In this example, application of IBL focuses on the development of research skills through the practice of problem-solving aspects of textual references and the application of critical thinking with regard to the nature of Jesus Christ's being. The development of information literacy combined with collaborative inquiry helps make known the importance of students' experiences in their process of learning, thus assisting them in the identification and analysis of Christological thought through strategic group discussion and the construction of a matrix of ideas. These strategies provide scaffolding in the cognitive formation of theological concepts and encourage higher learning. It is important to note that the students' developments in practical learning skills need to be viewed as an important part of a unit's teaching objectives, learning outcomes, student assessment and the lecturer's unit evaluation. In this way, inquiry-based learning offers a reflexive practice where the students and lecturer become co-learners.

Context

The Graduate Certificate course in teaching religious education offers a mandatory unit in foundational theology. This unit is delivered to practising teachers seeking accreditation to teach religious education in Catholic schools. The students who make up the class generally come with mixed abilities and various levels of teaching experience from primary and secondary schools, and it is important to assist their theological learning by discussing key concepts and ideas and nurturing their sense of inquiry. A constructivist learning approach has been adopted, as a pedagogy readily appreciated by practising teachers who were used to facilitating inquiry and reflective methods in their integrated curriculums in the schools where they taught.

---

1   In regard to transformative and constructive learning, see respectively:
    Jack Mezirow, "An Overview of Transformative Learning," in *Lifelong Learning: Concepts and Contexts*, ed. P. Sutherland & J. Crowther (New York: Routledge, 2006), 24-38.
    Lev Vygotsky, *Mind and Society: The Development of Higher Mental Processes* (Cambridge, MA: Harvard University Press, 1978).

Pedagogic Framework: A Constructivist Approach

Constructivism may refer to either an epistemology or a pedagogy. As a theory of knowledge the seminal works of Piaget and Kant provided its basis, and as a way of learning it defined human experience as the seat of knowledge.[2] Jack Mezirow, Lev Vygotsky, Jerome Bruner and Barbara Rogoff highlight research and theory in constructivist pedagogy.[3]

Epistemologically, constructivism derived aspects of its rationale from Piaget's theory of cognition. Claims that linked scientific and technological advances to providing the ultimate truths about the world objectified knowledge and reality. Piaget questioned this view of reality arguing that our senses, which coordinated our action, influenced the way we perceived and thought about the world, and this experience embodied the way knowledge was made.[4] Kantian constructivism made the link between empiricism and rationalism. According to Kant, neither the knowledge grounded in experience nor the knowledge constructed by the mind could operate in a vacuum. Empirical knowledge required sensory experiences and rational knowledge needed conceptual schemes to make meaning as they constructed experience. The construct of experience was thus facilitated by mental categories such as space, time, motion and previous knowledge. For Kant, knowledge acquired empirically and rationally was realised in these conceptual areas because these elements characterised our experience of the world.[5]

Piaget and Kant's contributions to constructivism led to the following assumptions. Knowledge within the realm of sensory experience is rationalised symbiotically through human conceptual constructs. In effect, living and thinking co-construct our human experience of the world and contribute to a collective body of knowledge. This construct of meaning provides the framework for our cognitive formation and higher learning.

As a model of learning, Vygotsky's Social Development Theory is one of the foundations for constructivism. Various levels of social interaction in human

---

2   Jean Piaget, *The Child's Conception of Space* (New York: Macmillan, 1956).
    Emanuel Kant, *Critique of Pure Reason*, trans. P.Guyer and A. W. Wood (Cambridge: Cambridge University Press, 1998).
3   Mezirow, "An Overview," 24-38; Vygotsky, "Mind," 1978; Jerome Bruner, *The Process of Education* (Cambridge, MA: Harvard University Press, 1960); Barbara Rogoff, Eugene Matusov and Cynthia White, "Models of Teaching and Learning: Participation in a Community of Learners," in *Handbook of Education and Human Development* (Oxford, UK: Blackwell, 1996), 388-414.
4   E. von Glaserfeld, *Radical Constructivism: A Way of Knowing and Learning* (London: Falmer. 1995).
5   K. Howe & J. Berv, "Constructing Constructivism, Epistemological and Pedagogical," in *Constructivism in Education: Opinions and Second Opinions on Controversial Issues*, ed. D.C. Phillips (Chicago, Illinois: The University of Chicago Press, 2000), 19-40.

experience help promote voluntary attention and logical memory, which then lead to the formation of concepts.[6] While much of Vygotsky's research was conducted in the context of children's language learning, broader applications of his framework have been conceived.[7] Such applications highlight the importance of social interaction in the role of education. Apropos, the principles of Mezirow's transformative learning theory encompass two aspects of adult learning. Instrumental learning is identified in the generation of understanding through exploration of cause and effect (reason), and communicative learning in a social context has been given to enact feelings (emotion). Cognition through reason in the context of social interaction offers consonance with learning modes generated through Vygotsky's Social Development Theory. In the context of social interaction for the promotion of conceptual learning, constructivist learning methods for adult learning may be devised. Mezirow's learning theory and the learning methods generated through Vygotsky's socially aware education theory offer practical learning approaches for adults to aid their development of new schemes and gain new perspectives. In this way, the concept of "transformative learning" may operate meaningfully in a social context for adult learning.[8]

An example highlighting this working relationship may be demonstrated in an inquiry approach where cognitive and socially interactive scaffolding activities were utilised for adult learning in foundational theology.[9] Here, inquiry-based learning involved the construction of a matrix of ideas, where a framework for analysing and synthesising theological information engaged a study group's conceptual formation through social interaction for their individual learning. Put simply, students were asked to work on a learning problem together and then afterwards on their own. The specific scaffolds for this activity included the facilitator's (lecturer's) choice of most appropriate articles to serve as reference for analysis, the study group coming to consensus in naming key principles for the texts, collaborative learning at Rogoff's apprenticeship level,[10] discussion and guided participation in referencing relevant excerpts from one of the texts,

---

6   Vygotsky, "Mind," 57.
7   J.V. Wertsch, *Cultural, Communication, and Cognition: Vygotskian Perspectives* (Cambridge: Cambridge University Press, 1985).
8   For Transformation theory of adult learning see Jack Mezirow, "Transformation Theory of Adult Learning," in *In Defense of the Life-world*, ed. M.R. Welton (New York: State University of New York Press, 1995), 39-70.
9   Scaffolding: Educational terminology used to describe joint construction of learning in a given field between learner/s and facilitator, with a gradual withdrawal of support from the facilitator.
10 Barbara Rogoff identifies three types of collaborative, social learning. Apprenticeship, guided participation and appropriation assume community, interpersonal and personal processes of learning respectively. See Rogoff, Matusov and White, "Models," 338-414.

including identification of its key principles, and the facilitator's modelling of written analysis for one of the textual references in matrix.

These activities incorporate various learning approaches which are meant to hone students' skills in working collaboratively in whole class and small groups, whilst encouraging independence in their research methods. These scaffolds were chosen so that learners could ultimately use the referenced ideas from their completed matrix to inform their writing of a comparative essay canvassing prominent theological thought about Jesus Christ and the Kingdom of God. It was understood that as the learner became more competent in the field of theological language, the understandings of various theologians and other theological concepts in general, the learning supports would be withdrawn at different stages during coursework to reflect the increasing academic level of scholarship expected of students.[11]

This constructivist learning approach provided students with guided instruction on theological concepts, mainly relating to the nature of Jesus Christ, and was used to encourage their practice in analysis and synthesis of various theological writings. Teacher and student participation and engagement in activities were coordinated to encourage learning that helped change students' meaning structures through reflection about the theological content of the information they were working with, and by becoming cognisant of the active process in their learning and the possibilities it held for empowering their learning independence.

Why Adopt Inquiry-Based Learning in Theology?

Learning about theology involves an active process of discovery involving one's mind, emotions and spirituality whether focused in systematics, biblical study, missiology/pastoral studies, church history or moral theology. This assertion is made to highlight the importance that constructivist pedagogy, transformative learning and inquiry-based learning approaches can apply to all areas of theological learning and should not be considered just the domain of practical theology. Learning about theology and religion is meant to go beyond lecturing and tutoring, and it needs to be active and creative. Teaching instructionally solely in the cognitive domain sells short the purpose for seeking learning about God. Using inquiry-based learning as an educational tool in theology offers methodological pathways to navigate and execute transformative learning in adults.

---

11   Jerome Bruner, *Toward a Theory of Instruction* (Cambridge, MA: Harvard University Press, 1966).

According to Mezirow, to assist in changing the meaning structures in adult cognition, reflection in content, process and premise schemes and perspectives are significant. Content reflection relays learning with present meaning schemes and draws from personal experiences, process reflection helps develop new meaning schemes, and premise reflection has the ability to enact learning through meaning transformation by engaging deep consideration of a larger view of things.[12] Inquiry-based learning assists students in "learning to learn," and acknowledges the importance of the cognitive, affective and spiritual areas of learning in academic theological endeavour. These areas need to be addressed in unit objectives for student learning outcomes. When thinking about what is expected from students in undertaking study in foundational theology, it bears noting that teaching can be a one-way passage for delivery of information without knowing how or if the information has been received until summative assessments have been done. Inquiry–based learning takes the emphasis off instruction and promotes the staged development of student skills by providing opportunity to incorporate diagnostic, formative and summative assessments in a set unit of work. Being able to receive and provide varied types of feedback from and to students during a unit of work assists the learning of the whole class and individual students, and improves the overall unit of work.

Inquiry-Based Learning and the Matrix of Ideas Process

a) Learning Outcomes for the Unit in Foundational Theology

The following learning outcomes were listed for the foundational unit in theology:

- Demonstrate an appreciation of the role of religion in the human search for meaning
- Understand the significance of Jesus Christ for the Christian faith
- Appreciate the origin, structure and mission of the Church
- Demonstrate an understanding of Christian hope in the context of Catholic eschatology
- Develop in written form a theological presentation of a particular theme in theology.

In addition to the stated outcomes for the unit, the learning module that encompassed the matrix of ideas was specifically designed for students to be

---

12　Jack Mezirow, *Cognitive Processes: Contemporary Paradigm of Learning*, ed. Sutherland (San Francisco, IN: Jossey-Bass, 1998), 5-12.

able to locate key elements and ideas in theological writings and to produce an expository text on a theological concept using the matrix of ideas. The criteria for assessment for these tasks included a written demonstration of comprehension in the form of the matrix. An analysis and synthesis of theological texts was also to be provided via interpretations presented in the matrix, as well as a comparative text explaining the Christological understanding of various theologians. The delivery of this learning module sought also to increase student motivation and to help them learn to transfer knowledge of this research strategy to other learning projects.

The learning outcomes listed infer either cognitive and affective or cognitive only student outcomes. The aim of student appreciation is included in outcomes one and three, which call for reflection on a particular function or concept. Heartfelt appreciation demonstrates feelings and emotions, and demonstration of these requires more than the production of an essay or an exam. The demonstration of appreciation in an area of study invites the student to reflect on certain aspects of content, process or premise as suggested by Mezirow.[13] While inquiry-based learning methods and activities can be devised to account for demonstration of appreciation, it is clear that the reflection that is being sought during such sessions remains always an invitation for the student to become involved in this way. Discussion and reflective writing activities may encourage appreciative comment for aspects of unit content by the student, but a demonstration of appreciation should not be forced from students to satisfy assessment criteria of the unit. For some lecturers, this may call into question whether student outcomes should reflect the affective domain of learning. In broaching this topic, it is clear that for effective transformative learning at tertiary level, the inclusion of affective outcomes as well as the cognitive is important, because adult learning necessitates change in an adult's meaning structures. Feelings, emotion and reflection are crucial for moderating and transforming the schemes within these structures.[14]

In planning to accommodate cognitive and affective outcomes in this foundational theology unit, a learning module was devised to provide deep knowledge in one area of the unit's content so as students became familiar with the level of inquiry required for exploring a theological concept. It was also

---

13 Jack Mezirow, *Transformative Dimensions in Adult Learning* (San Francisco: Jossey-Bass, 1991).
14 For the importance of the affective, emotional and social aspects of transformative learning see Jack Mezirow, *Learning as Transformation: Critical Perspectives on a Theory in Progress* (San Francisco: Jossey-Bass, 2000).

hoped that through inquiry and completion of an analytical framework (namely the matrix of ideas) that a deep knowledge of a particular topic (the Nature of Jesus Christ and the Kingdom of God) would provide an appreciation for the concepts and understandings addressed in unit outcomes one and three.

With regard to the aims set for the inquiry-based learning module, critical-thinking, problem-solving and creative skills were encouraged, whilst an appreciation for undertaking and an awareness for applying the matrix strategy to other situations were hoped for in the affective domain.

The Content and Schedule of the Unit

The contents of the foundational unit in theology included the following topics:

1. Human experience, the question of God
2. The nature and purpose of theology
3. Christian belief in Jesus as the fullness of God's self- revelation
4. Mystery of the Triune God
5. Revelation and faith in Catholic theology
6. Transmission of divine revelation in scripture and tradition
7. History and development of the Church
8. Church according to the documents of Vatican II and contemporary theology
9. Christian hope and Catholic eschatology: heaven, hell, purgatory and last judgement.

The teaching schedule for unit content was organised in the following way. The winter intensive unit was held on four separate Saturdays with six hours of lecturing and tutoring conducted on each of the days. The topics for days one to four are:

DAY 1
- God, Religion, Faith
- Theology, language, sources & methods
- Revelation 1: God's self-communication to humankind
- Revelation 2: The Nature of Revelation
- Revelation 3: Scripture, Tradition, Dei Verbum

DAY 2
- Jesus of Nazareth: Ministry, Miracles, Parables
- Christology 1: Jesus of Nazareth, The Kingdom/Reign of God
- Christology 2: Jesus the Christ

DAY 3
- The Triune God
- The Church 1: History and Development
- The Church 2: In the Light of Vatican II

DAY 4
- The Church 3: Models of the Church
- Christian Hope and Catholic Eschatology
- Heaven, Hell, Purgatory and Last Judgement

The inquiry-based learning approach was incorporated in this unit as a one-off module that included the facilitation of a matrix strategy for interpreting theological text on a particular theme. Before the module was delivered, students were asked to consider the essay topics prescribed for the major assessment item, and to choose one they would like to write about. This was done to field student's learning preferences and it provided insight into what motivated their interest, and what they felt served their professional needs. The essay topics offered exploration of revelation, scripture and tradition: Church as a mystery of faith and sacrament, elements of Christology in presenting the nature of Jesus Christ and elements of eschatology in the light of Christian understanding of hope. Students were informed that they could change this decision later if they wanted to write about a different topic, but were made aware that this initial preference would determine the references and content of the matrix modelling session, and the theme of their matrix assignment. Various study groups unanimously chose the Christology topic for the matrix construction. The completed matrix assignment was a precursor meant to inform the essay assignment for the same unit. Interestingly, most students went on to write about the Christology topic in the major essay, but a couple of students chose different topics offering another matrix of ideas contextualizing their research for a new topic.

In summarising the learning process for the initial assignment, the group worked collaboratively in choosing the field of study for the matrix construction. As a community of learners, the students took responsibility for the research topic and the facilitator (lecturer) provided the research references for the inquiry module. Group activities that followed provided supportive interactive learning through co-operative problem solving. The students who subsequently used the matrix format to assist them in researching another essay topic had personally appropriated the inquiry process and developed their learning independence. The character of this inquiry-based learning demonstrates "apprenticeship" learning when students learn in community; interpersonal learning when involved in "guided participation" with the facilitator modelling the matrix; and personal learning when the matrix format had been "appropriated" by individual students as a strategy for researching, analysing and synthesising information.[15]

Procedure of Inquiry-Based Learning Module

Matrix of Ideas

At the end of day one of the winter intensive program, students were asked to vote for their essay preference for their major assessment as explained previously. This allowed the lecturer to make the necessary preparations in regard to choosing the references required for the execution of the inquiry-based learning module. In this case, four appropriate articles covering Christological elements were chosen:

1. Michael Paul Gallagher, *Questions of Faith* (Dublin: Veritas, 1996)
2. Dermot A. Lane, *Christ at the Centre. Selected Issues in Christology* (New York: Paulist Press, 1991)
3. Michael Casey, *Fully Human Fully Divine: An Interactive Christology* (Liguori Missouri: Liguori Triumph, 2004)
4. Brian McDermott, *Word Become Flesh: Dimensions of Christology* (Collegeville, MN: Michael Glazier The Liturgical Press, 1993).

In choosing articles for an activity such as this, it is important to note that the lecturer requires deep knowledge of the texts, so they can identify and judiciously offer guidance for reaching consensus on the key ideas during the collaborative and modelling stages of the learning process with the students.

Towards the end of day two, further preparations were made for the IBL module. Based on the preferences offered by the students in the previous session, Gallagher's text was prescribed as the pre-reading exercise in preparation for an inquiry-based learning session. In preparation for the upcoming session, students were asked to list four elements or topics with associated key ideas that

---

15 Barbara Rogoff, "Developing Understanding of the Idea of Communities of Learners," *Mind, Culture and Activity* 1, no. 4 (1994), 209-229.

they thought pertinent for Christological discussion from that reading. Their choices would be shared with others in collaborative learning.

At the beginning of day three and before lectures and tutoring began on the Triune God and the Church history, the inquiry-based learning sessions commenced. The class was divided into groups to share their offerings from the reading and they were asked to deliberate carefully on each group member's list of four elements and ideas for the purpose of making an amended list based on a group appraisal. After this collaborative learning session, the groups rejoined the class and a guided participation session was conducted where the lecturer facilitated the learning for the construction of the matrix. A grid (seven down by five across) was presented to the students and they were invited to state an element of Christology and its associated key ideas they had identified in Gallagher's text. The object of this activity was to provide a forum where students felt comfortable to exchange their ideas, and to come to class consensus as to which elements and ideas were represented in Gallagher's writing. When consensus was reached the lecturer wrote the entry into the grid. This process was repeated for the remaining three elements and associated key ideas. Concurrently, the lecturer had to bear in mind the Christological elements and key ideas canvassed in the other three articles, and moderate discussions so that the final four topics chosen for the matrix would be able to represent the content of the four texts evenly. The elements established as significant to the reading were Kingdom of God, parables, miracles and preaching and praxis. Another two rows in the grid were added, one to highlight main scriptural references used by the theologian to support their ideas, and another to accommodate students' interpretations of the elements of Christology presented in the various theological writings. The elements, key ideas, and interpretation established through collaborative learning for Gallagher's text are shown in figure 1.

After modelling the appropriation of Christological elements and keys ideas for Gallagher's text, the students were given the task to undertake independently the same process and to complete the matrix by identifying and analysing key ideas for the same Christological elements represented in the other theologian's articles. Students were referred to the unit outline for details on how to present their matrix. Note form was acceptable for students to articulate concise analysis and synthesis of key ideas in the matrix. A written response of several hundred words was to accompany the matrix to compare and contrast key ideas and understandings about the Kingdom of God as presented in the articles studied.

Figure 1. Elements of Christology, key ideas and interpretation achieved through collaborative learning, guided participation and modelling the matrix construction

Guided Participation for Modelling the Matrix

Elements	Key Ideas Author and Text: Michael Gallagher, *Questions of Faith*
Kingdom of God	Points to a new relationship with God for all people: i.e. to be closer to God will lead to more loving relationships with others → Trust in God is the way to salvation
Parables	Were used frequently by Jesus when speaking to the masses and always included an element of surprise/unexpectedness & related to the "Kingdom" Representation of God in parables as being intimate & merciful, seeking downtrodden people
Miracles	Were specially used → not just as an act of kindness but as a "sign" of presence of Kingdom – a new closeness of God and the new levels of love that were possible for all people
Preaching and Praxis	Jesus was seen as a prophet who delivered a powerful message for the future, calling for people to set aside the urge to be powerful and trust in God as a way to the Kingdom.
Main Scripture References	Mark 1:42—Healing the Leper Mark 2: 27—Picking corn on the Sabbath
Interpretation of Key Ideas	Jesus' actions were often against Jewish tradition, which caused tension among Pharisees and ultimately resulted in His death. Jesus' messages were challenging and inviting, representing God as the Father "Abba" who loves and forgives all people. Reciprocal love & forgiveness of all people would result in their knowing the Kingdom of God.

Summary of Procedure

The purposes for developing this matrix was to help students strategise a research framework where they could systematically locate and identify common and dissimilar attributes from various theological writers. The benefit to the student for using this research tool was that it offered a ready reckoner for comparative writing pieces where analysis and synthesis of key ideas was required.

The construction of a matrix of ideas in this application was grounded in the text of various theologians. After the students unanimously nominated an essay topic for study, and prior to the inquiry-based learning session, the lecturer chose four articles, each containing various key elements and ideas. As a way of initiating the learning process, students were asked to read a selected text, and through a process of collaboration, direct questioning and discussion, the lecturer guided students' learning participation and modelled the writing of key elements and ideas for one of four authors in the matrix. Students were then directed to read individually the other three articles and independently to identify and comment on the key ideas for these writers. Key ideas were written next to each Christological element, and the students' interpretation of each of the author's representative comments was also entered into the matrix. The students were asked to write about the Kingdom of God in the light of the studied theologians, using their completed matrix as a guide.

Student Examples

The following student examples of work show a completed matrix of ideas from student A, and two excerpts taken from larger written responses that compared and contrasted key ideas and understandings about the Kingdom of God as presented in the studied articles, from students A and B. Their work has been presented without the lecturer's comments or grade.

In figures 2 and 3, student A has demonstrated a completed matrix of ideas based on four theologians' Christological understandings. In less than 1,000 words, the student has concisely presented the ideas of these writers and provided interpretations of their work in note form. The student demonstrated an ability to locate relevant ideas and understandings from theological writings. Students' Written Responses A and B have demonstrated written analysis of a theological concept. The students used their matrix of ideas to structure their thoughts for the comparative text.

The cognitive outcomes for this learning module were made known through the execution and independent completion of the matrix and accompanying written task. The act of problem-solving through inquiry and the processing learning strategies thus offered the prospect for changing student perspectives for the way they come to view their own learning. Inquiry-based learning assisted student performance with learning the matrix of ideas technique. The potential of transformative learning here is realised when students are able to transfer this knowledge and use it to assist them in other research tasks.

Figure 2: Student's Matrix of Ideas Page 1.

Completed Matrix of Ideas from Student A
(Figures 2 and 3 copied with permission of student Debra Jackson)

Christological Elements	Gallagher, Michael. *Questions of Faith.* Dublin: Veritas, 1996.	Lane, D.A., *Christ at the Centre. Selected Issues in Christology.* New York: Paulist Press, 1991.
Kingdom of God	Points to a new relationship with for all people i.e.: to be closer to God will lead to more loving relationships with others - trust in God is the way to salvation	Kingdom of God is central to preaching of Jesus 3 themes: God's presence in creation and activity in history together with historical experience of monarchy are the basic principles of the K of G in pre-Christian scripture as they inform messianic expectations
Parables	Were used frequently by Jesus when speaking to the masses and always included an element of surprise/unexpectedness and related to the "Kingdom" The Parables represented God as being intimate and merciful, seeking out those who were downtrodden	Most are about the meaning and relate to Jesus' perception of it. Lane suggests all contain a 3-fold pattern: Advent, Reversal and Action, urging people to act now to change their ways because the K of G is coming. We must have vision and praxis.
Miracles	Were especially used not just as an act of kindness but as a "sign" of the presence of the Kingdom - a new closeness of God and the new levels of love that were possible for all people	Nearly all are signs of the coming of the K of G. Performed by Jesus to vindicate the claim that "the K of G is at hand" Are also about the transformation that the K of G will effect.
Preaching and Praxis	Jesus was seen as a prophet who delivered a powerful message for the future, calling for people to set aside the urge to be powerful and trust in God as a way to the Kingdom	Jesus' entire ministry is devoted to the coming of the Reign of God - followed 3 themes: • The present- a privilege to experience (ACTION) • God is at hand - the age of fulfillment (ADVENT) • Prepare to repent & convert to the demands of the K of G (REVERSAL)
Main Scripture References	Mark 1:42-Healing the Leper Mark 2:27-Picking corn on the Sabbath	Dt 26:5-9 Presence of Yahweh in history Ps 93:1-2,96 Yahweh as creator Mk 1:14-15 Jesus begins to proclaim "the K of G is at hand" Lk 4:21 Jesus' Galilean ministry Mt 5:3 Beatitudes (REVERSAL)
Interpretation of Key Ideas	Jesus' actions were often against Jewish tradition, which caused tension among Pharisees and ultimately resulted in His death. Jesus' messages were challenging and inviting, representing God as the father "Abba" who loves and forgives all people. Reciprocal love and forgiveness of all people would result in their knowing the Kingdom of God	Two traditions linked - God as creator & God as Sovereign. Creative tension exists between present and future—emphasis on 3 elements: Action, Advent, Reversal The unity between vision and praxis effects change and transformation in the world - symbolic in Jesus' personal life style

Figure 3: Student's Matrix of Ideas Page 2.

Christo-logical Elements	Casey, M. *Fully Human Fully Divine: An Interactive Christology.* Liguori, Missouri: Liguori Triumph, 2004.	McDermott, B. *Word Become Flesh: Dimensions of Christology.* Collegeville, MN: Michael Glazier, The Liturgical Press. 1993.
Kingdom of God	Entry to the K of G is compared to parables of the Growth of Seeds. We are a part of God's plan and will all share in the K of G when he is ready—nothing we do will change his authority on that.	Jesus spoke of 2 themes in relation to K of G - Forgiveness & Mercy God called for decisions - those open to grace would receive salvation, those closed to the proclamation of the kingdom's coming would be judged
Parables	Parables of Growth of Seeds were used by Jesus to express that there is no need for anxiety about outcomes of our work if we trust in God (i.e. instructions of the nature & dynamics of K of G) Reflect renunciation of control	Unique to Jesus Stories of ordinary life God's reign being the plot Contain excess or surprise Allowed Jesus to describe characteristics of God Allowed Jesus to show people that God's reign is mysterious but effective in their lives
Miracles	Were resisted as part of renunciation of control	Performed as "signs" of the coming of "the reign of God" Participation reflected an open mind to trust in God Usually performed on first time spectators Generated curiosity as to "whose higher power" the miracle had come from - God or Evil?
Preaching and Praxis	Emphasis was placed on the K of G as the Father's work. Jesus' trust in God was absolute and encourages us to live like him. To enter the K of G we must do God's work and not resist what he wills for us.	Emphasis on K of G Authoritative teacher but not scholar - he did not appeal to tradition He ate with sinners - a praxis example - God does not discriminate
Main Scripture References	Mk 4:1-9—Parable of the successful harvest Mk 4:26-29 The Parable of the Faithful Servant Mk 4:30-32 The Parable of the Surprising Growth Mt 6:31-32 Trust in God the Provider	Mt 12:28 & Lk 11: 2—Jesus & Beelzebul Lk 7:23—Jesus declares forgiveness by God Mt 20:1-16—Parable of labourers in vineyard Lk 5:30—Praxis example eating with sinners
Interpretation of Key Ideas	If we have faith we will find treasure in heaven—the K of G—here our hearts will find home God is the primary agent who controls our entry into the K of G We are called to be like Jesus	Jesus' ministry was to teach of God's reign Jesus' reference to K of G can be found in all literary sources, thus is authentically identified as his ministry. He quickly gathered disciples to help spread the good news

Student Written Response A
(Copied with permission of student Linda De Marco-Zompit)

McDermott agrees with Lane on the anticipatory role of Jesus' miracles. Gallagher, Lane and McDermott indicate the establishment of new human relationships based on mutual love as the decisive actions that bring the Kingdom of God to fruition. Casey points out that by Jesus totally surrendering to God's will, and through his loving words and actions, sets the example for everyone. Therefore, each person's call and mission is, then, to reach out his own potential to love unconditionally, beyond human limitations. Lane stresses the fact that Jesus proclaimed that the Kingdom had never been so close and accessible (Luke 17:21, Mark 1:15). This is a call not to wait for its final manifestation, but to act now, in the present moment (Matthew 25:1-15).

Student Written Response B
(Copied with permission of student Debra Jackson)

The Kingdom of God is a divine act of salvation and is futuristic, that is, it is coming. This is the central message that Jesus delivers during his ministry, according to the authors of each of the texts studied. Each writer suggests that Jesus' use of parables indicated that the Kingdom of God was taking shape during the present time of Jesus, as most were based on the "Reign of God" being near/coming.

Whilst all authors attribute Jesus' preaching and praxis, the performing of miracles, healing and exorcisms as being part of His ministry, McDermott, Lane and Gallagher referred to miracles as being performed as "signs" of the presence or coming of the Kingdom of God. In contrast, Casey's emphasis of miracles was more to do with Jesus' renunciation of control by not performing miracles. Casey was the only author to address the concept of us being called to become more like Jesus, requiring his followers to recognise his extreme demands which were often life denying - this being necessary to show that one's trust in God is absolute.

Conclusion

Methodology, examples of students' work and outcomes for a transformative method of learning theology have been identified and explained. In this process, the inquiry-based learning approach focused on the resolution of a problem regarding the nature of elements for explaining Christology. Christological elements and ideas were explored in the writings of Gallagher, Lane, Casey and McDermott with a matrix of ideas offered as a guiding framework.[16] For the students, the learning process was person-centred, and because it was treated as a module within the unit, it did not dilute the prescribed content of theology for that unit. For the lecturer, it presented challenges in its required intensive planning and in executing faithful delivery of all unit material. The module was aimed at developing learning skills such as critical thinking, problem solving and communication skills, which were enhanced by collaborative learning, guided participation and modelling techniques. These skills applied to constructivist learning approaches have been highlighted as significant by a recent Report from the Grattan Institute, for redressing some shortcomings said to exist in Australian schools and areas of tertiary education.[17] The unit of work accounted for cognitive and affective outcomes, and the inquiry-based learning module represented within it aimed at realising the transformative learning potential of the adult students.

---

16 Michael Gallagher, *Questions of Faith* (Dublin: Veritas, 1996), 85-89.
    Dermot Lane, *Christ at the Centre: Selected Issues in Christology* (New York: Paulist Press, 1991), 11-32.
    Michael Casey, *Fully Human Fully Divine: An Interactive Christology* (Liguori, Missouri: Liguori Triumph, 2004), 87-100.
    Brian McDermott, *Word Became Flesh: Dimensions of Christology* (Collegeville, MN: Michael Glazier The Liturgical Press, 1993), 36-75.
17 Ben Jensen, "Catching up: learning from the best school systems in East Asia," Grattan Institute Report, February 2012, 14.
    http://www.grattan.edu.au/publications/129_report_learning_from_the_best_main.pdf

15 | TRANSFORMATIVE LEARNING IN CHURCH HISTORY

TIM COOPER

Abstract

Church History is well suited to delivering transformative learning. But this potential is truncated if we constrain ourselves to the traditional, western-centred paradigm that emphasises first the Mediterranean world, then the West's contribution to contemporary global Christianity. An effective way of delivering transformative learning is through a thoroughly revised narrative that looks East as well as West and that does not see western, European Christianity as inevitable and normative. This revised narrative reveals the essential nature of the History of Christianity, which suggests that, rather than Western triumphalism, suffering and even extermination are the normative patterns for the Church in history. This essay explores these themes and identifies some resources to facilitate the kind of transformative learning prompted by such a changed perspective of Church History.

• • •

Introduction

This is a great time to be teaching Church History. Over the last two decades there has been a steady flow of new publications, many with a notable determination to bring in a truly global story, not just a Western one. This opens up potential for genuinely transformative learning. There is nothing like the encounter with a foreign, unknown and surprising story to overturn students' existing assumptions and to challenge their worldview, shaped as it is by the cultural norms of contemporary Western society. This new material with its new direction can be harnessed to new learning technologies. The rapid development of online learning has sent a fresh new breeze through student assessment. This has brought its challenges and difficulties; it has taken time to come to grips with what these new learning technologies can offer. But they offer a lot.

In this essay I would like to explain how this cluster of new developments in the field of Church History can combine to produce a transformative learning experience for our students (which I hope might also prove illustrative and useful for those who do not teach Church History). Let me begin by offering a few generalisations about those students, based on my own experience of teaching in a New Zealand state university. Chances are, our students are Western Christians. If they know any Church History at all (and that is not a reliable assumption), it will focus only on the Western experience. Without even thinking about it, they will assume that the story of how the faith ventured west from Jerusalem is pretty much the only story to tell. They may be aware of how Christianity has—until recently, at least—sat at the centre of Western society, closely allied to the State. They will be unaware of just how much this conditions their perspective on the nature of the faith they hold. They will be blind to the ways in which the prevailing culture of comfort, affluence, materialism and consumerism has led them to see the faith in a particular way. This will incline them to expect a Church History that is shaped around material security and steady advance. If there is any truth at all in these generalisations, these students will be in for a shock when they encounter a story that is truly global. Hopefully, they will never see the faith in quite the same way ever again.

The Global Story

As I begin to teach my survey course on the history of Christianity, I set out in a conventional direction. That is, I head west. Over ten lectures I work out from the book of Acts towards Rome, past the conversion of Constantine and on to the leadership of Pope Gregory the Great (c.540-604). He ushered in changes that would eventually result in the conversion of Europe.

At that point I take my students back to the beginning, back to Acts 2:8-11, and to all those Jews who had come to Jerusalem for the Feast of Pentecost: "Parthians, Medes, Elamites and residents of Mesopotamia, Judea and Cappadocia, Pontus and Asia, Phrygia and Pamphylia, Egypt and the parts of Libya belonging to Cyrene, and visitors from Rome." That list has a very strategic construction, since Luke begins with those people who lived to the East of Jerusalem. And why not? Why would the faith not also go East as well as West, carried in much the same way by word of mouth, through Jewish networks, along trading routes, and propelled by persecution? I hope to surprise my students with this story of how Christianity went East through Syria, Persia, India, Southeast Asia and into China by the 7th century. I want them to see how this Syriac-speaking Church-of-the-East might well have had closer connections—certainly closer linguistic connections—to the earliest Church in Palestine than did the Greek-speaking Church in the West. I also show them how the faith went south into Africa, not just along the northern coast but deep inland as far as Nubia and Ethiopia.

In the early 4th century the persecution of Christians in the West came to an end and the long existence of relative comfort, status and security began. In the East, it was entirely the opposite. In AD344, for example, in what is now Iraq, Bishop Simon of Seleucia-Ctesiphon was led outside the city of Susa along with a large number of Christian clergy. Five bishops and one hundred priests were beheaded before his eyes, and last of all he himself was put to death. For the next two decades and more, Christians were tracked down and hunted from one end of the [Persian] empire to the other. At times the pattern was general massacre. More often, it was intensive organized elimination of the leadership of the church, the clergy. As fast as the Christians of the capital elected a new bishop after Simon, the man was seized and killed.[1]

The rise of Islam in the 7th century represented something of a reprieve for Christians in the East, since it was a further two or three centuries before there was anything like a Muslim majority.[2] Christians found important roles in medicine, education and in public service. Catholicos Timothy (the Patriarch of Baghdad from AD780 to 823) is a fascinating figure in the history of Christianity. He was arguably the most significant Christian spiritual leader of his day, much more influential than the Western pope in Rome, and on a par with the Orthodox patriarch in Constantinople. Perhaps a quarter of the world's Christians looked to Timothy as both spiritual and political head. At least as much as the Western pope, he could claim to be the successor of the ancient apostolic church.[3]

---

1   Samuel Hugh Moffett, *A History of Christianity in Asia: Volume I: Beginnings to 1500* (Maryknoll, NY: Orbis Books, 1998), 140-141.
2   Diarmaid MacCulloch, *A History of Christianity: The First Three Thousand Years* (London: Allen Lane, 2009), 261.
3   Philip Jenkins, *The Lost History of Christianity: The Thousand-Year Golden Age of the Church in the Middle East, Africa, and Asia* (Oxford: Lion Books, 2008), 3-7.

As the centuries progressed, though, the experience of Christians under Muslim rule grew steadily worse. In the middle of the 11th century the Seljuk Turks swept through the Persian Empire and they, too, set about systematically dismantling the institutions of the Church. For example, when they took Edessa, an ancient centre of Eastern Christianity, they killed or enslaved the entire population of around 47,000.[4] The Mongols replaced the Seljuk Turks in the 13th—they came with Christian connections and the Eastern Church once more experienced a reprieve.

Not far from [AD]1350 there were said to have been Nestorian metropolitans in China, India, Samarqand, Turkestan, Kashgar, and two other centres, each with six to twelve suffragan bishops. Early in the 14th century the Nestorian Patriarch is reported to have had a hierarchy of twenty-five metropolitans and from 200 to 250 bishops. In the middle of the 14th century Nestorianism seems to have been spread over more territory and to have been more prosperous than ever before. In general, the four centuries between 950 and 1350 saw a very considerable extension of the eastern frontiers of Christianity, with especially wide expansion in the 13th and 14th centuries. Christian communities were to be found clear across Eurasia from the Atlantic and the western and eastern shores of the Mediterranean to the China Coast and from Scandinavia and north of Moscow to South India.[5] Christianity was, therefore, a truly global faith. Few would have seen that collapse (in Asia, at least) was imminent.

The 14th century was brutal all round, and not just in Asia. A mini-ice-age drastically reduced food production, creating competition for scarce resources. The Black Death preyed on the trade routes, devastating whole populations. The Mongol rulers converted to Islam. The worst of them, Tamerlene, was the scourge of Asian Christians. The Church-of-the-East was brought to its knees. The office of the Nestorian catholicos remained vacant from 1369 to 1378, and possibly longer, and the Jacobites remained without a head from 1379 to 1404. Whole Christian communities were annihilated across central Asia, and surviving communities shrank to tiny fractions of their former size.[6] Waves of violence crushed Christian communities throughout Asia, Egypt, Nubia, Armenia and Georgia. The Church was not entirely wiped out across this vast territory, but it came close. In China, it vanished from sight.

---

4   Jenkins, *The Lost History of Christianity*, 116.
5   Kenneth Scott Latourette, *A History of the Expansion of Christianity*, Vol. 1, *The First Five Centuries* (London: Eyre and Spottiswoode, 1938), 591-2.
6   Jenkins, *Lost History of Christianity*, 130.

That left Europe as the last bastion of global Christianity, sheltered as it was by its alliance with the State. When European missionaries ventured out three or four centuries later they thought of themselves as breaking new ground in Asia, Southeast Asia and China. The modern missionary movement certainly provided the impetus for a new expansion of global Christianity over the last two centuries. But that earlier thread of persecution is unbroken. In any number of places, Christians have experienced slaughter and massacre on a scale that is difficult to credit. The most glaring example is in the Middle East. Now, it is almost entirely Muslim, though significant Christian populations remain in places like Egypt, Lebanon and Syria. In 1900, around 4,355,000 Christians lived in the Middle East out of a total population of some 44 million. Around 31 percent of Syria was Christian. In the Ottoman Empire, which comprised the Middle East, the Balkans and North Africa, 46 percent of the population was Christian. Half the residents of Istanbul were Christian.[7] How that has changed today, largely as the result of sheer physical extermination. As many as a million Armenian Christians were killed in 1915. Seven years later around 100,000 Christians were killed in Smyrna. These figures were not unusual.

> Whatever the reasons, the long-term effects would be the same: across the Middle East, Christian communities vanished one after the other, like lights being switched off. Before 1914, Christian pockets were numerous and widespread, while by 1930, most had vanished or were in the process of disappearing.[8]

That was true in other places as well. Mark Noll tallies "the death of perhaps 70,000 Roman Catholics in Viet Nam in 1851, of countless others in Madagascar during the century's middle decades, of 25,000 Catholics in Korea in 1866, of 100,000 Catholics in Indochina in 1885, of perhaps 50,000 Catholics and Protestants during the Boxer rebellion in China in 1900."[9] Even today, this ghastly brutality continues. What was once a significant Christian population in Iraq has all but disappeared—Iraqi Christians have either died or fled. Depending on how the situation in Syria plays out, the same may happen there, too.

---

7 For these figures, see Jenkins, *The Lost History of Christianity*, chapter 5.
8 Jenkins, *The Lost History of Christianity*, 163.
9 Mark Noll, *Turning Points: Decisive Moments in the History of Christianity*, 2nd ed. (Grand Rapids, MI: Baker Academic, 2000), 284.

Transformative Learning

Having heard that story, it should be easy to understand why presenting only the Western perspective is so inadequate, and why scholars have been calling on us to adopt a more global perspective. Anne Thayer urged the need to "de-center the West from the overall story of Christian history."[10] In a similar vein, Wilbert R. Shenk challenged us to "move beyond the conventional framework, which is governed by the assumption that what happened in the course of Western Christendom is universally normative for Christian history."[11] In a strongly worded article, Paul Spickard identified the laziness, neglect and imperialism implied in the traditional Western-centred approach to Church History. "Until recently, every English-language textbook history of Christianity has presented the faith as if it were a European possession—occasionally on loan to people in Asia, Africa or Latin America, but never really theirs."[12] On similar grounds, Andrew F. Walls called for "no less than the reconception of the task of the Christian historian."[13]

In my view, the very best guide on this is Philip Jenkins. His book, *The Lost History of Christianity*—lively, engaging, unconventional, provocative—is a pure gift to all who teach Church History. The broad outlines of the story I have just related I learned from Jenkins. His perspective is an eye-opener.

> The particular [Western] shape of Christianity with which we are familiar is a radical departure from what was for well over a millennium the historical norm: another, earlier global Christianity once existed. For most of its history, Christianity was a tricontinental religion, with powerful representation in Europe, Africa, and Asia, and this was true into the fourteenth century. Christianity became predominantly European not because this continent had any obvious affinity for that faith, but by default: Europe was the continent where it was not destroyed. Matters could easily have developed very differently.[14]

---

10 Anne Thayer, "What's New in the History of Christianity?" *Religion Compass* 1 (2004), 2.
11 William Shenk, "Towards a Global Church History," *International Bulletin of Missionary Research* 20 (1996), 50.
12 Paul Spickard, "It's the World's History: Decolonizing Historiography and the History of Christianity," *Fides et Historia* 31 (1999), 16.
13 Andrew Walls, "Eusebius Tries Again: Reconceiving the Study of Church History," *International Bulletin of Missionary Research* 24 (2000), 106.
14 Jenkins, *The Lost History of Christianity*, 3.

Jenkins makes a strong case that we need to acknowledge this story and present it to our students. If we do, there is enormous potential for transformative learning. "When we move our focus away from Europe, everything we think we know about Christianity shifts kaleidoscopically, even alarmingly."[15] I would like to draw out the main ways in which I think this true.

To begin with, there is the reality these scholars all have pointed to: Christianity is *not* only a Western phenomenon. Generally, our students will assume that it is. They will have read the book of Acts, in which Luke intended to relate only one part of a large complex story in a very strategic manner, working out from Jerusalem generally in the direction of Asia Minor, Greece and Rome. A very similar story was always possible, this time heading for Persia and India. But students are conditioned to think only of the West and to relate Christianity only with Europe—a perception that is only affirmed, in my experience, among the general populace and in the media. For them to witness the extensive, vibrant, important Church-of-the-East is to challenge those assumptions. Students will have to rethink their perspective on the nature of the faith they hold when they examine the commonalities and differences with Western Christianity: when they see, for example, the feminine imagery so prevalent within the liturgy of the Persian Church;[16] when they consider that the Nestorians—who flavoured this Church-of-the-East so strongly, who were so critical in Eastern missions—were declared to be heretics by the Council of Chalcedon in AD451; when they learn that in some parts of Syria even today the liturgy is given in Aramaic, demonstrating more ancient connections than many of those of Western denominations. All of this is both troubling and exciting when they realize, as Shenk has said, that Western Christianity is not normative Christianity. True, students will encounter some odd ideas among these Eastern Christians, but Western Christians have produced their own fair share of distinctly odd ideas over the centuries. Western Christianity is not the "gold standard" by which the faith is to be measured,[17] but our students tend to think that it is. Perhaps there is an additional challenge for Roman Catholic students, if they take seriously claims to papal primacy over all Christians. Those claims gain some perspective when students measure the reach of Catholicos Timothy; when they realize that Baghdad was a far more likely centre of global

---

15 Jenkins, *The Lost History of Christianity*, 5.
16 Dale T. Irvin and Scott W. Sunquist, *History of the World Christian Movement*. Vol. 1. *Earliest Christianity to 1453* (Maryknoll, NY: Orbis Books, 2001), 63-5.
17 Jenkins, *The Lost History of Christianity*, 3.

Christianity than was Rome in the first millennium and more; when they find Christians in India or Southeast Asia who may have a vague awareness of this place called Rome somewhere to the west, but who would be baffled by any claims of jurisdiction from the bishop who resided there. In this and other ways the global story brings the Western experience into perspective, into context. In the process, the initial assumptions of our students are challenged and overturned.

Nowhere is this more powerful than in the story of persecution I have just related. At the end of my course I tally up all the massacres we have encountered across two thousand years of the History of Christianity, all the persecution and suffering we have witnessed. What this demonstrates is, I conclude, that suffering, setback and persecution are the normative experience for the Church. Comfort, security, wealth, privilege and status are not the norm. If this is true, the Western Christian experience is not normative at all, it is an aberration. If history continues for another ten thousand years it may well disclose just how much of an aberration it is. If we think that the faith began with the execution of Jesus Christ, why would we be surprised? Why would we expect anything different? "It is through many persecutions that we must enter the kingdom of God" (Acts 14:22). I am pretty sure that most of our Western Christian students believe deep down that if they encounter suffering or hardship then God is not doing God's job properly; God has let them down. Such thinking would seem an indulgent fantasy to those hundreds of thousands of Christians slaughtered during the 14th century. Try telling them they can expect a comfortable existence as of right. If that thinking exists at all, it is a Western distortion, made possible only by the Western experience.

There is plenty to challenge our students, then, but also much to encourage in the age of modern Western secularism and pluralism. The Church has been displaced from the centre of society; it now stands at the margins. It has no prior right to speak in the public square. We might mourn or regret the passing of Christendom, to the extent that it ever existed, or we might see that the Church has done very well when it has stood at the margins. In fact, the margins may be—thinking historically and globally—exactly where the Church is supposed to be. Our students might be heartened when they read the account of Catholicos Timothy's conference with the Caliph over the relative merits of Islam and Christianity.[18] They may find in that discourse a model for open and respectful

---

18 John W. Coakley and Andrea Sterk, eds., *Readings in World Christian History: Volume I: Earliest Christianity to 1453* (Maryknoll, NY: Orbis Books, 2004), 231-42.

dialogue while also maintaining one's integrity and convictions. They will learn that Christianity has been here before, one faith among many, unsheltered by political and cultural patronage. That is not anything they should fear; it may be what they should expect.

At that point in the course where we have surveyed the calamitous 14th century, I suspend the story to offer a lecture in which I ask the students to reflect on what they are learning. I challenge them with some difficult questions that arise from the dark side of the Church that we have encountered and the Christian experience of marginalisation, persecution and extermination. Tertullian said that the blood of the martyrs is the seed of the Church. But is it? Or is it always? What are we to do with 17th century Japan, where the Church was all but wiped out within a few decades?[19] What about all those Christian communities like lights being switched off all through Asia in the 14th century? What about Iraq, which in a few years may have no more Christian citizens? In light of all this, what can we make of the claim of Jesus (in Matthew 16:18) that "I will build my church and the gates of Hades will not prevail against it"?

What we cannot do, therefore, is to offer our students a triumphalist account of Church History—any such account would have to overlook rather too much in the way of reality. Perhaps if we confine ourselves only to the Western experience it is just possible. We could, perhaps, relate a story only of saints, heroes and martyrs—the Church constantly in advance. But a global perspective puts a stop to that. Very often there is little triumph there.

And yet, the Church remains. Whatever the figures are worth, around two-thirds of the world's population can be described as Christian. For all the suffering and setback, the Church has endured. Where it dies off in one place, it seems to spring up in another. The global heartland might have shifted around, but there has always been one. Jesus is building his Church after all, but not by the means our Western Christian students might expect. Or perhaps it can be said that Jesus is quite capable of building his Church in whatever context it is found—privileged or persecuted. Certainly that is true. But the danger for our students is in thinking that can happen only through privilege and not through persecution, especially when the normative experience of historical, global Christianity looks a whole lot more like persecution than it does privilege. An encounter with the global story of the History of Christianity will make that clear, and in the process

---

19   Diarmaid MacCulloch, *Christian History: An Introduction to the Western Tradition*, 2nd ed. (London: Epworth Press, 2006), 198.

facilitate a learning experience that is genuinely transformative.

This is what makes all the effort to refocus our teaching worthwhile, but it is a lot of effort. For one thing, there is much less to go on in the way of both primary and secondary evidence. Because Christians were so often the losers in the story of global Christianity most of the evidence for their existence has long been lost. How different that is in Europe, where one can find evidence wherever one cares to look. The language barrier is a challenge, because the languages of the East are so much more foreign and inaccessible than the cluster of languages in Europe. And because this story has lain in relative neglect, with the occasional honourable exception, there is not the same amount of scholarship to draw on. Yet it is there, in increasing availability.[20] Perhaps what would also help us to overcome these practical difficulties is to partner with those who teach the history of Christianity in Africa and Asia. They might be best placed to open our eyes to the riches of what is there, for our sake and the sake of our students.

Online Learning

There is one very effective tool now at our disposal: online learning technologies. These are helpful whatever the nature of student learning, but I have found them especially helpful in this attempt to convey the global story in such a way as to facilitate a transformative learning experience for my students.

In my experience, deep down in their hearts both students and teachers have little fondness for online learning, by which I primarily mean online discussion. Students find it contrived. Rather than producing an authentic, engaging discussion they tend to jump through the hoops, achieving the minimum requirement but rarely going much beyond it. Their teachers sense this as well, which can leave them feeling frustrated and averse. Some give up on it entirely.

It is my conviction that if students and teachers are not enjoying online learning, all that means is that they have not yet found the right way of doing it. I got just the spark I needed when Dr Rod Sims, an Australian academic and learning-design consultant, visited my university in 2010.[21] He proposed the idea of online activities rather than discussions. From there I developed what

---

20   See Appendix 1 for a list of those resources I have found most helpful, in order of importance.

21   Rod has included some of the exercises and samples of student work in his book, *Design Alchemy: Transforming the Way We Think About Learning and Teaching* (Springer, 2014), 197-204.

are creative role plays. I ask my students to speak in the voice of a person from the past. If they can speak credibly in that voice, I know they have learned something. So I ask them to contribute one post of anywhere from around 150 to 350 words in length. Each post is worth five percent of their overall mark. The students may choose from three options: two creative role playing exercises and one standard online discussion. They contribute their individual posts on a group page, so the students will end up compiling something as a group. By way of illustration, Appendix 2 offers a series of examples.

The most obvious thing to observe is how well suited Church History is to these online activities. There are endless possibilities. I think it is important to include dimensions of irony and humour. Anachronism is an especially useful way of lightening the tone. In my instructions to the students I emphasise that I am not looking for scholarly prose and I will reward humour. This sends a clear signal that they can have fun with these, and they do. Other exercises are more sober and reflective. Whatever the case, students enjoy these activities and they really do learn something. To offer a few comments from formal teaching evaluations, one student said, "When I first read what was required I thought it was stupid—but actually it turned out to be my favourite part of this course and really made me think and retain the information which I had to work with." A second student "really enjoyed the online discussion. That was a lot of fun, it involved surprisingly high level engagement with the content, and it helped my writing skills in a different way than I had experienced at University." Another said that the best thing about the paper was the online activities: "It was so cool being able to get into character of some of the players in the historical scenarios. Apart from a lot of fun in being creative, it was educationally effective … I can REMEMBER much easier the people and situations around the historical events because of those scenarios I was involved in."

I think that comment indicates something else, as well. I am asking students to place themselves in the shoes of another person. They have to remove themselves from their own context to enter a very different one. As the exercises in Appendix 2 demonstrate, some will ask students to encounter the context of global Christianity. So, online activities are useful for reinforcing transformative learning. Students are required to think both creatively and personally. They will develop insights that are uniquely their own. And those insights can be powerful drivers of changed assumptions. Online learning, therefore, is a useful ally when it is well deployed and when it reinforces the global nature of the material being taught and studied.

We have, therefore, a great subject to teach and a great time in which to teach it. There is so much potential for transformative learning, though it remains a challenge. I hope this brief essay has been a practical encouragement to take it up.

Appendix 1: Useful Resources for the Global Story

Philip Jenkins, *The Lost History of Christianity: The Thousand-Year Golden Age of the Church in the Middle East, Africa, and Asia* (Oxford: Lion Books, 2008).

Dale T. Irvin and Scott W. Sunquist, *History of the World Christian Movement*. Vol. 1. *Earliest Christianity to 1453* (Maryknoll, NY: Orbis Books, 2001).

Dale T. Irvin and Scott W. Sunquist, *History of the World Christian Movement*. Vol. 2. *Modern Christianity from 1454 to 1800* (Maryknoll, NY: Orbis Books, 2012).

Samuel Hugh Moffett, *A History of Christianity in Asia: Volume I: Beginnings to 1500* (Maryknoll, NY: Orbis Books, 1998).

Samuel Hugh Moffett, *A History of Christianity in Asia: Volume II: 1500-1900* (Maryknoll, NY: Orbis Books, 2005).

Ian Gillman and Hans-Joachim Klimkeit, *Christians in Asia Before 1500* (Richmond, Surrey: Curzon Press, 1999).

Kenneth Scott Latourette, *A History of the Expansion of Christianity*, vol. 1, *The First Five Centuries* (London: Eyre and Spottiswoode, 1938).

Kenneth Scott Latourette, *A History of the Expansion of Christianity*, vol. 2, *The Thousand Years of Uncertainty AD500-AD1500* (London: Eyre and Spottiswoode, 1938).

Paul R. Spickard and Kevin M. Cragg, *A Global History of Christians: How Everyday Believers Experienced Their World* (Grand Rapids, MI: Baker Academic, 1994).

Diarmaid MacCulloch, *A History of Christianity: The First Three Thousand Years* (London: Allen Lane, 2009).

Robert Louis Wilken, *The First Thousand Years: A Global History of Christianity* (New Haven, CT: Yale University Press, 2012).

Adrian Hastings, ed., *A World History of Christianity* (Grand Rapids, MI: William B. Eerdmans, 1999).

Martin Marty, *The Christian World: A Global History* (New York: The Modern Library, 2007).

John W. Coakley and Andrea Sterk, eds., *Readings in World Christian History: Volume I: Earliest Christianity to 1453* (Maryknoll, NY: Orbis Books, 2004).

Christoph Baumer, *The Churches of the East: An Illustrated History of Assyrian Christianity* (London: I.B. Tauris, 2006).

Lamin Sanneh, *Whose Religion is Christianity? The Gospel Beyond the West* (Grand Rapids, MI: William B. Eerdmans, 2003).

Lamin Sanneh, *Disciples of All Nations: Pillars of World Christianity* (Oxford: Oxford University Press, 2008).

Appendix 2: Examples of Online Exercises

This is a selection of online activities I have developed. You are free to use them if you wish, or you might adapt the approach to suit your own interests and temperament.

1. It is hard work being a theologian. For this reason, both Origen and Tertullian are heading for a seaside holiday. Unwittingly they find themselves sharing the same train compartment. So begins a lengthy and at times fraught discussion on matters of Theology. The two men are joined by one Mrs Edith McGillivray—a woman unknown to history but important in this conversation as one who might ask questions of them both, challenge their thinking, or poke holes in their logic. (In other words, Edith serves as a neutral figure in the conversation.) In your post you will carry on the conversation among these three tourists, building on the conversation already developed by any students who have made their posts before you. You might broach any topic of Theology that would interest the two men (we are, of course, less sure of Edith's own interests, but assume they are wide-ranging) though there's no doubt they will be sure to discuss a proper Christian perspective on the place of classical philosophy.

2. Let's say it is the early 5th century and a group of notable theologians have gathered together for a Theology conference in Constantinople. The theologians are Gregory of Nyssa, Gregory of Nazianzus, Basil of Caesarea, Jerome, John Chrysostom, Cyril of Jerusalem and Cyril of Alexandria. It is the evening before the conference begins and they are all sitting together in a pub in the suburb of Chalcedon. They are telling each other what they have been working on lately and, being opinionated, they are each telling the others where they have gone wrong; they are also talking about Augustine in his absence. Who knows where the conversation will lead, but Theology will be at the heart of it. You are one of these theologians (take your pick). Write a post that is their contribution to what looks like a genuine conversation.

3. You may not be aware that Catholicos Timothy wrote his own blog, but he did. In the year 781, he made a post on this blog describing his two-day conference with the Caliph (conveniently supplied to you in a document on Blackboard). Being a man who likes to encourage discussion, Timothy has a comment feature on his blog. Imagine you are either a Christian or a Muslim living under Muslim rule: write a comment in response to Timothy's post. In this way you will help to build up and carry on a genuine exchange between the two sides in the commentary. You are also welcome to write as Timothy

himself, who from time to time was not averse to inserting his own comments in response to the comments of others.

4. Imagine you are a Christian living under the Seljuk Turks or the Muslim Mongols and you are experiencing persecution. Each night in your journal you reflect on the day's events in a way that is designed to encourage you or other Christians who may read it. Write a journal entry. In it, describe your experience of persecution during that day (or what you have witnessed of the persecution of others) and offer some theological reflection on that experience. In other words, how do you make sense of the pain and persecution you have to endure, and how do you encourage yourself and others to persevere under it?

5. Imagine it is 30 January 1077. Pope Gregory VII and King Henry IV of Germany (Holy Roman Emperor) are holding a press conference before international media assembled at a convention centre on the outskirts of Canossa in the Italian Alps. Henry has just made his penance before Gregory, and Gregory has just welcomed Henry back into the fold. You are a journalist at the press conference. Ask a question of either Gregory or Henry and write their answer. In your post, begin the question with Q: and the answer with A: If you are not the first student to make a post, follow on from the previous question and answer. You are welcome to challenge an earlier answer from Gregory or Henry and to ask your own follow-up question. So this should look like a genuine line of questioning at a press conference.

6. You'll find on Blackboard two primary documents that are letters written by concerned Christians to the pope. The first was written by Catherine of Sienna, a famous and influential Italian mystic associated with the Dominican order, to Pope Gregory XI in March 1376. The second was written by an anonymous German priest or monk on the occasion of a visit by a Cardinal-Legate (a representative of the pope) in 1451-2.
EITHER imagine you are a nun or a monk living in the year 1452 (a fairly random date). It is your turn to write a brief letter to Pope Nicholas V concerning the condition of the church. **OR** imagine you are the pope. Write a reply to Catherine's letter or to the letter written by the unnamed monk.

7. Those in your group who choose this option will create two sets of diary entries. One set is written as a member of the German Christian Movement who supports the Nazi regime. The other set is written as a Christian in Germany who is actively working to protect the Jews. In each case the first entry should be for Tuesday 12 May (a random date) and each subsequent entry should be for each following day. You can be creative with your content—

try to develop a story of this person's life day by day—but each entry should contain some reflection on how this person's faith is shaping their actions or perspective. So this should look like a genuine portion of a person's diary. To be clear, you need write only one diary entry and from only one perspective.

8. Imagine it is 1956 and debate is raging in the *Christian Life* magazine over the article that was published in its March edition, "Is Evangelical Theology Changing?" (available on Blackboard). Write a letter to the Editor from the position of either a Fundamentalist or an Evangelical. If you are not the first to write a letter, respond to those who have. Begin each one with "Dear Sir." In other words, make this look like a genuine exchange of letters to the Editor.

16 | CROSS-CULTURAL MISSION AS A TRANSFORMATIVE LEARNING EXPERIENCE

A REPORT

MURRAY HOUSE

Abstract

Theological Field Educators provide opportunities for the students to integrate learning with the practice of ministry. Avondale students' cross-cultural experience in Fiji was a capstone event with "just in time" learning. It had a maturing effect upon the student's ministerial readiness. Students' sense of their call to ministry and their development of a ministry identity were enhanced. They understood better the importance of "servant leadership." Students focused on creating community and its importance for a vitalised ministry. It involved them in ministry outreach and relationships that stretched and nurtured their giftedness. They developed a passion for prayer and the need for the Holy Spirit in their lives. Students' self-understanding grew. It increased their levels of confidence as ministers. All students recommended that intercultural learning be incorporated into their theological education.

• • •

Introduction

In recent years, seminaries have designed Mission Immersion Experiences (MIE) as capstone experiences in ministry formation.[1] Unfortunately, published quantifiable data on the MIE impact upon ministry students has been lacking. I have sought to address this gap in research by measuring the impact of the MIE's role in improving students' awareness of their ministry identity, commitment to mission, and spirituality. After 18 days in Fiji we measured changes to these categories of ministry readiness and student confidence in their growing competencies for ministry.

Upon their return to classes, students were asked to write a 500-word reflection paper on what they had learnt and experienced. Common themes evident in these papers informed the research and also informed the development of 81 survey questions. All ten student participants were surveyed and their anonymous responses collated. Questions were consistent with Avondale's curricula objectives and graduate outcomes.

This MIE proved to be a capstone event that maximized the integration of learning and the practice of ministry. It had a maturing effect upon the students' ministerial readiness with a hothouse style formation in a unique cross-cultural context. In this article, students' evaluation of the impact of this MIE will be shared. Seventy-five percent of Avondale's ministry competencies were experienced in Fiji. The data confirms that this Fijian MIE was a transformative learning experience. Student self-understanding grew. They realised their need to rely on God. It indeed was a sacred moment.

History and Preparation

Avondale College of Higher Education ministerial training involves six areas of ministry formation.[2] In these six areas, 54 competencies are targeted. Students engage in these competencies in their eight semesters of training. An ideal capstone event would see these competencies being extended and the students' skills maturing as they immerse themselves in active ministry. It was hoped that the MIE would enable the formation of fresh paradigms and learning.

---

1 One example is the Baptist Theological Seminary at Richmond, Virginia.
2 See Figure 1: Personal development, relationships, pastoral care, proclamation, evangelism & discipleship and leadership.

Avondale and Adventist church leaders in Fiji began planning for this MIE eight months before the students arrived. During this time they prayed as communities for the success of the MIE. The ten Avondale student participants were selected from amongst 3rd and 4th year Bachelor of Ministry and Theology students from a group that volunteered. Only three of those who wished to go were left behind because of the financial limitations and limited English proficiency. The preparation of students for the MIE involved attendance at a cross-cultural orientation seminar. Some of this was conducted by a Fijian pastor, now working near Avondale College of Higher Education. In addition, regular prayer sessions were held over a three month period.

Figure 1 below shows the percentages of competencies from each area of ministry. What areas of ministry would the MIE impact? Which ones would be weakest and which ones strongest? The figure below shows how the areas of Personal Development and Proclamation were the areas most impacted by the MIE.

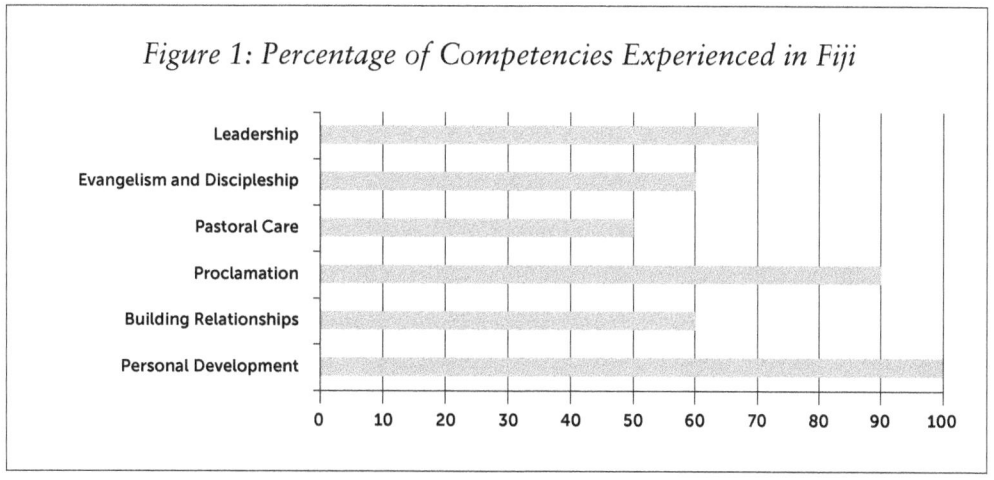

Students completed the survey within one month of their return. The results indicate that a high level of skill maturation, spiritual impact and readiness for ministry resulted. Avondale lecturers learnt new ways to improve these events. Students want more involvement in ministry, individual opportunities for leadership and intentional times for reflection to maximize their transformative experience.

Servant and / or Guest

The time in Fiji was designed as an active ministry MIE in contrast to those that are more reflective. It is therefore surprising and significant that 100% of the personal development competencies were experienced by the students. They spent up to 4 hours preaching across the 18 days. By serving others through the Word they needed to spend time engaged with the local culture with enthusiasm and sensitivity. Learning how best to engage with others necessitated a critique of their own bias and values. This gave relevance and form to their presence within the immersion. Their involvement in servant roles did not hinder the students' engagement in personal growth.

Purely reflective MIEs have their advantages but these Avondale students personally grew by their service to others. It is vital that this generation experience meaningful service as learning. The nursing model from the 1990s literature shows us the transformative influence of service.

Impact on Personal Spirituality

It was inspiring to see the impact of the spiritual Fijian people on the Avondale students participating in the MIE. Their generosity of spirit awakened spiritual sensitivities within our students. One student stated, "It was worth the whole trip, to see and understand personally the need for prayer in our ministry, the need to deepen our experience with God and to pray for and encourage others."[3] Of the 70 responses on spirituality, only two were not optimal responses (see Figure 2). Students felt they were God's instruments. They developed their self-understanding and encountered the great need to rely more on God. This impact flowed through to the student-led morning worships which were full of challenge, encouragement and personal testimony. God "showed up" each night to convict hearts as He used these students in their ministry to others. It indeed was a sacred encounter when they could encounter the blessing of God upon them. This was an experience that truly transformed the students and left them feeling they were ready to be used again. It is expected that the MIE will be a source of rich encouragement and formation in the lives of these students for their future years of ministry.

---

3 Taken from a student reflection paper.

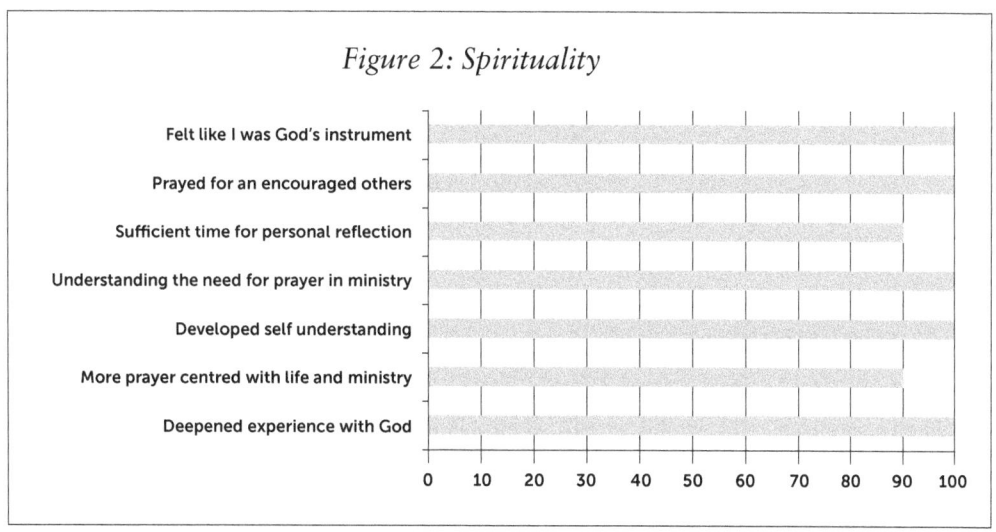

Figure 2: Spirituality

Relational Skill Development

The questions on relational skills included "respect for others," "attitude to local leadership" and their "relationships with each other." Eighty-four of the students' responses (from a maximum of ninety) in this area of relational skills were positive. The students mixed well with local members, pastors and attenders. It was encouraging to see the good relationships developing within the team and with others.

Our ministerial students took seriously their opportunities to mentor younger church members. At Navua, formal training was conducted. The Fijian Adventist youth movement ensured that youth camped at the church for two months prior to opening night. Each day these youth went visiting and praying for the people they hoped would attend the meetings. The sacrifice, enthusiasm and devotion of these youth acted as a catalyst for Avondale students to deepen their commitment to God and His mission. They realised that they were receiving more than they were giving.

Fijian hospitality overwhelmed the students' capacity to respond with service. Their generosity of spirit in relationships, the gifts of food, sharing of their homes and heart impacted students deeply. This formed openness to a learning of God's activity in the lives of others.[4] Students became the recipients of God's

---

[4] Joseph S. Tortorici and Shenandoah M. Gale, "Intercultural Immersions and Cultural Competency: Preparing Seminarians to Minister in Today's Global Reality," *Reflective Practice: Formation and Supervision in Ministry* 32 (2012), 209-220, accessed August 3, 2013, http://journals.sfu.ca/rpfs/index.php/rpfs/article/viewFile/167/166.

blessings through the Fijians' hospitality and graciousness. In return, students modelled a more relational approach than the local culture was using. Fiji Adventism was still using the missionaries' 1950s approach. In the light of the students' ministry, this older approach was seen to be lacking. Local members and leaders were pleased to see another model.

Ministry Readines

Students' sense of their call to ministry and their development of a ministry identity were all rated by the students at 100% positive (see Figure 3). They felt that their spiritual giftedness had been extended. They understood better the importance of servant leadership. Student focus on creating community and its importance for a vitalised ministry also received one hundred percent positive response. Eighty percent of students felt that they were equipped for the "unexpected" in ministry and that the mentors in their lives had effectively modelled ministry. Nine out of ten students realised that they had learnt to manage their time better. However, only 50% felt that they had been given opportunity to exercise leadership in the two weeks of the evangelism initiative. That can be addressed in future planning so that each student has more to do that would meet their expectations of a leadership role.

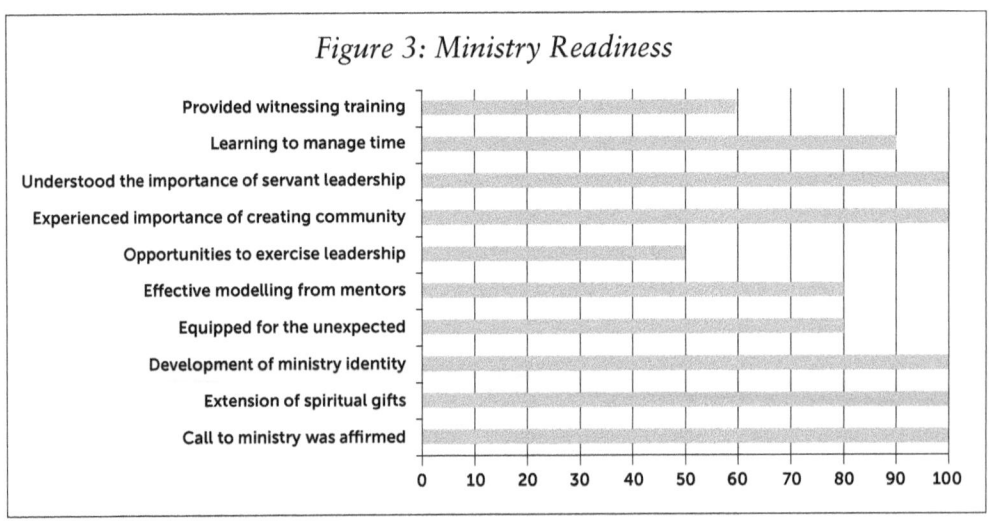

Figure 3: Ministry Readiness

All ten students recommended that this be an annual event offered to all our ministry students. They had seen and endorsed the relevance of their training in their Ministry course. One hundred percent of students indicated this experience had built their confidence in what they had to share with others and had better prepared them for ministry.

Cross-cultural Ministry Skills

Eighty percent of students felt that their cross-cultural ministry skills had grown and 90% felt that they had learnt to be more sensitive in another culture.[5] Ninety percent of the students were now more willing to serve God in the Island Mission fields despite the fact that 30% of the students had had no previous cross-cultural ministry experience. All the students also reported that they had an increased passion for the lost.

In this cross–cultural immersion, students were in a hothouse of personal development and skill maturation in preparation for lifelong learning and ministry. The new ministry context enabled students to experience competencies not previously developed.

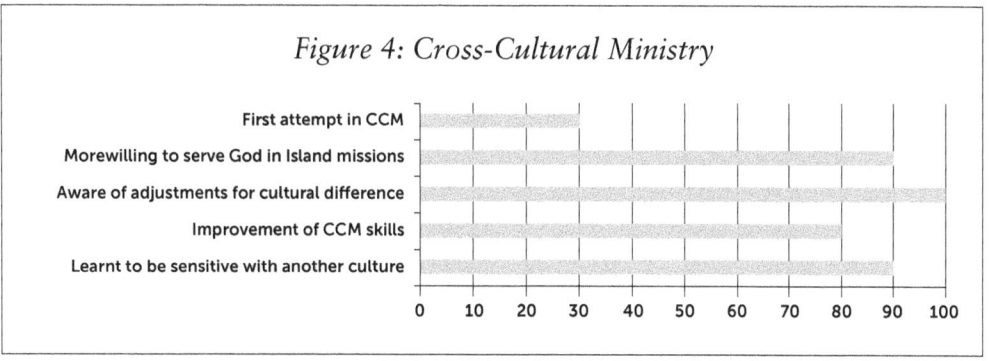

Figure 4: Cross-Cultural Ministry

Organization of the MIE

In this series, students were impressed with the great food and accommodation and were 100% satisfied in that area. One in five students felt that their personal finances had been negatively impacted. Eighty percent of the students were satisfied with the level of their involvement in financial management the MIE. One student felt that the planning of the program could have been improved and that the mentoring by Avondale's team leader could also have been stronger.

---

5 Tortorici and Gale, "Intercultural Immersions and Cultural Competency," 216. Wesley's students experienced similar outcomes. This transformative learning is the basis of building cultural competency.

Conclusion

The trend towards an increasing cultural diversity within Australia accompanied by a reduced percentage of Anglo-Australians requires that more cross-cultural learning be incorporated into Australian theological education. Cross-cultural learning would enhance the effectiveness of our graduates and equip them for the ministry they will face. The Avondale data confirms that MIEs can be transforming curricula.

This Mission Immersion Experience placed our students in an entirely new and challenging context. It served as a capstone event coming at least one semester prior to their graduation. The students' time in Fiji provided opportunity for Avondale ministry students to focus on the needs of the lost and on what they can do to reach others for Christ. It involved them in ministry outreach and relationships that stretched and nurtured their giftedness. The Fiji experience bound them together as a group and enriched their readiness for ministry. They developed a deeper passion for prayer and the need for the Holy Spirit in their lives. Cross-cultural ministry increased their levels of confidence as ministers and nurtured their ministerial identity.

Participants' unanimous recommendation that all students receive such an experience must be noted and actions taken to use further opportunities for student empowerment through MIE. Avondale is seeking ways to ensure that intercultural immersion is a consistent part of the ministerial students' preparation for ministry. Going forward, Avondale needs to provide a greater intercultural immersion experience for all its students and by this means extend our students' spirituality and their giftedness for new and challenging contexts.

17 | FROM PLACE TO PLACE

A COMPARATIVE STUDY OF 5 MODELS OF WORKPLACE FORMATION AT 2 COLLEGES ON 1 CAMPUS

DARREN CRONSHAW AND ANDREW MENZIES

Abstract

Workplace or service learning is an important and growing context for teaching and learning theology. This is not just about providing unstructured off-campus "ministry experience" but placing and supervising students in a service context and inviting thoughtful reflection on what they experience and learn, integrated with their broader studies. As a linked series of case studies, this essay analyses vocational/professional education in five courses based at the two colleges housed at one campus in Mulgrave, Melbourne: Supervised Theological Field Education and Urban Neighbours of Hope internship in community development and urban mission, both at Stirling Theological College—University of Divinity; and Tabor College Victoria's Teacher Education, Christian Counselling and Vocational Practice courses. We suggest possibilities for workplace learning that places learners in stretching workplace contexts as a means of apprenticeship, and consequently raise implications for integrated practical placements and learning-in-context pedagogy.

Transforming Theological Education

Theological education is in an interesting place as we grapple with changes on at least two fronts. On the one hand, the relationship of faith and society is changing as fewer people participate in church and yet more people are looking for life-giving approaches to spirituality, leadership, values, meaning and community. We live in a world that is changing rapidly—moving on from where we have been but not always sure where we are going. Thus we express our context as postmodern, postcolonial, post-Christendom, post-secular, post-hierarchical, post-book, post-industrial, post-moral, post-national, post-almost-everything. A present challenge for theological education is to prepare Christian leaders who are equipped to exegete their classic texts as well as engage their contemporary context, and to communicate the resources of Christian tradition in relevant ways to a changing society.

On the other hand, the world of education is changing. As theological educators we want to cultivate the craft of our teaching. At our best we realise the need to commit to ensure we foster helpful *learning* for students. New paradigms in student learning that focus on transformative learning fit well in theological education. Foundationally, we want not just to promote cognitive development. Our aim is to transform people and their inner lives, and equip them to transform the world around them.[1] This is the terrain of our formational and transformational agenda in theological education.

A recent investigation of where transformative approaches to education are happening at their best in theological education is Les Ball's *Transforming Theology* project.[2] Ball asks where theological education is starting with student experience and where it could be better utilised; where it is fostering transformation; and where it is taking students outside the classroom to workplace contexts that can be significantly transformational in themselves, especially when combined with guided reflective practice.

Ball points out that most theological education providers say their courses are transformational and start where learners are at and aim for holistic development, but challenges us to evaluate to what extent this is delivered. He affirms programs and pedagogy that are taking account of student experience

---

[1] Darren Cronshaw, "Transforming Theology: Student Experience and Transformative Learning in Undergraduate Theological Education, by Les Ball (book review)," *Higher Education Research and Development Journal* (forthcoming 2014).

[2] Les Ball, *Transforming Theology: Student Experience and Transformative Learning in Undergraduate Theological Education* (Preston, Vic: Mosaic Press, 2012); Cronshaw, "Transforming Theology (review)."

and fostering transformation. For example, theology students are learning from reflective journaling, collaborative assessment, dialogue with followers of other or no religion, problem-based instruction, case studies, educational field trips, and appreciative inquiry (AI). Students often say their most formative learning—and when their experience is best taken into account—is in spiritual formation and Supervised Theological Field Education classes. But as Ball maintains, there is scope for more systemic development of learner-centred and transformational pedagogy and curriculum.

This essay focuses on the transformative ingredient of field placements and workplace formation. Theological colleges have a long history of including ministry experience in their programs, but it has not always or consistently been integrated or given real value. As authors, our experience as students in different colleges included some *ad hoc* loosely monitored ministry experience programs where we were left to ourselves and some excellently developed and properly supervised programs of field education. Both of us have been involved in designing field placement programs and supervising students and student cohorts. And we are curious observers of the innovative curriculum for workplace-based training that is being developed in other higher education fields in order to develop professional practice and identity. Students are spending significant time experiencing and reflecting on their envisioned vocational place, whether training to be teachers, healthcare providers, chaplains or Christian ministers. As such, we are eager to investigate how we can best utilise places outside the classroom for mission and transformational outcomes that theological students require.

Research scope and methodology

In the form of questions, what we are investigating is what is the proper place for off-campus training in a curriculum, i.e. learning in the context of action and work? How can we best utilise off-campus places for learning and teaching? How do theological educators ensure that spaces of learning beyond the classroom become *places of learning*? What is the student experience when their place of learning is a workplace, church ministry or service context? And where is the best place to send theological students? Church work is one obvious context. But theology and the mission of God are broader than just what happens in the ecclesial world. If theological education wants to equip people for being relevant to the world, then we need more placements in schools, social service agencies, advocacy groups, innovative mission contexts and so-called "secular" contexts.[3] This leaves us asking how can we best place learners in stretching placements and help them grow and apprentice as leaders? How can we best help learners engage with people in church and society, and reflect and learn from those experiences? What can we learn about the placement of theology students in church and community service contexts for learning and teaching? How can these placements form faculty and college foci and programs?

The method employed in this project was Appreciative Inquiry. We were looking for where the field education on this campus expressed its highest aspirations, where it was happening at its best and what other teachers could most learn from it. The qualitative data-collecting methods of the project were to collect and analyse curriculum and promotional documents about the courses; conduct expert interviews of the five course designers or coordinators; conduct interviews of students from each of the programs; and to describe, analyse and compare the five programs.

For the sake of focus and comparative value, and to reflect on a context we teach in, this essay deals solely with field education and workplace formation for students from two colleges on one campus, but in five programs:

1. Supervised Theological Field Education at Stirling Theological College (Stirling);
2. Urban Neighbours of Hope course in community development and urban mission at Stirling;
3. Teacher training at Tabor College Victoria (Tabor Vic);
4. Counselling training at Tabor Vic; and
5. Master of Arts in Vocational Practice at Tabor Vic through Open Seminary.

Case Studies

1. Stirling Supervised Theological Field Education
Supervised Theological Field Education (STFE) at Stirling is a program that includes a placement in a church, aged care facility or other ministry context, with a supervisor, evaluation and feedback committee from the ministry placement, and an action-reflection peer group on campus. It has been employed in its current format for over a decade at Stirling.

---

3   A point previously made in Cronshaw, "Transforming Theology (review)", inspired by Ball, *Transforming Theology*.

STFE has two primary frameworks that are employed. The aim of the program is to guide the development of students to be theologically reflective. The program is also built upon a praxis loop (practice, theory, practice) whereby students, often over a two-year cycle, learn to locate their operating theological framework through placement-based case studies.

The program has beneficial effects for the college and students. The college is able to keep in touch with patterns and currents in church and community service placements: what is taking time, where demands are, what are the maps, what individual creative abilities are emerging, what things are taken for granted, and how culture is changing. Students value the place of practice being integrated within their academic world. They report they are often tested in placements—practically, personally, professionally and in terms of skill. The 360-degree reflection process incorporating supervisors, feedback groups and peers is often helpful to give students feedback on their vocational strengths and needed learning goals. For these reasons also, it is hard for students to avoid emerging challenges and issues possibly confronting their longer-term vocational direction.

The theological education sector recognises that one of the key and growing contexts for transformative theological education is workplace or service learning. This is not just about providing unstructured "ministry experience" but placing and supervising students in a service context and inviting thoughtful reflection on what they experience and learn, integrated with their broader studies.[4]

Student feedback on Stirling's STFE program emphasised the importance of it to their formation for ministry and chaplaincy.[5] Comments revolved around the surprisingly high degree of trust and disclosure generated among peers. There were several comments about tough issues being named and that there was little room for escaping presenting issues. The role of the qualified supervisors was overwhelmingly positive and appreciated and some students have maintained informal, ongoing mentoring-type relationships after the conclusion of the STFE program.

2. *Urban Neighbours of Hope*

The Urban Neighbours of Hope (UNOH) course in community development and urban mission was based at Tabor Victoria (through a UNOH employed

---

[4] Penny Galbraith, Stirling STFE Coordinator, Interview with Andrew Menzies, 10 September 2013; Alan Niven, Stirling Vice-Principal and Lecturer in Pastoral Theology, Interview with Andrew Menzies, 10 September 2013.
[5] Stirling STFE Student Interviews with Andrew Menzies, 29 January 2014.

teacher) and from 2013 is now offered through Stirling. UNOH is a missional order of the Churches of Christ that works in some of the poorest suburbs of Melbourne, Sydney, Auckland and the slums of Bangkok. The course is designed to equip UNOH workers or apprentices by helping them reflect on the issues they face in urban community development. The academic units of the course are designed between UNOH and Stirling, and students usually complete the units as part of a University of Divinity Bachelor of Theology or Master of Divinity.

Students enrolled with this program are UNOH interns first; however, a requirement of the placement is formal participation in the prescribed theological study. Units typically involve class time in UNOH contexts in Bangkok, Dandenong and their own placement through STFE, which is designed to create space for the same model used for Stirling ministry students to introduce interns to theological reflection. The ultimate purpose is to equip UNOH workers for thoughtful mission participation among the urban poor. The arrangement is essentially a form of industry partnership.

As a result of the placement and class experience, students are expected to develop a theological rationale for what they do and why; to consider the practical skills available and needed; and to understand the complexity of the task of urban mission among the poor. The course helps develop the self-understanding of UNOH workers.

Peter Blair, UNOH Director of Training, emphasised the importance and benefits of students knowing why they were engaged in mission among the poor rather than "wishy-washy" romantic understandings. They also appreciated that they were engaging in something bigger than just the mission of UNOH by participating in a theological college and its wider scholarship as well as learning from other students, not just from UNOH. Value was also expressed for the importance of UNOH workers gaining some sort of academic qualification for their futures.[6]

There was a wide range of feedback from UNOH interns and workers interviewed.[7] The variance possibly reflects the changing nature of the course delivery as noted above but also the wide variety of people participating in the program. Some UNOH workers were specifically in UNOH for "hands-on" work among the poor and felt that academic discipline was irrelevant or hard. Others expressed gratefulness for the wider horizons presented by the linking of their ministry with UNOH and formal theological studies.

---

6   Peter Blair, UNOH Director of Training, Interview with Andrew Menzies, 20 September 2013.
7   UNOH students, Interviews with Andrew Menzies, 29 January 2014.

3. Tabor Victoria Christian Counsellor Training

Christian Counsellor Training at Tabor College Victoria requires students to complete between 80 and 200 hours of supervised counselling in placements in addition to prescribed coursework. This is taught through the Bachelor of Arts or Graduate Diploma in Christian Counselling programs, and prepares students according to industry requirements prescribed by the Psychotherapy and Counselling Federation of Australia (PACFA).

The aim of the placements is to help students step off from academic coursework and learn to function as a "team player" in the function of a healthy, professional, therapeutic environment. The placements are where students engage in real experience and learn how to be a "safe" practitioner. A guiding theory of the program is praxis, where counselling theory is tested and reflected upon with supervisors and when students return to classes for further formal content. A significant part of the placements is in helping students gain an understanding of their own natural counselling technique and reflecting on where modifications are required. Students are supported directly in their placement with a supervisor associated with their counselling context and by Tabor in a fortnightly, moderated, online group of other students using Google Hang-Out.

The frameworks employed are aimed at integrating a balance between theory at college and practice in the placement through four foci: increasing self-awareness, understanding therapeutic practices, interacting with the professional body standards and practices, and working in a team.[8] These are qualities that a counsellor needs as a professional, and are best learned in the context of practice rather than merely in a classroom.

Getting 80-200 hours of placement and supervision is a challenge for many students, and sometimes expensive if they need to pay for the professional supervision. But students often get experience in multiple contexts and have to engage with live issues with real clients. One student spread her practicum over a primary school, working with at-risk youth, a city church counselling centre and an outer-suburban church-based centre. She faced ethical issues, had to debrief with her supervisor and move beyond theory to authentic engagement with her clients. She said their practicum was especially helpful for developing her own counselling style and working out how to adapt it to client needs.[9]

---

8 Arthur Wouters, Tabor Vic Head of School—School of Arts and Social Sciences, Senior Lecturer in Counselling and Psychology, Interview with Andrew Menzies, 17 September 2013.
9 Counselling student, Interview with Darren Cronshaw, 14 January 2014.

4. Tabor Vic Teacher Training

Tabor Vic trains teachers, but this is highly regulated through the Australian Institute for Teaching and School Leadership (AITSL), which includes strict professional experience requirements (teacher rounds). Tabor also has its own clear commitment to seeing professional experience as integral in their teacher training courses. The ultimate aim is not merely to produce good teachers, but to form teachers who will help children have positive learning experiences. The quality of teaching and learning of the children is what is in mind. The work placements of student teachers in schools are naturally central in this. All academic work leads into preparation for placements, or comes out of it, or develops frameworks for the next placement.

Professional experience is sandwiched through the course. For example, Graduate Diploma Education (Primary) students in term 1 are equipped with lesson plan and classroom management skills. The aim of the first five-week placement in term 2 is to help the students move from novices to develop confidence. They are not "thrown in the deep end" but carefully scaffolded through increasing responsibility. Starting with observation orientates student teachers to classroom management and gives them ideas on good teaching that they can adopt or adapt, and then try themselves when they are responsible for a small group and then the whole class.[10] The students return to their academic work in term 3 with newfound motivation to learn and a wealth of school experience to draw on. The aim of the second five-week placement in a new school context in term 4 is to get the student teacher "ready to teach". At the end of their course Graduate Diploma students will have done 55 days of professional experience—from observation through managing small groups to managing a whole fortnight of class teaching. Tabor is phasing out the Graduate Diploma and phasing in a Bachelor of Education (Primary or Secondary), which will follow a similar sandwiched structure with 100 days over 4 years. The student teacher writes teaching plans, a daily observation and a daily reflection and uploads these for the Practicum Coordinator to view. Experienced teachers supervise students in their placement and provide regular feedback. Tabor sources placements and pays schools, but a challenge is finding sufficient teachers who are willing and able to provide quality supervision.[11]

---

10 DipEd student, Interview with Darren Cronshaw, 13 January 2014.
11 Ulrike Mason, Tabor Victoria Head of School—School of Education, Interview with Darren Cronshaw, 28 May 2013.

Tabor Vic students do their practicum, and after graduation, teach in a wide range of schools: government, private, and "Christian." Since Tabor is a Christian Higher Education provider, its graduates are especially sought after by Christian schools. To help prepare student teachers to teach with their Christian values, whatever school they end up in, Tabor is adding a new subject in 2014, "Contexts and Philosophies for the Christian Educator." Mason and her team are developing this subject to explore intelligently the intertwining and at times conflicting philosophies and expectations that frame contemporary schooling, and to help them reflect on how their own faith impacts and is influenced by different Australian education systems.[12]

Teacher education has a whole different level of expected workplace formation, compared to theology or ministry programs. One hundred percent of education students do practical placements, as do 100% of counselling students who want to be qualified with Australian Counselling Association (ACA). But there are lessons we can learn from teacher education for workplace formation for other courses. Most importantly, there is intentional integration of professional experience throughout education courses. Workplace formation is not stuck at the end of courses or independent of classroom learning, but integrated as an intentional part of the total program. Moreover, the student teacher's professional experience is intentionally staged. It is not a "sink or swim" scenario, but neither are student teachers given only nominal responsibilities. Their level of challenge and responsibility is developed from that of "novice" to that of "ready to teach" over their program. The aim of the program is not that teachers will be trained, but it goes one step further: that students will learn well.[13] By correlation, the aim of ministry training programs is not that church leaders will be trained, but that the mission of the church will be done well—that disciples are formed.

5. Tabor Vic Vocational Practice
A program that focuses more specifically on the mission and practices of the church is the Master of Arts in Vocational Practice (MAVP), a six-semester course for experienced practitioners. There are currently cohort-based streams for church leaders and Aid & Development workers. Tabor Vic is aiming to prepare people for various vocations, not just in churches but also in other spheres of influence. Inspired by Parker Palmer, they want students to discern

---

12 Tabor Victoria—Communications, "Two years, and nearly 60 teachers," *Tabor Talk* (December 2013).
13 Mason, interview.

where their passions engage with world needs.[14] The course is taught in South Africa, where Wynand de Kock started it in 2000 as Open Seminary as part of a church plant, and now also in America at Palmer Seminary since 2012, and in Malaysia focused on aid and development since 2013. This essay, however, focuses on the experience of church leaders doing the course in Australia, where it has been taught since 2006.[15]

The practitioner/students meet as peer groups for their learning and assessment tasks. Students say this is what really helps make the course function at its best, although admittedly a (rare) poor cohort can make for a poor semester too. Their first assignment each semester is a collaborative social inquiry paper that a cohort group works on together to investigate broadly the topic of interest. Collaborative assessment is a good tool for mutual learning and teamwork; skills that are in themselves integrally important for ministry.[16] Then the whole class meets for a mid-semester intensive, usually off-site in a relevant learning context. For example, church leaders have their class in a local church that exemplifies the topic of study—whether worship, spiritual formation, community building, missional service, evangelism or doing theology in vocational context. The MAVP is less focused on a teacher-learner paradigm and is more about gathering experienced learners together with apprentice learners. Guest Lecturers are not specialist gurus but rather experienced learners assisting others in their growth in ministry.[17] The unit is rounded off with end-of-semester individual reflection papers including local action plans. Each of the six subjects seeks to bring the workplace experience of the student into conversation with other practitioners, the academic lecturer, and a practitioner-teacher and their local context. The MAVP semester incorporates an extended 20 weeks to allow extra time for collaboration and reflection and to help busy ministers finish their assignments well. De Kock would like even more time to allow students to

---

14 Parker J. Palmer, *Let Your Life Speak: Listening for the Voice of Vocation* (San Francisco: Jossey-Bass, 2000), 10.
15 Wynand de Kock, MAVP designer and Tabor Victoria Principal (at time of interviews), Interviews with Darren Cronshaw, 18 Jan 2011; 28 May 2013; see also Darren Cronshaw, "Australian Reenvisioning of Theological Education," *Australian eJournal of Theology* 18, no. 3 (2011), aejt.com.au/__data/assets/pdf_file/0008/398924/Australian_reenvisioning_of_theological_education_In_step_with_the_Spirit.pdf; Darren Cronshaw, "Reenvisioning Theological Education, Vocation and the Kingdom of God," *Zadok Papers* S195 (2012), 10-15; www.tabor.vic.edu.au/study/ma/church-practice
16 Darren Cronshaw, "Reenvisioning Theological Education, Mission and the Local Church," *Mission Studies* 28:1 (2011), 91-115.
17 de Kock, Interview, 2011; Cronshaw, "Reenvisioning Theological Education, Vocation and the Kingdom of God," 11.

implement and evaluate their interventions, although others say the semester units are already too long and intense, especially because students are in ministry contexts already. The course does not appoint students to a field placement as such, but requires students to be in ministry (using a broad definition) and offers them space for reflection.[18]

The aim of the course is to help practitioners to cultivate a theological approach to study and ministry that engages questions from their ministry context. Assignments typically identify a live pastoral concern, reflect on it drawing on sacred texts (biblical studies, systematic and historical theology), identify gaps in knowledge and work towards a generative theological response, and indicate where that might lead in purposeful action. The ideal of the theological response and action is that it be "generative" rather than "stagnative." This is Erik Erikson's social psychological maturity level of generating an outcome that leads to further reflection and action steps and being a stakeholder in the next generation.[19] De Kock comments:

> Seeing yourself as a stakeholder in the coming generations opens possibilities for the future. Our theology should not only answer our questions but also create opportunities for the next generation to build on what we develop here. Theology never finds a final answer, just the best answer for our time.[20]

Les Ball, among others, critiques a compartmentalised and foundationalist theological curriculum.[21] Traditional programs tend to start with introductory units in various sub-disciplines and add advanced knowledge in later years. However, students—especially those who are in the midst of ministry—come with a wealth of experience to draw on for reflection and classroom interaction. Ball suggests an alternative three-stage curriculum of *establishing a hermeneutical and skills base* in first semester, the *application and development of the level 1 base* over the next four semesters, finishing with *personal integration and synthesis* in final-semester reflective practice or capstone units. So instead of introductory units and selecting majors, the ideal progression is thus from equipping the learner with skills development, guiding them through theological discovery, and leading to personal integration.

---

18 de Kock, Interview, 2013.
19 Erik H. Erikson, *Childhood and Society* (St Albans: Triad, 1977 [1950]).
20 de Kock, Interview, 2013.
21 Ball, *Transforming Theology*; Cronshaw, "Transforming Theology (review)."

The MAVP offers another model of approaching curriculum differently—starting with the student's experience and centring on an aspect of the practice of ministry, rather than a "Schleiermacherian" traditional discipline division of theological studies. As students grapple with issues of church practice, they draw on different disciplines—biblical, historical and systematic theology—but the course is not designed around those categories. The course is structured around functions and practices of church with six subjects: worship, formation, community, service, evangelism, and the doing of theology in vocational contexts. De Kock starts with student questions that emerge from life and ministry practice rather than a syllabus of biblical sources and traditional answers. The pedagogy assumes we learn best by doing theology inductively rather than deductively; starting with live questions and drawing on tradition, rather than studying tradition and looking for application.[22] For example, one practitioner investigated online churches and how they can foster community through online connections, another examined how denominations can train leaders for the churches many pastors will retire from in the coming decade, while another evaluated why a majority of young adults said they feel at ease communicating the gospel but only a minority do it.[23] Another minister wrote a personal philosophy paper on intergenerational ministry and how to integrate his older and younger people, while another (in South Africa) evaluated Alpha and then designed their own contextually adapted program that proved more fruitful. Brian Macallan said it is very much a practical theology methodology that starts with questions from the local context rather than working top-down.[24] Starting with student experience is pedagogically critical to enhance learning but it is also critical for ministry to enhance effective practice.

Feedback from churches, as reported by de Kock, is that they appreciate their leaders not being removed from their ministry context and that the assignments and teaching offer tangible benefits to congregational life. Moreover, people say they appreciate the MAVP and its high relevance and resonance with healthy congregational life and mission; there is less perceived or actual disconnection between what is studied and the churches' reality, and yet it helps them to progress beyond where they are.[25]

---

22 de Kock, Interview, 2013.
23 MAVP student, Interview with Darren Cronshaw, 13 December 2013.
24 Brian Macallan, Tabor Victoria MAVP Coordinator and Senior Lecturer in Theology, Interview with Darren Cronshaw, 22 January 2014.
25 de Kock, Interview, 2013.

Re-envisioning Mission Placements

An earlier voice for workplace formation came from Robert Banks in *Reenvisioning Theological Education*.[26] He appealed for a distinct mission focus in training, by which he meant that education and formation, at their best, always placed students where they could *do* what they studied, which was at least in part field-based. He grappled with integrating action and reflection, theory and practice, and, inspired by Donald Schön, did not want merely action following reflection, or theory that is then applied in practice, but "reflection-in-action," or formation that occurs while learners are in the midst of mission.[27] Banks argued for further development of internships of mission placements and faculty taking their classes into the midst of ministry beyond the walls of the classroom. But the best workplace formation is not just about working in a place outside of a college, but to do so with supportive and structured challenges, supervision and learning clusters.

The best of workplace formation at Tabor and Stirling happens when "ministers"-in-training have a peer group to guide them in their theological reflections arising from their ministry experience, or when UNOH workers are stretched by the experience and complexities and realities of ministry among the poor, or when classroom lessons prepare student-teachers for their placement and help them debrief afterwards, or when counsellors-in-training have an actual practice context to develop their own counselling style, or when experienced practitioners develop action plans for the questions and challenges they are facing. Not everything is directly transferable, but we hope that programs will learn lessons from the principles and practices of other different programs.

This essay has discussed the values and frameworks of workplace learning in five courses, and where they function at their best, but there is more that could be explored. Moreover, there are at least three other programs based at the Mulgrave campus. Stirling's Master of Theological Studies offers practising ministers one subject per semester on Bible, mission and leadership subjects related to gospel, church and culture themes, designed to help ministers reflect on the mission challenge of their contexts and always with practice-focused assessment. Tabor Vic has Theological Field Education subjects. Moreover,

---

26   Robert Banks, *Reenvisioning Theological Education: Exploring a Missional Alternative to Current Models* (Grand Rapids: Eerdmans, 1999); discussed in Cronshaw, "Reenvisioning Theological Education, Vocation and the Kingdom of God," 9.
27   Donald A Schön, *The Reflective Practitioner: How Professionals Think in Action* (New York: Basic, 1983), 68; in Banks, *Reenvisioning*, 139.

Tabor Vic's MAVP (Aid and Development) is distinct from the Church Practice-focused MAVP. Each of these three programs would also be worthy of investigation. Another potential area of further research is to explore more deeply the experience of students in the programs, perhaps like Colin Hunter, a master-teacher of Supervised Theological Field Education, did at Whitley College over a decade ago with a cohort of students.[28]

What Sort of Christian Leaders do our Churches and Society Need?

Where and how do we best place students to learn from their practice of their ministry or other vocation? This is our question as researchers and as teachers. We have learned from the five programs at Mulgrave, but we would like to learn more from other sources and continue to develop our practice of facilitating workplace formation. As alluded to at the outset, we place this essay in the context of not just changing educational models but a changing society that calls for new approaches to leadership. There are also changing expectations and requirements from our churches. The Church of Christ and Baptist Church movements that we, as pastors and teachers, belong to are rethinking what kinds of leaders we need for the 21st century. We are asking, "What are the nature and capacities of leadership that will best help empower our churches for their common mission?"

Paul Cameron, the CEO of Churches of Christ Vic-Tas, of whom Stirling is a Partner Agency, is calling the whole movement into a process of renewal. An important element of this is reviewing what kinds of leaders are needed for "communities of hope and compassion," whether local churches, mission communities, agencies or orders. Cameron suggests the new type of leader needed for the 21st century will be able to:

1. Guide a transformational faith experience and introduce people to Jesus
2. Promote and lead spiritual formation for community members and help people know God deeper
3. Identify, develop, and support other leaders, including apostles, prophets, evangelists, pastors and teachers (Ephesians 4)

---

28 Colin James Hunter, "Supervised theological field education: A phenomenological enquiry" (DMinStuds thesis, Melbourne College of Divinity, 2003).

4. Build, inspire, and lead a "team" of both staff and volunteers
5. Develop and communicate a compelling vision
6. Motivate and develop a Community of Hope and Compassion as a "mission" outpost or a community of missionaries
7. Interpret and lead change with appropriate directions, process and timing
8. Manage conflict, and allow it to energize creative moments
9. Maintain personal, professional, and spiritual balance
10. Be a lifelong learner, using every experience to learn to work smarter, not faster
11. Provide leadership for high-quality, relevant worship experiences that speak to the heart not just the head
12. Navigate successfully the world of technology.

Cameron asks if people in ministry are evidencing these characteristics, and if we are developing leaders who can lead 21st Century churches and other mission communities with these sorts of characteristics.[29] This is the pressing missional agenda of theological education, and our changing educational, missional and church contexts all point us towards workplace formation as the best place to learn these characteristics.

Conclusion

Higher Education providers are developing some innovative curriculum for workplace based training. Some universities are prioritizing community placements across their programs. Certain courses are being redesigned to develop professional practice and identity. Students are spending significant time experiencing and reflecting on their envisioned vocational place, whether training to be teachers, healthcare providers, chaplains or Christian ministers. Ball suggests theological education could learn from human service professions, especially teaching, social work and nursing. These professions almost universally expect integrated practical placements. Some universities have completely redesigned their courses around professional practice, for example devoting the whole third year to clinical practice and reflective learning, and refocusing course aims

---

29 Paul Cameron, "CCVT Renewal Challenge: A Conversation Paper," in *Tension Summit* (Discovery Church, Mt Evelyn, 2013), 11-12; drawing on Jill Hudson, *When Better Isn't Enough: Evaluation Tools for the 21st Century Church* (Herndon: Alban Institute, 2004).

around professional identity and skills for a changing work context as well as traditional content.[30]

The theological education sector recognises that one of the key and growing contexts for transformative theological education is workplace or service learning. This is not just about providing unstructured "ministry experience" but placing and supervising students in a service context and inviting thoughtful reflection on what they experience and learn, integrated with their broader studies. The sector needs ongoing analysis in how best to place learners in stretching contexts to apprentice them as leaders. This essay has sought to identify insights and lessons in workplace learning from five different programs on one campus and propose implications for integrated practical placements and learning-in-context pedagogy for other places.

Appendix: Semi-structured interview schedule (Appreciative Inquiry)

1. Explain your program's history and how it operates now? How are students admitted? What percentage of your students go through this model?
2. What is the aim and purpose of the program?
3. What theoretical/ theological/ pedagogical frameworks inspired and shape it?
4. What is the value of workplace formation for the college, and for the student?
5. Give us an example of where you have seen formation at its best in work placements.
6. Where do you see the strengths of the program? Where could you see the program improving and developing?
7. Anything else you'd like to add?

Acknowledgements

The students at the two Mulgrave campuses (Stirling and Tabor Vic) who participated in this project's interviews have given of their time for the benefit of future cohorts of students—we have learned from them, in the classroom and now through this project. We acknowledge the support, inspiration and sharing

---

30 Cronshaw, "Transforming Theology (review)."

of wisdom provided by course coordinators in many ways: Dr Ashley Barker, Dr Wynand De Kock, Rika Mason, Peter Blair, Dr Arthur Wouters, Rev Penny Galbraith and Rev Dr Alan Niven. We also appreciate the interaction of 2013 conference attenders at the MCD Faculty Day (6 June), the Higher Education Research and Development Society of Australasia 2013 conference (2 July), SCD Learning and Teaching Conference (27 September), and the Australia New Zealand Association of Theological Field Education Conference (2 December).

SECTION SEVEN
ENLARGED HORIZONS

18 | CHINESE THEOLOGICAL EDUCATION IN AUSTRALIA

THE WAY AHEAD

FELIX CHUNG

Abstract

In response to the theme of "Learning and teaching theology in Chinese in Australia: some ways ahead," this essay investigates the characteristics of Chinese churches in Australia, which are shaping the future learning and teaching of theology program in Chinese. This essay seeks to analyse the characteristics of Chinese churches in Australia and its impact upon the aim, focus, and curriculum design of Chinese theological education. Special attention will be devoted to missiological orientation and multicultural composition. Recommendations for future theological education in Chinese in Australia conclude the essay.

• • •

Introduction: Overview of Chinese Theological Education in Australia

Chinese theological programs in Australia were originally initiated by churches. At the 1991 regional conference of the Chinese Coordination Center of World Evangelism (CCCOWE), Chinese church leaders decided to offer theological education in Chinese to meet the needs of the increasing number of Chinese churches in Australia.[1] In 1993, with the help of Bible College of Victoria (now Melbourne School of Theology, MST), a Chinese Department of MST was established to offer a Chinese theological diploma course that was accredited by Australian College of Theology (ACT). Today, there are three bible colleges offering ACT accredited Chinese theological courses: MST Chinese department, Brisbane School of Theology Chinese program and Chinese Theological College Australia Inc., which is under the supervision of Presbyterian Theological Centre (Sydney). All have Chinese faculty and the Dean to deliver the Chinese program. Moreover, two other theological colleges offer certificate courses in Chinese, namely, Presbyterian Theological College, Victoria (PTCV) and Morling College in Sydney.

The relationship between churches and theological education is a significant factor in its future development (Aleshire 2008, 129).[2] Thus, the characteristics of Chinese churches in Australia are worth studying. Nevertheless, there are some other important factors which may contribute to the future development of Chinese Theological Education in Australia. Factors including Chinese cultural values, Australian and global contexts, partnership with Australian Churches and theological consortiums, and second generation Chinese churches are all significant (see Figure 1). This essay focuses on the analysis of the characteristics of Chinese churches in Australia and their relationship with future Chinese theological education.

Figure 1: The future development of Chinese Theological Education in Australia: Significant factors

---

1 "The Origin of Theological Education," *History*. Chinese Department, MST College Website. 2013. Source: htte3wp://www.mst.edu.au/. Accessed in August, 2013.
2 Daniel O. Aleshire, *Earthen Vessels: Hopeful Reflections on the Work and Future of Theological Schools* (Grand Rapids: Eerdmans, 2008), 129.

Historical Development of the Chinese Church in Australia

The first period of development: before 1970

Chinese had come to Australia even before the Gold Rush period.[3] "Between 1848 and 1853, over 3,000 Chinese workers on contracts arrived via the Port of Sydney for employment in the NSW countryside."[4] However, many believed that it was the Gold Rush in the 1850s that caused the "first great influx of Chinese people into Australia …. During 1851-1861, half a million immigrants headed to the goldfields of Ballarat".[5] As early as 1857, Anglicans in Melbourne had already begun their Chinese ministry through the local Anglican churches.[6] Little Bourke Street was "a bustling centre for Chinese cultural and business activity,"[7] and was the place of missionary ministries. In 1884, the Presbyterian Church in Sydney also started its Chinese mission ministry among the Chinese immigrants:

> The Chinese Presbyterian Church has its roots in the work of the Presbyterian Chinese Mission begun by the Presbyterian Church of NSW in Sydney in the 19th Century. In its early years, the work of the Mission was held in rented premises in 1884, in a house on the corner of Nithdale and Goulburn Streets, and later in 1889, in new premises on the corner of Elizabeth and Goulbourn Streets. It was not until 27th May 1893 that the first church building dedicated for the use of the Chinese Mission was opened in Foster Street. By 1897, the Foster Street Mission had been raised to the status of a sanctioned charge and the following year saw the induction of Rev. John Young Wai as its first minister, together with three Chinese elders to form the first Session of the Chinese Church.[8]

At that time, outreach ministry to Chinese was mainly initiated by either the Chinese leaders of the local Australian denominations or local church leaders.[9]

---

3   The first Chinese might have arrived as early as 1818, being known as John Shying (Mak Sai Ying). Source: Asiaeducationfoundation, "Chinese in Australia - Gold rush". http://asiaeducationfoundation.wikispaces.com/Chinese+in+Australia+(Gold+Rush). August, 2013.
4   Asiaeducationfoundation, "Chinese in Australia - Gold rush".
5   Asiaeducationfoundation, "Chinese in Australia - Gold rush".
6   "History", Anglican Chinese Mission of the Epiphany (Est. 1901). Source: http://www.acme.org.au/history/. August, 2013.
7   Museum Victoria, "History of Immigration from China,"2013. Also refer to "History," Anglican Chinese Mission of the Epiphany (Est. 1901).
8   Chinese Presbyterian Church. Internet article. Source: http://www.cpc.org.au/content/cpc-church-history. Accessed in August, 2013.
9   Chinese Presbyterian Church. Internet article; also "History", Anglican Chinese mission of the Epiphany (Est. 1901). Source: http://www.acme.org.au/history/. Accessed in August, 2013.

The main driving force was missional, not social or denominational. The first generation of the Chinese church in Australia, therefore, was planted as a result of missional ministries among Gold Rush workers and other Chinese community.

Unfortunately, many of these early Chinese workers, including the converted Christians, chose to go back to China to settle down, especially after the 1901 "Immigration Restriction Act" (White Australian Policy). By the time of Federation, the Chinese population in Australia was very small, around 29,000.[10] The population even dropped sharply after that.[11] Hence, Chinese churches were not fully rooted in Australian soil in that period.

The second period of development: 1970-present

This situation had begun to change in the decade of 1970-1980, particularly after the abolition of the White Australian Policy.[12] The first wave of Chinese immigration included Chinese from Vietnam, Indio-China and East Timor. They became refugees and migrants to Australia owing to the social and political instability in their countries. Missional ministries to them were revived.[13] Several independent churches such as the Evangelical Chinese Church in Melbourne, Grace Chinese Christian Church in Sydney and Melbourne Chinese Christian Church were planted because of the missional ministry to the Chinese immigrants. Denominational churches such as St Matthias Anglican in Melbourne also started their Asian and Chinese ministries by providing social services to the migrants.[14]

During that period, the planting of Chinese churches in Australia was mainly initiated by individual Christians or home groups.[15] They saw the needs to have

---

10   Charles Price, "Asian and Pacific Island Peoples of Australia," in James T. Fawcett and Benjamin V. Cariño, *Pacific Bridges: The New Immigration from Asia and the Pacific Islands* (New York: Centre for Migration Studies (1987), 176.
11   Museum Vitoria 1, "Overview Graph: Population," Origins. Museum Victoria, 2013. Source: http://museumvictoria.com.au/origins/getpopulation.aspx?pid=9. Chinese population of Victoria dropped from 25424 in 1857 to 2817 in 1928.
12   This corresponded to the considerable increase in the diversity of cultures represented in the population after the end of the White Australia policy. See Philip Hughes & Stephen Reid, compiler, *All Melbourne Matters: Research of Church in Melbourne for the Future of the Church and City, the Citywide Report* (Victoria: Christian Research Association, 2009), 61.
13   Source: http://www.ecci.org.au/about-us/our-history. Accessed in August, 2013.
14   This information is from a conversation with one of the pastoral leader team member in 2004.
15   One example is the Grace Chinese Christian Churches in Sydney. See their church history. Source: http://gracechurch.org.au/new/index.php/2012-07-25-12-25-07. Accessed in August, 2013.

bible studies in homes or suburbs; churches were then started.[16] Overseas students and new immigrants were their target groups.

In the 1980s, preparation for the return of Hong Kong and Macau to China caused another immigration wave. With immigrants and overseas students from areas such as Taiwan, Malaysia and Singapore, the total number of Chinese residents in Australia increased rapidly.[17] Missional ministries to Chinese in Australia were then carried on through local churches and organisations. Chinese churches and Christians in Australia were taking up their responsibility to reach out to the local Chinese community. Since then, they have successfully planted several churches through church planting ministry. For example, Melbourne Chinese Baptist Church began their service by renting a room in the Baptist Seminary in 1986 with the help of the Baptist Union of Victoria and Kew Baptist Church. Then, they planted two other Chinese Baptist churches in the 1980s and 1998.[18] The Evangelical Chinese Church grew from one congregation in 1986 to 11 congregations in 2005; from fewer than 20 church attendees to more than 1000 church attendees through planting new churches and conducting worship services in different dialects.[19] The Chinese Methodist Church in Australia grew into a national denomination within 20 years by planting churches in different major cities.[20] These are outstanding examples of Chinese churches in missional ministry reaching out to Chinese Australians.

After the 1989 Tiananmen Square Incident, the then Prime Minister Bob Hawke granted all students from Mainland China the right to settle in Australia permanently. Since then, immigration from Mainland China increased rapidly and many Chinese came through "family reunion immigration." Together with "skilled and business immigration," Mainland Chinese has become the largest

---

16 Melbourne Chinese Baptist Church planted Central Chinese Baptist Church and Eastern Chinese Baptist church in that way. See MCBC, "History." http://www.mcbc.org.au/eng/history.html. Accessed in August, 2013. Grace Chinese Christian Church also began from a home group bible study. See their church history. Source: http://gracechurch.org.au/new/index.php/2012-07-25-12-25-07. Accessed in August, 2013.

17 In Victoria, for example, the Chinese population from China alone increased from 8537 in 1986 to 93,327 in 2011. Chinese from Hong Kong and other countries also increased sharply during that period and reached its peak in 2011. For more information, see Museum Victoria, *Origins*, 2013. http://museumvictoria.com.au/origins/getpopulation.aspx?pid=9. Accessed in August, 2013.

18 See MCBC, "History." http://www.mcbc.org.au/eng/history.html. Accessed in August, 2013.

19 See "History of Evangelical Chinese Church." Source: http://www.ecci.org.au/about-us/our-history. August, 2013. Also see S.K. Ho, "Pastoral case study," *Theology and Spiritual Formation* 8, 15-18 (2003). MST.

20 That information was collected through a conversation with the local Chinese Methodist Church in 2005.

single people group of immigrants who shaped the profile of the Chinese community in Australia in the 21st century. In 2005, Chinese immigration was on the list of the top three source country (after New Zealand and Britain).[21] Outreach ministry to them became a major focus of many established Chinese churches and local churches in Australia in the 21st century.

Another new phenomenon of the Chinese church movement is the rise of a second generation among the Chinese churches. They are mainly English speaking, bi-cultural Chinese-Australian churches. The second generation Chinese speak excellent Australian English. They embrace Australian culture and identify themselves as Australians but always preserve core Chinese cultural values in their worldview. Ministry to them becomes a challenge to many Chinese and Australian Churches. However, there are some successful cases. For instance, Grace Point Chinese Presbyterian Church which was planted by the Chinese Presbyterian Church in Surry Hills, Sydney in 1999, continued its growth by planting new ministries in English services.[22] New Life Evangelical Church also planted their English youth service and the service is growing by itself. These successful examples give us a clear message that missional intents and activities are still the distinctive characteristic of Chinese churches in Australia in the 21st century.

In summary, Chinese Australian churches or Chinese churches in Australia are mainly formed and planted by missional efforts. Today, Chinese churches are quite aware of the responsibility of reaching out to the new Chinese immigrants, settled Chinese Australians and temporary Chinese residents from overseas. The awareness of the sense of missionary responsibility is the characteristic of Chinese Churches in Australia. That has important implications for the future of theological education in Chinese in Australia.

---

21 Source: Stephen Castles & Mark J .Miller, "Migration in the Asia-Pacific Region." Internet article. Published by Migration Information Source. http://www.immigrationinformation.org/Feature/display.cfm?ID=733. Accessed on 15th January, 2014.
22 See History, Grace Point Chinese Presbyterian Church. http://bcpc.org.au/page.php?p=4. Also refer to the 'History of Grace Point Church, the English service'. Source: http://www.gracepoint.org.au/ourHistory.html. Accessed in August, 2013.

Characteristics of Chinese Churches in Australia

a. The missional characteristic

Historically speaking, the development of Chinese churches in Australia is always associated with the missional intention and activities of churches and individual Christians (see Figure 2). Chinese churches in Australia can be broadly divided into three categories according to their church planting methods: churches planted by missionaries or local Australian churches; churches planted by local Chinese churches; and churches planted by individual Christians.

Figure 2: Characteristic of Chinese Churches in Australia: Missional

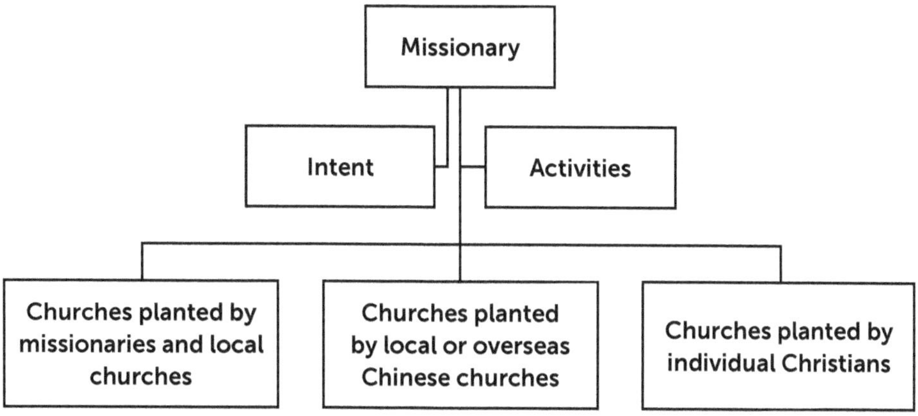

```
                    ┌─────────────┐
                    │ Missionary  │
                    └──────┬──────┘
              ┌────────────┴────────────┐
        ┌─────┴─────┐              ┌────┴─────┐
        │  Intent   │              │ Activities│
        └─────┬─────┘              └────┬─────┘
              └────────────┬────────────┘
    ┌─────────────┬────────┴────────┬─────────────┐
┌───┴──────────┐ ┌─────┴────────┐ ┌──┴───────────┐
│ Churches     │ │ Churches     │ │ Churches     │
│ planted by   │ │ planted by   │ │ planted by   │
│ missionaries │ │ local or     │ │ individual   │
│ and local    │ │ overseas     │ │ Christians   │
│ churches     │ │ Chinese      │ │              │
│              │ │ churches     │ │              │
└──────────────┘ └──────────────┘ └──────────────┘
```

b. The multicultural characteristic

Another significant characteristic of Chinese churches in Australia is their multicultural characteristic. Chinese churches in Australia are multicultural in their composition of church members. Many of them come with different theological emphases or denominational distinctives. They speak different dialects or languages or have been subjected to different home cultural influences (see Figure 3). However, they have preserved traditional Chinese core values at the same time.[23] That forms the multicultural characteristic of Chinese church in Australia.

---

23 For details of the Chinese cultures, please refer to my book, *Chinese Qinqing Mission Theology: An Interdisciplinary Approach* (Saarbrucken: VDM Verlag, 2009).

Figure 3: Characteristic of Chinese Churches in Australia: Multicultural

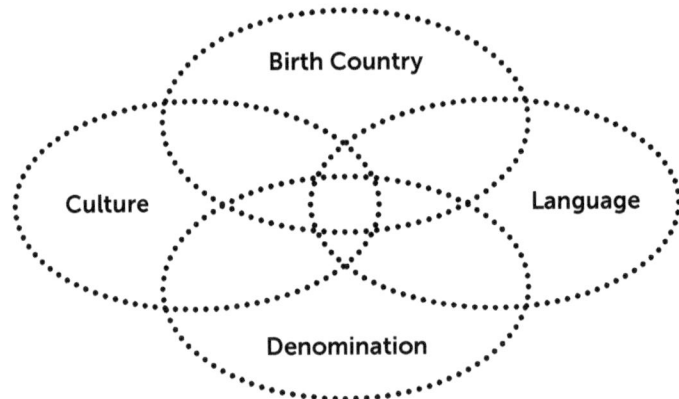

In Australia, the multicultural characteristic has both positive and negative impacts upon the development of churches. The positive side is that it becomes a driving force of church growth and development. Some Chinese churches have developed from a mono-cultural church to a multicultural church because they saw the need of serving their church members who came from different cultural background. For instance, New Life Evangelical Church Cantonese congregation has developed English and Mandarin services because of the growing number of second generation Chinese and Mandarin speaking families in their congregation. This has spawned the now second generation and Mandarin speaking NLEC churches.

The negative side of the multicultural characteristic is seen in the intercultural conflicts arising from cultural miscommunication. This might reflect the lack of theological and practical knowledge in transitioning from a mono-cultural church to a multicultural church.[24] In addition, conflicts, miscommunications and confusion have occurred because of the diverse cultural backgrounds. The establishment of independent churches was thus always a way out for those who were not satisfied with local churches or denominations. Splitting off from a local church was also an alternative for those who would like to stay with their own group.

The diverse cultural background of Chinese churches in Australia poses challenges to the pastoral leadership teams in church. The acknowledged problems

---

24 For the practical way of transitioning from mono-cultural church to intercultural church, please refer to Rob Brynjolfson & Jonathan Lewis (eds.), *Becoming an Intentionally Intercultural Church: A Manual to Facilitate Transition,* 2nd ed. (Canada: WEA, 2004).

associated with the multicultural characteristic need immediate attention from the educators in Chinese theological education. As Chinese churches in Australia are always missional and multicultural, the aim and mission (statement) of Chinese theological education should always be missiologically and interculturally focused, which will then outline the curriculum, teaching pedagogy and even the requirements for faculty members.

The Future Theological Education Program: A Suggestion

The strong missiological and multicultural characteristics of Chinese churches imply that bible college graduates are expected to be able to minister or work in a missional and intercultural setting. This should be the aim of theological training in the future of Chinese theological education. This aim should be reflected in the mission statement of theological colleges, should govern the design of curriculum, and should be accomplished through the teaching pedagogy in Chinese theological education (see Figure 4).

Fig 4. The reltionship between the aim, mission statement, design of curriculum and teaching method of Chinese theological education.

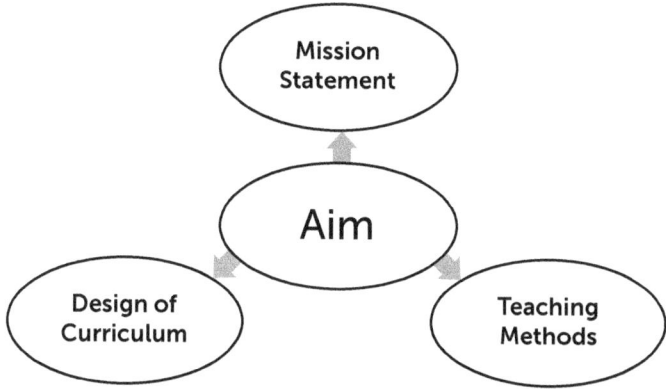

What is the issue?

According to John Kao, a well-known former Chinese Christian leader in Canada, Chinese theological education in Canada should have its unique characteristics. He listed nine characteristics, but only one is related to missions: "Theological students join short term missions and church planting" (my translation).²⁵ None of the nine characteristics related to intercultural formation, skill, knowledge or commitment. This unavoidably leads to a misconception that the only responsibility of theological colleges is to provide opportunity to their students to participate in short term missions. This is a very conservative and passive approach to intercultural education in theological programs.²⁶

David D'Amico believes, "Those preparing themselves for ministry for the 21st century should become aware that serving in God's kingdom will require diverse preparation."²⁷ Obviously, missional and intercultural training is part of this diverse preparation. In order to accomplish the aim of future Chinese theological education, the following significant questions should then be asked: Who are the students? What is the curriculum? How to train? Who does the training? (See Figure 5)

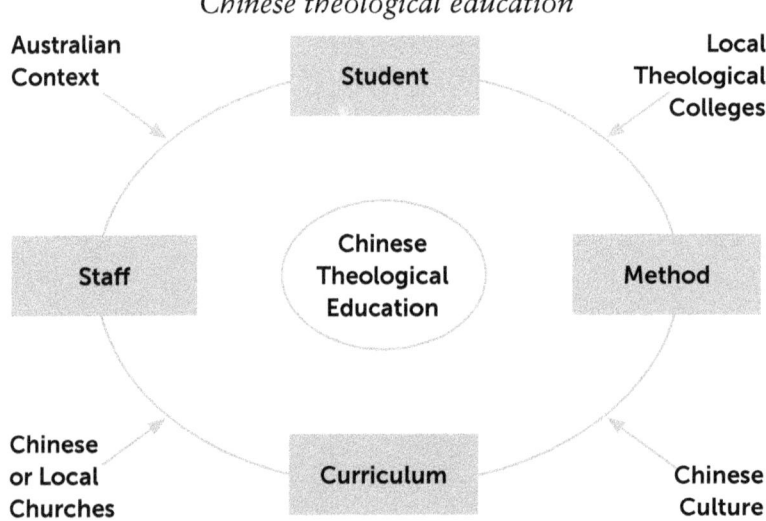

Fig 5. Significant factors to be considered for the future Chinese theological education

---

25 Original Chinese is "神學生參與短宣、植堂". 高雲漢 (John Kao), 「加國華人神學教育」(Chinese Theological Education in Canada)". 加拿大華人基督聯會 (Association of Chinese Evangelical Ministers (Canada)). Internet article. Source: http://acem.ca/ch/index.php?option=com_k2&view=item&id=457: 加國華人神學教育&Itemid=87. Accessed in August, 2013.

26 As early as 1995, David Harley had already pointed out, "Some have questioned whether specialised missionary training is necessary. They argued that all that is needed for effective missionary service is reliance on the Holy Spirit and faithfulness to the Scriptures." This belief is still very popular among some Chinese church leaders. Refer to David Harley, *Preparing to Serve: Training for Cross-cultural Mission* (Pasadena: William Carey, 1995), 7.

27 David F D'Amico, "Christian Ministry in Global Context," in *Preparing for Christian Ministry: An Evangelical Approach*, ed. David Gushee and Walter Jackson (Grand Rapids: Baker, 1996), 303.

Who are the students?

In order to fulfil the aim of future of Chinese theological education in Australia, careful selection of students is a crucial step. In other words, a clear selection criterion and graduate profile of students should be stated by the theological institution.

David Harley has listed "spiritual maturity, realistic view of mission, God's call, support of home church or mission agency, effective in ministry, character, relational skills, health, academic adequacy, work experience or professional qualification" for the consideration of a potential student's suitability to receive missionary training.[28] Although these characteristics are for missionary training, I see the relevancy of applying these requirements to the future of Chinese theological education in Australia because of the missionary and multicultural characteristics of Chinese-Australian churches.[29] A certain selection criterion of students may also be added due to the unique denominational and theological distinct of the theological institution.

Regarding the graduate profile of Chinese students, Kao has once listed his expectation on a Chinese seminary graduate in the Canadian setting: [30]

- He is a good pastor, has the burden of leading, caring, showing kindness, protecting, and feeding. (他是好牧人，有領導、愛護、餵養的負擔。)
- He is a servant of Christ, has a humble heart and an attitude to serve. (他是基督的僕人，有謙卑服侍的心態。)
- He is a witness of the Lord, has a heart and mind to suffer and even be a martyr. (他是主的見證人，有殉道喫苦的心志。)
- He is an elite soldier of Christ, has ability to transcend difficulty and overcome temptation. (他是基督的精兵，有超越困難、得勝試探的能力。)
- He is a voice of God, has the light and message from God (他是神的代言人，有從神而來的亮光與信息。)
- He is an ambassador of Christ, has the eloquence to persuade people to be reconciled with God. (他是基督的大使，有勸人與神和好的口才。)

---

28 Harley, *Preparing to Serve*, 59-68.
29 I agreed with Harley except for the "professional qualification," since many non-professional background students from Chinese theological colleges became great ministers and missionaries after they received theological training as their first undergraduate training.
30 高雲漢(John Kao), 「加國華人神學教育」 (Chinese Theological Education in Canada). 加拿大華人基督聯會(Association of Chinese Evangelical Ministers (Canada)). Internet article. Source: http://acem.ca/ch/index.php?option=com_k2&view=item&id=457:加國華人神學教育&Itemid=87. Accessed in August, 2013. This is originally published in Chinese, English is my translation.

- He is a steward of Christ, has faithfulness in taking care of God's household affairs. (他是基督的管家，有處理神家事務的忠心。)
- He is a priest of God's house, has a loving heart to heal, to pray for others, to exhort and comfort. (他是神家的祭司，有代禱勸慰、醫治的愛心。)
- He is a sinner saved by grace, has an experience of being forgiven and pardoned by God. (他是蒙恩的罪人，有蒙神赦免，饒恕的經歷。)
- He is a partner of gospel ministry, has a big heart to work with others in ministry. (他是福音的伙伴，有與人合作事奉的廣大心懷。)
- He is a workman who does not need to be ashamed, and who has training to handle the Word of truth correctly. (他是無愧的工人，能按正意，分解真理之道的修養。)

The attributes of this graduate profile indicate a requirement of a spiritual aspect or pastoral character of a Chinese minister in a Western cultural context (Canada). Interestingly, this profile is formed according to the great commissioning of Jesus Christ. Yet there is only one characteristic that is related to evangelism and mission of the church.[31] Nothing else mentioned is related to the preparation of a minister to serve in a multicultural context. However, his profile does reflect the expectation of the spiritual character of the Chinese minister in a church context. This is highly related to attitude and character, not skills or knowledge.[32] Notably, missional formation is missed out in this profile. Certainly, there is a need for all Chinese theological colleges to set up a student profile that gains a balance between spiritual, ministerial and missional formation. Since the Australian context is missional and multicultural, the inclusion of these two areas is important.

What is the curriculum?

The curriculum should also be shaped by missional and intercultural formation. This is particularly important in the Australian context. Today, Australia is gradually becoming a mission field itself. Multiculturalism has already posed a challenge to Australian churches in many aspects. The 2011 Census revealed

---

31 He is the ambassador of Christ, has the eloquence to persuade people to be reconcile with God .他是基督的大使，有勸人與神和好的口才。)

32 In Chinese there was a time when the Rice Christian issue troubled the Christian churches. Spiritual character is important to separate a servant of God from a Rice Christian. This corresponds to Ball's observation in theological education in Australian context as well. See Les Ball, *Transforming Theology: Student Experience and Transformative Learning in Undergraduate Theological Education* (Preston Vic: Mosaic Press, 2012), 20.

that "over a quarter (26%) of Australia's population was born overseas and a further one fifth (20%) had at least one overseas-born parent."[33] In metropolitan Melbourne, "Approximately 30 per cent were born in a non-English speaking country. There are more than 180 languages spoken in metropolitan Melbourne, with around 10 per cent of the population speaking a language other than English at home" in 2001.[34] Among these figures, Chinese alone comprise 3.9% of the total Melbourne population, with 2.5% of the Australian population speaking a Chinese language in 2009.[35]

Most importantly of all, the ratio of Christianity in the national population is turning downward. "Since the first Census…, there has been a long-term decrease in affiliation to Christianity from 96% in 1911 to 61% in 2011.[36] If Catholicism (25%) is deducted from this figure, the actual Protestant portion is only 35% of the total population.[37] Those who claimed that they had no religious affiliation comprised 22.3 % of the total population.[38]

Such research has shown an urgent need for the reform of Chinese theological education in Australia. Chinese theological educators have the responsibility to revise the curriculum in order to respond to the challenges to Christianity from the changing context and worldview of Australian society. There are two implications for this reform. The first is the need to focus on the missional training of theological students in Australia, in both English and Chinese programs. The second is to include intercultural communication and formation in Australian theological curriculum to prepare theological students for intercultural ministry. "Mission to your neighbours" is a realistic task of the Great Commissioning in Australia now.

However, there is a lack of flexibility in the design of curriculum for training future church ministers and preparing them to serve in the current Australian

---

33 ABS, Australian Government, "2071.0 – Cultural Diversity in Australia, Reflecting a Nation, Story from 2011 Census." Internet public document. Source: http://www.abs.gov.au/ausstats/abs@.nsf/Lookup/2071.0main+features902012-2013.
34 Melbourne City Council, "A City of Opportunity: A multicultural strategy document for the City of Melbourne 2005-2009." Internet public document, 2005. Source: http://www.melbourne.vic.gov.au/AboutMelbourne/ProjectsandInitiatives/Documents/multiculturalstrategy05.pdf. Accessed in August, 2013.
35 Hughes & Reid, *All Melbourne Matters*, 53.
36 ABS, Australian Government, "2071.0 — Cultural Diversity in Australia, Reflecting a Nation, Story from 2011 Census." Internet public document. Source: http://www.abs.gov.au/ausstats/abs@.nsf/Lookup/2071.0main+features902012-2013.
37 ABS, Australian Government, "2071.0 – Cultural Diversity in Australia.
38 ABS, Australian Government, "2071.0 – Cultural Diversity in Australia.

context. The overwhelming biblical-theological emphasis in the curriculum of the Master of Divinity and Bachelor of Theology programs hampers the preparation of students to meet missional and multicultural challenges. To facilitate the renewal of focus, the content of the curriculum should be re-examined. I recommend two different ways to achieve that renewal.

The first suggestion is a diverse curriculum of Master of Divinity (MDiv), that is, to offer the MDiv in different streams (focuses) to meet the needs of the stakeholders. For instance, Singapore Bible College formulates its MDiv curriculum into three streams: Biblical Studies Concentration; Intercultural Studies Concentration; and Ministry Studies Concentration (see Figure 6). Approximately one-third of the curriculum of all three concentrations is practical units. This design clearly reflects the ministry focused intention. This may be one way of forming the curriculum of future Chinese theological education in Australia.

The second suggestion is the diversification of the degree courses. For instance, Hong Kong Alliance Bible Seminary separates the Master of Divinity training from the Master of Christian Studies (MCS) training. Those who graduate from MCS cannot be accredited toward the first two years' study of the MDiv degree. This stems from the belief that the MDiv aims at training ministers and the MCS aims at training Christian lay leaders.[39] This model of diverse degrees and different aims of curriculum for different degrees can be incorporated into Australian Chinese theological education (see Figure 7).

Fig 6. Diversification of Curriculum: 1

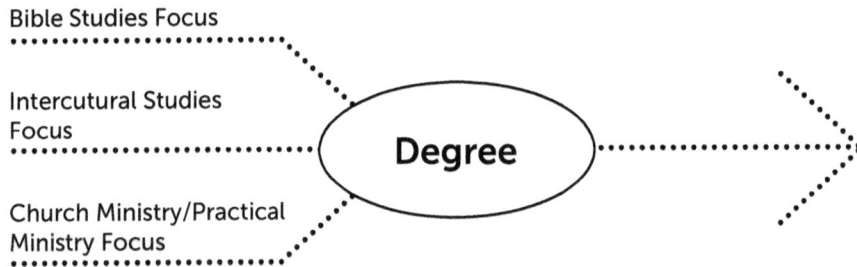

---

39 梁家麟 (KL Leung), "神學教育與關係網絡的建立 (The build-up of theological education and relationship network)" 教牧分享 (Pastoral Sharing) Vol. 188 March (2013), 17.

Fig 7. Diversification of Curriculum: 2

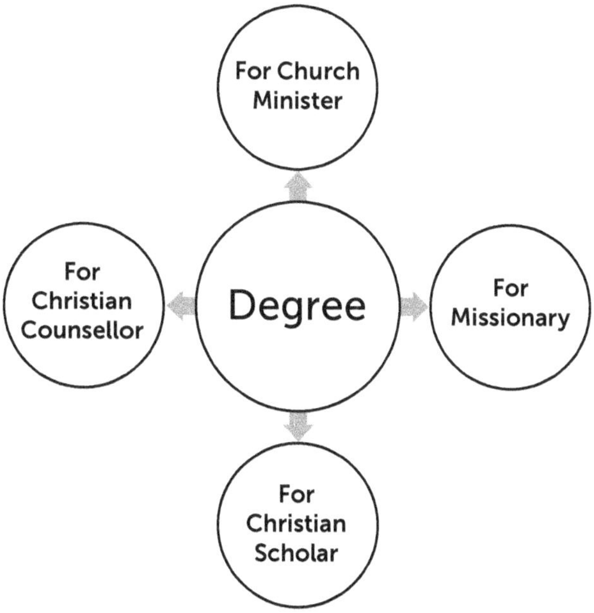

```
                    ┌─────────┐
                    │For Church│
                    │ Minister │
                    └─────────┘
                         ↕
  ┌─────────┐       ┌─────────┐       ┌─────────┐
  │   For   │       │         │       │   For   │
  │Christian│ ←───→ │ Degree  │ ←───→ │Missionary│
  │Counsellor│      │         │       │         │
  └─────────┘       └─────────┘       └─────────┘
                         ↕
                    ┌─────────┐
                    │   For   │
                    │Christian│
                    │ Scholar │
                    └─────────┘
```

The addition of practical units to the core units category in a degree course is always debatable. However, one has to consider that "the commitment to multicultural learning experiences is not a political or even primarily an educational one; it is biblical."[40] Therefore, a curriculum that has a missional and intercultural focus should be regarded as a response to the Great Commissioning. In the Australian context, it also means a response to the challenges of society. The revision of the curriculum helps to renew a missionally and interculturally focused program. The achievement of the aims requires us to implement curriculum through an integrative learning method.

How to train?

This essay argues that an integrative method of teaching helps to achieve the aim of future Chinese theological education. Using PTCV as an example, the English program uses an integrative approach to accomplish the shift of focus to missional training through teaching pedagogy, both formal and informal. PTCV stresses the importance of integration in teaching. Biblical lecturers will

---

40   Ellen L. Marmon, "Cross-Cultural Field Education: A Transformative Learning Experience," *CEJ* Series 3, Vol. 7, No. 1 (2010), 72.

teach not only biblical knowledge, formation, theology and history, but also the implication and application of the Word of God in ministry and life situations. There are some important events that place missions and an intercultural focus within the educational structure: (i) college missions under the leadership of faculty members every year; (ii) missions chapel every week on Thursday; (iii) preaching chapel; (iv) pastoral care groups led by the faculty members.

PTCV also offers ACT accredited intercultural studies program for candidates and private students. The program aims at training worker to serve in a multicultural context. From time to time, PTCV also invites missionaries to come to speak at the chapel services or to introduce the ministry of their mission organisations.

The student body at PTCV holds their own prayer meetings regularly to pray for missionaries they support. They also organise their own fund raising events for the support of missionaries. The lecturer of missiology organises evangelism activities for the students and a Chinese mission seminar for the Chinese churches in Melbourne once every two years.

To conclude, mission formation in PTCV uses intentional class-room teaching, sharing of values, group and individual mentoring and supervision, life-experience shaping, direct participation, praying and preaching to shape the missional and intercultural formation of our students (see Figure 8). Most important of all, PTCV has a multicultural faculty to drive that agenda in theological education. Such teaching and learning pedagogy as that of PTCV can be incorporated into future Chinese theological education in Australia.

Fig 8. Theological Education: Ways of Influence. Source: (Felix Chung 2006)

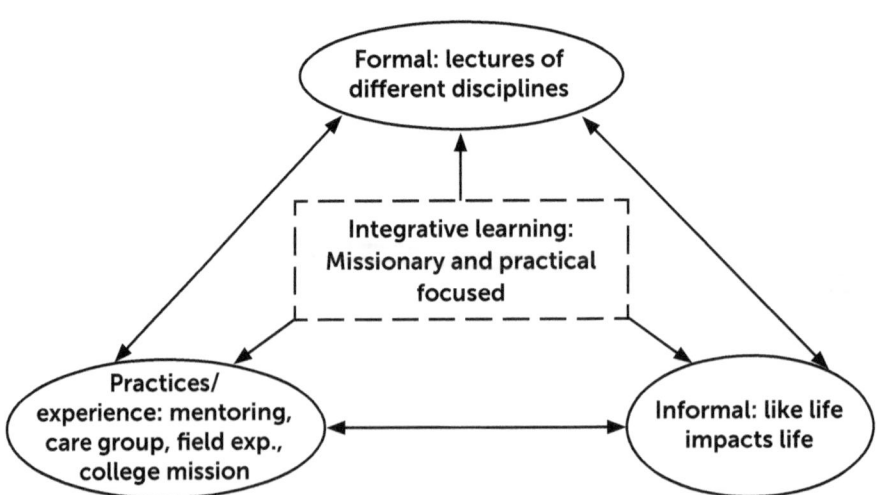

Since missional or intercultural formation can be achieved by intentional formal and informal education, there are two implications. First, future theological education in Chinese is not to produce a one-off product, but to form the foundation of the transformation process of students.[41] The curriculum should not aim at teaching all biblical books and schools of theology within three years, but to build the foundation of their biblical, theological, ministry, spiritual and missional formation, which is a life-long process for the students.

Second, the church can play an important role in forming the missional and intercultural orientation of theological students before they start their theological study in bible colleges. Some churches may question the quality of the theology students without being aware of the fact that many of these students are nurtured by the church before they come to the college. A recall of the role of the church in a theological student's formation is necessary.

Rodolfo Rudy Girón discussed the lifelong process of missionary formation and suggested that church is important in the ecclesiastical (level 2).[42] The recent rise of discipleship training programs or lay leadership training programs in different theological colleges, or tailor-made programs at the church level, illustrates such impacts. PTCV has been offering in-house short courses in Chinese to prepare students for entering formal theological education for full-time ministry.[43] The curriculum focuses on practical units, as well as clarification of basic concepts in theology, missiology and ministry. This can assist students to prepare themselves for formal theological education and formation.

Who does the training?

As "teachers are part of the 'hidden' Curriculum,"[44] the search for suitable faculty members is important for the future of Chinese theological education in Australia. Obviously, the diverse preparation for theological students to minister in a multicultural context is mainly achieved through teaching. Therefore, one

---

41 鄒永恆, "Learning in Theological College: A Learning process of Transforming Life"(神學院的學習: 轉化生命的學習過程) . Sept., 2010. Published in Chinese. 教學與成長: 華人教會基督教教育. Internet Article. Source: http://chinesechristianeducation.blogspot.com.au/2010/09/blog-post_8796.html. Accessed 2013.
42 Rodolfo Rudy Girón, "An Integrated Model of Missions," In William Taylor (ed.), *Too Valuable to Lose* (Pasadena: William Carey Library, 1997), 25-40, at 31.
43 The in house certificate course became an ACT accredited certificate course in 2014.
44 John D. Hendrix, "Teaching: A Little Piece of Holy Ground," in Gushee and Jackson, *Preparing for Christian Ministry: An Evangelical Approach*, 222.

must look for those who have intercultural experience and missional commitment to teach in a multicultural context.

Generally speaking, the pastoral team of Chinese churches or faculty of Chinese theological colleges in Australia is often multicultural. For example, MST Chinese department has a multicultural teaching and administrative team, who are from Mainland China, Hong Kong, Macau and Malaysia. To the Chinese faculty members of Chinese bible colleges, serving together by itself is a cross-cultural experience. That means an ability to communicate effectively in a multicultural context, like Australia, is a must for all lecturers who teach Chinese theological programs.

One further point should also be noted. The "multiple cultural backgrounds are thrust together often resulting in vast differences of preferences and expectations," and "distinct differences in worldview and spiritual expectations … will vary between the host culture … and other cultures, often leading to judgment and disillusionment."[45] This hints at a need to recruit someone who has cross-cultural experience, intercultural skills and knowledge in order to minimise potential cross-cultural miscommunication.

What qualifies a Chinese lecturer to teach in a theological seminary or college in Australia? Harley's recommendation for missionary training can be an example for us to learn from:

> Those … are expected to demonstrate the qualities of a spiritual leader. They should be examples in faith, in prayer, in commitment to Christ and concern for evangelism. They should be willing to live simply and sacrificially, requiring no less of themselves than they do of their students.[46]

This requirement particularly suits Chinese culture with its anthropocentric, pragmatic, moral and spiritual emphases. In addition, the lecturer needs to be a bi-lingual or tri-lingual speaker (preferable languages now are English, Mandarin and Cantonese); otherwise he or she would not be able to communicate well with students, churches and consortiums in Australia. Besides, he or she should also have some years of experience in pastoral ministry, demonstrate spiritual maturity in life and ministry, have had local Chinese ministry experience and be

---

45 David Wells, "Understanding the Tension," in Brynjolfson & Lewis, *Becoming an Intentionally Intercultural Church: A Manual to Facilitate Transition*, 2-3.

46 Harley, *Preparing to Serve: Training for Cross-cultural Mission*, 55.

academically qualified to teach research programs in Australia. There is a great need to train future Chinese theological lecturers in Australia. In the future, academic staff should be fostered locally rather than imported from overseas in order to minimise issues of cross-cultural mal-adaptation.

It must also be noted that cultural shock is another issue regarding the multicultural characteristics. Using Mezirow's term, a "disorienting dilemma"[47] can happen both in a multicultural faculty and among Chinese theological students in a diverse theological educational context. Many students who study in a Chinese theological college will unavoidably experience cultural shock, either in getting along with their fellow students, or simply by just living in Australia. To a certain extent, this is not a bad thing because cultural shock is also the factor that "triggers the process of transformation."[48] That transformation is helping to shape students' intercultural experience and formation.

On one hand, offering knowledge, theory, skills, experience and self-evaluation learning opportunity in intercultural education to the students is desirable. On the other hand, helping them to go through cultural disorientation is also important. Therefore, there is an urgent need to recruit a faculty member who has cross-cultural and missionary experience with academic qualification (see Figure 9).

Fig 9. The Chinese Faculty: Requirement

---

47   Marmon, "Cross-Cultural Field Education: A Transformative Learning Experience," 73.
48   Marmon, "Cross-Cultural Field Education: A Transformative Learning Experience," 73-74.

Conclusion

In summary, this essay has suggested a missional-intercultural focus to provide direction for the future of Chinese theological education in Australia. It has argued that Chinese churches in Australia are missional and multicultural in their history and composition. Such characteristics correspond to the current changing facets of Australian Christianity, culture, and values. An in-depth discussion of student profile of a similar context in Canada also revealed some defects in current programs of missional and intercultural preparation for theological students. Two recommendations have been given to resolve the issues of curriculum, focusing on the need for more appropriate curriculum design and the possibility of using more effective teaching pedagogy. Finally, a list of requirements for suitable Chinese faculty is suggested, as faculty are the most pivotal agents in implementing such recommendations.

19 | NUNGALINYA COLLEGE – EMPOWERING INDIGENOUS CHRISTIANS

JUDE LONG

Abstract

Nungalinya College in Darwin celebrated its 40th anniversary in 2013. Initially a cooperative venture between the Anglican Church and the United Church (later the Uniting Church), the College's ecumenical nature was further enhanced when the Catholic Church joined in 1994. Graduates from the college include most of the key Indigenous Christian leaders and ministers of the Indigenous Churches within those denominations. Ironically, 40 years after the foundation of Nungalinya, the challenges facing Indigenous Christian leaders are greater than ever before. Falling levels of literacy, increasing dysfunction within communities, poor health and low life expectancy are all contributing to a significant leadership issue for the Indigenous Church of the future. While Nungalinya seeks to provide pathways that will empower Indigenous Christians, the mismatch between Indigenous and Western learning methods, the lack of access to Scriptures, learning materials and teaching in heart languages, and the restrictive nature of government accreditation and funding requirements all contribute to the difficulty of the task. However, there are signs of hope. There is a great hunger among Indigenous Christians in remote communities to be equipped for ministry and also to be able to understand and survive in dominant culture.

Background

This essay reflects on some of the challenges of theological education for Indigenous Christians. This is an immense topic and one that is of great interest to many in the church today. There is a growing awareness of the importance of recognising the first nations of this country, and from a Christian perspective of recognising and supporting the Indigenous Church.

However, Aboriginal and Torres Strait Islander peoples are as diverse as the nations of Europe! They speak different languages, have different cultural traditions and different histories of contact with dominant culture. Many groups have been decimated by that contact and lost much of their traditional culture and language. However, particularly in the more remote regions, there are many people groups who do not speak English as their first language, and operate from a totally different worldview and culture from that of mainstream Australia.

The purpose of this essay is to focus on the particular issues facing Indigenous Australians when it comes to theological education. There are very few Indigenous students at mainstream theological colleges, but that does not mean that there is not a great desire for theological education or that Indigenous Christians are not participating. What it does indicate is the importance of providing culturally relevant theological education in an environment that will enable Indigenous people to feel safe. There are a number of Indigenous theological Colleges in Australia endeavouring to do this including Wontulp-Bi-Buya in Cairns, Yalga-Binbi in Townsville and Nungalinya College in Darwin.

I can only speak from my context which is working at Nungalinya College in Darwin with Aboriginal people from remote communities in the Top End of Australia. The needs and challenges of Aboriginal people in southern states or urban centres are different but just as acute. However, this essay addresses the particular challenges for theological education for Aboriginal people from remote communities in the Top End.

Nungalinya College

Nungalinya College was originally envisaged as a training institute for non-Indigenous people planning to be involved in mission to Indigenous people. However, in what was a visionary and quite counter-cultural decision, it was instead decided to provide theological education for Aboriginal and Torres Strait Islander people. When we consider that the College was founded only six years after Indigenous Australians were recognised as citizens of Australia and allowed to vote, this was a brave but vital decision.

Nungalinya College celebrated its 40th anniversary in 2013. Starting as a partnership between the Anglicans and the United Church (the forerunner of the Uniting Church), it is now an ecumenical partnership between the Anglican, Catholic and Uniting Churches, with the Catholic church joining in 1994. Currently over 200 students from 41 different communities, speaking over 15 different languages, are studying at the College.

Historically, the Top End of Australia was divided up between the denominations so that they did not compete with one another in mission. Ironically, the Catholics and Anglicans had the sea regions with plenty of water, while the Baptists had desert regions. However, what this means today is that in many remote communities there is only one church, although Pentecostal churches are now spreading to some communities. There are some really good things about this.

One of the questions regularly asked is how do we cope with the three main denominations working together. From the student perspective it simply is not an issue, largely due to the circumstances described above. Because the students are from different people groups with different languages, for them different denominations and different ecclesial practices are seen as a part of being from a different culture. Just as they are interested in sharing their stories and culture, they share their different ecclesiologies. The students really enjoy learning from one another and see Nungalinya College as a culturally safe place to come and share across cultural boundaries.

Today, Australian society struggles with the legacy of dominant culture's interactions with Indigenous peoples. There are many horror stories of what went on in missions, although it needs to be clarified that government compounds were also called missions. The shameful history of the stolen generations hangs over us all. However, it cannot be denied that the positive effect of the missions in the Northern regions was to preserve the lives of Indigenous people, and in some cases intentionally to preserve their languages and cultures. At Nungalinya College's anniversary celebrations, one of the senior elders of the Uniting Church, the Rev. Rronang Dhalnganda Garrawurra, shared how grateful he was to the missions for saving Aboriginal people and helping them keep their language. This is a story that is not often heard.

The missions also focused on providing education for Indigenous people in literacy and numeracy in English and biblical training, but also in practical skills such as farming, carpentry, car maintenance and the like. Sadly, this was frequently at the expense of local languages, but in some places a bilingual, two-directional learning was embraced.

In the early days of Nungalinya College, most students had been educated in church mission schools and had reasonable literacy in English. Most of the students were men, and they would come and live on campus full time with their families for up to five years. They studied right up to degree level. A number of these students were ordained as ministers in the Uniting and Anglican churches and include some of the most senior Indigenous church leaders in Australia today. The College was largely funded by the churches and dedicated donors throughout Australia.

Today we are finding that the literacy level of Aboriginal students has severely declined, with the result that their ability to undertake theological education is reduced. This does not appear to be improving. Church leaders and elders are unanimously very concerned about their young people. The cultural clash for young people is disconnecting them from traditional culture and its values and structure, but they do not have the skills to survive in dominant culture either. It is not surprising that there are high levels of youth suicide, substance abuse and gambling, and a significant lack of hope affecting the young people in remote communities.

The educational models and structure of Nungalinya College are now very different from those early days. This is due to decisions and opportunities that have arisen and been embraced by the College. Some of these are very positive, some less so and many Indigenous leaders mourn the loss of that vibrant community of learning that existed in the 1970s and 1980s.

A major difference today is that the College receives substantial amounts of government funding. However, like all government funding, this is a two edged sword. Firstly, it restricts the College to offering government accredited, Abstudy approved courses. Secondly, it requires all students to study by mixed mode—that is 50 % by distance, and 50 % face to face intensives. While this can work in some places, studying by distance is extremely difficult for students who may share a house with 15 other people, have no personal property, no desk, no chair, no paper, no computer. The actual living conditions for Aboriginal people in remote communities are extremely difficult and a constant challenge for our students is how they can keep their study papers and then have time and space to work on them. You know that old joke about the dog ate my homework—I did actually receive some At Base material with a big bite out of it! However, looking at the positive aspect of this change, enabling students to continue to live in their communities rather than move to Darwin for years at a time is, on balance, a much better model. We are very grateful for the funding to pay the travel and accommodation expenses for students to come to study intensives in Darwin.

The second major difference today is that the College actually has more female students than males. Currently 70% of our students are women. There are a number of reasons for this. One is that Aboriginal men are more affected by the issues of substance abuse and violence, and many are in gaol. Secondly, there are cultural issues that make it more difficult for Aboriginal men to become church leaders.

Currently, Nungalinya College is offering three courses:

- Foundation Studies – Certificate I in Education and Skills Development.
  This is a secular course in literacy and numeracy to which we have added a theological curriculum. Students develop their literacy using the Bible as the "technical text" they work with.

- Certificate II in Media and Discipleship – Certificate II in Creative Industries.
  Once again we have taken a secular course and added a theological curriculum. Their final project is the production of a short 5 minute video of their own faith journey.

- Certificate III in Theology and Ministry.
  This course has been offered at Nungalinya College in various forms for many years. It is the qualification that some of the community pastors and even ordained ministers have.

In 2014 there will be added a Certificate II in Music as well as an exploration of the possibilities of offering either a Certificate IV in Theology or a higher education Diploma.

Obstacles to Theological Education for Aboriginal People

The reader might be surprised by the low academic level of the courses that we are offering at Nungalinya College, so that brings me to exploring some of the obstacles that our students currently face. Rather than just talk about them abstractly, I will focus on the challenges for just one group of students which will hopefully give a real picture of what life is like.

This group of students comes from a very small community of fewer than 200 people. There has been something of a revival in that community with God speaking to people in dreams and visions, and a little church has been growing.

It is an exciting time and the church members are really keen to learn the Bible, to be equipped to lead the church, and to continue to tell others in their community about Jesus. A number of their key leaders are studying at Nungalinya. However, here are some of the challenges that they face in terms of their theological study and also being leaders in their community, as follows.

1. Access

The community we are focusing on is quite remote and does not have mobile phone reception. In order to arrange for students to come in, our Dean rings the public phone in the street and hopes someone will answer and that it is not a child who just wanders off while you hang on the phone for half an hour wondering what happened. In order to get these students to College we charter a plane to fly them to a larger community where they can catch a regular flight. Not all communities have the problem of no mobile phone reception, but the issue of contacting students is a significant problem for all the communities from where we draw students. Students regularly change their phone numbers, lose their phones, do not have phone credit, are not actually in the community when we call, have lent their phone to a family member who has taken it somewhere else and so on. Therefore contacting students - and also church leaders - is often a frustrating and time consuming task.

2. Very low literacy

For most of these students, English is a 3rd or 4th language and one that is hardly ever spoken in the community unless dealing with any non-Indigenous people who work there. So not only do they have to learn literacy, but it is in a language that they struggle to understand. One of the students from that community could not even recognise the letters of the alphabet when she came in. From a worldview perspective, some students even need to learn that each time they open the Bible all the books are in the same order – that is a concept they do not have. However, it is also not just an issue to do with teaching in English. Many students do not have good literacy in their own languages. Some Aboriginal languages are so complex that very few people can actually read in the language at all. There is a great deal of debate about how best to teach literacy. Many would argue that it is best to learn literacy in your own language first, and in most cases I would agree. Ongoing work in the area of literacy development for Aboriginal people, whether in English or their own language, is essential if some of these major obstacles are to be overcome.

3. Health

In this community there is a small clinic. However, we had a situation last year where the clinic was closed for a number of months, because a 14 year old girl committed suicide by hanging herself outside the clinic—with the result that the people were too scared to go there. One student from the community came in with a burnt foot and we eventually took her to hospital only to discover she had gangrene and had to have two toes amputated. Many students suffer chronic health issues, so we have an Indigenous student support officer at the College who arranges medical appointments and check-ups when students come in for intensives.

4. Violence

The church leader of this community is a student at Nungalinya College but was unable to come in last year partly because he was hospitalised with a machete wound to his arm after trying to break up a fight. Many of the women who come in to study have experienced assault and violence, and many live in fear. Statistics show that Indigenous women in the NT are 23 times more likely to be victims of domestic violence than non-Indigenous women. As the research also says that probably 49% of assaults are unreported, the situation is actually even worse than the statistics show. We had to have the husbands of two students removed from campus by the police this year because they had assaulted their wives who had come in to study. Violence and fear are an integral part of the lives of many Aboriginal people in remote communities and, if the statistics are to be believed, it is getting worse.

5. Substance Abuse

A lot of the violence in communities is related to alcohol and substance abuse. Again from this same small community, a couple came in together to study. While at the College, the husband became extremely drunk and abusive and the police had to be called. While he was very repentant and really wants to follow Jesus, the alcohol continues to be a trap for him. When his wife came in last year, I asked how he was going and it was so sad because she said, "Why is it that the women always have to be the strong ones?" He is currently on the drink in Katherine. These stories are repeated across the communities that our students come from. However, perhaps the biggest issue is the overwhelming spectre of death.

So many people in the communities die young – through suicide, accident or chronic illness. Life expectancy for Aboriginal people in the NT is about 61 for men and 69 for women. Youth suicide is a huge issue in the communities our students come from. Children as young as nine are committing suicide, usually by hanging. There is also a ripple effect from the high mortality rate. "Sorry time," as it is called when the community grieves the loss of a member, means that everything stops. This causes immense disruption to education and work. However, even more than this is the emotional and spiritual effect on the community. Living with tragedy all around you saps your strength, challenges your faith and disrupts normal life. Yet most of our students display immense resilience, hope and trust in God in the midst of tragedy.

I have explored some of the personal issues that our students face when attempting theological education. However, there are other structural and educational obstacles that also impact significantly on Aboriginal people successfully completing their study.

6. Educational Models

Currently at Nungalinya College we teach within the Vocational Education and Training sector (VET). This is the only avenue available to teach accredited courses prior to Higher Education. For those unfamiliar with VET education, it is competency-based education designed to teach people skills. It works fine in areas like carpentry, truck driving, workplace health and safety, or even computers and business. However, there is little opportunity for personal development, reflection and knowledge increase. Theology does not fit well into this skills-based model. How do I measure whether some can pray competently, or the number of healings or miracles? Unlike traditional theological education where you learn the content of the bible and theology, VET education provides only a very limited opportunity for students to learn the content.

Secondly, there is a fundamental mismatch between Aboriginal and Western learning styles and philosophy. Traditional Aboriginal learning methods are constructivist, incremental and repetitive. Independent critical thinking, which is a core element of most Western teaching models, is neither encouraged nor expected. Learning takes place through established ceremonies with knowledge passed down from elders to young people in small pieces. You do not actually accumulate enough knowledge to be a leader, including a church leader, until you are reasonably old. When we add to this model the reality that life expectancy for Aboriginal people is significantly less than for non-Indigenous people, we end up with a vacuum in leadership because those with the knowledge and experience have passed away before the new generation of leaders has developed. This is what we are currently seeing in the Aboriginal churches in the north.

7. Language

A second major issue is the issue of language. Missiology has clearly identified that people need to read the Bible and express their faith in their heart language, the language they speak at home. While there has been, and continues to be, a strong desire to translate the Scriptures into Aboriginal languages, only one full Bible exists and that is in Kriol which is not one of the traditional Aboriginal languages. The difficulty is that there are so many different languages and the number of speakers of each language is quite low, so this translation work is incredibly expensive per user. At Nungalinya College we are currently teaching in English. In a class we may have up to six different language groups in a class of 25 students. Some of us have a small amount of one language, but how can we cater to this diversity? We are exploring the use of Indigenous Assistant Teachers, but even then they will not speak all thelanguages present in these mixed classes.

8. Gospel and Culture Issues

The relationship between gospel and culture is a huge issue that is very difficult to confront. Different Aboriginal people groups have quite different approaches to how gospel and culture interact and this is then reflected in their practice. However, one of the significant issues that affect theological education and church leadership is the issue of power. Ceremony men within communities hold a great deal of power. For many it becomes an either/or issue. They may feel that in order to embrace the gospel fully they have to repudiate their ceremonies, or *vice versa*. This is also a very difficult issue to discuss as most ceremonies are secret and gender specific.

Future

Well, I have painted a pretty bleak picture and on my bad days I feel like throwing my hands in the air and giving up. But there is hope. We see and celebrate the little steps our students are making and gain encouragement from that. To be in a chapel service where a student gets up to read the Bible but before she does so shyly says, "I have never read the Bible before" is immensely rewarding. What then is the way forward?

1. Local Initiatives

I think the first thing to say is we must move away from a mentality of one size fits all. Aboriginal people are as diverse as the different nations of Africa or Europe. Too often we lump them all together. The needs of Aboriginal people in remote regions are very different from those in urban environments, yet both have immense challenges to face.

There is a great need for consultation, empowerment and support for local initiatives. However, at the same time these need to be more integrated. There are many different groups currently providing services and education in Aboriginal communities with a great deal of duplication and waste. The local Indigenous church is a key to listening and working with the community and a more strategic approach to supporting the local community is essential. This requires a flexible approach to funding that listens to the needs of the local people and provides different models to meet different contexts. For example, in the case of students studying at Nungalinya College, while we have received church funding to run a small crèche for the preschool children of students, there is no government funding available to pay for the children's travel expenses so that has to be met from donations to the College. The funding can be used only for the individual student. Empowering younger people, especially women, to receive education means that the needs of children must be considered and supported.

2. Indigenous Teachers

One of the biggest needs for the future is to have capable, godly, well-educated Christian leaders and teachers for the Aboriginal churches. Sadly, the old generation that had a foundation from the mission times is passing away and a new generation needs to be mentored and supported to take up leadership. It may seem obvious, but effective Aboriginal theological education requires Aboriginal teachers and these are in very short supply. A long term strategy to build learning pathways from the lowest levels of literacy learning through to degrees and even doctorates is needed.

However, these pathways need to have the opportunity for Aboriginal people to learn in ways that are closer to their traditional ways, preferably in their own language, and at their own pace. For this to happen there needs to be pressure brought to bear on the government which throws millions of dollars every year at Indigenous education to develop new, local and culturally appropriate models for funding. At the same time the churches should be exploring ways to provide education that possibly falls outside the accredited and government funded models.

Part of building that pathway will be working with the Aboriginal churches to identify Aboriginal people with the gifts, ability and commitment to become the teachers of the future. Only when we have Aboriginal teachers who can teach in their language and contextualise the gospel in their cultures will good theological education start to happen. This is a key element of Nungalinya College's strategic plan for the future. We now have Aboriginal graduates coming as Assistant Teachers at the College. However, this will only be from Uniting Church communities as that is the only funding available for them at present.

But we cannot have Aboriginal teachers without support mechanisms. Alongside these teachers will need to be mentors who can encourage and provide assistance when needed.

3. Indigenous Theologies

Lastly we need to support the Aboriginal church as it seeks to develop Aboriginal theologies - plural. This builds on the previous points. The development of Aboriginal theologies requires culturally relevant theological education as well as access to the Scriptures in their own languages. In addition to this, for Aboriginal Christians in remote communities, the connection with the land is so important that theologising needs to take place on their country. These ideas are quite alien to us and often are brushed aside because of practical concerns, but until these sorts of issues are recognised, the development of truly Aboriginal theologies will be hampered.

What Can Colleges and Churches Down South Do to Help?

1. Cross Cultural Awareness

Firstly, many people down south have very little understanding of the realities of Indigenous culture and life. I find very few people are even aware that Aboriginal people in remote communities do not speak English. The provision of intentional cross-cultural training and experiences for non-Indigenous theological students would be a great step towards changing mainstream Australian Christian culture. I know some colleges and churches are connecting with their local Indigenous people and are having opportunities for immersion experiences for students and congregational members. These sorts of experiences are vital and potentially life changing for many people and these sorts of opportunities need to increase.

2. Training for Ministry with Aboriginal people
Mission to Aboriginal people has become something of a forbidden subject since the Stolen Generations report. However, the Aboriginal Churches are saying we want people to come and help. Not come and run the church, but to walk beside, to support, and to provide help with theological education out in communities. This requires long term commitment and language learning. However, rather than raising funds and sending missionaries, a better model would be to encourage people to use their other skills and training to get employment in communities. There are many opportunities for work as teachers, medical staff, even managers and retail. However, it needs to be recognised that this will be an extremely challenging ministry that will not be for everyone.

3. Partnerships and Support
Lastly, there may be ways that theological colleges and churches can support colleges like Nungalinya College and other Indigenous theological colleges. Opportunities for Assistant teachers to study by distance at another institution while working at an Indigenous College for example would be helpful. However, there would need to be attempts to allow for a more contextual approach and greater flexibility than most courses currently offer. Offering scholarships for students to come and study at Colleges down south in my view is not a great option, and what often happens is that those educated in that manner stay in the cities and never return to their communities resulting in an ongoing brain drain where the brightest and best leave. One College has offered to teach the Certificate IV in Training and Assessment to our Assistant teachers for free as part of their mission responsibilities.

Another idea is that theological colleges form partnerships with Indigenous Colleges and have regular cross-cultural intensives in those places. We are already developing this option for Uniting Church candidates for ministry. Many churches are partnering with Nungalinya College through financial support but also through volunteers either individually or in teams coming to help at the College. While assistance with teaching is not really an option except for those with the appropriate qualifications and experience working with Aboriginal people, there are many practical tasks on campus that volunteers help with. This greatly assists the College to get on with its core business of providing theological education.

Conclusion

Hopefully, this essay has provided some insights into the issues facing the Aboriginal church in my region of the Northern Territory. The issues are huge, and the answers will not happen in the short term. Our motto at Nungalinya College is "Empowering Indigenous Christians." That is what it must be about —not doing things and making decisions for people, but walking beside people, listening, and building slowly for the future.

I conclude with the words shared at our 40th anniversary celebration by Gaymarania Pascoe, a church leader from Maningrida:

> Nungalinya is so important for us as students from different communities can gain understanding, knowledge and wisdom and be qualified as ministers, pastoral, youth workers, leaders and musicians. A seed has been sown that has been growing well. Today Nungalinya College has shown us a better future and a stronger future where God wants us to be:
>
> > Strong in Christian faith
> > Strong and faithful in our Christian beliefs
> > Strong and caring for the needs of others
> > Literate and strong leaders in our communities
> > Workers for the kingdom of God and Disciples for the Lord Jesus
> > And many more.
>
> These are things we remember and celebrate on our 40th Anniversary.
>
> I believe God has poured out his blessing to all people, of all languages and races. Nungalinya College is the gate for our communities far and wide and the key to the world.
>
> That is Nungalinya College.

www.ingramcontent.com/pod-product-compliance
Lightning Source LLC
Chambersburg PA
CBHW051329110526
44590CB00032B/4462